THE AMERICAN EXPLORATION & TRAVEL SERIES

[*Complete list on page 422*]

WILLIAM
BOLLAERT'S
TEXAS

WILLIAM BOLLAERT'S TEXAS

EDITED BY W. EUGENE HOLLON

AND RUTH LAPHAM BUTLER

Published in Co-operation with
THE NEWBERRY LIBRARY, CHICAGO
by the
UNIVERSITY OF OKLAHOMA PRESS : NORMAN

TO
THE MEMORY OF
EDWARD E. AYER

PREFACE

THE PAPERS OF WILLIAM BOLLAERT were acquired by Mr. Edward E. Ayer in 1902 from Quaritch, and presented by him to The Newberry Library in 1911. They have been used from time to time by students, and quotations have occasionally been made from them, as in Joseph W. Schmitz, *Thus they lived: Social Life in the Republic of Texas* (San Antonio, 1935) and in William R. Hogan, *The Texas Republic* (Norman, 1946). But they have not been published in full until now.

The Texas manuscripts consist of six diaries and notebooks and two volumes of journals, from December, 1841, to April 11, 1844. The latter represent a second stage in the preparation of a finished manuscript for publication. In some instances Bollaert copied entries from the diaries without change; in others he wrote a fresh version which often embodied information not contained in the diaries; in still others he omitted from the version in the journal material that is of more interest and freshness in the diary form. The task of the editors was to choose the version that seemed to them most informative and readable, without any way of knowing what Bollaert himself would have done when he prepared his final draft. He might have removed the dash which in some places encumbers the journals as printed here, and have substituted smooth-flowing and readable sentences.

The journal itself constitutes the heart of the first fourteen chapters of this present book. The last two chapters come from one of the notebooks that Bollaert did not rewrite. Chapter divisions are the editor's, although about half of the chapter titles are Bollaert's own. Where additional narrative seemed necessary to clarify the original account, the editors have supplied it, as so indicated.

Mrs. Butler is responsible for the transcript of the text, and for general editorial assistance; Mr. Hollon for the choice of materials to be included, for the editor's narrative, for most of the notes and bibliography, and for the index.

The editors are grateful to Mr. Joseph Wolf of The Newberry Library for information on Bollaert's family, procured in part through the kindly offices of Mr. R. P. Graham-Vivian, Windsor Herald, and to Miss Llerena Friend, custodian of the Barker Library, University of Texas, and Seymour V. Connor, former Texas state archivists, for their co-operation in helping to track down obscure facts relating to various Texas personalities and historical happenings. The following persons on the faculty at the University of Oklahoma provided assistance from time to time: Professors Hans A. Schmitt and Max L. Moorhead of the Department of History; Professor Lawrence S. Poston, Jr., Department of Modern Languages; Dean Ralph W. Clark, College of Pharmacy; Professor George J. Goodman, Plant Sciences Department; and Professor Arthur H. Doerr, Department of Geography. David Carlson, former graduate student in history at the University of Oklahoma, provided assistance in digging out facts and figures from the library.

W. Eugene Hollon
Ruth Lapham Butler

September 29, 1956

INTRODUCTION

BY STANLEY PARGELLIS

BOLLAERT'S JOURNALS PRESENT as good a picture of social life in Texas on the eve of annexation as any record that has survived. When he landed at Galveston in February, 1842, Texas embraced, or claimed to embrace, all land east of the Río Grande to Red River on the north and to the Sabine on the east. In less than one-tenth of this vast area lived a population of 75,000. Most of them were within an arc of one hundred miles from Galveston Island. San Antonio could claim perhaps 5,000, mostly Mexicans, but it lay on the western fringe of the frontier, subject to frequent harassment by marauding Comanches and Apaches. North of San Antonio was the newly established city of Austin, still more a city on paper than in fact. Nearly two hundred miles farther north, the present metropolis of Dallas was little more than a crossing on the Trinity River. To the southeast some 150 miles was a cluster of settlements in the vicinity of Nacogdoches.

Although it was virtually bankrupt, the Republic's potentialities loomed so great as to make its future a matter of importance to the United States, Mexico, France, and England. To England it offered the possibilities, if settlers could be brought in from Europe, of providing both a source of cotton that would relieve her from dependence upon the United States and a free trade market for her goods. There were many Englishmen in Texas when Bollaert arrived, and considerable English capital. Vast acreages could be had for little more than the asking and the promise of settlement. Attracted by the lure of wealth, men of all nationalities came to Texas. Few had had the experiences which William Bollaert, at thirty-five, had passed through.

The Bollaert family in England was an obscure one, though several of the Bollaerts in Holland, who lived in Middelburgh, find a place in the *Nieuw Nederlandsch Biografisch Woorden-*

XI

boek. One of them, Nathan, was in the 1790's house-director of the communal orphanage there. Some indication of the family's humble position in England appears in the marriage certificate of William's sister, Jane Sarah, who in 1844, at the age of twenty-seven, married William Marsden, a clerk. She was a sempstress, made her mark on the certificate instead of signing, and was living at No. 1 Labour in Vain Court, in the then parish of St. Mary Mounthaw. Although her father, Andrew Jacob Bollaert, is set down as an apothecary, his name is not listed in the registers of the Apothecaries' Company. Either he was not an accredited apothecary, or he qualified abroad before coming to England. The parish registers of St. Mary Mounthaw record the burial, on December 6, 1835, of Henry Jacob Bollard [*sic*], aged twenty-two, of Labour in Vain Court. There was another brother living in London, Samual Johannes, a bookseller, who married Jane Carter in 1853 and had four children.

William Bollaert, eldest of the family, was born on October 21, 1807, at Lymington, Hampshire. At the age of thirteen his talents were already such that he was permitted to enter the Royal Institution as a laboratory assistant in chemistry. There he remained for five years, working with William Thomas Brande, professor of chemistry, with Michael Faraday, assistant and later professor, and with Sir Humphrey Davy, an occasional visitor. In this field he was competent enough, while still in his teens, to make some original discoveries in benzoic acid, and to publish his results in the *Journal of the Royal Institution* in 1823–24. In 1825 his father became blind, and the young man had to give up the laboratory.

Thrown thus upon his own at the age of eighteen, he chose to go to Peru as an assayer and chemist at the famous silver mines of Guantajaya in Tarapaca. He did much more than his job at the mines required, studying the geography, geology, and natural history of Peru so effectively that in 1827 he was asked by the Intendente Castilla, who later became president of Peru, to make a survey of the province of Tarapaca. "Leaving Arequipa, at the foot of its snow clad volcano, we passed desert plains with their vast tracts of moving hemispherical sand hills (*medanos*), which have been known to overwhelm the traveler under their shifting masses. The district of Tarapaca—with its rocky mountains, its desert steps, and its mines of silver—was next examined; and Mr. Bollaert believed that the huge range of Lirima, in the Cordillera Real, will, upon further investigation, prove to be the culminating point of the New World."[1] He was one of the first "white" men to cross the desert at Atacama (now Chile), exploring the country and searching unsuccessfully, for he lost his way, for the meteoric iron of Atacama. The unsettled state of the country, as a new republic, and the monetary crisis in Europe combined to put an end to mining operations, and, in 1830, Bollaert returned home. He returned as he had gone, around Cape Horn, and via Rio de Janeiro, where he picked up a smattering of Portuguese (he had learned Spanish in Peru). He had a natural gift for languages. His trip from Valparaiso to Rio was made on board the *Adventure*, during its famous scientific cruise with the *Beagle*.

Back in London in October, 1830, he returned to the study of chemistry, in the hopes of getting the assistantship at King's College, which had been established two years before. Those hopes, he wrote, were "sorely and unexpectedly disappointed. This changed my views of life; my strong natural propensities had been thwarted."[2]

It must have been as a consequence of his frustration and despair that he formed the desperate scheme of going to East Africa, exploring the coast south from Zanzibar, proceeding to Lake Nyasa—not to be discovered by Livingston until 1859—and investigating the possibilities of an expedition across the continent. According to the obituary notice in the Royal Geographical Society *Journal* for 1877, he tried to get financial support from the Society and the government, but of course failed. Until corroborative evidence is found, this episode in Bollaert's life, probably related by him to his friends in later life and remembered by that

---

[1] Bollaert read this paper, on "The Geography of Southern Peru," in 1851. *The Journal of the Royal Geographical Society of London*, Vol. XXI (1851), xciii, 99-129.

[2] Bollaert, *The Wars of Succession of Portugal and Spain, from 1826 to 1840* (2 vols., London, 1870), I, 85.

one who wrote the obituary, can best be regarded as showing his state of mind at the time. Death in the unknown continent would have seemed to him then a fitting end.

He was psychologically ready, therefore, when he met Sir John Milley Doyle in September of 1832, to listen to that adventurer's proposals. Doyle was trying to raise a group of officers and men to go to the aid of Dona Maria II of Portugal, a girl of thirteen, whose father Pedro, former emperor of Brazil, with the help of a small fleet under a retired British naval officer, had captured Oporto the preceding July from his brother Miguel, a reactionary who had proclaimed himself king a few years earlier. A few secret meetings with Doyle's handful of officers were enough to persuade Bollaert, and on October 6 he sailed as a volunteer to put his scientific training to a new test, in artillery and engineering. For nine months he lived in the beleaguered city of Oporto. Food was at a premium, especially at only a private's pay. A meal of salt fish and potatoes, washed down by a bottle of thin, sour, highly colored new port, cost him a little more than a penny. He did his job there, served for a time as quartermaster, was wounded, was hospitalized with inflammation of the lungs following exposure and lack of food, was put in command of a rocket brigade—still on a private's pay— was awarded a war medal and created Knight of the Order of the Tower and the Sword, and finally saw Maria II crowned in Lisbon before he left for England in 1833.

Bollaert confessed that at heart he was a liberal, as Pedro was. Yet his next fantastic six years were spent in behalf of the conservative cause in Spain. Somewhere he had met Baron Maurice de Haber, whose chief business was raising funds for the reactionary monarchs, and in March of 1834, he left England in a fast cutter to carry dispatches from Haber to Miguel and to Carlos, the pretender to the Spanish throne. These are years for Bollaert of diplomatic intrigues, of false passports, of being smuggled over the border of Spain among the mountain guerrillas who were Carlos's chief strength, of acting as agent in Bayonne, of supplying Haber with information, of carrying money when it could be raised, of acting as interpreter, of giving advice on a high diplomatic level to Don Carlos, and of traveling to Holland, to Karlsruhe, and to Rome, where for a short time he was treasurer of Dom Miguel, who had thrown in his lot with Carlos.[3] It was exciting, tremendously exciting, but in 1840 he was back in London, with less in his pocket than might have been expected.

Then, after a year or so, began Bollaert's Texan experiences. He read William Kennedy's *Rise, Progress and Prospects of the Republic of Texas* (1841), and had, as he says in his journal, "a strange inkling to know this Republic." There was more to it than this. Kennedy had been promised by Samuel Houston a 4,500,000-acre grant southwest of San Antonio, and Bollaert must have met Kennedy's London agent, William Pringle, who suggested to him the possibility of going to Texas and investigating it with an eye to persuading emigrants to settle there. He may well have met Kennedy in London and have formed with him the friendship that was to last until Kennedy's death. The journal gives several hints that he meant to make Texas his permanent home. "My now adopted country," he says in one place, and again, he petitioned for and was granted admission to the Texas bar. A career as promoter and land agent, and in time as representative of English commercial capital, might open for him. It is going perhaps too far to suggest that such a contingency explained the lengths to which he went to make friends with every one in Texas, or his enrolling in the Texas Navy. But when Kennedy, having been appointed British consul at Galveston, turned back his grant to the Republic, Bollaert's opportunity for acting as a colonization agent must have dimmed.

He had two reasons for leaving Texas. The agitation for annexing Texas to the United States caused the British residents of Galveston and Houston to protest to Aberdeen, the secretary of state for foreign affairs, that their expectations would be ruined if the United States were to gain a monopoly of North American commerce. Bollaert (misspelled "Bollant") signed the petition.[4]

[3] All of these experiences are related in some detail in Bollaert's *The Wars of Succession of Portugal and Spain, from 1826 to 1840* (London, 1870).
[4] *The Southwestern Historical Quarterly*, Vol. XIX (1916), 91–93.

His health, too, was poor; the "yellow and intermittent fevers" he picked up there did not improve an incipient tubercular condition. So he left Texas, as he wrote, after nearly two years, "with a broken heart," and if it had not been for a girl in England he would have tried to go elsewhere in the New World.

Bollaert sailed from Galveston on July 10, 1844. He had had to borrow a little money to get home. He had even left his watch with one friend as security. For a few days on shipboard he was ill, and then his natural spirits and curiosity prevailed, and he kept the same kind of notes about the voyage as on the trip out. He docked at London on September 15—"Poor me, without a dollar." On his birthday his good friend, Charles Plimpton, a barrister, gave him a dinner and loaned him five pounds. In December he got a job in charge of the Spanish department of Rickards, Little & Company as a merchant clerk. For some months he played with the idea of joining another foreign venture, but in August, 1845, he decided "to take the bull by the horns," and stay with his job, do some writing, and marry a girl he had met eight years before, Susannah McMorran of Stamford. The wedding, for which Pringle and Charles Plimpton each gave him ten pounds, took place on November 22, 1845, in Stamford, at St. George's Church. In the marriage certificate, under the heading "Rank or profession," Bollaert appears as "Esquire," of 26 Devonshire Street, and his father as "Surgeon." In later years he seems to have referred to his father as a doctor, but the name is not in the rolls of the Royal College of Physicians. On October 7, 1846, a son, Charles William Alexander, was born.[5]

The "hard going" continued for some years. Bollaert's salary was reduced by twenty pounds a year during the depression of 1847, his wife helped support the family "with the needle," on February 15, 1848, a daughter, Francisca Maria Augusta, was born, and, on December 25, 1849, another daughter, Caroline Bingley Melanie Kate. Bollaert was living then in Dalston, a

---

[5] Charles in later life seems to have followed in his father's footsteps. He is recorded in the *Journal of the Anthropological Institute* for 1879 as a "local secretary (abroad)," living in Rosario.

middle-class suburb in the parish of Hackney. Two more daughters were to make their appearance, Emily Martinez, on June 15, 1851, and Alice Henderson, on January 1, 1853. William was then listed as a merchant, and with the end of the depression his situation had improved.

In 1850 he took a trip to Gibraltar and Ceuta, and in 1851 to Spain, both probably on business. In 1853 and 1854 he made a second trip to South America, landing at Santa Marta and proceeding to Panama, Quito, Lima, and Valparaiso. His account of this journey omits more of his personal references than usual, so that the auspices under which he made it are unknown. It was probably to survey business possibilities, for a few years later, in 1859, he had something to do with the formation of the Equadorian Land Company, which had a colonization program and planned to erect commercial establishments and to carry on scientific researches in connection with various scientific societies. These were activities that Bollaert might in time have organized in Texas had it not been for annexation. This company also had to yield when local political connections put an end to these fairly extravagant hopes. On this same trip he investigated the coal mines of Chile, crossed the Andes, and returned home via the Argentine Republic, Paraguay, and Brazil. This was his last long journey. Thereafter, except for brief trips to the Continent, he remained in England.

Hard times began again. In the 1860's the return of his old illness kept him chained at home, and in 1863, perhaps because the annual fees were too great for his slim purse, he resigned as a Fellow of the Royal Geographical Society. At the time of his death he was living at 4 Camden Gardens, Sheperd's Bush, not at all a fashionable district, and since his name does not appear in London or suburban directories of the period, it is probable that he lived in lodgings. His daughter Emily, a spinster, was looking after him when he died, on November 15, 1876, from "paralysis of the functions of speech and swallowing, complicated with congestion of the right lung."

All his life Bollaert aspired to be a writer, and not on scientific subjects alone. The bibliography he assembled in 1865 contains no less than eighty articles and three books, the last then still in progress. The majority of the articles appeared in scientific journals, principally in the transactions or journals of the Royal Geographical Society, of which he was a fellow, of the Ethnological Society, of New York and of London, of which he was a corresponding member, of the Society of Antiquaries, and in the memoirs of the Anthropological Society, of which he was one of the founders in 1863 and its honorary secretary for two years. The subject matter of his scientific articles covered many fields. He wrote on "the Chirihuanos or travelling doctors of Peru" for the Medico-Botanical Society, of which he was one of the founders and subsequently a corresponding member. He had articles, among others, on the llama, on New World numismatics, on the electrical theory of earthquakes, on the history of the Incas, on Indian corn, on a mastodon found in Chile, on gold ornaments in ancient Indian tombs in Ecuador, on salt and saline bodies in general (for which he received a bronze medal from Prince Albert, president of the Society of Arts, in 1853), on the coal deposits of Chile (for which he was elected a corresponding member of the University of Chile), on the alleged introduction of syphilis from the New World, on the astronomy of the Red Men of America, on the Maya alphabet, and on ancient Peruvian figurative writing.

His Texas experiences produced a variety of articles, most of them at a time when he was trying to earn a few pounds during the hard days in London in the late 1840's. The *United Service Magazine* for November, 1846, carried an abridgment of the early part of his journals under the title, "Texas in 1842—Cruise of the Lafitte, by a traveller." The same magazine printed his "History of Texas in Two Parts" in 1847, an article on "Blackbeard's Island," also in 1847, and in 1851, "The Life of Lafitte the Pirate of the Gulf of Mexico." His "Notes on the Coast Region of Texas" appeared in the Geographical Society *Transactions* for 1844, as did in 1850 his "Observations on the Geography of Texas." He had an article in the Ethnological Society *Transactions* for 1850, "On the Indian Tribes of Texas," and one in the *Transactions* of the Linnean Society that same year, "On the Botany of Texas." In addition to these, he wrote on "Hunting in Western Texas, San Antonio Bejar" in the *Sporting Review* in 1848, and "On the Natural History of Texas" in the *Sporting Magazine* for September and October, 1851. Altogether there were ten articles connected with Texas.

Twice he tried his hand at drama. On his return from Peru the first time, he wrote "The Last of the Incas; A Play in Three Acts," the manuscript of which was stolen from him in 1846. In 1840, on his return from his experiences with Carlos and Miguel, he wrote "Argia—or Creon the Tyrant of Thebes; A Tragedy," which remained in manuscript. His interest in music, evidenced on several occasions in the journal, was responsible for *Seis Canciones Españolas del Peru y Chile*, published in 1832 and again in 1848.

Bollaert's articles, as a general rule, were better than his books. He was a careful scientific observer and a good reporter of what he saw. His scientific articles consist of a series of factual statements. He could also relate interestingly enough a personal incident or an anecdote. But when it came to putting a book together, he lacked the faculty of organization and of drawing conclusions. His best book, *Antiquarian, Ethnological and other Researches in New Granada, Ecuador, Peru and Chile, with Observations on the Pre-Incarial, Incarial and other Monuments of Peruvian Nations* (London, Trübner & Co., 1860), is composed of a succession of unrelated topics held together precariously by the narrative of his personal experiences. The second book, number 28 of the Hakluyt Society publications (1861), was a translation from Pedro Simon, *The Expedition of Pedro de Ursua & Lope de Aguirre in Search of Eldorado and Amagua in 1560–1*. Bollaert did not write the introduction. His most pretentious work, in two volumes, *The Wars of Succession in Portugal and Spain, from 1826 to 1840* (London, Edward Stanford, 1870), is again less real history than a series of statements of fact, and of anecdotes interspersed with his own experiences. Had he ever published his Texas journals, they would probably not have differed greatly from the form in which they are reproduced here. Little essays, such as the one "On Titles," would have been run in haphazardly. Roughnesses in sentence structure would have been smoothed out, and doubtless other tales would have been remembered and added.

Bollaert's career provides substantiation of the accuracy and authenticity of his observations on Texas. He wrote down what he saw, he saw much that a less well trained observer would have missed, and he remembered what he heard. Few travelers at that time covered as much territory as did he. His picture of life in the frontier republic, therefore, can stand as one of the most interesting, most unprejudiced, and most sympathetic that has come down to us.

CONTENTS

	Preface	IX
	Introduction, by Stanley Pargellis	XI
I.	*Arrival in Texas* [February, 1842]	3
II.	*Galveston Island* [February–March, 1842]	14
III.	*The Cruize of the Lafitte* [March, 1842]	38
IV.	*From Galveston to Matagorda and Back* [April–May, 1842]	55
V.	*Matagorda Again and Then to New Orleans* [May–June, 1842]	83
VI.	*Visit to Houston and Vicinity* [June–July, 1842]	100
VII.	*Galveston Revisited* [August–September, 1842]	126
VIII.	*Random Observations* [October, 1842–August, 1843]	153
IX.	*Austin and Back to Columbus* [August–September, 1843]	179
X.	*San Antonio de Bejar* [September–October, 1843]	208
XI.	*The Valley of the Guadalupe* [October, 1843]	242
XII.	*From Columbus to Montgomery* [November–December, 1843]	261
XIII.	*From Montgomery to Huntsville* [December, 1843–January, 1844]	284
XIV.	*Down the Trinity to Galveston* [January–April, 1844]	311
XV.	*To the Kennedy Grant, at Last* [April–July, 1844]	332
XVI.	*Homeward Bound* [June–July, 1844]	360
	Appendix I: Colonization Contract Between the Republic of Texas and William Pringle, James Grieve, and Associates	380

William Bollaert's Texas

Appendix II: Notes for a Life of Wm. Kennedy,
  by W. Bollaert   385
Bibliography   390
Index   397

ILLUSTRATIONS

	Facing page
Bollaert's Sketch of the Texas Squadron	72
View of Galveston Harbor	72
General Houston	73
Doctors' Office	104
President's House	105
The City of Austin	105
San Antonio from the Top of the Alamo Church	232
Broken Bridge over the San Antonio River	232
Texan Farm in Montgomery County	233
Huntsville	264
The "Scotch Hermitage"	264
Page from Bollaert's Journal	265

MAPS

The Republic of Texas, 1842   page 22

WILLIAM
BOLLAERT'S
TEXAS

I

ARRIVAL IN TEXAS

[February, 1842]

THE WHYS AND WHEREFORES of my going to Texas is not all important to relate, but for some time ere I left England for this country from what I had read and heard of it gave me a strange inkling to know this Republic.[1] I had perused much that had been written on the country, but it is to Mr. Kennedy's *Rise, Progress, and Prospects of Texas*,[2] published in 1841, that I obtained the information I sought for. On my friends and acquaintances being made acquainted with my project of going, and probably settling in Texas—they drew long faces, shrugged their shoulders, expostulated, suggested Australia, Canada, etc., but Texas!—pitied my determination—but gave me their blessing. I need hardly mention that to most people in Europe—Texas was an almost unknown country; there were vague ideas regarding its locality—that Galveston Island had been the abode of pirates and other strange folk—and that a handful of American Backwoodsmen and a few foreigners from every quarter of the globe had rescued from the bigotted and ignorant and debased Mexicans a considerable portion of territory. Many sanguinary conflicts had been the consequence of this crusade of civilization, but the Battle of San Jacinto fought on the 21st of April 1836 under General Houston had settled for ever the separation of Texas from Mexico.

I made arrangements to go from London to Galveston direct,

---

[1] In Bollaert's first draft of the first page of his journal he states: "My object in going to Texas was to assist in the survey and examination of a large tract of country comprising about 4½ millions of acres situated west of San Antonio, with a view to colonize it with emigrants from Europe."

[2] William Kennedy, *Texas: The Rise, Progress, and Prospects of the Republic of Texas*. This work was based upon the author's personal observations and research while serving as a British diplomat in Texas. Its chief design was to promote amicable Texas-British relations and obviously it had considerable influence upon Bollaert's attitude towards Texas. See Bollaert: "Notes for a Life of Wm Kennedy" in Appendix II.

3

but this, I do not generally recommend, without a large number of persons or Emigrants were starting—but would recommend starting, say, from Liverpool, to N. Orleans, and from thence by a steamer to Galveston. My fellow passengers on board the ——— (I cannot say the "Good Ship") consisted of a French Gentleman, his family,[3] and servants, about settling in Texas, a German merchant and a few Steerage passengers consisting of Carpenters, Blacksmiths, Tailors, etc. On the 9th December 1841 we left London. On the following morning a cutter ran foul of us and carried away our jib-boom, etc.—bad weather caused us to bear up and come to anchor off Deal for some days in company with a large fleet of outward bound vessels. A fair wind from N. E. then wafted us out of the channel carrying us into the "trades."

My companions were agreeable enough—but the Captain! Before we left London, he had given occasional proofs of inebriety, but I had hoped that his duties as a seaman and navigator when at sea would reclaim him from the intemperate use of the bottle. Alas, the brute, pardon the word, was in a state of intoxication the whole voyage. He seldom changed his clothes unless they were falling to pieces—he seldom if ever slept in his berth. The cabin passengers fortunately had state rooms—such as they were—thus the *Captain* would sit and booze by himself after we had retired nightly, fall drunk under the table and then groan—and sleep. He had a horror of even moderate cleanliness and in a short time the cabin became perfectly pestiferous. The few days we remained at St. Thomas';[4] the *Captain* led a life of drunkenness and dissipation, but I was fortunately located on shore with a kind and hospitable friend, thus evading in some measure his brutality and wretched conduct. How is it that some means are not resorted to—to ascertain, say by some examination by competent persons in the principal ports of Britain, as to the knowl-

---

[3] Bollaert later visited the French gentleman and his family on their plantation in Montgomery County. For his observations on their trials and hardships in the new republic, see Chapter VI.

[4] St. Thomas is one of the principal islands formerly owned by Denmark and belonging to the Danish West Indies group. These islands were purchased by the United States in 1917 and are now generally referred to as the Virgin Islands.

edge of masters of vessels in navigation at least.[5] Ours was not even a seaman, but being part owner of the vessel being the stipulation of his getting the command, the care of the ship entrusted to his mate. One day our worthy commander assayed to "take the sun." He had previously taken some huge draughts of bottled beer. He could not succeed in making the meridian observation: he smashed his sextant to pieces and then threw it over board! Drink had commenced making ravages upon his mind and it was with difficulty he was prevented by remonstrances from throwing the chronometer over board.

Wednesday, January 19th, 1842: We made Antigua,[6] passed between this island and Guadalupe, saw Montserrat.[7]

Thursday, January 20th, 1842: Abreast of Nevis, got sight of St. Kitts, St. Eustache, and at 10 A.M., St. Saba; bore N. by W. 8 miles. We passed over Avis shoal—6 P.M. shoals of fish. All the islands seen as yet have high rugged peaks and of a dark colour—particularly Nevis. The West India Islands are known as the Antilles and the Colombian Archipelago. They are divided into three parts, viz.: the Great and Little Antilles, and the Bahama or Lucayo isles, and belonging to England, France, Spain, Denmark, Sweden, and the Republic of Hayti.

Friday, January 21st, 1842: 6 A.M. Saw St. Thomas'. In rounding "Frenchman's Rock" encountered a heavy squall. 11 A.M.

---

[5] [*Note at the end of Chapter I*] In the autumn of 1842 I made some mention to the Geographical Society to suggest to Captain Fitzroy R.N. and one of the elder "brethren of the Trinity House" owing to the ignorance and inability of many masters of vessels—some of whom had come under my notice during some 16 years sailing about the world—the necessity of an examination as to capability in navigation as well as seamanship—1843—I find that Capt. F. introduced a bill into Parliament—but after some discussion withdrew it for the present on being informed by Mr. Gladstone who "said that the question of subjecting the masters and mates of merchant vessels to an examination previously to granting them certificates, was under the consideration of the Government."—Bollaert.

[6] An island in the colony of Leeward Islands, Lesser Antilles, British West Indies.

[7] In the British West Indies, situated southwest of Antigua.

came to anchor. 1 Danish and 2 Dutch Men of War in harbour. These good people very fond of saluting each other—a great expenditure of powder. A fleet of some 60 merchant ships in port from all parts of the world, this being a Free Port.

The Agents of the West India Steam Packet Company busily employed in building a wharf for the expected steamers. Coal is brought at present from England, but it is reported that a coal has been discovered in the Island of Porto Rico. There is no yellow fever here just now—but those of a bilious and congestive character not uncommon. 6 A.M. 78°

Saturday, January 22nd, 1842: Saw some fine specimens of sulphuret of copper with traces of Galena, from the copper mines of Virgin Gorda, these mines are working by a company composed of English speculators and others, under the superintendence of Captain Hitchen. The average per centage of copper in the ores 32 per cent. A great outlay has been made and have got down to a 30 fathom level. Traces of silver said to have been found.

This being a free port, or at least a very trifling duty paid, consequently commercial affairs are generally brisk. Here can be purchased from Day and Martins blacking to Attar of Roses, from Morrissons pills to English and French preserved meats, etc. The shops and stores are not so finely set off as those of Regent St. but they nevertheless contain costly commodities, and the jingling of Spanish dollars and dubloons, particularly at the Bank which is situated on the main street, is very interesting. I strolled to the cemetery (known by the name of Gregory). Many were the monuments erected to the memory of the departed, some of beautiful Italian marble and exquisite design and workmanship; numberless wooden crosses mark the spots where those who die in the Lord— sleep the sweet sleep of death. I stood alone in this receptacle for the mortal body, a blistering sun shone above me, the blue heavens without a cloud, but a gentle breeze cooled the air. The cemetery was covered with huge spring nettles and large gay tropical flowers. I saw nothing in unison with a grave yard. There the scorpions, and lizards running about, in and over the tombs, pushing themselves up so unconcernedly; the myriads of mosquitos buzzing about and now and then pretty birds flying about. The stately coco-nut and plaintan[8] to be seen at every step, in the distance sugar plantations, and all over the island covered with a dense tropical vegetation.

There are two or three good hotels in the Town, the charge about 2 to 2½ dollars per diem. The sovereign exchanges for five dollars—Spanish dubloon 16 dollars. The dollar is divided into 15 old bits or 12 new bits and 3 stivers,[9] 5 stivers an old bit or 75 stivers=to 1 dollar. *When one knows how to go to market here,* things are not expensive. The favourite drinks here are lemonades and sangarees, the last made with maderia [*sic*], iced water, sugar, and nutmeg. Good Havana segars are scarce—but the segars made on the island is of good tobacco, and very fair ones 20 for 3 pence. A long cheroot is manufactured here and smoked principally by the Negro men and women. Nineteen-twentieths of the population of the Island are Negros [*sic*] and "darkies" of different shades. The Negros appear to be a pretty bustling race, full of fun and talk, eternally rowing each other, but seldom come to blows. Slavery under a very mild form exists here, but at 6 P. M. all of the ferry or passage boats (these are conducted by slaves for the benefit of their masters) are hauled up and chained to the shore to prevent any drunken or disaffected Negro escaping to the Island of Tortola[10]—for on the arrival of a runaway Negro at that Island (which is in the vicinity), they are free. Often they can find no work and return to St. Thomas' again.

I met with some planters who complained of "Emancipation" and "The Saints." Some talk loudly of the *ruin* of the West Indies, but this has yet to be seen. The produce of sugar may not be so great for awhile, but then there will be a more general commercial intercourse and greater consumption of manufactured goods. At all events slavery is a harsh term, and if sugar and rum is to be the principal result—it is a pitiful affair. But, slavery as it appeared

[8] Plantain—a tropical plant very similar in appearance to the banana tree.
[9] A stiver is a Dutch coin formerly worth about two United States cents.
[10] The chief island of the British Virgin Islands.

to me in St. Thomas' is very unlike what has been represented by many of the champions for the "Black Man."

During the day it is hot on shore, but on board under an awning it is pleasant when the sea breeze sets in. It is said that there is very little difference between winter and summer in these latitudes.

There is one Catholic Church, one Danish, and occasionally the Episcopal or English minister comes over from St. Croix.[11] This may be called a rocky mountainous island. It contains two or three small sugar plantations. There are no rivers or streams; here and there a small spring, and the well water pretty good; but they are dependent on rain water for drinking.

At present the shores of the Bay, with the town upon its three hills being covered with verdure, is very picturesque. There are a few trees, no timber, but plenty of brush-wood.

The principal houses are well built, of stone, with venetian blinds before the windows, but the habitations of the "darkies" "down town" have no very particular regard to the rules of architecture.

There is one newspaper, written in Danish and English—not quite so large as the *Times*. Neither is the St. Thomas' establishment so large as that of Printing House Square. The newspapers give full particulars of Court Affairs in Denmark, the health of his Danish Majesty and his wish for the welfare of his colonists—scanty political or literary information, advertisements, and winds up with an occasional "Reward of 50 dollars for a runaway Negro."

January 25th, 1842: The Steamer "Tay" of 1700 Tons came in from England. This is the first of the line that has arrived. A Ball was given to the Officers and passengers the following Evening.

January 26th, 1842: The Steamer "Clyde" arrived.

The mornings and evenings are beautiful at this season of the year, yet during the heat of the day, all hands appear at their different vocations. The Spanish part of the population dines

[11] More commonly spelled Santa Cruz and formerly a part of the Danish West Indies.

about 1 P.M. and sleeps a short siesta. In this I think they are judicious, because they rise very early. No one in this island, and I should think it is the same on nearly all the rest, knows what hard work is—thus with common industry and intelligence, but with great care to one's temperate habits, even the inhabitant of the North will enjoy good health and in a few years become independent. But the motto of many in these delicious islands is "A short life and a merry"—thus they sometimes go to "Gregory" rather prematurely. Nature is most prolific in all her operations in these climates, the productions are of a costly nature, thus the manufactured commodities are easily obtained in exchange.

During the short time I was at St. Thomas', the moon was in her full. This gorgeous nocturnal luminary I had never seen so bright before, although I had previously resided in tropical countries. Its brightness to me was of a peculiar description and in the "stilly night" to a northern eye looked unnatural and the glare looked anything but the "soft silvery beams of Cynthia."[12] It is said, I believe, by some philosophical writer that the moon's rays give out heat, indeed they appear to have that character.

There are about 2000 slaves in the island. Moreover, some free blacks. Some are let out as low as 3 dollars per month, but for one who is a good cook, almost any salary may be obtained.

There is a regiment of Danish troops—and a nightly armed patrol composed of free blacks—commanded by Creoles. The inhabitants are very polite and hospitable, and even in this warm climate much addicted to dinners, parties, concerts and dancing.

While I was here a good Equestrian company was performing.

February 1st, 1842: Left St. Thomas', passing Porto Rico. Saw the Mona passage. Continuing our course along by Santo Domingo, fell in with shoals of flying fish[13] and immense flights of gulls.

---

[12] Cynthia, the emblem of the goddess Diana, is a poetic name for the moon used from Shakespeare's day through the nineteenth century. It was one of Bollaert's favorite literary symbolisms.

[13] My readers will recollect the old anecdote, that a young sailor told his mother, among other things that he had seen flying fish in the Seas and Rivers of Rum on shore at Jamaica. The old lady would not believe him—but I beg to assure

February 5th, 1842: Blue Mountains of Jamaica seen—the High land of Cuba— 5 P.M. upon the "——— Shoal," S. end this A.M. 4^{fm} water—This Shoal is four miles broad and 8 long composed of Rocks and white sand.

February 7th 1842: Off Mon[tego] Bay—numerous Sugar Plantations seen. On the 8th it was thought we were below the Great and little Cayman Islands[14]—but at 2 A.M. on the 9th the man at the helm heard a noise as of breakers on the starboard bow. The master and mate [were] asleep and before the latter could be roused we were within 10 minutes of our destruction. It was dark and cloudy. After considerable confusion we stood to the S. and W. and at daylight we only found ourselves ½ mile from the "Cayman Brac."[15] A fresh and fair breeze from N. and E. soon extricated us from our difficulty and we passed between the Two Caymans. This breeze seemed to have no salutary effect upon the Captain. The bottle was his only companion.

February 11th, 1842: Made Cape Mandes,[16] Island of Cuba. It is low and this part has the reputation of producing some of the finest sorts of tobacco. At noon made Pt. San Antonio.[17] Weathered at and laying up about N.W.

February 13, 1842: Sailed through shoals of Portuguese Men of War—sea weed and drift wood—

February 16th, 1842: Fell in with N.E. Gales which cooled the temperature of the air from 85° to 60° in a few hours.

---

my readers that this is literally the case. The same old dame did give credence to mountains of sugar. The Spaniards often gave the name of *Pan de Azuca*[r] (Sugar Loaf Mountain) to such rocks or mountains having a conical appearance. —Bollaert.

14 "Alligator" Islands, northwest of Jamaica.

15 The middle one of the Three Caymans, the others being Little Cayman and Grand Cayman. These British islands are located about seventy-five miles due south of Trinidad, Cuba.

16 Bollaert obviously meant Cape Mangles (there being no Cape Mandes), from his description of the region. Cape Mangles is situated on the southwestern coast of Cuba and is noted for its production of superior tobacco.

17 Point San Antonio is on the extreme western tip of the Island of Cuba.

February 18th, 1842: 8 A.M. Flight of wild duck—drift wood and sounded in 35 fathoms; at noon in 20 fathoms. Northerly gale increased, with that ahead.

February 19th, 1842: 6 A.M. 60°. Noon 52° when the land to the E. of Galveston seen.

February 20th, 1842: A deputy pilot came on board, but we were fortunate in the arrival of Mr. Temple, the able pilot of Galveston, to carry us over the *Bar* the following day. Glad enough was I to get on shore once more safe on terra firma. I may mention here that the Captain continued his drunken line of conduct, indeed exceeded rather his love of liquor. He was taken sick, delirium tremens came upon him "and his reeling brain conjured up a multitude of fancies, far more horrible than ever tantalized the wildest maniac." He would sit upright on his bed, his countenance the image of dispair. His eyes were alternately fitfully glancing, or fearfully rolling in their strained sockets, as if in pursuit of ever changing objects. Startled at the entrance of any one into his room, at times incapable of recognizing the person—He would fear and shriek that his attendants wanted to rob or murder him. Terror would beam from every lineament.

"Fiends!" he would exclaim, shrinking backward and elevating his hand for defence.

"Snakes! See them crawl!—see, see, they are at my throat—they want to suck my blood—keep them off!" The expression of his features, his intense agitation, his motions were all those of one upon whom ten thousand reptiles were trailing their scaly bodies. In one of his paroxysms he beat himself dreadfully—bit his tongue in two and suffered much. But through the unremitting attention of his medical men and the family who had hospitably received him into their house—he recovered.

He took again to drinking soon afterwards and it was with difficulty he was persuaded to leave Galveston. The ship got a fresh cargo of cotton and arrived safely in Liverpool.

But to return to my narrative. On my landing I found by letters awaiting me that the affairs in which I felt an interest were going on better than I expected. And having a particular and pressing letter of introduction to a countryman, I proceeded forthwith to present it. After the ordinary cut and dried expressions of welcome to "this new country" I was invited to take tea—or in this country called supper.

During the meal somehow or another my host discovered that I unfortunately "had a will of mine own" and that I would not gulp down or digest his views relative to men and manners and things in Texas. It might prejudice on my part, but I had come to the determination to consider the world honest until I had discovered personally the reverse and to me it appeared so extraordinary that my host, who had been established here some time, apparently doing a good business, should wish to bias my mind against "Texas and the Texans." My very recent arrival prevented me replying more than *"nous verrons,"* but from the moment I did not bend to his strange view of things, he withdrew his patronising smile. How could I acquiesce with him? I had nursed in my mind the little I knew of Texas with some fondness and it would have shown a fickleness indeed and a want in me, as the Yankees say, "of the natural dignity of man," to have thrown over board and destroyed my fond hopes, perhaps through the prejudice of another.

The scanty supper was cleared away by a couple of hulking dirty slave wenches. The tallow candle shed an ambiguous light. The room was cold and cheerless, not such as one would expect in the domicile of an Englishman. No comforting cheer made its appearance, although mine host did not appear to have "taken the pledge," for there was a certain reddish blue and yellow tinge on his proboscis and cheeks. A "norther" had set in. It howled and shook the wooden habitation. I rose to depart, begging that Mr. ———— would be good enough to send one of his Negroes to show me the Hotel. His reply was the following: "It is very late to send any one out on such a night as this—but there are two Hotels up Town," and he came to his door showing me the way out. The night was pitch dark, pointing in the direction I should go—and then he closed his door.

"Bravo," said I, and I laughed heartily at the position I found myself in, and thought within myself I will never accept another "pressing letter of introduction." During my progress "up Town" I fell into several ditches, got into several quagmires, got into one or two *cul-de-sacs*, when at last I got into an avenue something like a street, but all was dark. I saw the light in the lower part of a house. I proceeded to the window and saw several persons huddled round a "stove." I entered when it was soon perceived that I was a "stranger." I approached the fire to light a segar. I was politely offered a seat when the bar man opened the conversation: "Stranger, I guess you came in on the Brig today?" I replied in the affirmative—told all I thought would be interesting to my hearers. The night wore apace and although the Boarding House was full of people, the "stranger" was accom[m]odated.

It was made known to me some months afterwards that the above individual in question wrote a very lachrymose letter to London informing the party who had given the letter of introduction "that he was sorry if I was a dear friend of his, for *he* could not fold me to his heart, etc.," and spoke of my immoral conduct, etc. The history of the business is that my acquaintance with Mr. Kennedy, and not permitting slander to be heaped upon him, was the cause of, the mantel of protection—that my letter of introduction anticipated—was not thrown over me.[18]

[18] The author has included at the end of this chapter two clippings from the *Civilian and Galveston Gazette*, March 2, 1842, and March 5, 1842. Neither article appears very relevant to the narrative (hence is not reproduced), except that the first one, which is extremely critical of Bollaert's friend and countryman (William Kennedy), probably was written by the above Englishman in question.

II

GALVESTON ISLAND

[February–March, 1842]

BEFORE CONTINUING THE NARRATIVE it may not be out of place to say something relative to the Island of Galveston. On approaching its shores it is seen to be very low and uninteresting, but there are land marks such as "The Three Trees," which are a collection of small trees eleven in one group and two single ones about the centre of the island, and houses along the beach. Formerly there was some difficulty in making the bar, or pass, into the harbour owing to the erroneous latitude and longitude that was given. This and other natural points have been well ascertained, and there being no want of pilots, makes this place easy of access.

The present name of the island was given to it by Lorenzo Závala, in honor of the Intendente General of New Spain, Don Jose Conde de Gálvez.[1] It was formerly known as the "Isla de San Luis," and its eastern P[t]. called "Punta de las Culebras," so that the island was at times denominated "Snake Island," from the number of these reptiles inhabiting its small lakes and bayous. It was a wilderness like unto the surrounding country, being occasionally inhabited by Indians (the Carancuhaus[2] principally) lured to it for hunting and fishing. It was the occasional resort and rendezvous of the sea-rovers who frequented these seas, more particularly from the time and previous to Jean LaFitte[3] establishing his headquarters at Barrataria, a noted locality to the westward of the Mouth of the Mississippi.

Here a few words (the life of LaFitte)[4] relative to this indi-

---

[1] Bollaert is in error. During the period that Bernardo de Gálvez, not Don José Conde de Gálvez, served as Spanish governor of Louisiana (1777–83), he ordered a survey of the Texas coast. It was at this period that Galveston Island was named in his honor, a few years before Lorenzo de Zavala was even born.

[2] This word has several spellings, but generally it is "Karankawa."

[3] More commonly "Laffite," although either form seems correct.

[4] Laffite held a strange fascination for Bollaert, who during his stay in Texas

vidual may be interesting: Jean LaFitte was a native of France. He ran away from his paternal roof and after some time we find him in command of a *Privateer*, using the Venezuelan flag against the Spaniards or against their property in the shape of their merchant vessels. Establishing his headquarters with others of his calling at Barrataria about the year 1805 (some accounts say 1809). But just before the Battle of New Orleans in 1814 his excesses and depredations called forth the interference of the authorities of Louisiana. A flotilla was dispatched from N. Orleans by Gov. [W.C.C.] Claiborne, which succeeded in routing out of their nest the freebooters of Barrataria. LaFitte and his followers escaped, but their vessels, fort, habitations, and booty to the amount of 500,000 dollars fell into the hands of captors. Previous to this event the British commanding officer in these seas made overtures to LaFitte to join him against N. Orleans. This was not acceded to by this Sea-Rover, who placed in the hands of Gov. Claiborne the correspondence of the British officer, and although the ban of outlawry had been issued against him and his followers, it was considered advisable to promise a pardon should they redeem themselves by assisting in the protection of N. Orleans. This LaFitte and many of his followers did and received President Madison's pardon 5th February, 1815.

LaFitte did not lay fallow but obtained or purchased a Privateer's Commission from the Colombian Government, or their agent in the United States, and occupied himself in concert with others to arrange for active operations. In 1816–17 we hear of Galveston Bay being the residence of "a motley mixture of freebooters and smugglers, under the Mexican flag, being in reality little less than the re-establishment of the Barratarian Band, somewhat more out of the reach of Justice" headed by a person styled Commodore Aury,[5] who in conjunction with some Americans

continued to collect data on the famous pirate. His article, "Life of Jean Laffitte, the Pirate of the Mexican Gulf," published in 1852, in *Littell's Living Age*, Vol. XXXII (1852), 433-46, was probably one of the first authentic biographies of Laffite ever printed.

[5] An account of Louis-Michel Aury's activities on Galveston Island is found in Harris Gaylord Warren's *The Sword Was Their Passport*, 143.

was allied to the Mexican Patriots. The celebrated General Mina[6] with many followers came to the island on his way to Mexico, October, 1815, expecting the cordial co-operation of Aury. This was not carried into effect. When Mina set sail, Aury only accompanying him on the coast of Mexico with his daring band composed of 300 warriors, but after performing prodigies of valor and sufferings of no ordinary description, fell a martyr to the cause he had upheld on the Peninsula.

Aury, it would appear remained some little time at Matagorda, retiring from it, and it is believed he then went to Colombia.[7]

After the departure of Mina and Aury the persons then at Galveston consisted of about 30 or 40 persons, including sailors, etc.; some six of them formed a new government, and they appear not to have considered it convenient to have "neither knowledge or belief of a Mexican Republic." LaFitte and many followers joined the above individuals—their numbers rapidly increased amounting at one time to nearly 1000 persons. A Fort and habitation were erected about the spot now known as Sacaroppa (called then Campeache). They soon had a fleet of more than a dozen vessels.

In 1819 General Long[8] arrived in Texas with armed forces. After four failures in the field he attempted to get LaFitte to form a coalition with him. This he failed to do. Long went afterwards to Mexico. He was taken prisoner and ultimately assassinated by a Mexican soldier. In this same year the Government of the U. States was very desirous of dislodging LaFitte from the island, communicating with him on the subject—but it was not until 1821 that he was forced to break up his establishment and then "cleared out," which he did in an armed Brig. He cruised about

[6] Francisco Xavier Mina was a Spanish liberal who failed in his efforts to overthrow Ferdinand VII and fled from Spain in 1814. He hoped to strike another blow at the autocratic Ferdinand VII through an invasion of Mexico. He and his men landed on Galveston Island on November 22, 1816, whence they launched their expedition against the Spaniards in Mexico. For a time things went well, but Mina was eventually captured and executed on November 11, 1817, at the age of twenty-eight years. *Ibid.*, 146–48, 160, 168.

[7] Aury died at Isla de Providencia (Old Providence) in 1821. Walter Prescott Webb and others, eds., *The Handbook of Texas*, I, 78–79.

[8] Dr. James Long's ill-fated venture in Texas is covered adequately in Warren's *The Sword Was Their Passport*, 233–54.

for a short time in the Gulf, went to the island of Margaritta near the Orinoco and [was] reported to have died in Yucatan in 1826. Although there is no very positive information relative to him after that period, it is generally supposed that he died some years afterwards there or in one of the West Indian Islands.[9]

We will retrace our steps a little to mention that in 1818 General Lallemand[10] with French emigrants—chiefly of Napoleon's old soldiers—formed a settlement which they called the "Champ d' Asile" near Galveston, but were dispersed by the Spaniards.

In July, 1821 S. F. Austin entered Texas with 17 companions, when the terms for colonization entered into with his father Moses Austin were settled. One of these 17 is a gentleman now living on the island. He informs me that Texas was then an almost unknown "wilderness," that the island had not one habitation, its previous piratical possessors having destroyed the abodes. The island was covered with long, thick grass. The bayous and ponds full of alligators and snakes. Mosquitoes in myriads. Game and fish were in extraordinary abundance. It was then concerted to make the island at some time or other what we now see it. Mr. Kennedy says, "In 1836, there was hardly one arrival in a month of shipping at the port. In 1837 there were but 7 houses on the island. In May 1839, there were thirty sailing vessels in the harbour at one time—three steamers plying regularly between it and N. Orleans, and the same number between it and Houston."[11]

This brings me to the period I am now writing.

February, 1842: There appears to be a more fixed population than formerly, the building of houses, moving and removing them continually going on.[12] Vessels from various parts of the world

---

[9] Bollaert's first assumption, that Laffite died at Yucatán in 1826, is the accepted version.

[10] See J. A. Dabbs, "Additional Notes on the Champ d'Asile," *Southwestern Historical Quarterly*, Vol. LIV (1950–51), 347–58, for an account of Charles François Antoine Lallemand's activities in Texas.

[11] Kennedy, *Texas*, II, 407.

[12] The houses are built of wood and so constructed that even a three-story house can be moved from one end of town to the other at pleasure. It is not a question of moving one's furniture, but one's house into the bargain.—Bollaert.

continually arriving. The steamers from N. Orleans bring passengers, emigrants, and goods, returning laden with cotton and other produce. What is known as the Market Place—Strand and Tremont St., Church St., and Custom House—shew a scene of comparative bustle. The greater number of the inhabitants are from the U. States, with a sprinkling from every part of the world. The English language is the one spoken, but "Buenas dias," "Bon Jour," "Bon Giorno," "Guten Tag," "Ya Ya," etc. and an occasional jabbering of the Lipans and Coshattis[13] is heard.

Although the following was written a little later in the season under a specific heading, I beg to introduce it here:[14]

Life in Galveston

I am quite a convert to the "creature comfort" system, it is a good one, and I speak most feelingly on the point, having lived at one period of my life, and for three years on a sandy desert, six months in a besieged city and more over . . . . Some villainous authors[15] have treated Texas most scurrilously, they have called her hard names—have gone so far as to report that this was the last country created—of shreds and remnants; its geological formation clearly shows at no very remote period, its shores and beautiful prairies were under water, but then there is quite enough above the sea already, to offer a happy home to thousands.

But to my subject, "creature comforts"—and let me premise that this is naturally almost a barren island, there is abundant pasture, but only three clumps of young trees—water may be obtained very near the surface, thus in dry weather the gardens can be easily watered; if there be any inconvenience, it is that the temperature is rather too elevated, for northern vegetables and plants, but then there are so many others that require considerable heat for their production, and these we can have.

About sunrise, prudent and judicious people will rise, prepare

13 Alabama-Coushatta.
14 This article obviously was written by Bollaert. A marginal note in his handwriting states, "from the *Commercial Chronicle.*"
15 Edward George Earle Lytton Bulwer-Lytton.

their toilette, clad themselves lightly, walk or work in their gardens, then ride or bathe on the sea shore—at half past 7 A. M. bells may be heard ringing about the city from the different Hotels; but in the tones of that of the Tremont, I can almost fancy the accompaniment of the words "come to breakfast come!" The bells ring for about five minutes—they stop short—the sluggards hold a counsel of war with themselves, as to the propriety of "turning out." Now then, under the Tremont Verandah, the boarders and others meet—words of recognition take place—some of the individuals may indulge in the 'weed' per humo and per masticato.

A small bell is now rung, when all take their places at the breakfast table—the ladies at the top. We all appear to suffer a little langour, the air is sultry—the sea breeze has not set in—we get this meal—which is a most excellent *dejeuner a la fourchette*—retire, light the gentle Havana, discuss the politics of the day—a small quantity of whittling going on—but the quantity of wood thus destroyed will depend upon the excited state of the times, etc. Then those who have business attend to it—idlers may return to their rooms, read—and these idlers and visitors read a great deal—Bulwer's last novel of Zanoni is here, this is a great favorite —then before dinner, billards or nine-pins may be played. At the bar[16] of the Tremont lunch is laid—but to partake would be sinful, considering the excellent dinner that Capt. Seymor has in preparation, which is enhanced by the promptitude of his domestics. "Come, come to dinner come," the bell announced this most important of meals. We congregate again under the Verandah— impart to each other news, etc.—probably take an iced mint-julip —the ice comes from the U. States—a glass of Madera and bitters, etc. etc. Then the little bell's inviting strain says "Dinner's on table." In a moment the crowd of carnivorae march for the dining room, where a *dinner* will be found prepared and arranged so as to meet all tastes and wishes. Moreover one may enjoy a bottle of wine, as the duties are low. Generally speaking they do not sit

[16] The *Bar* is generally a large apartment on the ground floor of an Hotel. New wines and liquors, lemonades, etc. may be had at one bit, less than 6ᵈ per glass; that is, each person taking the quantity he pleases. At the common drinking places "groggeries" or "drunkeries" ½ bit is the charge.—Bollaert.

long at table—but sometimes a few of the jovial ones huddle together, and oftimes a few songs are heard. Not many of my Texan friends sing, but they appear very fond of singing and music. Towards 4 or 5 o'clock, parties are made to go fishing on the beach with the seine—or a gallop on the prairie till dark—when "come, come, come to supper come" is the signal to prepare to this meal—it is generally a tea supper à la fourchette—a quiet smoke in the Verandah—long chats—and then each one off to some evening party or other—where if there be no dancing there is music and singing—pretty good hours are kept—but it does not require much pursuasion to sit for an hour or two and in the cool of the evening, sip a mint julip or two—touch the guitar and sing the song most loved.

[*Bollaert resumes his journal.*]

The approach to the coast of Texas by sea is, as I have before mentioned, anything but interesting, being so very low and destitute of trees. Emigrants (from Europe in particular) have been much disappointed on arriving in Galveston, that they have left this country immediately, departing either to the U. States or to their homes. But even on this nearly sandy island of Galveston, with a little attention, the ground yields every thing in the vegetable world, and even some of the more northern products.

Emigrants who have had the perseverance to go up the Bay on Buffalo Bayou[17] to Houston and its vicinity become more reconciled and by extending their journeys into Montgomery County to the east [north] where the white man finds a climate he can work in without the help of Negroes, many emigrants settle. But when they go, say toward the west and journey by Washington—the upper parts of the Colorado, on the other side of the Guadalupe or on toward San Antonio—the European emigrant is perfectly satisfied and delighted with the appearance of the country. As an instance, two Englishmen started from their native country—one on his way to Texas and the other to Illinois. On their

[17] Buffalo Bayou was eventually widened and deepened to form the Turning Basin and the Houston Ship Channel.

arrival at N. Orleans, the one destined for Texas heard such reports about this country that he returned immediately to Europe *disgusted with Texas!!* The other who was bound for Illinois came to the determination to pay a visit to Texas and see for himself. After remaining a day or so at Galveston, he journeyed westward; he is now delighted with the country and has settled in the vicinity of Gonzales on the beautiful Guadalupe river.

I became acquainted with General Mirabeau Lamar,[18] expresident. The suavity of his manners, his pleasing address, kindly feeling and expressions relative to my native country, with the offer of his good services should I require them, was grateful and flattering. I cannot omit to mention here that his subsequent attentions and friendliness I feel proud to mention; his kindness and readiness to give me at all times advice and information relative to Texas affairs.

I [also] became acquainted with D. G. Burnett,[19] who had been the first president of Texas, and from his society, conversation, and labours, I must ever remain his debtor.

A Mexican prize was brought in, but though of no great value was a sufficient cause to call forth a pleasurable "excitement." Party spirit was running high, the greater portion of which is as yet a sealed book to me. One thing, however, I soon discovered that it was the old political bloodless war of "Outs versus In's."

The political forces in Texas at this period were aligned behind either Sam Houston, now serving his second term as president of the Republic, or Mirabeau B. Lamar, the former president. The latter's administration was none too successful and the Houston forces were making the most of his magnificent failures. Lamar, who had visions of extending the boundaries of the Republic to the Pacific Coast, had dispatched the Texas Santa Fé Expe-

---

[18] Mirabeau Buonaparte Lamar was the second president of the Republic (December, 1838–December, 1841). His term was sandwiched between Houston's two terms. The two men were bitter political enemies, as Bollaert frequently demonstrates.

[19] David G. Burnet served as ad interim president of Texas, March, 1836–October, 1836.

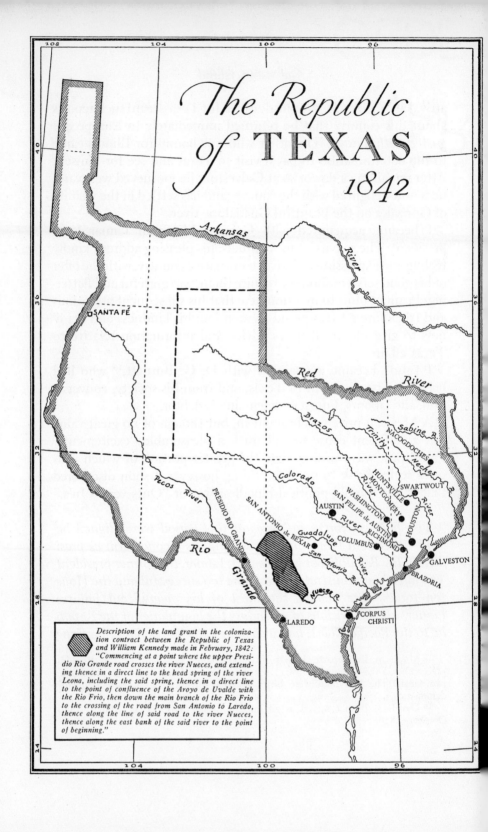

The Republic of TEXAS 1842

SANTA FÉ

Arkansas River

Red River

Brazos

Trinity

Sabine R.

NACOGDOCHES

Neches

Pecos River

Colorado

HUNTSVILLE

MONTGOMERY

SWARTWOUT

WASHINGTON River

SAN FELIPE de AUSTIN

PRESIDIO RIO GRANDE

SAN ANTONIO de BEXAR

AUSTIN

Guadalupe

COLUMBUS

RICHMOND

HOUSTON River

Rio

San Antonio R.

River

GALVESTON

Grande

San Antonio R.

Nueces R.

BRAZORIA

LAREDO

CORPUS CHRISTI

Description of the land grant in the colonization contract between the Republic of Texas
and William Kennedy made in February, 1842:
"Commencing at a point where the upper Presidio Rio Grande road crosses the river Nueces, and extending thence in a direct line to the head spring of the river
Leona, including the said spring, thence in a direct line
to the point of confluence of the Aroyo de Uvalde with
the Rio Frio, then down the main branch of the Rio Frio
to the crossing of the road from San Antonio to Laredo,
thence along the line of said road to the river Nueces,
thence along the east bank of the said river to the point
of beginning."

dition in 1841, hoping to establish commercial relations with New Mexico and to bring that region under Texas' political control as the first step in his expansion program. Actually, the city of Santa Fé was within the limits of Texas as its boundaries were established by the first congress of the Republic, and she had carried on a thriving trade with St. Louis and other cities of western United States for more than two decades. But Texas was getting none of the trade, hence Lamar's decision to cut a road from Austin to Santa Fé and thus divert that lucrative business to the impoverished Republic.

Santa Fé wanted no part of Texas, and certainly the Mexican government did not recognize Texas' spurious claim to the New Mexico province. Although the majority of the members of Congress were opposed to the plan and refused to appropriate money for it, President Lamar nevertheless carried through his scheme. Members of the ill-fated expedition eventually were captured by Mexican troops, placed in chains, and marched off to Mexico City—two thousand miles away. Santa Anna, once again head of the Mexican government, retaliated by sending a Mexican army under Rafael Vásquez to Texas in March, 1842. Before retiring across the Río Grande, the Mexicans captured and temporarily occupied the towns of San Antonio, Goliad, and Refugio.

Meanwhile, Lamar had left office and Houston had taken over for his second term. The country was in panic. The Republic had no standing army. Houston declared a state of emergency, proclaimed a blockade of Mexican ports, and eventually ordered the Texas government moved to Houston. William Bollaert was an interested spectator to the rapidly developing events as they unfolded in Galveston during the latter part of February and the month of March, 1842.

I attended a public meeting held at the "Tremont Hotel." The subject moved by the *Outs*, to address the President, General Houston, relative to individuals comprising the unfortunate Santa Fé expedition, and moreover to hear a report from a gentleman who has just returned from Mexico, having visited the greater number of them, working in chains in that City and other parts. The recital of the treatment these unfortunate men were suffering, elicited many eloquent speeches and more than once I heard growled in an under tone, "War to the knife." This expedition, which turned out so unfortunately, left Austin to transverse the wildnerness in June 1841, being composed of traders, amateurs, and a military force, about 300 in number.[20]

For sundry reasons, but more particularly for want of orders at Austin, the expedition had been delayed, and moreover the original number contemplated was 1000 men. After much suffering, having somehow or other deviated from the proper track and ultimately through the traiterous conduct of a fellow named Lewis,[21] the expedition fell into the hands of the Mexican authorities of Santa Fé in October of the same year. The greater number were made prisoners at Anton Chico, on the River Puercos [Pecos];[22] they were taken to San Miguel some 15 miles up the Puercos, and after considerable anxiety as to their fate, they were marched the immense distance from Santa Fé to the city of Mexico to be exhibited to the citizens of that place in chains and working like unto felons in the streets. Much had been expected—politically and commercially—from this adventurous trip—in the first place it was hoped that a direct transit for trade would be thus opened from Austin, the capital of Texas, to Santa Fé, which would materially increase foreign trade to the port of Galveston; and secondly, the Texan government was led to believe that the inhabitants of Santa Fé would sympathize politically with them, and in the end declare themselves free from the usurped power of

[20] Among the personnel of the Santa Fé expedition were Thomas Falconer, English traveler, and George Wilkins Kendall, publisher and editor of the New Orleans *Picayune*. Both published books relating to the venture soon after they returned from prison in Mexico.

[21] Captain William P. Lewis turned traitor and persuaded his comrades to lay down their arms on September 17, 1841. Bollaert mentions Lewis in his notes several times, invariably pointing out that "he broke his Masonic oath."

[22] Bollaert was quoting from Falconer's account of the expedition. Falconer applies the name Puercos to the Pecos in almost every instance. He evidently adopted the incorrect spelling from Lieutenant Zebulon Montgomery Pike's map. Thomas Falconer, *Letters and Notes On The Texan Santa Fé Expedition, 1841–1842*, 37n.

Santa An[n]a and the Centralist party. The principal guide of the Texans, Wm. P. Lewis, turned traitor, and moreover Santa Anna had reinforced the military power considerably in that direction under his creature General A[r]mijo.[23]

But to return to the subject of the meeting: Every proposal regarding the future welfare of the prisoners was carried nem: con: Public and private resources were to be put into requisition, more particularly the good services of the Government of the United States were to be requested, and that His Excellency, the President of Texas, General Sam Houston be made acquainted with the wishes and desires of the people of Galveston and its vicinity upon this matter. Simultaneous meetings were held throughout the country in aid of the captives' relatives and friends. I may observe that when they were first made prisoners, some of them were shot, others badly treated, and it was feared that those who had arrived safely in Mexico might be at least decimated.

On the 23rd of February General Houston arrived at Galveston from Austin, the Congress having closed session for the season. On my introduction to the President, he gave me a friendly welcome to the country. He had been twice called on to be its chief magistrate and spoke in the most kind manner of a Gentleman, a friend of mine informing me that he [Houston] had appointed him Consul-General from Texas to Great Britain. I need hardly mention the name of the person in question, but I mean Mr. Wm. Kennedy.[24] About this time he [Kennedy] arrived from San Antonio, having been there to see that part of the country owing to the Texas government having conceded to him a grant of land of considerable extent in that quarter—for the introduction of European Emigrants under certain stipulations.

March 2nd, 1842: This is one of the great days in Texas—the

---

[23] Governor Manuel Armijo of New Mexico had learned of the expedition and had detachments out awaiting the arrival of the Texans.

[24] Although William Kennedy was a British citizen, President Houston appointed him Texas consul to London. Kennedy served in the position for only a few months before returning to Texas in 1842 to become British consul in Galveston, a position he held until annexation of Texas by the United States in 1845.

anniversary of its Independence—the 4th of July of these parts. On this day, 2nd of March 1836, the declaration was made. It was a bold and daring act, but such as freemen dare do, and such as freemen will maintain. Richard Ellis[25] was President—General Houston represented Refugio County in that period. I need hardly add that this day was one of rejoicing and the evening passed in suppers and balls. The more humble citizens patronizing what is called in this country "A Dutch Ball." I offer this following from the pen of a Galvestonian:

Have you ever attended a Dutch Ball? No. Very well, I have—and with your permission, will enlighten you. In the first place, I know not why they are denominated *Dutch* Balls. Certainly not on account of their being principally patronized by that worthy class of emigrants, the Germans. Is it because a Dutchman first introduced them here? Or is it that the entertainers seek patronage from that industrious people? Or why is it? The deponent answereth not.

One dollar is the price of admittance. I paid my fee and entered. The room was small and badly lighted; the music—such as serves our *other* Balls. The attendance—slim; only ten or twelve Ladies and some twenty *Lords*. Although it was rather a failure in this instance. But then—this was the commencement of the season. A larger ball room, music, lights, ladies—will increase and multiply as the season advances.

I only aspire to a general description, and cannot entertain you with an account of how this belle was ornamented and that beau equipped. In fact, these balls are intended more for *use* than ornament, for dancing than gazing. Republican simplicity is the order of the day. The women make themselves as tidy as circumstances allow, holding a correspondence in colors, and an adherence to any particular fashion in utter contempt. The men, I am sorry to say, carry this contempt for dress a *little* too far—with some exceptions.

[25] Richard Ellis later served as a senator in the first four Texas Congresses. Lewis Wiltz Kemp, *The Signers of the Texas Declaration of Independence*, 79, 98–106.

Country dances, cotillions and waltzes, followed each other in rapid succession. Partners were rather scarce and in demand, but I managed to 'hold my own' among the competitors. "In Rome etc." is my motto, and from being a dignified spectator, I soon became a jolly and eager participant. Some of the ladies made their *debut* 'on the light fantastic toe,' but they were encouraged and prompted, instead of being criticized and sneered at—and did very well.[26]

March 10th, 1842: We have been for some days on the *qui vive*, owing to reports that a large armed force of Mexicans was approaching San Antonio. I may here remark that at the commencement of the Texan revolutionary struggle, all flew to arms—but for the better organization of armed men, the citizens formed themselves into volunteer companies and thus comparative order commenced. But as the Mexican armies increased in numbers, it was found requisite to have a standing army in Texas, to cooperate with the citizens. This regular army had been disbanded, there not being any more use for it; moreover, the expense of maintaining it was considerable.[27]

March 11th, 1842: The news was confirmed that the Mexicans had entered San Antonio, 500 in number, and that 3000 might be expected.[28] It was likewise reported and credited by many that three Mexican transports were expected off the Coast at Passo Caballo,[29] with troops, arms, ammunition and provisions.

Bollaert chooses at this point to describe the activities in Galveston, upon receipt of the news of the capture of San Antonio,

[26] This article probably was written by Bollaert and published in an English newspaper.

[27] Although this action by Houston was doubtless a judicious one, it antagonized many soldiers and officers and became a cause of much bitter criticism of the President.

[28] Vásquez captured San Antonio on March 5, and the first unconfirmed reports reached Galveston four days later.

[29] Pass Cavallo is between Matagorda Bay and the Gulf of Mexico and separates Matagorda Island from Matagorda Peninsula.

through newspaper clippings. The following items relative to the invasion were taken from the March 11–16, 1842 editions of the Civilian and Galveston Gazette *and pasted in the journal under the same dates.*

An express has just arrived from Austin announcing the retreat to that place, of a body of troops who had marched to the aid of the citizens of Bexar. It also brings positive intelligence of the surrender of Bexar to the Mexican forces by abandonment.[30] The Proclamation of Arista,[31] also received by the same Express, must remove every doubt of the most skeptical, in relation to the invasion and its purport.

We are pleased to learn that the Executive has at last determined to act in the National defence.

From the following paragraph, which appears in the form of an Extra from the office of the *Houstonian,* of the 9th inst.: we are glad to find that the official organ of the President is at length awake and calling out vigorously "TO ARMS! SAN ANTONIO TAKEN!!"

Additional information received this morning leaves no doubt that a large MEXICAN FORCE is within our borders, and have captured San Antonio and Goliad, and invaded Victoria.

There is no reason longer to doubt. J. D. Morris[32] and Mr. Van Ness[33] are in the hands of the enemy!

---

[30] The Mexican troops abandoned the town of San Antonio, in Bexar County, on March 9, four days after its capture.

[31] Mariano Arista in 1842 was general of the Mexican Army of the North. His proclamation, issued at Monterey, informed the Texans that it was hopeless for them to continue their struggle for independence and promised amnesty and protection to all who remained neutral during his planned invasion. Bollaert has more to say about Arista's proclamation in a later portion of his journal.

[32] John D. Morris in 1842 was a representative to Congress from Bexar County. *The Handbook of Texas,* II, 237.

[33] George Van Ness was a lawyer in San Antonio and one of the prisoners taken by the Mexicans during the Santa Fé expedition. The news of the capture of Morris and Van Ness was retracted in the March 15, 1842, issue of the *Civilian and Galveston Gazette;* however, Van Ness was later captured when the Mexicans returned to San Antonio in September, 1842. *The Handbook of Texas,* II, 832.

News from the West.—Mr. Cleaveland arrived here at 12 o'clock on Wednesday night with news from Victoria. Capt. Ferguson[34] had been taken by 300 Mexican troops, near Corpus Christi, and escaped. The detachment that took him were going to Copano to receive provisions, 6 vessels having been sent there with provisions. They reported 14,000 troops east of the Rio Grande.

At 11 o'clock yesterday an Express from Austin arrived bringing news of the abandonment of San Antonio, and its being in possession of the Mexican forces. The Expresses came to the President.

We have just learned the arrival of an express announcing that Victoria has been taken by the invading army.

The Coast Guards will meet at the Merchant's Exchange, at 10 o'clock this morning.

The President has given his sanction to prepare the steamer LaFitte for sea, and has subscribed one hundred dollars for the purpose.

A very large public meeting convened at 8 o'clock on Wednesday evening, at the Merchant's Exchange, to receive the Report of the Committee appointed to confer with the President. J. S. Sydnor[35] was called to the Chair, and H. Stuart[36] and A. J.

---

[34] Alanson Ferguson was a congressional representative from San Patricio County in 1842. *Biographical Directory of Texas Conventions and Congresses, 1832–1845,* 82.

[35] John S. Sydnor ran a profitable commission and real estate business in Galveston in 1842, and later served as mayor of the city (1846–47). *The Handbook of Texas,* II, 700.

[36] Hamilton Stuart founded the *Civilian and Galveston Gazette* in 1838 and remained a faithful supporter of Sam Houston as long as the latter held public office. *The Writings of Sam Houston,* IV, 424.

Yates,[37] Esqs. appointed Secretaries, the latter of whom took his seat.

Mr. Brown[38] from the Committee read the resolutions formerly passed, the letter of the Committee to the President, and his reply thereto. The latter was received with considerable hissing on the part of the audience.

The following Resolutions were adopted:

1st, Resolved, That this meeting will, tomorrow morning, aid in the enrolment and equipment of two hundred men for immediate service.

2d, Resolved, That a committee of two be appointed by this meeting, to communicate to the President, the intelligence received from the West this afternoon, and also to request him to appoint Gen. A. S. Johnston, Major General, to take command of the forces raised for the defence of the Republic.

3d, Resolved, That lists be now opened for the subscription of the names of such persons as wish now to enrol themselves.

4th, Resolved, That a committee of ——— be appointed to solicit contributions from the citizens, to the amount of five hundred dollars, for the purchase of ammunition.

5, Resolved, That the President be requested to order the preparation of the brig Wharton for sea.

6, Resolved, That a committee be appointed to procure the arms required by Mr. Jack[39] in his letter, and forward them to Brazoria.

7th Resolved, That a committee of vigilance be appointed to meet daily, to consult on the exigencies of our position, and call such meetings, and take such measures as they may deem necessary, and receive the names of such as will enrol themselves for service when called on.

[37] Andrew Janeway Yates practiced law and published the *Daily Advertiser* in Galveston at this period. Opal Rosson, "The Life of Andrew Janeway Yates" (unpublished M.A. thesis, University of Texas, 1939).

[38] George William Brown had just moved to Galveston from Virginia to practice law. *Biographical Directory of Texas Conventions and Congresses,* 57.

[39] William Houston Jack was a senator in the Texas Congress in 1842 and commander of the Brazoria County Militia which was formed to help repel forces under Rafael Vásquez. *Ibid.,* 111.

The meeting was successfully addressed in its various stages by Messrs. Love,[40] Brown, and Potter, Esqs. with great effect, and the whole spirit of the meeting was characterized by a determination to act promptly, in the defence of our country, and in the infliction of deserved chastisement upon the Mexicans, whether sanctioned or opposed by the Executive. We were much delighted with the noble spirit of independence which breathed throughout the addresses, delivered on the occasion. We cannot avoid expressing our peculiar satisfaction at the second address of our fellow citizen Mr. Brown.

The several committees were promptly appointed by the Chairman, and we regret that we have not room for the insertion of the names. The meeting adjourned until 12 o'clock the next day.

Adjourned meeting at the Merchant's Exchange, Thursday morning 10th March, 10 o'clock. J. S. Sydnor in the Chair, A. J. Yates, Sec'y.

On motion of Col. Love.

Resolved, That the President be requested to order the preparation of the brig Wharton for sea.

On motion of Col. Potter, the Express from Capt. Wm. J. E. Heard,[41] at Victoria, was read.

On motion of the Secretary, the Committee appointed by the Chairman last evening were requested to wait on the President forthwith, with the foregoing resolution, and the express just read.

Resolved, that the Committee of safety be requested to make arrangements for the departure of the steamer New York to New Orleans, and that a committee be sent out in her to procure aid.

Adjourned to meet at 1 o'clock P.M.

One o'clock, P.M. 10th March. Citizens met pursuant to adjournment.

[40] James Love was a successful planter with extensive holdings on the Brazos River. He was a staunch supporter of Lamar and used his home in Galveston as a rallying point for the political opponents of Sam Houston. *Ibid.*, 126.

[41] William Jones Heard served under Houston at the Battle of San Jacinto and was later elected chief justice of Wharton County. J. L. Kemp, "San Jacinto Roll" (MS., Texas State Archives).

Col. Love stated that another express had been received by the President, announcing the abandonment of Bexar by its citizens, and its being in the possession of the enemy. Also, that the President was preparing a proclamation which would be issued this evening.

On motion of Col. Love, Resolved that the committee of vigilance be requested to have all the horses on the island driven up and those who are about to depart for the army, be supplied.

Adjourned until to-night at 7 o'clock.

We annex the official orders for the organization of the Militia of this Brigade:

HEADQUARTERS, 2D BRIGADE
HOUSTON 9th March 1842

COL. A. A. M. JACKSON, SIR,

From positive information just received from the West, we learn that the Mexicans are in possession of the frontier towns and are marching to our country.

You will hold your command in readiness to execute such orders as may be directed to you, in a moment's notice.

You will communicate to me as it regards the protection of Galveston, and should it be necessary to extend farther protection you will use all means to effect that object.

E. MOOREHOUSE[42]
Brigadier General

Order No. 7

HEAD QUARTERS,
4TH REG'T 2ND BRIGADE
TEXAS MILITIA
GALVESTON, March 10, 1842

"The companies composing beats one, two, three and four, as well as the volunteers, will muster in their respective beats, to-morrow morning, at 9 o'clock. The companies composing beats no. 5 and 6, (Bolivar and Edward's points) will muster in their

---

[42] Edwin Morehouse participated in several Indian campaigns during the period of the Republic. *The Writings of Sam Houston*, I, 521.

respective beats, immediately on the promulgation of this order. Commandants of companies will make duplicate returns of their numbers and equipments to the Adjutant without delay. By order of

THOS. BATES
Act'g Adjutant

ALDEN A. M. JACKSON
Col. Commanding

THE MEXICANS IN OUR COUNTRY
Late and Important News from the West!!

Just as our paper was going to press we were furnished through the politeness of Mr. Winney, with a duplicate copy of original letters received from officers commanding our forces in the West, from which we make the following extracts:

San Antonio, March 4th, 1842. Two of our spies were shot at running in from the Medina, again this evening near the Leona, four spies were hailed and charged. They all got in safe. Our two spies (Mr. M'Culloch[43] and Mr. Miller[44]) were either cut off or behind the enemy.

JOHN C. HAIGHT.
Commander

BEXAR, March 5th, 1842.

The spies have just come in, and report the enemy within six miles of town, covering about one hundred acres of ground, and have 150 camp fires.

F. S. GRAY,
By order of JOHN C. HAYS
Col. Commanding

[Here Bollaert resumes his narrative.]

The town of Galveston was thrown into "intense excitement!"

[43] Ben McCulloch served as a scout for Captain Jack Hays of the Texas Rangers in 1842. He represented Gonzales County in the first legislature of the state of Texas and during the Civil War as a brigadier general in the Confederate Army. Walter Prescott Webb, *The Texas Rangers*, 84.

[44] Washington D. Miller was Sam Houston's private secretary in 1841 and later helped edit and publish the *National Register* at Washington-on-the-Brazos. *The Writings of Sam Houston*, II, 289.

In the first place the sessions [courts] broke up abruptly. The Chief Justice Morris,[45] who a few hours before sat gravely on the bench, was in the saddle armed and accoutred for war. The "gentlemen of the bar," busy raising companies of volunteers. The worthy chief clerk, Mr. Bates,[46] booted and spurred, looked the bold dragoon. Public meetings called, which were attended to suffocation. Money, clothes, provisions, etc. liberally subscribed.[47] Many sold their lots of land, some their Negroes, others their very houses, horses, oxen, etc., so as to raise funds for the various purposes that might be required. The Texans wrote to their friends and relatives in the United States to aid and assist them in this hour of need.[48] Fresh news arrived: the inhabitants of San Antonio had fled from their homes. Some of the merchants had burnt their goods to save their falling into the hands of the enemy and the whole of the western country was up in arms.

Generals Lamar and Johnson were already off and Col. Potter took a great number of friends under his command. A corps called the "Galveston Guard" was organized to remain on the island to protect the women and children. The company of "Fusileers" and "Coast Guards" made arrangements to equip the steamer "La-Fitte"[49] for a cruize at sea to intercept the reported transports, and give confidence to the people down the coast. Many were the

---

[45] Richard Morris was nominated district judge, First Judicial District, by President Lamar, September 18, 1841. *First Biennial Report of the Texas Library and Historical Commission, March 29, 1909, to August 31, 1910,* 205.

[46] Thomas Bates came to Texas from Mobile, Alabama in 1839 and soon afterwards was appointed chief clerk of the First District Court by Lamar. *The Papers of Mirabeau B. Lamar,* V, 268.

[47] Bollaert helped fit out a company of volunteers by contributing his services to several fund raising activities.

[48] Among the many contributions donated by the citizens of Galveston were large quantities of liquor. But the "Coast Guard" unanimously voted to sell it and use the funds for more essential equipment. *The Civilian and Galveston Gazette,* March 15, 1842. Despite a resolution by the "Coast Guard" that all military companies follow its example, the crew of the *Lafitte* did not choose to do so, as evidenced from Bollaert's subsequent account.

[49] The activities of the *Lafitte* are described in detail by Bollaert in Chapter III. The only official records of the *Lafitte* that could be found in the Texas State Archives was the list of the crew (*Index to Navy Muster Roll*). Jim Dan Hill, in *The Texas Navy in Forgotten Battles and Shirtsleeve Diplomacy,* neglects to mention this vessel at all.

difficulties to overcome ere the "La Fitte"[50] and two small craft bade adieu for a while on the 14th to the island, with prayers for success.

Although Houston considered the present situation somewhat as "a tempest in a teapot," he nevertheless was forced to accede to public clamor and make some show of military defense. Volunteer companies were being formed hastily in various towns and counties and were being rushed to the aid of the western frontier. But the rumored invasion by sea of the Mexican fleet posed a serious threat to such coastal settlements as Galveston. "I have not one dollar at my disposition,"[51] Houston wrote at this time. To make matters worse, the Texas Navy was scattered—part of the fleet had previously sailed off to Yucatan to assist that Mexican state in its struggle for independence from Mexico, and part was laid up in New Orleans awaiting repairs. Only the Wharton *and* Zavala *were in home waters, lying idle at Galveston because of lack of funds for repairs.*

On March 15, 1842, the Civilian and Galveston Gazette *carried this notice: "We were pleased to learn that the President assented on Sunday morning to the fitting out of the brig of war* Wharton *and the steamer* Zavala, *at the solicitation of Col. Jackson and Mr. Frankland, on the condition that they should be*

[50] The following newspaper clipping, dated March 16, 1842, is included in Bollaert's journal:

"The departure of the gallant band of Texian soldiers, who left on board the La Fitte, Monday evening last, could not fail to give joy to every true patriot.

"We visited the vessel a short time previous to her sailing, and was pleased to witness the enthusiasm which prevailed among all on board. We read to the crew the letter received from Mr. Morris, but that did not appear to have the least tendency to check their ardor. The spontaneous reply was, 'We have fellow citizens detained in prison and servitude in Mexico, and we are determined to release them!'

"The noble spirits who have gone on that expedition are determined never to return until they have planted the tree of Civil and Religious Liberty within the gates of the City of Mexico, and when they shall once have crossed the Rio Grande, their march will be onward, and cannot be impeded by all the influence of the Executive, together with those of his friends who are disposed to GO THE WHOLE in the advocacy of his measures, 'right or wrong.' "

[51] Executive Letter Book, No. 40 (Handwritten copies of official correspondence on deposit in the archives of the Texas State Library.), p. 52.

fitted out by the citizens. Immediately on obtaining the assent Messrs. Frankland and Co. offered to fit out the Zavala at their own expense, and it is expected both vessels will be at sea in 24 hours. The Zavala is to be placed near the mouth of the harbor.

"Videttes are stationed along the coast which give communications from San Luis to this place every six hours.

"The steamer La Fitte, schooner Santa Anna,[52] and sloop Washington, fully armed and equipped by the Coast Guards, under Capt. Swingle, sailed for Copano and elsewhere yesterday. We expect to hear a good account of them shortly."

I could not resist all this excitement. The recollection of having smelt powder in the old world prompted me to lend a willing, although feeble, hand in the new adopted country.

But before I proceed—I must not omit to mention that there was one who discountenanced such violent operations; he knew the Mexicans well, and it was his opinion that—the present entré of the enemy was at most a marauding party and that a few days would prove his assertions. This was General Houston.

Old Sam kept his head, and future events proved that the invasion was but a marauding party that quickly retreated south of the Río Grande. Nor would Houston support a large scale retaliatory invasion of Mexico, as his political opponents demanded. "To defend a country requires comparatively but little means— to invade a nation requires everything," he argued. "To conquer Mexicans in Texas is one thing—to battle with Mexicans in Mexico is a different kind of warfare."[53] Fortunate indeed for Texas that Houston now governed, and not Lamar!

But before the excitement had abated (only to break out once again when the Mexicans recaptured San Antonio the following September), William Bollaert, the English traveler, signed

[52] There is no official notice of this ship, although Bollaert makes frequent mention of it. He subsequently identifies it as a revenue cutter with one gun, and states that it was renamed the *Borden*, doubtless because of the stigma of Santa Anna's name.

[53] *The Writings of Sam Houston*, IV, 73.

on the LaFitte *as a waister*[54] *to do his part for his "now adopted country."*

The *Outs* were at this moment in opposition and a violent "War Party." Some of them appeared to anticipate that could a large number of volunteers be procured from the States, that soon (as they said) they might revel in the "Halls of Montezuma," etc., etc. Well, all that could be spared from Galveston [were] being sent to the war—some by land and some by sea. I will now introduce to notice, extracts from my journal of the "Cruize of the LaFitte."

[54] Index to Navy Muster Roll (Texas State Archives). A waister on a naval vessel was formerly one of a class of old men who had been disabled or grown gray without rising in the service. On a whaling vessel it was a green hand who was usually placed in the waist of the vessel until qualified for more responsible duties.

III

THE CRUIZE OF THE LAFITTE

[*March, 1842*]

THE CRUIZE OF THE LAFITTE was under the command of Captain John Wade,[1] Captain J. Haviland his second in command. The company of Coast Guards, with volunteers for the cruize amounting to 100 men, accompanied by Captain Swingle and his company of Fusileers of 50 men, armed with patent rifles, having bayonets, habited in modest uniform. The "Coast Guards" more with an eye to uniformity, adopted Red Woolen Shirts, white trousers, and straw hats, armed with muskets, and pistols, pikes, and boarding sword. But there was no scarcity of hatchets, tomahawks, and Bowie Knives for close quarters, if necessary. We had a fine long brass gun in the bows and two iron carronades[2] on either side; plenty of ammunition, provisions and sundry other comforts on board, in the shape of "small stores" not forgetting the "Pig Tail," or as known in this country under the name of "Honey Dew" plug tobacco, and segars.

Monday, March 14th, 1842: Got over the Bar to sea, the "Santana"[3] (commanded by Captain Hitchcock)[4] and the little "Washington" (by Captain Boylan)[5] in company.

---

[1] This chapter was edited by Bollaert and published in the November, 1846, issue of *Colburn's United Service Magazine* (pp. 341–55), under the title "Arrival in Texas in 1842, and Cruise of the Lafitte."

John M. Wade was one of the five men in charge of the "Twin Sisters" during the battle of San Jacinto. He was a printer by profession who worked on the *Telegraph and Texas Register* at Columbia and Houston. He must have had some experience at sea, although there is no mention of it in Samuel H. Dixon and Louis W. Kemp's *The Heroes of San Jacinto*, 85–86.

[2] A carronade is a short piece of muzzle-loading ordnance used in ships.

[3] See footnote 52, Chapter II.

[4] Lent Munson Hitchcock enlisted in the Texas Navy at New Orleans in 1836. He later settled in Galveston where he held several public offices until his death in 1869. *The Handbook of Texas*, I, 817.

[5] James D. Boylan served in the Texas Navy throughout its entire existence,

Tuesday, March 15th, 1842: During the night kept a westerly course 2 or three miles from land. Went inside Passo Caballo Bar, anchored at Decrows.[6] This is a low point of land but a good depth of water for vessels; here are a few houses and gardens.

Wednesday, March 16th, 1842: The "Fusileers" went on shore to exercise. Rumors increasing relative to the Mexican invasion. The crew of the "Lafitte" divided into watches, divisions, etc. I had the honor of being nominated to the rank of Sergeant, having in my division all of those foreigners who were not as yet very good English scholars. We drilled and exercised with musket and boarding pike. All took to soldiering very kindly but there was a fear that they might kill one another in their anxiety to attack.

Some of us supped on shore with Baron ———[7] and his party of settlers. They had just arrived from France, as emigrants, with the intention of going to San Antonio, but the present crisis perplexed them. Nevertheless, they were all for aiding, abetting, and assisting in the struggle. One of the Baron's party was so exhilarated at our warlike attitude that he begged of me to obtain permission to join as a volunteer—this was acceded to. I enrolled him in my

and served as commander of several ships, including the Yucatán flotilla in May, 1842. *The Writings of Sam Houston,* II, 103.

[6] Decrows Landing was named after Daniel Decrow, a member of Stephen F. Austin's Old Three Hundred families. Decrow operated a sloop between the Brazos River and San Jacinto Bay until his death in 1837. In addition, he owned a large farm in Matagorda County. A sketch of Decrow is found in Lester G. Bugbee, "The Old Three Hundred," *Quarterly of the Texas State Historical Association,* Vol. I (1897), 108–17.

[7] Baron P—— some months afterwards—not succeeding in his expectations became deranged—it is feared by drink—and shot himself.—Bollaert.

In Bollaert's miscellaneous notes (File No. 84) the following newspaper clipping (undated) is found: "Baron Ernest Philabeaucourt (the French Count who arrived in this Bay [Matagorda] in March last, with his family and a party of twenty emigrants) committed suicide, by shooting himself through the lungs, while on board the sloop Cutter, on her last trip from Galveston to this port. He was landed at Deckrow's Point, where he lingered for two days before dying. Baron Philabeaucourt is represented by those who know him intimately, as having been a gentleman of accomplishments and great worth of character. He had voluntarily forsaken the gay society and titled associations of the circle in which he moved in Paris, and sought out a new home in Texas for himself, his own family, and the members of his household who accompanied him. The cause of his rash deed is unknown."

division, but his inclination was manifestly to assist the commisariat department on board and was made cook of my mess.

Thursday, March 17th, 1842: At day break got under weigh and stood out to sea; when a few miles north of Espiritu Santo inlet[8] —a sail to windward was seen and coming down fast on us. We soon made her out to be a large Brig—beat to quarters. Now I had another appointment conferred upon me—"First Rammer and Spunger[9] of No. 3 Gun." We anticipated that this was one of the Mexican transports we had come out to look for. The "Fusileers" were stowed away out of sight, the greater number of "Coast Guards" likewise, and all as "quiet as coons." The determination to be at mischief was interesting. The Brig coming down upon us with a fair wind. We, steaming towards her with American Colour flying. The Brig ran up the banner of the Stars and Stripes. Alas! She proved to be from Mobile with lumber! There was one consolation and gratifying circumstance—namely, "our Rifles were ready," and ready were we.

A short time after this disappointment and when off the inlet, we saw a small sloop on shore apparently under suspicious circumstances—bore down toward her. The gig was manned and away went our boys. The breakers off the bar were running high; our brave fellows dashed into the foam, with the hope of getting safely through the breakers into smooth water. We watched our companions with considerable anxiety. They disappeared from our sight and in a few moments the boat was seen bottom up with all hands clinging to her. Our commander heard the shouts from those on board, "By —— they're swamped!" He cast one of his deep and scrutinizing looks toward the wrecked party. "Order! Silence! he shouted—those brave fellows will never sink— they've

[8] Espiritu Santo Bay (Holy Ghost), also called San Bernardo Bay, is in southern Calhoun County between Matagorda Island and the mainland and between San Antonio Bay and Matagorda Bay.

[9] Guns on naval vessels a century or more ago were held in position for firing by a series of ropes and blocks. The latter took the recoil of the gun when it was fired. It was the rammer's job to ram the shot or powder down the barrel before the shot, and if he was also the "spunger," he wielded the swab to clean the bore of the cannon after discharge. Usually each gun had a crew of five or six men.

got Jim Haviland with them—see, they are walking in the shoal breakers—they land—the boat is drifting ashore." At this period we discerned the whole of the boat's crew standing in a line on the shore, each shouldering an oar, so as to make themselves more visible to us. We gave them three cheers. The little "Washington" came along side the "Lafitte." We threw on board of her dry clothes and provisions for the gig's crew. We then bore off to Aransas Pass—got over the bar, and came to anchor for the night.

Friday, March 18th, 1842: At daylight, up anchor. Our gig and the "Santana" joined us. We were glad indeed to see our companions. We had a full and particular account of their "scrape" or "difficulty" and that the sloop had accidentally run on shore, her cargo being only flour.[10] 10 A. M. Came to anchor at Live Oak Point. This spot is the residence of Mr. James Power,[11] an old empresario settler. He received us most hospitably. Had "Beefs" (Oxen) killed for us, supplied us with milk and fish. He was here with his family and had secreted in various parts of his house and behind doors an armament of loaded rifles and muskets, in case of a sudden attack. Here we took in water, and parties went on shore to wash clothes, fish, "oystering," "gunning" etc. In this vicinity roams about the "last" of the Koronks or Carancahuas Indians. They have the reputation of being cannibals. Mr. Power informed me that a chief by the name of "Capitan Francisco" told him that "a white man's heart was the sweetest meat he had ever eaten."[12] Mr. Power had with him a young Carancahua boy. He had but a sorry reputation, namely "thief and liar." Then he had taught some of Mr. Power's children to eat dirt; that when

[10] Bollaert does not give the name of the Mexican vessel captured, nor is there any record of this incident in the Texas State Archives.

[11] James Power was a partner in the Power and Hewetson Colony and one of the early empresarios of Texas. He was very prominent in affairs of the Republic, being one of the signers of the Declaration of Independence (1836) and largely responsible for seating Sam Houston in the Convention of 1836. *Biographical Directory of Texas Conventions ond Congresses,* 156.

[12] The Karankawa chief was undoubtedly "pulling Power's leg." Although the Karankawas did have the reputation of being cannibalistic, they and other Southwestern tribes frequently boasted of such acts that were obviously untrue.

41

he had committed himself in any way he would "take to the woods" for a time.

The country about here is a higher and better land than at Galveston and the live oak tree is a great addition to the generally low character of the land. The soil is somewhat sandy but good. Fresh water from wells. The peach trees were in blossom—vegetables thriving and the graceful "sword-leaved" Palmetto chooses its abode and displays its large white cluster of flowers, surrounded by triple ranks of pointed leaves bristling like the bayonets of the grenadier guards.

Saturday, March 19th, 1842: The cloudy wintry weather gone; it is now bright and clear, with refreshing southerly breezes. 10 A. M. got under weigh, and at 2 P. M. came to off Copano.[13] Our commander went on shore. He found that all the men had gone off to the West on the news reaching them of the "invasion," leaving the women and children at home, and that 300 volunteers a few days since had passed through the "Mission" (Refugio)[14] on their way westward.

5 P. M. came to anchor off Black Point,[15] the object being to cut and take in wood, which is the musquit [mesquite] of the acacia or mimosa species. These bays are full of sandbanks and shoals, one has to keep the "lead" or the "pole" going, and it requires some attention to navigate in the channels.

Sunday, March 20th, 1842: Black Point has an abrupt loamy coast, the land covered with musquit grass, which bears a good name for cattle. The breeze sweeping over the prairies was laden with the sweet smelling perfume of its flowers. I was tempted into a ramble with a friend. We took our guns; rabbits in great abundance, but the axe of our wood-cutters had commenced to scare the deer away. Whilst we were moralizing upon the extraordinary

---

[13] Copano Bay is an extension of Aransas Bay in western Aransas County and southern Refugio County.

[14] Nuestra Señora del Refugio.

[15] Black Point was an old Spanish landing place. It is a point where the Aransas River empties into Copano Bay.

history of the country, the cattle and game all over the country, the fish that filled the bays and rivers, we pictured in our imagination, the shores of these bays lined with habitations—nay, noisy towns conducting commercial relations even to the Pacific Ocean, but all now appeared so still and quiet. My companion was a young Spanish merchant. He had just acquiesced in this view of the subject, observing, "*O mi patria, es tú, que has perdido la joya del mundo, la America. No diré nada contra los Ingleses y los Americanos sus descendientes, porque es razonable que el principe. O el gobierno que no cuidan sus estados deben perderlos.*"[16] He nevertheless breathed a very heavy sigh—there was a brief pause—then a slight noise. "*Caramba! Que es eso?*" said he. And then we heard a rattling sound. "*Por Dios Amigo, es una culebra*"; and at that moment a large rattle snake reared its head, with the intention doubtless of not being over civil. Fire! was the word. Two bullets brought the beast to the ground; we took the "rattles" (some 12 in number) from his tail on board for a trophy. Snakes of various sorts are found about here and an occasional "scorpion," centipede, and a few alligators. Sharks are seen, but they are not very common. Turtle [are] in great abundance. In our rambles today saw the Nopal (Opuntia) and some species of cactus in flower.

Monday, March 21st, 1842: Wooding all day. The express we had sent to Refugio returned, but brought no news of importance. A party has just joined us from the interior, informing us that on the 7th inst. some Mexicans surprised near to St. Patricio a party of Texans, killing Messrs. Carnes, Snodgrass, Wells, and Willis, and 4 Lipan Indians. The following day these Mexicans arrived at Corpus Christi distributed a proclamation signed by General Arista, calling upon the Texans to return to "their duty," etc. etc. etc. The same enemy then retreated to the Rio Grande.

---

[16] Bollaert frequently dropped into Spanish. "Oh my country, thou hast lost the jewel of the world, America. I will say nothing against the English and the Americans, your descendants. But it is reasonable when princes or governments know not how to preserve their dominions, they should lose them."

Tuesday, March 22, 1842: 8 A.M. Got under weigh for Live Oak Point.[17] Arrived at noon and took in water. I may observe here that independent of the warlike organization of our ship, we were divided into messes: No. I Mess included the Captain, the principal officers, in a word—even among us Republicans— the "elite." And a good example they set to the rest on board. Then came No. II Mess. This was located between the steam-boilers and the "caboose," having on the left flank the purser's store room and adjoining it the store room belonging to No. I Mess. No. II was known as the "Great" or "Rowdy" Mess, and it was esteemed no inconsiderable honor to belong to it. Yet, there was the one duty belonging to it that was not patronized; namely, each day one of the Mess had to superintend the cooking, laying the table, and then worse than all, to wash up the greasy plates and pannikins. We of No. II dispensed with knives and forks, using our fingers and bowie knives. No. I Mess would in its arrogance taunt us somewhat, alluding at the same time to their little comforts.

No. II Mess appointed a "committee of three" to investigate the conduct of No. I, and if guilty of any points unbecoming our "natural dignity" to punish No. I in some manner or another. After a few minutes the committee declared No. I "guilty"—that the said No. I should be politely waited upon by another committee of three of No. II Mess, inviting them to an evening party in our part of the ship. (It is particular here to bear in mind that No. I's store room was in our vicinity.) Sergeant B[ollaert] had to organize the instrumental and vocal parts of the affair and solicited to write a song for the occasion. Judge B——, who was acting as Boatswain's Mate, was appointed to look after and prepare the drinkables. General —— to rig up some temporary seats. Col. —— to arrange the docorations, and Capt. —— to look after the rest of the "fixings," such as bread, cheese, butter, tobacco and segars.

The appointed time arrived: No. I Mess ushered to their seats

[17] Live Oak Point is on Copano Bay, some distance north of present Corpus Christi, the entrance to which is Aransas Pass.

most respectfully. Bright claret sparkled in the brighter pannikins. The conversation became animated, the song went round, and a more joyous set of faces [were] seldom beheld. Well, the claret gave out. Whiskey punch was introduced when Sergeant B[ollaert]'s song was loudly called for, or as he was familiarly called on board "Blowhard." These were not moments for apology as to colds, coughs, sore throats and the other innumerable ills that vocalists on lands are victims to. He began: "Comrades, I beg respectfully to offer for your attention the following ditty—The Red Rover Song."[18] I got immediate promotion for this, and moreover I was to be forever exonerated from washing up the dishes, etc.

No. I Mess sang their quota of songs, when I offered another lyric in honor of our brethren in arms who were probably face to

---

[18]

Dedicated to the Galveston Coast Guards

Red Rovers, Red Rovers, huzzah!
Red Rovers, Red Rovers, huzzah!
By sea or by land, we are ready—our band,
Red Rovers, Red Rovers, huzzah!

In the gloom of the night when billows are dashing,
And our path is lit up by the fierce lightning's ray
To guard our dear coast—to repel the invader
Is the joy of the Red Rover—the rover so gay.
Red Rovers &c.

In battle for glory and our bright rising star,
O what joy in each breast when we meet the base foe;
And the fame of our actions will resound—aye, afar,
And many will envy the Red Rover in war.
Red Rover, &c.

Then our cruise being over, our coast free from harm
And anchored in port—there are other alarms;
But they are of love's joys—the enduring caress:
By the girl of his heart—the Red Rover is blest.
Red Rover, &c.

Although the text of both this and the following song were removed from the manuscript, Bollaert published them in his article on the cruise of the *Lafitte* in *Colburn's United Service Magazine* (November, 1846), 351.

face with the enemy in the West. It was as follows: "Trumpets Sounding."[19]

Now then comes the gist of this tippling "frolic." The claret, whiskey, segars, songs, etc., had commenced to raise certain and somewhat confused ideas in the minds of No. I Mess, when to their astonishment—clean pannikins were put on the table— and as if by magic, one dozen of fine champagne graced the board. In a few minutes, "pop-pop-pop" went the corks, and the glorious liquid was quaffed with extacy. No. I Mess to a man rose and cheered us for our "kindness and hospitality." We were lauded to the skies—and set down for regular "up street" boon companions.

"Steward!" cried the Captain, who was at the head of No. I Mess. "Come Here." The Captain whispered something into his ear. "Yes, sir," was his reply! In a few minutes he returned with a woefully looking cast of countenance. "Tis gone," he ejaculated. "Where," asked the Captain. "I guess you've just drank your own

[19]
> *Trumpets sounding, war-steeds bounding—*
> *Heroes Grasp the spear and shield;*
> *Banners waving, dangers braving,*
> *On they rush to glory's field.*
> *The warriors have departed*
> *In brave and gallant row,*
> *Strong of arm and lion-hearted*
> *To conquer the base foe.*
>
> *Arms are clashing, swords are flashing,*
> *Dealing death at ev'ry blow:*
> *Scatter'd! flying! dead and dying—*
> *Mark! the foeman's overthrow.*
> *Hear the war-cry loudly swelling—*
> *"Remember Santa Fé;"*
> *And the shouts of triumph telling*
> *"We've conquer'd and are free."*
>
> *Martial story, wreaths in glory*
> *Ev'ry hero's hallow'd name;*
> *The holy fire their sons inspire*
> *Who struggle for fair fame.*
> *Such the story—all impelling*
> *To scorn the tyrant's chain;*
> *Each generous heart high swelling*
> *To fight it o'er again.*

champagne." This was too good a practical joke to be offended at. All laughed heartily. No. II was unanimously declared to be a "Bully Mess." The whiskey punch went round for a short time afterwards, when each returned to his berth or hammock—having previously as a finale, sang the following song: Air—"I'd be a Butterfly."

I'd be a jolly tar, born on the ocean,
Where billows and wild waves are dashing around,
Sailing along whilst the waves are in motion,
'Tis joy to my heart—the fierce cannon's sound.
  I'd be a sailor with grog for my portion,
  Seldom with such is much sorrow found,
  I'd be a jolly tar born on the ocean,
  When Neptune is stirring the blue waves around.
    I'd be a jolly tar, I'd be a jolly tar,
    When Neptune is stirring the blue waves around.

Landsmen may laugh at a sailor's devotion,
May talk of the joys and pleasures of land;
Think you a bold tar would alter his notion,
And leave his gay berth for a home on the strand?
  When the base tyrants have vessels in motion
  Old Jack will be there with true steel in his hand.
  I'd be a jolly tar, born on the ocean,
  When tempests are raging or gales blowing bland.
    I'd be a jolly tar, I'd be a jolly tar,
    When tempests are raging or gales blowing bland.

The following was one of the effusions of the evening:

Texas Song

By Col. ———

For a while, adieu the smile,
  And the joys our home surrounding,

47

> *And welcome now, with a soldier brow,*
> *The trump of the battle sounding!*
> *For the hand of War—would strike our "star"—*
> *Away in its early beaming.*
> *But it long shall be o'er the Texans free,*
> *With a sacred glory streaming!*
> *Then on! Be brave! And if a grave*
> *Await our rights' contending,*
> *'Tis sweet to fall, 'neath the battle pall,*
> *The home of the heart defending!*
> *For the hand of War . . . .*

Wednesday, March 23rd, 1842: I accompanied Captain Wade and others in the "Washington" to Corpus Christi. It blew hard from S. E. Arrived at 3:30 p.m. It is high bluff land, with muskit timber. Messrs. Kenney[20] and Aubry are the principal traders here. Their log house is fortified and they have a piece of artillery. We learnt that Carnes and his party had been for some time past doing military duty here, but had left for San Patricio where they were surprised and murdered by the Mexicans, Dr. Cameron alone escaping. Cameron[21] we found had gone off to join the volunteers.

This spot at present may be looked upon as a good point for trading into Mexico. When the question is settled between the two countries, then Corpus Christi will become a place of some "importance."

Thursday, March 24th, 1842: Left for Live Oak Point. Met the

[20] Henry Lawrence Kinney arrived at the site of Corpus Christi in 1832 and by 1840 had established a trading post and employed forty men as his personal soldiers. He continued to promote Corpus Christi for several years and is closely associated with, and responsible for, the town's early development. He formed a partnership with William B. Aubrey in 1841. Homer S. Thrall, *A Pictorial History of Texas*, 579.

[21] Poor Cameron was afterwards brutally murdered by the Mexicans.—Bollaert. Ewen Cameron was a leader in the Mier Expedition of December, 1842, and subsequently became a Mexican prisoner. He was one of the leaders in the ill-fated escape from Salado (February 11, 1843) and was later captured and shot by order of General Santa Anna. Thomas Jefferson Green, *Journal of the Texian Expedition against Mier*, 285.

"Santana" coming down the bay on her way in pursuit of a Mexican spy who is on one of the islands. We are informed that General Burleson[22] has got hold of three spies, two of whom had been condemned to be shot. General Houston has issued a proclamation to the volunteers which, as it does not breathe "War to the Knife" and "Onwards," makes the President unpopular with the War Party."[23]

Friday, March 25th, 1842: After my duties were ended for the day, and they commence pretty early, for independent of my other two appointments, I am Captain of the Larboard Waisters, I went gunning. The birds "mighty shy," but brought on board a few ducks. On my getting on board I found them all in high glee at the escape of the Mexican spy named "Incarnacion." The party sent after him pounced upon him at a rancho or hut and secured him. There were several "beefs" about where they took him, and they thought that it would be no bad plan to take some fresh beef with them on board. They tried in vain to "lasso" or catch one of the animals who was a wild fellow. There was a fine mule ready saddled at the rancho when "Incarnacion" suggested to his captors, he being a "first rate" herdsman, if they would let him have the mule and a lasso, he would soon catch the "beef." This was immediately acceded to, when the wily Mexican, after pretending for some time to catch the "beef," got far out into the prairie and when at good starting distance, galloped off as fast as he could, leaving his former captors in no very good humor. It was this "smartness" and "sloping" of "Incarnacion," the Mexican, that

[22] General Edward Burleson served the Republic for many years. He was elected brigadier general of the militia in 1837 and vice-president of the Republic in 1841. Largely through the efforts of his old political enemy, Sam Houston, he was defeated for president of the Republic by Anson Jones in 1844. Dixon and Kemp, *Heroes of San Jacinto*, 125–26.

[23] On March 17, 1842, Houston wrote to Washington D. Miller: "My calculations from the first have all been realized. I told you of this last winter, and when I heard that the Mexicans had taken Bexar, I predicted its evacuation by them. Fools only pursue phantoms and children will chase butterflies. The people and the frontier did nobly, but at Houston and Galveston they acted thoughtlessly, if not foolishly." *The Writings of Sam Houston*, II, 508.

caused the hilarity on board, and it was put to the vote and carried, that the Captors of "Incarnacion" merited a "leather medal."

Saturday, March 26, 1842: Went to La Mar[24]—½ hours sail opposite to Live Oak Point. There are six to eight habitations, the residents preparing to "break up their establishments." Here we heard that some Comanches (Note: I am subsequently informed that they were Waccos and not Comanches) had come down as low as 30 miles below Goliad and killed a Mr. and Mrs. Gilleland,[25] taken away their two children, but the children were rescued 2 or 3 days after their capture. The little boy being severely speared, but his recovery hoped for. Some of the murderous Comanches were shot. We hear that the two Mexican spies that had been condemned by General Burleson had been hung near Goliad.

Sunday, March 27th, 1842: Messrs. McKinney[26] and Jones arrived from the Army, gave us confirmation of the news. They proceeded to Corpus Christi. It is believed by many that an invasion by Mexico is about to be attempted, so much so, that all those families westward are removing down toward the Coast and Galveston—that is—they are upon the "slope." Many of them unfortunately know too well the sanguinary character of their enemies. All this is bad for the crops and retards numberless operations for the well-being of the country.

Monday, March 28th, 1842: The majority of "Fusileers" will

[24] James Byrne laid out the town of Lamar (Aransas County) and named it after Mirabeau B. Lamar. The community had twenty houses in 1839, but a century later it contained only one store and a total population of twenty people. *The Handbook of Texas*, II, 14.

[25] Johnson Gilleland and his wife were killed at Goliad by Comanches in the spring of 1840. Their two children were taken prisoners but later released. Rebecca J. Gilleland Fisher, "Capture and Rescue of Mrs. Rebecca J. Fisher, née Gilleland," *Quarterly of the Texas State Historical Association*, Vol. III (1899–1900), 209–13.

[26] This was probably Thomas F. McKinney, one of Austin's Old Three Hundred colonists, who settled in present Brazos County in 1824. Thrall, *Pictorial History of Texas*, 589.

remain here a few days with Captain Swingle, awaiting more information from the army.[27] The rest go homeward to Galveston with us, for it appears pretty clear that there are no Mexican transports just now on our coast. 4 P.M. Got under weigh, and brought up inside the bar for the night.

Tuesday, March 29th, 1842: Morning—got under weigh, took the "Santana" in tow over the Bar. The musquit wood is not the best for raising steam and with a heavy swell, we do not make much head way. 5 P.M. Came to anchor off St. Luis. Here we saw President Houston's Proclamation of Blockade of Mexican Ports.[28]

Wednesday, March 30th, 1842: 5 P.M. [A.M.] Got steam up. Strong breeze from N.E. made our "Smoker" roll and creak. On our making the east end of the island found the Brig of War "Wharton" and Steamer "Zavala" there, the former waiting for a fair wind to go out cruizing, the other as a guard ship. As we came up along side the town with our prize, part of our company who had remained on shore had got our two pieces of artillery down to the shore and saluted us, so did the arsenal. All the inhabitants came to meet and welcome us home—pleased enough that we had taken the schooner.

Thus ended the "Cruize of the Lafitte," taking only one small prize, but doubtless had we got a chance, we should have distinguished ourselves. For some time we shall bear the title of "Red Rovers," our sea uniform being red shirts. We are called Sea Fencibles, but our legal appelation is "Coast Guards."

In a few words the whole of the present excitement appears to be owing to some 500 Mexicans under General Vasquez had entered San Antonio, had committed no particular depredations, but distributed a Proclamation signed by General Arista calling upon the Texans to return to their "duty," etc. etc. promising that, if they (The Texans) did not do so soon that a large Mexi-

[27] If there is no work for them, will return by land to Galveston.—Bollaert.

[28] Houston's proclamation of blockade against Mexico was issued on March 26, 1842, and revoked on September 12, 1842. *The Writings of Sam Houston*, II, 537; III, 156.

can Army would overrun the country. General Houston looked upon this as bombast, but his political opponents at this "entré" of the Mexicans formed the "War Party" and their motive was to get a large number of volunteers from the U. States and fight the question out at once. This view of the subject did not meet with the approbation of General Houston or his government.

Throughout the month of March, 1842, Houston was hard pressed from all sides, for the popular cry now was to invade Mexico. A self-styled Committee of Safety at Houston petitioned the Chief Executive: "Will the executive approve of and permit the prosecution of immediate offensive hostilities against Mexico under the Texian flag, provided men and means for the purpose can be procured from abroad free from charge upon the Texas Government? For the promotion of said object, will he order the officers and men now in the field to concentrate at such point or points as in his judgment will best promote the furtherance of such design? Will he clothe, with legal authority, one or more agents to be sent abroad to solicit and co-operate with the people of Texas in the enterprise? Will he issue letters of marque and reprisal, for capturing all Mexican property on the high seas? Will he issue orders to our naval commanders to harass the commerce, and seize all vessels which they may find under the Mexican flag, until our independence shall be acknowledged by Mexico?"[29]

At near-by Galveston the general enthusiasm was "so great that it has extended to the fair-sex, and several of the good ladies of our city, have been industriously engaged, for the last few days, in moulding bullets and making cartridges for the use of the army. There has been contributed within two weeks past, by the citizens of Galveston about twelve thousand dollars in provisions, munitions of war and money. The steamer LaFitte and two other vessels armed and equipped have proceeded down the coast."[30]

Meanwhile, Houston heard rumors that General Burleson was at San Antonio with 1,500 men and Clark L. Owen at Victoria

[29] Printed in *Houston Morning Star*, March 19, 1842.—Bollaert's notes.

with 1,000, all burning to cross the Río Grande for revenge, and damning the President that he would not let them go on. His only political action now was to assume an attitude of offensive warfare. On March 17, 1842, he wrote Gail Borden at Houston: "The news by express from Austin up to the 13th inst. is that the enemy have evacuated San Antonio, after having plundered the place. They were laden down with baggage and march slowly. Colonel [Jack] Hays is harrassing them on their march. They only march about eight miles each day. The troops from Austin and those on the frontier are marching to overtake and beat them. War shall now be waged against Mexico, nor will we lay our arms aside until we have secured the recognition of our Independence. Until then I will never rest satisfied, nor will the people of Texas. We invoke the God of Armies."[31]

On March 22, 1842, the President informed General Alexander Somervell that should "you find your forces sufficient in strength and organization, you are at liberty to cross the Rio Grande, if you deem it discreet, entering the country by way of Laredo, or the most eligible crossing and taking such towns above Matamoros on the Rio Grande as you think proper—taking care not to advance upon Matamoros with an insufficient force, as no certain co-operation can be assured by sea."[32]

For obvious reasons Old Sam was moving coolly and deliberately in the execution of his plans. He had no intentions of letting Somervell do more than put on a show of strength on the Mexican frontier, while thwarting Burleson's plan of invasion. Four days after ordering Somervell to the Río Grande, the President issued the previously mentioned blockade of Mexican ports— another smoke screen, of course. What he really wanted was to have all farmers who could, return home and plant their crops and not let the Mexicans goad the Republic into a war it could not afford, politically or financially. Had he been able to control

---

[30] Printed in *Civilian and Galveston Gazette*, March 21, 1842.—Bollaert's notes.
[31] *The Writings of Sam Houston*, II, 509.
[32] *Ibid.*, 530.

the malcontents, trouble with Mexico might well have ended without further ado.

With the excitement of the Mexican invasion subsiding temporarily, William Bollaert remained in Galveston throughout April and the early part of May, 1842, except for short trips by land and sea to some of the near-by settlements.

IV

FROM GALVESTON
TO MATAGORDA AND BACK

[*April–May, 1842*]

EVERY STEAM BOAT that has come in from N. Orleans brings volunteers, and unfortunately not having Mexicans to fight with, have commenced fighting among themselves. Several serious difficulties have been the consequence. It was thus found convenient to allow them to go to Corpus Christi to defend if necessary that part of the frontier should it be attacked.

April 7th, 1842: Today there was a "Batallion Inspection" in Galveston composed of the "Fusileers," "Coast Guards," "Galveston Guards," and "Artillery." We had marching and countermarching to our heart's content, being reviewed by the Lt. Col. Commanding. This gentleman is Captain of one of the Houston Steam Boats; his blue jacket was replaced by a fine uniform coat and epaulets. Mounted on his charger, he made a speech thanking us for our discipline and services, at the termination of which there was nearly a dead silence. At this a friend of his stepped up to him and whispered something in his ear. The Lieut. Col. advanced nearly to the center of the column, saying "Gentlemen, I shall be happy to take a drink with you all at Shaw's Hotel" (which was opposite). Three cheers followed this magnanimous determination of Lieut. Col. O'Brien.[1] It was this day that I was initiated into the merits of mint julips and other "drinks,"[2] pre-

[1] This was probably Owen O'Brien, whom Sam Houston ordered, on March 20, 1842, to transfer the archives from Austin to Houston. *The Writings of Sam Houston*, IV, 84.

[2] Drinks: Plain mint julip; fancy do., cupped do., strawberry do., arrack do., race-horse do., sherry cobbler, Rochelle do., arrack do., claret do. Tip and Ty. Fiscal agent veto. I.O.U. Tippe na pecco. Moral Suasion, Vox populi. Ne plus ultra. Shambro. Pig and Whistle. Citronella jim, Egg Nogg, Sarpent. Silver top, Poor man's punch, arrack do., iced do., spiced do., epicure's do., milk do., peach

pared under the superintendence of my worthy friend and comrade Judge B——. This sort of soldiering is not unpleasant and for volunteers it must be confessed we are not particularly disobedient to orders.

Commodore Moore[3] took a Mexican vessel laden with salt,

---

do., Jewett's fancy, Deacon. Exchange. Stone Wall. Virginia fancy. Knickerbocker. Smasher. Floater. Siphon. Soda punch. Soda Mead. Gin sling. Cocktail. Tom and Jerry. Negus' and mulled wines. Whiskey. Brandy. Gin. Apple toddy. And each all for the sum of one bit. Dinner generally good at all the hotels. Brft. about 9 or 10—Dinner 2 to 3. Supper or tea 7.—Bollaert.

[3] During my absence from Galveston, Commodore [Edwin Ward] Moore was off this port with his fleet on their return from Yucatan, the government of that country having paid him the stipulated sum for sundry assistance—some $35,000. He is now in New Orleans to refit—pay his men off and get new crews.—Bollaert.

The following may serve as a memoranda relating to the Texan Navy—entitled "Notes for Memoir on the Texas Navy":

Liberty—Schooner, 5 guns—Texas vessel of war commanded by Capt. [William S.] Brown.

Independence—do. 7 guns. National V. Taken by two Mexican Brigs, the "Libertad" and the "Alvarado," off Matagorda after a running action of four hours—17th March [April], 1837—in which Captain [George Washington] Wheelright was severely wounded (The "I" took several prizes).

Brutus—Schooner—11 guns. This vessel took several Mexican prizes, attacked the forts of Sisal—bombarded the Town, but escaped unhurt herself. Her commander was Captain [James D.] Boylan. Brutus lost in Galveston, October 6, 1837 [in a storm].

Invincible—Schooner, 7 guns. Commanded by Captain [Henry L.] Thompson. She was attacked by the Mexican Brigs "Libertad" and "Alvarado" and running into Galveston Port struck upon the Bar and was lost.

Potomac—Brig, guns 14. Captain [John W.] Taylor—went ashore in Galveston Bay [in] 1841.

Zavala—Steamer, 10 guns. Captain [J.T.K.] Lothrop. She went to Yucatan and assisted in the capture of the city of Tobasco, 1840 then kept in defense of the harbour. At present a wreck with a broken stack caused by the gale of September 19, 1841.

San Jacinto—Schooner, 5 guns—Captured some Mexican vessels—lost on the Las Arcas Islands on the Yucatan Coast, 1840 September.

San Antonio—Schooner, 7 guns—Captain [William] Seeger. Took several prizes. Now absent from port and supposed to be lost.

San Bernard—Schooner, 7 guns. Captain Downing H. Crisp—Was at the taking of Tobasco and captured several prizes. The gale of September 19, 1841 drove her ashore—where she now lies.

Wharton—Brig, 18 guns. Captain [J.T.K.] Lothrop. Attacked Tuxpan and has been laying in N. Orleans for the six months.

Austin-Ship [Sloop-of-war], 20 guns. Commodore E. W. Moore. At the taking of Tobasco. Made some prizes and has been laying in N. Orleans for the last six months.

but in bringing her in by some maneuver or another she got aground near the San Bernard River.

During the early part of April, 1842, Bollaert attended a public concert in Galveston, the object of which he explains below. Two accounts of the incident that followed appear, one in the regular journal[4] and the other in a separate article intended for publication.[5] The following anecdote of his amusing experience is a combination of the two writings. No changes have been made in the originals by the editor except the rearranging of some of the sentences.

The War-Party was apparently popular, and to its standards rushed those who knew but imperfectly the real state of affairs, who had but little else to do or who fond of an adventurous roving life, preferred following the drum to the plough. However,

Archer—Brig, 18 guns. In ordinary. [The *Archer* never saw active service and was allowed to rot in Galveston harbour].

Borden, or *Santana*—Revenue Cutter. 1 gun. Captain Simpton.

Tom, *Toby*—Privateer, 5 guns. Captain N. Hoyt. Took several prizes.

Terrible—Dº. 1 gun. Captain [John K.] Allen. 1st privateer fitted out.

Washington—Dº. 1 gun. Captain [George Washington] Wheelright. Took one prize.

Gualateca—Dº. 7 guns. Captain [?] Thompson.

—Bollaert.

In July, 1839, Edwin Ward Moore became commander of the navy of the Republic of Texas, and between 1840 and 1841 he sailed off the Mexican coast to hasten peace negotiations between Texas and Mexico. He later made a *de facto* alliance with Yucatán, and captured the town of Tabasco. On September 18, 1841, Moore received orders to guard the Yucatán coast in conformity with the Texas-Yucatán treaty and on December 13, 1841, he left Galveston with three ships to join the Yucatán fleet at Sisal. Upon his return to Galveston, he was commissioned by Houston to blockade the Mexican coast, but when funds for the blockade were withheld, Moore, financed by Yucatán, joined to break the Mexican blockade of Yucatán. By June 25, 1843, the Texas Navy controlled the Gulf. On June 1, 1843, Moore had received Houston's proclamation accusing him of disobedience and suspending him from the Texas Navy. A court later found Moore not guilty of charges of disobedience, except on four minor charges, and the Texas Congress gave him the right to continue in the navy. *The Handbook of Texas,* II, 228.

[4] "Bollaert Papers," The Newberry Library, File No. 87.

[5] *Ibid.*, File No. 86.

those citizens who were established on their plantations and farms, thought with Houston, that it would be quite time enough to turn out, when the enemy had arrived within rifle shot.

A Volunteer Company had been formed at Galveston, its object being to proceed to the frontier, but as an addition to their funds was necessary for its complete equipment, and its Colonel being a German Professor of Music, he came out boldly in an advertisement on the propriety of getting up a concert, the proceeds of which were to be given to the Company, at the same time interesting the editor of the principal newspapers for a helping hand on the occasion, that document winding up with the following: "We need not remind our readers of what Shakespeare said about the individual who was so unfortunate as to have no music in his soul. They will all recollect that that close observer of human character pronounced such fit only for the vilest uses."

Reader, pardon me—for now I am obliged to speak somewhat directly of myself. I was invited to take part with the professionals! on the occasion and solicited to sing a Spanish song or two, there being several families from San Antonio (where Spanish is spoken) who intended to patronize the concert—which was held at the Tremont Hotel. The audience arrived when it was first treated to the tuning of what had been once a piano, but more appropriately now might be called a collection of tin kettles. Well, the piano was screwed up to G#, and after a considerable time passed in tuning—the audience tired of waiting—the concert commenced with a quartette. Before it was concluded, there was a regular break down. Our Prima—and only Donna—a delicate young lady, Mrs. Sealsfield found that the instrument was in as base a B flat as one could possibly wish. It was no go. Never was so indulgent an audience, and rounds of applause followed. The Colonel now tried to give the "Largo il Factotum," but what with the tinkling tones of the piano, and his own tremulous husky voice, having had a severe fit of the ague in the morning, he made, to use a common expression, a mess of it. Still, he came in for his share of applause.

According to the program it was my turn. A Spanish song was given, at the end of which "Bueno, bueno, mui bonito" from the

Spaniards—but from the Texas citizens resounded "Give us a song from the old country." I gave them one, breathing as much of trumpets, drums, powder, and shot etc. as the most Hector-like could wish for. Encored of course, and amongst other protestations of eternal and everlasting friendship were the following: "Now if that stranger wants a town lot here, I'll give him one." "If he stops in the country and will run for Congress, he has my vote." "They say he's a lawyer; why, we'll make him a judge ere long."

My companions in arms tried a duet. They floundered about like a merman and mermaid on dry land. The audience, bless their kind and benevolent souls, took it all in for Gospel. It was now suggested that as the piano was in such a "fix," another should be sent for. When Mr. Power offered us his, half a dozen Niggers brought it from his house. In the interim it was suggested that the audience and singers should return to the Bar of the [Tremont] Hotel and "take a drink." This however only extended to the male part of the audience (and I may here mention that during the considerable time I was in Texas I never saw a woman in the bar room of an inn or hotel, or one in any way under the influence of liquor).

The second piano arrived, when after much screwing and thumping, it was pronounced to be tuned, when a flute solo by a violent-tempered Irishman, with piano accompaniment was announced. It commenced—went on a few bars—they tried back —if anything, the second piano was worse than the first. Our Nicholson became infuriated, he cursed etc. the piano. Up jumped the lady performer horror stricken at the imprecations, when he rushed out of the room, swearing that he "would be d——d" if he would be made a fool of by any such piano on this side of the Atlantic." This of course produced roars of laughter and more amusement than any vocal or instrumental display by us possibly could have done.

D. Guillermo (that's me) was pressed. "Tus ojos excitan," came next. Some Spanish families being there and the majority of the concourse understanding that language, bravoed it "Encore Encore," but instead of it I sang my new song of "Red Rovers." Thunders of applause and thus I was obliged to put down their bellowing—to bellow again. "By G——! said one, "I'll give that stranger a league of land." "By G——, I'll give him a town lot." By G——, he's a brick, etc." But one kindred spirit, s^d. "Sergeant Blowhard, come let's take a drink." Aye, and good bottled beer was the tipple. More songs were sung—I wound up with "My Little Maid and that Bonnet." Encore D—— the encores—these Texans believe that I have a potent pair of lungs.

After the concert the "exclusives" had returned to the Ladies Parlor of the Hotel in which the concert was held, and "Mr. B[ollaert]'s company particularly requested by the Ladies." When did beauty ever plead in vain and there were some there meriting this appelation? A Petite Souper was ready, after which singing and music commenced and this in fact was the real concert, when we were favoured amongst others, with many lyrical compositions of the other side of the Atlantic, including some real and original negro melodies. The moments flew gaily along. Cynthia was getting low in the horizon, but in the blue heavens the souls of despairing virgins (stars) did twinkle so sweetly. Each thought of his couch, but one Syren had stolen a march upon my constancy. How philosophically we can apologyze for our peccadillos. "Mr. B." said a cozy looking apparently to me, elderly gentleman with whom I had a casual acquaintance, "will you have the goodness to see this lady into the hall?" This I did. She was young, very pretty, interesting and intelligent, in fact, one of the first American ladies with whom I had had the honour of personal acquaintance.

In course of our brief conversation, I mentioned that there were but two things worth living for:

"Pray tell me."

"But you must keep it to yourself."

"That I will."

"Then Lady, one is ambition."

"And the other?"

"No, I do not think I ought to mention the other. You are yet too young."

"Pray tell me."

"Then it is love!"

"You are quite right, Sir."

Arriving at the hall door, we learned from a Negro that Mr. —————— had requested that I would see the lady homeward. Somehow I could not relinquish the well-rounded arm that was enfolded in mine. I led onward and in the direction of her domicile—my cosy friend bringing up the rear. Arrived, what think you awaited me in the shape of retribution! Said she, "I hope the dear boy is not awake." In mere astonishment and dumbfoundness-trembling I ejaculated, "Whose boy?" "Why my dear little Donald." Pray come and see Donald and I am sure Mr. Mac and myself will try to make you comfortable." I thought I had been flirting with Mr. Mac's daughter, Charles. It was his wife. Gods! Ye Gods!

I went home sunk many per cent in my own estimation. But like a good *roué*, went the next day to see "dear Donald," kissed him, and we all laughed over the story. I mention this ancedote to shew how young the American ladies marry, and in her case, tho' somewhat an exception to the rule, she retained her youth and freshness of appearance.

The winter in Texas has left us for some time past and the cold "norther's" bottled up in the Rocky Mountains until next season. The weather, although warm for an European, is delightfully tempered by the refreshing and invigorating southerly breeze. The air becomes pure, the sky clear, and the starry or moonlit nights beautiful.

Owing to the unsettled state of the country, some of the western settlers have returned to the U. States, awaiting more propitious times. It must be confessed that for the planter and industrious farmer it is not agreeable, to be worried on the one hand by Mexican invasion and on the other by Indian depredations. The Volunteers in the field are all towards the frontier. Trade is at a low ebb, and credit still lower—yet with all this, "Texas will go ahead."

April 10th, 1842: The "San Bernard," one of our Naval Vessels, D. Crisp,[6] Commander, (an Englishman) came in from Vera Cruz. Commodore Moore and the rest of the Texas fleet at Yucatan. General Houston and the Government are at Houston. Austin is considered for the present too far West for the residence of the Executive. A Mexican Prize sent into Galveston.

Galveston at times is an awkward port to get in and out of, but a small steamer "Tug" would affectually remove this difficulty; indeed, the "Neptune" and "New York" steamers answered this end with either coming or going out of the harbour.

April 13th, 1842: Morning close and sultry, few flashes of lightning and deep booming thunder. Thick dark clouds hanging about and occasional showers commenced which cooled the air considerably. The last showery weather has brought forward all sorts of vegetables and although the farmer has been abruptly taken away from his agricultural labours, to shoulder his rifle, kind nature is giving us a helping hand. 11 A.M.: A violent storm came on, blowing from N. but varying to NNE. The thick black clouds dissipated when it rained in torrents; sheet and forked lightning of the most vivid descriptions. This is what might be called "Elemental Strife." 12 P.M.: It is now blowing a hurricane. 1 P.M.: Most furious, with occasional hail. At 2 P.M.: commenced subsiding. Much damage done to the shipping and houses and gardens. The Post Office blown over, and the letters knocked into "pie."[7]

April 15th, 1842: Commenced a cruize in the sloop "Cutter" bound to Matagorda.[8] 6 P.M.: Abreast of the "Three Trees," or more properly, three clumps of trees.

[6] Downing H. Crisp was the son of a commander in the Royal Navy and served in the Texas Navy from 1840 to 1843. His ship, the *San Bernard*, was blown ashore at Galveston during the storm of September 19, 1842. *The Writings of Sam Houston*, III, 362.

[7] And this we were informed was but a "young gulf storm."—Bollaert.

[8] Matagorda, in present Matagorda County, had a population in 1840 of more than 1,500 people. It was an important Texas port until it was destroyed by a storm in 1894. Its population, according to the 1950 census, was approximately 1,250.

April 17th, 1842: At sun down got over the Bar of "Paso Caballo," and came to anchor below Cumming's, the pilot's house. Accompanied the Mast[er] of the sloop on shore to pass the evening at ———. This is a rude looking place. A host of large hunting dogs "bow-wowed" us from the landing to the log house. This log house was of an inferior description, but I have seen such habitations, built very neatly, well furnished, good beds with their attendant bars to shield one at night from the sting of mosquito, and even to a piano forte.

We perceived that the inmates were at supper; we were pressed to partake the evening meal with them, but we had supped. Seats were brought outside to us. I must confess that I was not very polite for taking several peeps into the interior of the log house, for the first glance convinced me that it was a "tall crowd." They soon dispatched their meal and one by one came out to see and welcome us. Our host introduced us to his guests, some of the tallest men that I had ever seen. They appeared the remains of a long lost race of giants, particularly one elderly man who was called Uncle Tilley. In standing up to speak with him I had to throw my head back so far as to feel an inconvenience. The dogs had ceased their barking, their presence being now only recognized by an occasional growl. After the ordinary topics relating to politics were dispatched, General Houston and his passive measures roughly commented on, we took a drink, lit our corncob pipes, and by turns these warrior citizens recounted particulars of the history of the country even from the time of Moses Austin, the Father of Texas.[9]

There was one there who had known the brave David Crockett, and nearly all the martyrs who have fallen for this country. When

[9] There was no low vulgarity in discussing the state of affairs, and altho' Houston and his passive measures were commented on, they generally appeared to think that he and his party knew the true position of Texas, and that "Old Sam," as they familiarly called him, knew how to get Texas out of the "scrape." ... It was here I heard of the "Fall of the Alamo," "The mournful day of Goliad," the dastardly butcheries of Santa Ana and his myrmidons at the Alamo and elsewhere, but as a retribution their defeat on the field of San Jacinto in glowing language such I can never forget, and from those who had been actors in those eventful dramas.—Bollaert.

speaking of Crockett, I had a rich treat in listening to how panthers, bears, wolves, etc. were to be hunted and caught. These hunters then exhibited their rifles—"real Kentuck"—of great lengths. Then came an exhibition of Bowie Knives, pistols and such-like "small gear," but Col. ——— who had lived long in the Western Country related the following melancholy story—of Guadalupe Leon:[10]

The mother of Guadalupe was of Indian origin and claimed the city of the Montezumas as her birth place. At an early age her marriage with Senor Leon was in a measure forced upon her, owing to certain properties and family connexions; thus the girl was sacrificed to cursed sordid interest. Here we will premise, that her consent was given most reluctantly to the said marriage—for a young Spanish officer, of true Castilian blood, had captivated her heart. Fortunately about this time the Spanish officer was ordered upon distant service. She might have wept in secret for the man she loved and her friends anticipated que en la ausencia hasta el amor se olvida! Her new liege Lord, Senor Leon, had an indistinct knowledge of the fact that he had had a rival but the object in question was far from the city of Mexico, and moreover, his marriage with the beautiful Carmen had been solemnized with considerable show. They had partaken of the marriage sacrament, they had been blessed by the Lord's annointed, and, in the eyes of her maiden friends and gossips, she was, for a time, the envied one. Senor Leon received the accustomed congratulations from his male friends, whilst sipping a glass of "gloria" and the tasting of the wedding pastries. Carmen of course received the visits customary on such occasions but when she retired to her chamber, the tear stole from her eyes—were they of joy? or were they, some of them at least, "para el official."

Time passed on, the Mexican revolution commenced; the officer in question we shall call by the name of Solis, had arrived

[10] The story of Guadalupe Leon appeared in Bollaert's handwriting in his journal, as well as in a newspaper clipping which he pasted opposite the pages. The printed version must have been published in an English newspaper. A note in Bollaert's handwriting at the top of the printed article states that the story was written "By W. Bollaert."

with his regiment, with others which had been ordered to the capital by the Viceroy to assist in keeping down by shew of armed strength the revolutionary system of things that were fomenting and which the Viceroy dreaded would soon be of serious moment.

But to be brief, in a night attack upon the Vice-royal palace, where Solis was on guard, he was severely wounded and carried to the first house that his men found open. The inmates received the wounded and senseless man, but the following morning he found it to be the domicile of Senor and Senora Leon, the latter his beloved Carmen.

For some time Solis was an inmate at Leon's house, but by kind attentions and unremitting care the wounded man recovered. He was promoted for his faithful services, and ordered with his regiment to a distant part to quell insurrection. To Senor Leon this was no very mortifying intelligence, but when it reached the ears of Carmen, and they were alone, "O Solis, is it true that you are to leave me?"

"Leave me, did you say? O God! O Holy mother of the Saints! You tremble, then thou hast not forgotten the times when we said we loved each other; when our hearts beat in unison; when thy hands were clasped in mine; when thy lips * * * !"

"No more, Solis, for thy dear mother's sake, no more. O yes, I do recollect all. O memory become benighted; yet when I see thee I cannot cease to love thee. Your absence, I had hoped, would have in some measure, removed the desperation of my feelings, but it now appears that fate made you a sufferer so that I might pity and love thee the more."

Carmen fainted in the arms of Solis, and it was long ere she became sensible of her position. Solis delayed his departure as long and even longer than was consistent with his duty. They had many meetings, there were no witnesses of their attachment for each other, but at last he was obliged to tear himself away from her.

Years rolled away. The torch of rebellion was lighted, revolution was in the ascendent, the power of Spain was dashed to the ground, a republic had been formed, the old Spaniards and those attached to their cause were banished, others fled into the wilds and the

Senor Leon traversed Mexico, crossed the "Sierra Madre" and Rio Grande, saw the beautiful vallies of the West and chose for a resting place the vicinity of San Antonio de Bejar.

Solis, when he found it was of no use longer to battle for the royal authority, and that the Viceroy had retired to Spain, left the military service—married and journeyed northward, and ultimately found a resting place at San Antonio likewise. He met his old friends. He was now married, his wife had given him a darling boy. Carmen had an offspring, and she was named Guadalupe.

Solis would not have settled in this spot, or even so near to it, had he known it to have been the residence of Carmen, but to retreat or advance further into the country he did not consider now very necessary, and thus located himself a few miles off from his friend, having prairie and woodland between them.

Years rolled onward, Guadalupe was called the beauty of the west, she had numberless admirers, but amongst them all Fernando Solis's son was the preferred companion. Guadalupe did not appear to have the least sympathy for the rest of her lovers. Fernando was her idol, and although he was somewhat younger than herself, his word was law to the loving and loved Guadalupe.

In the course of events Senor Leon died, and it was observed by the prying and meddling neighbors that Carmen from that day forth banished her triste and generally unhappy cast of countenance, and soon appeared joyous, living apparently in and for her daughter, and in making such suitable alliance as suited her Guadalupe's feelings and position.

"He comes not tonight," said Guadalupe sorrowfully. "He will roam so far for wild honey and beautiful flowers. I love his presents —yet I want them not. I want him ever by my side. O Querido Fernando!" Her mother who had listened to this discourse, grew pale, and became intensely agitated, repeating after her daughter "querido Fernando." "Daughter, I have oft heard thee speak of our old friend's son, and thy playmate, in terms of childish endearment, but until now I never thought that ———."

"Yes mother, I love him, from a child I must have loved him, it is not that stupid mawkish stuff that is called love amongst

66

young people, who talk a great deal of nonsense—write verses to each other—make huge protestations, they then quarrel!—they make up again—become *friends!* then enemies, then marry in spite of each other to give the lie to the world, or they in a most friendly and equitable manner—forget each other as lovers, return letters and verses—rings and trinkets, and then become most excellent neighbors."

"No mother, we love each other, we gaze on each other, we fall into each others arms, and we shed tears when we separate."

"Daughter, methought that our neighbor Zavalla's son was the favored one—indeed, his father has already proposed the alliance."

"O mother, did you consent?"

"No, but ———."

"Then mother mention not the thing again. If I ever marry, Fernando Solis shall be the husband of Guadalupe Leon."

Guadalupe's mother fainted, and when she recovered ejaculated:

"Oh Heavens, thou must not see Fernando again. Should he come, feign illness for a few days. I conjure thee my child, obey me and believe me it is not that I love the boy the less."

Senora Carmen wrote a letter despatching a person with it, with strict injunctions to deliver it to no one but Senor Solis, and return instanter with the answer.

The person presented himself at the hacienda of Senor Solis— delivered the letter. He read it, as it were, all at once, became faint, and all that escaped him was "Ay Dios Mio!" He acquainted Fernando that it was his positive wish, begging of him not to ask for explanation, nor to return any more to see Guadalupe. To the repeated enquiries and solicitations relative to so abrupt a determination, the only answer he could obtain was:

"Paciencia por el amor de Dios tongos pridad para tu padre infeliz."

Senor Solis commenced making arrangements to leave his hacienda, to settle he knew not as yet whither, but to start as quickly as possible from San Antonio. Fernando perceived all this, but could he leave his Guadalupe forever, and in such a manner? No, but his father divined his intentions—he implored

of him to relinquish the idea of again seeing Guadalupe, informing him that if he did he would for ever repent his disobedience
to parental wishes.

Some days passed, Guadalupe became intensely agitated at the
protracted absence of Fernando. The mother tried in vain to
console her, when Guadalupe rendered desperate, exclaimed
"then mother, if you love Fernando, why should not I love him?"

"O Guadalupe, forgive your poor mother. Fernando Solis is
thy brother!" She then briefly recounted the circumstances of her
ardent attachment to Fernando's father, their illicit intercourse
in Mexico, the ignorance of Solis that Guadalupe was his daughter
until she had acquainted him a few days since, and that the absence of Fernando was in accordance to injunctions from his
father. Guadalupe became as it were petrified, her eyes rolled
glaringly about, she took from a casket a dagger, and in brief space
she plunged it into her bosom, uttering "O mother! mother!
mother!!"

At that moment Fernando rushed into the apartment, he found
the mother wild and panic struck, the ruddy stream pouring from
Guadalupe's bosom. Life was ebbing fast, he clasped her in his
arms, he conjured her to tell him whilst the sparks of life remained, the mystery of this woeful transaction. She hung upon
him, saying "thy father, is my father, O Fernando thou art my
brother.' She sunk into the sweet sleep of death. Her mother
followed her shortly afterwards to the tomb. Fernando accompanied his father to a distant country to mourn in secret over
their sorrows.

During the recital of the story of Guadalupe, the old hunters
evinced by their short ejaculations their feelings, and an old
Negress, the only female about the place, when it came to the
denouement, tears streaming down her cheeks, exclaimed: "Gor-
amighty Sar what a mighty pity for dat poor young lady to take
on so and kill herself. Ah! I recollect very well when I was a young
woman in Virginny when Tom ———"

"Phillis!" said her master, "enough of your story bring some glasses—water—whilst I get a bottle of whiskey." This stopped the continuation of Phillis' narrative.

Our kind host and his guests pressed us to remain with them for the night. We declined and got on board our craft.

April 18th, 1842: About 2 o'clock in the morning, one Jim, a good sort of hard working fellow we had brought from Galveston to get him out of a drinking "frolic" and keep him from whiskey, woke us from a sound sleep, by a terrible groaning and moaning caused by a violent attack of *delerium tremens* or *potiomania,* swearing and shouting that someone was preparing to shoot him from the shore, for a debt of ten dollars, Jim begging us to secrete him from the individual. I went on deck in the hope of pacifying his disordered imagination. "Look," said he, "look, there he is— don't you see him behind that bush levelling his gun at me—ah! take care he is going to fire." I had great difficulty in persuading him that there was not even a bush upon the prairie. We got him down into the cabin and after a while he fell asleep. 8 A.M.: Got under weigh and in making for the custom house to present the ship's papers, got aground. What the reason can be I do not know why a custom house should be placed where it is, so much out of the way and moreover dangerous to get at. The proper position would be Decrows Point where there is deep water for anchorage and every facility of getting to it, and in a direct course to the town of Matagorda. I went from the Custom House in their boat to Decrows Point where I rejoined the sloop.

Among other strange yarns spun, was the following: On seeing a very large porpoise wanting the fin on its back, that some eight years since this said porpoise had been first seen by a Captain Hanson and had not since then left the bay and was known by the name of Tom Hanson, 4 P.M.: Left Decrows Point—with fair winds, ran on until 11:20 P.M., then came to anchor. The moon and stars shining brilliantly. The bay smooth and placid and the temperature very agreeable.

April 19th, 1842: At daylight up anchor. English brig "Iron-sides" at Tres Palacios[11] taking in a load of cotton. 10:00 A.M.: Came to anchor off Matagorda in 6½ feet, soft bottom, composed of alluvial stuff from the Colorado River. It took an hour with a fair wind to run in our boat from our anchorage to the town. This is rather inconvenient for the shipment of goods etc. And it is thought that "Tres Palacios" will take some of the export trade from Matagorda. I passed the evening at Dr. Hunter's,[12] who amongst other attainments is a great musician-violinist as well as harpist, but above all, I subsequently found him a kind friend, a good man and excellent companion. The society I met at his house, both of ladies and gentlemen, left nothing to be desired. Beauty, talent, and friendship. The "Belles of Bonavista" were there. They are "mild and fair, gentle as a zephyr's sigh![13] After our soireé a friend begged I would accompany him and two or three others to sup off a cold wild turkey. The night was beautiful indeed, it was too early on such a night to return to rest. On our arriving at his house supper was laid, but lo and behold the baker had forgotten to send bread. At this, being in a merry mood, I sang the words "Diavolo, Diavolo, Diavolo," being somewhat appropriate to our present difficulty of want of bread.

An old Negress had heard the chant of "Diavolo" from the kitchen—came into the room—exclaimed: "O Massa, I hear you sing tonight at the Doctor's, Diavolo, Diavolo, Diavolo. Do sing one verse for me—then I go knock the baker up and bring some bread." I complied; the Negress was in extasy. She started for the bread and now voilà we are at supper.

April 22nd, 1842: A musical party given at Col. L——, when Dr. H[unter] afforded all a great treat by his performance on the

[11] Tres Palacios Bay, a northeastern arm of Matagorda Bay, is located south of the town of Matagorda in western Matagorda County.

[12] Dr. Johnson Calhoun Hunter was a member of Austin's Old Three Hundred. Later he developed the Hunter plantation on Oyster Creek, which for fifty years was a landmark in the Richmond area. Bugbee, "The Old Three Hundred," *Quarterly of the Texas State Historical Association*, Vol. I (1897-98), 108-17.

[13] Since then they were married.—Bollaert.

harp. Taking the toute ensemble on this party—the music, dancing, and elegance, I could hardly believe that a few years since the
name of Texas was scarcely known.

April 23rd, 1842: In speaking of the want of depth of water
before the town of Matagorda—a gentleman observed: "We cannot have *all* we wish and want; our wars we pray will soon be over,
emigration must and will flock to our country. We have all good
health here in Matagorda, a fine climate, game, fish, turtle, cattle,
and poultry in abundance. I, who seldom ride now, have a score
in the prairie who take care of themselves." I took a ride into the
prairie with the said gentleman; in the distance, ridges of timber
were seen; nearer to us, horses and cattle grazing, and although
late in the spring, the prairie was covered with flowers. The shores
of the Bay skirted with shady groves that were fanned by the
southern breezes, that swept over the flowery plains, excelled the
choicest Parisian perfumes.

I fell in with a copy of "Impressions of America" by Power,
the actor. He says of Texas when speaking of persons who are in
"difficulties": "Numbers seek freedom from restraint within the
Mexican territory, where an infusion of blood will be productive
of strange events in Texas, and if this fine territory be not within
a very short period, rendered over-hot, a berth for its Mexican
population, coming events cast their shadows to very little purpose."[14] Alas, poor Power, I knew him, a fellow of infinite jest
and most excellent fancy. And moreover he was a Prophet as far
as regarded Texas.

April 25th, 1842: All the country round envelloped in as fine a
tropical thunder storm I have ever beheld. It was a grand specimen and seemed as if the "all shaking thunder" would "strike
flat the thick rotundity of the world!"

April 27th, 1842: A friend accompanied me across the prairies

[14] Tyrone Power, *Impressions of America, 1833-1835,* II, 90. Power went
down in the *President,* lost in a storm en route from America in 1841.

to Caney Creek; we passed two streams ere we reached our destination, the same evening, the cotton plantation of Mr. P——. I could not help remarking the peculiar and melancholy appearance the Spanish moss (Tillandsia Usneoides) in some places gives to the "timbers" or "bottoms." Its long, shaggy and hungry grey appearance, contrasting strangely with the deep green foliage. When much of this moss is seen growing, the locality does not sustain a good character for healthiness—"chills and fever" being common.

The Spanish moss when prepared, which is done by steeping it in water, part of it rots off, and is decomposed, leaving the long fibres which when dried in the sun take on a blackish appearance and is then used as horse hair is used in Europe and sells for from 4 to 6 cents per pound. During my ride I observed many of the feathered tribe of beautiful plumage, but particularly the turtle dove. It appears so tame that if started up from a track will gently descend again ahead and oftimes continues this for a considerable distance. It is a curious fact, that formerly game and birds could be taken very easily owing to the fact that they would allow the huntsman to come very near to them, even to knocking them down with sticks and stones; but as the wilderness gets settled, the game and birds get "scared" and thus hunting becomes more laborious.

I am informed that the wild indigo plant grows in these prairies. I am sorry to say I have not seen it, or any indigo made from it, although I am assured that the dye extracted is of a good quality.

Mr. P——'s plantation, although a recent one, is a thriving cotton estate—the lands are rich, but all these rich bottoms are occasionally subject to agues. The planter and his family may evade this local disease by building their residences in the prairie, say a mile or two from the "timbers" as Mr. Shepherd has done in this prairie at a spot called Bonavista. Others have followed his example. Returned to Matagorda, and in crossing [Big] Boggy, the ferryman Peter, I found, knew many of my acquaintances at Bayonne in France.

The rest of the time I remained in Matagorda passed pleasantly

Bollaert's drawing

Bollaert's Sketch of the Texas Squadron.

View of Galveston Harbor.

Bollaert's drawing

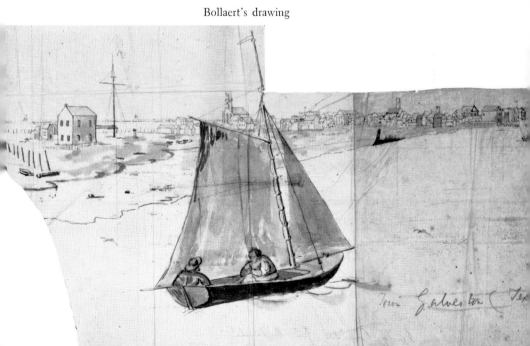

General Houston: *"His intimate friends have had much difficulty in persuading him to retain the Presidency. Others say that he wishes to annex Texas to the U. States, etc. etc. (Twaddle)."*

indeed, and I shall ever cherish a grateful remembrance for un-remitting attentions and kindness.

Some few years since there was a great fight between the first settlers about here and the Carancahua Indians; the Indians were defeated with great slaughter; since then their numbers have considerably decreased.[15] The bow and arrow, spear, tomahawk and scalping knife lie idle in their wigwams. They do not like work; they fish and hunt enough to support themselves and sell some. Now and then they bring in a panther's skin, or other pel-tries in exchange for blankets or whiskey. They now and then "appropriate" (steal is an ugly word). I saw some of them parad-ing the town, walking almost naked, one after the other. They looked robust and in good health, but no smile or joy was seen in their looks. Texas which means in the Comanche language the land of friends or happy hunting ground is now fast becoming the grave of the tribes of Red Men.

April 31st, 1842: Got to Decrows Point in sloop on our return to Galveston. The last "Proclamation distributing bout" of the Mexicans is considered by Santa An[n]a equal to anything a Napoleon did, or a Talleyrand conceived, and for the time being it has done some harm. The industrious inhabitants, farmers, and planters had to leave their peaceful occupations, shoulder their rifles and off to the frontier. The entry of the enemy into San Antonio would be trumpeted forth as a victory in Mexico to please the bigotted, and raise the shouts of "Viva Santana" by the Leperos; and although it had the effect of stopping emigration and will do for a time, it, according to the language of a friend of mine, "has reroused Texan energies and all our soul'd Brothers of the U. States have once more come to aid us." False reports are continually reaching the settlements, through Mexican spies of the "advance of the enemy." Parties go out to reconnoitre—*non inventus est* is the result.

[15] The Karankawas were defeated in several encounters with Stephen F. Aus-tin's colonists in the 1820's and 1830's. By 1844 most of the remnants of the tribe had fled to Mexico. Frederick Webb Hodge (ed.), *Handbook of American Indians North of Mexico,* I, 657–58.

I find a few notes in my journal on another subject. This is a "great" country, but should a stranger not be lucky enough to discover the right "diggings," he will never "go a head" but will stupidly lose his money and his time. But should he be aware of the simple arithmetical fact that $2+3=5$, goes straight forward, never minding to be considered a "smart man," but feel the natural dignity of man, he will be beloved and respected and by taking care of his own affairs, no one will meddle with his, and moreover he will keep out of "difficulties." The loafers and outcasts soon find their level, and with the assistance of whiskey go headlong to ruin, but the honest and industrious man, let him be from any foreign land, will find a *home* in Texas. He will soon feel that he is a man, municipal honors await him six months after his arrival in the country when he becomes a *citizen*. He is given, if a married man 680 acres of land, if single 340 and in a few years with industry and perseverance he has the gratifying feeling of being seated in the Congress of the Nation, assisting in the administration of his fellow citizens. This by some may be considered high coloured, but I will only confess that it has but the slightest "colour de rose" about it.[16]

May 4th, 1842: Wind dead ahead and strong current against us. 6 P.M.: Came to anchor between the San Bernard River and Cedar Creek.[17] As night came on saw a very large patch of prairie

[16] A friend of mine writes of Galveston in 1841.—Bollaert. [The following newspaper article was enclosed at this point. No date is given, but obviously it appeared in 1840 and was published in a Texas newspaper.]

Brazos, Caney, and Bernard lands have fallen instead of risen in value. Texas money has been daily depreciating although it is getting almighty scarce. Town speculators begin to look *blue,* but how they manage to *get so* the Lord only knows. Merchants are making money—*over the left shoulder.* Money is getting so abominably scarce that T.T. notes are harder to come at than specie used to be. In fine, unless Old Tip, is elected and sends us over a branch of the United States Bank, or General Hamilton obtains *the* loan—I don't see how the devil the loafers and lazy *town gentlemen* will much longer maintain their dignity. By the way— the latter gentry begin to look very chap-fallen and confoundedly shabby of late.

But let me not put all my readers in a bad humor when bidding them farewell. The industrious tillers of the soil and growers of stock are rapidly accumulating wealth and improving their lands and will continue to do so.

[17] This would put the travelers a few miles down the coast from present Freeport, Texas.

on fire, which as the night was dark, looked strange indeed. Its occasional vivid streaks of light, when the wind fanned the burning grass, then the huge black vapors rising and rolling about; it did not require a very considerable stretch of the imagination to picture some large city on fire; then the wind would alter the appearance, and being low land, the fire appeared to issue as if out of ocean depths, as if it were the extended crater of a volcano.

The prairies are generally set afire to burn weeds and old pasturage, so as to make room for the new grass. Many distressing tales are told of travellers and cattle being burnt by the prairie fires (but it scotches an occasional snake or so). The Indian plan, when surprised by a prairie fire, is to burn all the grass in their immediate vicinity, so as the fire sweeps over the ground (the celerity of which will depend upon the force of the wind) finding no combustible matter, they may, although surrounded by fire, escape.

May 6th, 1842: Our passage is retarded. Our provisions are nearly out and we have several passengers. It has been unanimously declared that there is a Jonas on board. One of our passengers up to this morning was a *desperate* chewer of tobacco and a w[h]ittler of sticks. The whittling could be tolerated even by a nervous person, but the huge pieces of tobacco that my friend kept continually in his mouth, distorted his features and certainly was affecting his health. I took the liberty of putting on a grave face, for he generally kept below expectorating in a large wooden spittoon.

"Friend," said I, "You don't look well this morning—you did not appear to relish your breakfast."

"Why Sir, I'm a bad sailor and thus I keep below, but, I do feel rather—" (nothing was the matter with him, but having heard the flattering tone of sympathy—it was requisite if only for politeness sake to feign some sort of sickness).

"Yes, I'm sure you do, but if you will permit me to give an opinion, I think that the weather being hot and debilitating, you *use* a little too much tobacco."

"Well friend, I think you are right—hem-ha-hem."

"You look a little bilious. I have some excellent pills and would advise you to take a couple directly. You will be comfortable before night and if the practice of chewing is not inveterate with you—don't *use* so much."

"Stranger, you speak like a book—give me the pills. I'll chew no more tobacco. Its killing me by inches, but I suppose I'll indulge occasionally in a segar."

"Undoubtedly, indeed the segar is a pleasant companion, particularly when one is travelling alone, and moreover it assists digestion."

My friend took the pills. He was better on the morrow, and kept his promise by chewing no more tobacco, but he punished me for some time afterwards by smoking my segars.

May 7th, 1842: Cloudy—occasional rains—airs N.E. but variable—cool.

May 8th, 1842: Anchored in Galveston. The President and Government at Houston. The majority of our warriors returned to their homes. The "War Party" is for keeping up the excitement and "go a head" even to the "Halls of the Montezumas." Weather becoming hot.

On Titles

Our worthy, industrious, and intelligent offspring in the new world, morally and physically better than their progenitors in many particulars—and this owing to their successful revolution against the Mother Country, and moreover, having respired the air of a beautiful region, nursed with the milk of freedom, and more than all enjoying *all* the proceeds of their individual and collective labours—having no large armies and navies—national debt—or expensive courts to maintain—indeed, with but a few years of labour—men thus situated must become rich. But their riches sometimes lead them for want of a continuance of excitement into immense speculations—such as founding new countries, cities, towns, etc., in the fastness of the savage wilds hitherto untrod but by the wild beast and the Red Man. But to our subject "Titles"—and this the Americans have inherited from the Mother Country like many other good and evil customs and manners. Washington and his brave companions in arms and in the forum—banished the shadow only of Royalty that shed its artificial hue around the American colonies. A Republican Government was formed. Its head was called the President, but the idea, charm, and prestige of title is still preserved: "His Excellency General George Washington, President of the United States of America." The members of the House of Representatives and Senators have the title of "Honorable." Judges and some others likewise bear this appelative title. It has been so often repeated that every other man one meets with in the states is a General, Colonel, Major, Captain, or Judge—but in reading of this it does not strike one so much as to hear it, more particularly when we are taught that pure democracy only exists in the United States.

I attended a patriotic meeting at G. The speakers were Generals, Majors, Captains, Judges, etc., but after an elequent speech from Judge B——, Colonel L—— quietly said to him: "Judge, take a drink," and in a jiffy my worthies were sipping as nice a glass of cold mint julip as was ever made behind a bar. With regard to the U.S.: there remain many of the old Revolutionary officers. Their titles they nobly bear—may they live to use them long—but the great mass of military names belong to militia officers, but such a militia and volunteers that would surprise even the iron strong nerves of John Bull. May their shadows never be less—and they are not pigmies. My prayer is that we may in time know one another better fraternize and whip the world when they require it. But to titles again. The Americans as yet do not relish titles as King, Queen, Duke, Marquis, Earl, etc., but say "The Earl and Countess of Alabama's carriage stops the way"—this would be "pretty enough"—but—dubb any of our good transatlantic friends with General, Colonel, Capt. or Judge, by G—— he'll cheerfully give you a drink—and such a thing is particularly good in hot weather. I have invariably found when the English and Americans quarrel, that it is because they do not understand each other, and sometimes their high-fed bloods will not concede. Let one or the other say "It may be so," and not "It is so," and then they'll swear by each other to the eternal d——t of Johnny Crappaud and all other nations. We like titles and why should they not—they live in a free country and why not treat them as well as [any] body else.

During the American war an attached friend of G¹. Washington's named McDonald, the bravest of the brave and foremost in the fight would never accept any other title than that of "Sergeant." Indeed, this title, speaking somewhat funnilly, is considered in Texas very distinguished because our military aspirants *run* for all the other high grades. Long live "Sergeant" Blowhard of Lafitte Expedition memory.

How to Obtain a Title

During one of my journeys into the interior in company with a friend, we were benighted on ———— Creek. After wandering about a considerable time we espied a light in the distance, and made for it. On approaching the log-house we heard a violent altercation, as if between a man and his wife, who turned out to be emigrants from the Emerald Isle.

"Arrah now Judy, you're not in auld Ireland now, be asey or I'll be after showing ye—ye're living in a free country, and that I'll get a divorce from Sam Houston."

"Dennis, Dennis is that the way you spoke to her, you for so many years called your own darlent Judy—and is it divorce ye mean—and would you go and live with another woman before the mother of ye're children was under the sod?" Here the poor woman burst into tears. At this juncture we arrived before the log house and requested hospitality for the night.

"Sure, yes, who are ye and where do you come from," said Dennis. I told our host that I was from the "auld country." Sobbing tears Judy commenced preparing supper—when both at intervals made known their griefs. My companion by some chance or the other called me accidently "Judge."

Judy brightened up—came towards me, put her hands upon her hips akimbo—"Honey, is it ye're a Judge? Would ye be a Christian man and listen and as ye're a Judge just explain to Dennis upon the enormity of wishing to separate from his darlent wife."

"Arrah Judy, don't tease the travellers, they are tired. But Judge—it's all her fault. She's good enough, but didn't I come home the other night tired from hunting—devil a bit of fire was there. She and all the children fast asleep—not even a pot of sweet potatoes cooked."

"Ah Dennis ye come home so late—Gentlemen-Judge, when he stops out so late, I know he's safe at the neighbors up the creek."

"I'll go to Houston and get a divorce—Judy! Judy!"

"You'll break my heart—but Judge give us your advice."

"Well, friends it appears to me, that you are very good people and if ye have a fault you love each other's society perhaps too much. I must say that it was very hard for Dennis when he came home to find no fire and sweet potatoes. But at the same time Dennis, you must consider that your wife had waited for you—it got late, and if she went to bed that was very natural."

"Sure Judge, you speak like a book," said Dennis.

"Arrah, see Dennis how the Judge explains the matter."

"Moreover my good friends, I suppose you are Roman Catholics."

Then they both crossed themselves.

Dennis replied, "Ah Judge it is many a long day we have not heard mass—not since we lived at San Antonio."

"Well, my friends you must be aware that according to the tenets of your church, a *divorce* is not permitted. It is one of the holy sacraments."

Then they crossed themselves again.

"Now I would advise you if you cannot live peaceably together to *separate*."

"Sure, that's a good idea," said Dennis.

"And the children," replied Judy.

"Why! Why! (here was a poser) Why, I would suggest, as you have 680 acres of land—you Dennis, build up a log house at the further end of your property, enclose a small part and let Judy live there. Let her have one of the big boys to work for her and take care of a cow or two. Then she can take care of the younger children. The other big boy can work with you."

At this, Mother, Father, and elder children shed tears. They looked at each other—Dennis flew to his darlent Judy—kissed her, came then to me, "Judge, many many thanks—No, I'll not leave the old woman."

"Ah Dennis, Dennis, I promise [to] let ye be out all night. I'll keep the fire on and have you a pot of sweet potatoes waiting."

We had our supper; nothing more was said of the divorce or separation. Some time afterwards Dennis sent me a present of a deer, two wild turkeys, and three brace of ducks, with a letter addressed to "Judge B."

The following article on titles appeared subsequently to this in the *Texas Times*[18] of October 19th.

Illegitimate Titles

In the Northern and Eastern States of the Union, a gratuitous bestowal of unearned titles is frequent—in the Middle States general—at the South a majority are thus *honored*;—but in Texas, the custom is almost universal. A happy man is he who has lived a year in this Republic without having been addressed as General, Colonel, Major, Captain, Judge, Doctor, or Squire. For our own part we have had both the civil and military vocabulary of titles exhausted on our devoted head. For two weary years we struggled manfully against the storm, but oh! how vainly!! We battled fiercely, not as the veteran soldiers of Europe—to earn a title— but, in the spirit of true republicanism, to avoid the wearing of

18 The *Texas Times* was published at Galveston.

unearned honors. Our efforts have been as futile as those of a majority of the aforesaid veterans.

We have abandoned all hope of maintaining our simple cognomen of Mister, and expect to die a martyr to the prevailing taste of the sovereign people; and if our friends should each write an epitaph separately, we think the inscription will read somewhat as follows:

> *The General died a true believer*
> *The Colonel liv'd "a gay deceiver."*
> *The Major died an easy death.*
> *The Captain's gone for want of breath.*
> *The Judge is freed from worldly pains*
> *Peace be to the Doctor's manes.*
> *The Squire died of persecution.*
> *Which has not ceased with dissolution.*

If the little army with which we are preparing to contend with Mexico should perish, (which God forbid), and Texas should erect a monument to their memory (which, judging from Republican precedents, will never be done), and an inscription should be placed on the monument, giving the fallen heroes their nominal titles, then will future generations suppose the two opposing armies to have outnumbered the countless hosts of Xerxes. The record would be to the following purport.

> *Forty Generals died like heroes*
> *To break the chains of modern Neroes.*
> *Eighty Colonels lie beneath;—*
> *In freedom's cause they suffer'd death.*
> *One hundred Majors shed their blood,*
> *Like water for their country's good.*
> *One thousand Captains led the van*
> *And all died fighting—to a man.*
> *No living soul was left to tell*
> *What on that woful day befell;*

81

But for each soul that took its flight:
One hundred foemen fell in fight.
The blood that in their veins congeal'd
This country's lasting freedom seal'd.

May 10th, 1842: Amongst other amusements[19] we have our
Fancy Fairs. A theatre is occasionally opened. Concerts and Balls
during their particular seasons. The present Fancy Fair was held
for obtaining ways and means to finish building of the Episcopal
Church. The Fair stall-keepers did some "trade." It was well attended, with refreshments in abundance. At one end of the room
a Gypsy's tent was erected, in which sat a fortune-teller, near to
her was the "Post Office" and for the small sum of two bits visitors
got a *billet-doux* such as:

MY DEAR FRIEND

This is a pleasant evening. Everything favorable to happiness.
I hope you are pleased. Does the world use you well? If it has not,
do not repine—bear up and you may be more successful—more
particularly if there is a lady in the question.

Your friend,
MARY

These Fancy Fairs, independent of the charitable ends they
meet, are distinguished apologies for a little small-talk. And why
not? *C'est l'amour, l'amour, l'amour.*

[19] At the period we are writing of, there was no lack of amusements at Galveston. There was horse racing, occasionally the "players" from New Orleans, a
traveling circus, concerts, such as they were, and dances denominated balls and
"Dutch Balls," fishing parties on the beach, these winding up with a "chowder
feast" made generally of the fish caught. . . . But the chief amusements are hunting, fishing, turtling expeditions, and boating.—Bollaert.

V

MATAGORDA AGAIN
AND THEN TO NEW ORLEANS

[May–June, 1842]

THE OUTS, OR WAR PARTY are strong in their invectives against the Executive for not organizing *coute que coute* active warlike operations. Moreover, as they say, any number of volunteers could be obtained from the United States.

But first, where are the ways and means? For war is not carried on nowadays by inspiration. Secondly, would it be politic? If the question can be settled even by a lengthy negotiation, thus good blood would be spared. True it is, the West is nearly "broken up," but in the eastern counties all is going on flourishingly, particularly on Red River and the "Cross Timbers." The President's political opponents have organized a sort of "Convention" to be held at Brazoria;[1] and considerable acrimony of feeling and opposition is evinced against the Executive for his wish of having the "Archives,"[2] sent from Austin to Houston, according to his view of the case, for their better security. The inhabitants of Austin will not allow them to be removed.

May 11th, 1842: An old Coshatte [Coushatta] Chief named

[1] Sam Houston wrote to Colonel Barry Gillespie on May 16, 1842, relative to the Brazoria meeting and others similar: "These incendiaries would not, I presume, exceed twenty in number; but they are composed of men who have some smartness, some means, and possess all the attributes of mischief. . . . Who are these men? They are not men who have shared in the toils of the Revolution; nor have they stood shoulder to shoulder with those who have embraced the perils of a well-fought field. They are men who have no principle but self; and aside from that feel no affections." *The Writings of Sam Houston,* III, 51.

[2] The Archives War was precipitated by Houston's order to remove the capital from Austin to the city of Houston, fearing that the Mexican Army would move on Austin. The people of Austin prevented the moving of the official records when efforts were made in December, 1842, for they were certain that the President wanted to make Houston the permanent capital. Their warlike action doubtless resulted in the restoration of the capital to Austin in 1844.

Colête[3] some 80 years of age made a long speech in his language at the Exchange. It was translated to his hearers, the principal points being that some white men had transgressed and taken some of their lands on the Trinity River, but he was ready with his warriors to aid the Texans against Comanches or Mexicans. It is well to be on friendly terms with our Indian Brethern, but they are generally looked upon as "loafers," when they have been attached to any Military expeditions. I took a pipe with the venerable Chief, but our "talk" was not of any great length. The Coshattees are supposed to be descendants of the ancient Natchez Indians, inhabitants of Texas at the time of the Spanish Conquest.

May 15th, 1842: Volunteers keep arriving from the U. States. Saw Mr. Falconer, who had accompanied the Santa Fé expedition. He intends, I believe, to write the particulars of this affair. Honors are continually showering upon me. Appointed 1st Corporal of the G. Coast Guards, but a *full private* is about the best position one can have. Rank and station cause much uneasiness—particularly the rank of Orderly Sergeant.

"Uneasy lies the head that wears a Crown."

Friday, May 20th, 1842: Left Galveston in company with Messrs. P. and M. 15 miles brought us abreast of the "Three Trees,"[4] the first is a clump of ten, the two others are single ones. An excellent ferry boat took our buggy and horses over to the island of St. Luis,[5] there by a smaller ferry to the main land; about dusk we arrived at Velasco;[6] here is an hotel with good accom-

[3] This was probably Colita, an aged Coushatta chief who was still alive in 1842. The Coushattas have a tradition that after the Battle of San Jacinto, Colita, their chief, carried the news of the victory to the border of Louisiana and brought the Texans back. Harriet Smither, "The Alabama Indians of Texas," *Southwestern Historical Quarterly*, Vol. XXXVI (1932–33), 92.

[4] The "Three Trees" was the site of a battle between Lafitte's pirates and a band of Caranchuas in 1819, at which time the latter was badly defeated. Thrall, *Pictorial History of Texas*, 135.

[5] San Luis Island is off the tip of what was commonly known as the Velasco Peninsula; it lies across San Luis Pass from the west end of Galveston Island.

[6] Velasco is in southern Brazoria County near the mouth of the Brazos River. It is one of the oldest towns in Texas, the schooner *Lively* having stopped there in 1821 to land the first of Austin's colonists.

[m]odation. One of my companions had assisted under John Austin,[7] June 26th, 1832 to take the Fort of Velasco. The Texans had 11 killed and 52 wounded; 173 Mexicans formed the garrison, one half of them were killed.

Saturday, May 21st, 1842: 8 A.M. Ferried across the River Brazos to Quintana.[8] The River is deep inside but the bar bears a bad name. Sailing vessels have been occasionally lost here. Swam our horses over the San Bernard River, but got the buggy and ourselves paddled over in a "dug out" or canoe. When one gets to a stream and there be no ferry-boat or canoe, the general plan is to put one's habiliments into one's saddle-bags, sling these across the shoulder, dash into the stream "á lo Indio" and swim across. On a hot day this is very refreshing, but during the winter months, and should it be blowing a "Norther," why then a ferry-boat is preferable. We slept within 15 miles of the town of Matagorda

---

[7] The battle of Velasco was probably the first case of bloodshed in the relations between Texas and Mexico. John Austin, one of the leaders of the Texas forces against the Mexican fort of Velasco, apparently was no relation of Stephen F. Austin's. The companion that Bollaert referred to as having assisted John Austin in the attack was Edward Miles, who later served in the battle of San Jacinto. Dixon and Kemp, *Heroes of San Jacinto*, 138.

[8] Quintana was once an important shipping port and a thriving community, but tropical hurricanes and the diverting of its trade elsewhere by an intercoastal canal have reduced it to a small fishing village of two or three dozen people. *Saturday, May 21st, 1842:* 8 A.M. Ferried across the Brazos to Quintana. This appears to be a flourishing country. Live oak is cutting up the River for the English Gov't—River has deep water—continuing along the Coast came to the River Bernard—dist. 9 miles—Here is a bad bar — no great width of River. It is now for the first time a pebble or so is seen and a little alluvial soil on the banks. To here and further on the Coast is of Sand—very few shells—and large quantities of drift wood which forms a sort of Barrier for the sand that is blown up by the S. and S.E. winds and this extends and gives height to the Coast. It is moreover very evident that these s^d. S. and S.E. winds blow up from the very shallow shores of the Gulf of Mexico—much sand and thus fresh Shores may be said to be forming daily—the dead shells with a small quantity of sea-weed and such plants that like a saline soil form in time habitable soil for man. In my travels I know of no coast that is forming so rapidly as this. The shores give pastures but they are rather rag[g]ed growing on a sandy and saline soil—but where there is an alluvial deposit there the pastures get better with Prairies. In the Bottoms and land adjoining them there the Timbers grow—Crossed Caney Creek 7½ miles from Bernard by fording thro' the Breakers—Keeping the Woods of Caney to our Right 10 miles brought us to Nigger Island—(mouth of Caney to Matagorda 25 miles) slept here.—Bollaert.

at Major S——. He has excellent quarters and the situation of his house is so desirable that it goes by the name of "Bonavista," and to add to the charm, he is blessed with a most amiable family.

In large cities and populous towns one is too much occupied either to read or study, more than the ordinary daily occurrences; but it is in village or country life where one enjoys a peculiar quietude; one has a zest for study, and for my own part I am like the Arabs of the Thousand and One Nights—I like a story, yarn, legend, or historical reminiscence.

Sunday, May 22nd, 1842: 5 A.M. started for Matagorda. At the ford met Mr. Powell and returned back to Major Sheppherd's. Reports from Corpus Christi that Mexicans intended taking it and establishing themselves there—Colonel Kenney[9] sᵈ. to be a prisoner on the other side of the frontier—that Austin had been superceded by General [Adrian] Woll, and that we may expect a visit daily from the enemy—*nous verrons!*[10]

Some wolves caught in these prairies. Yesterday middle of the day was warm. Prairies sultry. These prairies near to the bottoms might be made available for sugar plantations. It is rather too warm for general gardening, but good potatoes are grown.

Monday, May 23rd, 1842: Accompanied Mr. and Mrs. Shepherd to their plantation. Snakes in trees.

Tuesday, May 24th, 1842: Went to Matagorda. This night the Thespian Company of Matagorda played the "Two Thompsons" and "When Shall I Dine"—very well indeed in their pretty little theatre. My vocal powers were solicited—when I had the honor of singing, in the character of a hunter, Mr. Kennedy's much admired song of "Our Rifles are Ready" and the "Red Rovers," in the sea costume of the "Coast Guards."

[9] Colonel H. S. Kenney was a merchant at Matagorda in 1842. Lamar, *Papers*, V, 583.
[10] Austin was never visited by a Mexican army; however General Adrian Woll did return to San Antonio in September, 1842.

Wednesday, May 25th, 1842: Left Matagorda. We got on famously in the prairie with the buggy, having two fine horses, whisking along in great style, startling occasionally a wolf or deer. But when wending our way through the woods, a "land snag" caught one of the springs and "used up" the buggy. However, we mounted the horses and got to Mr. P——'s plantation, sending a score of Negros to fetch the wreck of our vehicle.

Thursday, May 26th, 1842: Went round the plantation. 10 miles brought us to Bernard River at Cowan's Ferry.[11] Three miles more brought us to Brazoria.[12] All this distance from Caney [Creek] is wooded. Some few mulberries ripe. Fine field for botanist. Talk not of starvation in Texas—sat down to a fine dinner at Mr. Bennet's and dispatched a bottle of fine Hock. Plenty large walnut near Gonzales—and might be floated down the Guadalupe, might be easily floated down into Espiritu Santo Bay in Spring—swift Currents—Large alligators—Fish—few flys— Wild vines—just ripening—Fossil fish found in digging well in forest near here—water 20 ft.

Friday, May 27th, 1842: 10 A.M. left Brazoria—passed Mr. Miles and other plantations. Came to Mr. MacNeel's;[13] dined— fine brick building—one of the oldest settlers. Plantations want rain—What a country for cotton, maiz, and sugar—if they had Niggers enough—The buggy got snagged again and all the springs broke. 9 P.M.: Got to Quintana situated at the mouth of the Brazos River.

11 Probably named after William James Cowen, who settled near Brazoria in 1835.
12 Brazoria was founded by John Austin (see footnote 7 above) in 1828, as a port and trading center for Stephen F. Austin's colony. It continued to be an important town after the Revolution, its population at one time amounting to approximately 5,000. A gradual decline followed after the Civil War, and today Brazoria contains approximately 1,000 people or less.
13 John Greenville McNeel settled in Brazoria County as a member of Austin's Old Three Hundred in 1824. His plantation, Ellersly, was one of the showplaces of early Texas. Kemp, *Signers of the Texas Declaration of Independence*, 25, 27–28.

Saturday, May 28th, 1842: 9 A.M. Got to San Luis; it was rather hot and sultry and we deemed it advisable to take it cooly. Left at 4 P.M. and arrived at Galveston at 9 P.M., much pleased with my trip. Some of the Santa Fé prisoners have escaped from Mexico and have returned to Texas. I may here mention that several Mexicans have been arrested on the frontier and the general opinion was they were spies; nevertheless, General Houston has ordered them to be liberated.

June 1842: Having expressed a wish to a friend that wanted to visit the coast of Texas up to the Sabine, from thence along to the Mississippi and New Orleans, I was invited on board the ———. I observed a large number of persons, rifles, and muskets, etc., on board the craft and a gun placed in the bows, and asked my friend the meaning of this warlike preparation. "You will see presently," said he, "and I promise that you will see the coast— *perhaps some strange things*—and moreover, New Orleans." When we had got fairly out to sea, the individual who was in command, shewed his commission as a Privateer, signed by Sam Houston. It would appear that information had been obtained in Galveston to the effect that one or two Mexican vessels with specie, would be, about this identical period, leaving some port or other of Mexico for New Orleans. Privateering is all very well, when too great a latitude is not given to the commission. . . .

June 1st, 1842: At 8 A.M. Tow boat coming down S.W. Pass with one ship and suspicious schooner. Got under weigh—calms and light airs—strange sail steaming rather in the direction of enemy's coast. We were to leeward of her. 2:30 P.M.: She hoisted her main gaff-top sail: thus it was evident she wished to slip from us. We had gained upon her, but this time being then ¾ miles to leeward. Wind shifting however brought us into her wake and at 15 past 5 P.M. came up to her and spoke her—send boat aboard. She proved to be a vessel bound to Tobasco under suspicious circumstances—lashed ourselves along side of her and commenced examination of papers but upon manifest "corn" only appeared but by prosecuting a little of the Paul Pry considerable quantities of what we thought proper to denominate "munitions of war." Sloped up—this added to considerable suspicious discrepancies on the part of the Captain ("A Bayonese"), the supercargo ("Felice Tormento") and two Spaniards or Mexicans—why by some strange transmogrification or other appeared to be the peculiar appelation of Henry Townsend and John Wilson. And moreover, the trepidation of a very useful appendage to a ship called the "Doctor" or cook—combined with the s^d. powder, lead, and probably other etc's., it was decided nem: con after due deliberation that the *Marie Elizabeth* should be immediately sent to Galveston as a prize. Her papers appeared to show that she belonged to a Mr. Power of New York, but we have an idea that Mr. Power is a Mexican in Tobasco. We were 20 or more miles from the mouths of the Mississippi, thus the *Marie Elizabeth* being over 3 leagues from land—going to the enemy's coast with munitions of war, constitutes her a prize.

The s^d. vessel had been dispatched by Schmidt and Company of New Orleans and consigned to Lobache and Company, according to her papers, but all these documents looked clumsy. 7 P.M.: Sent prize under charge of Lt. Boyland[14] and three others to Galveston—with a fine fair breeze—with dispatch to Colonel Hockley,[15] Secretary of War and Marine, and Mr. Smyth, our legal adviser—with orders to try and adjudicate her and awaiting further orders from Captain W——.[16] The tonnage of the *Washington* is 17½. We had during the chase, 15 in all—pretty well armed and disposed, and could have given "Jessy" if required—armed to the teeth with rifles, muskets, pistols, boarding swords, and bowie knives etc. 11 P.M. Came to anchor off the Mississippi.

Thursday, June 2nd, 1842: Sunrise got under [weigh]. Entered

[14] James D. Boylan. See footnote 5, Chapter III.

[15] George Washington Hockley came to Texas in 1835 and was Houston's chief of staff during the Revolution. Houston later appointed him colonel of ordinance, and later secretary of war. He went with Samuel M. Williams in 1843 to arrange an armistice with Mexico. Dixon and Kemp, *Heroes of San Jacinto*, 73.

[16] Probably George Washington Wheelright. See footnote 3, Chapter IV.

the S. W. Pass, bringing up at the Balize. This is a strange looking place, almost under water, the residence of the pilots who have an association in common and who appear to be in very good circumstances. Independent of their beautiful pilot boats, they have very pretty pleasure boats. The Houses are built of wood, well furnished, and there are towers or look-out houses to see the approach of shipping. The place is a perfect swamp, but the residents will not allow that it is as unhealthy as New Orleans. Perhaps on account of its vicinity to the sea breezes; but the weather was now getting warm. The mosquitos in abundance and the only hunting that of alligators.

We were most hospitably received by Captain Taylor. At great expense and trouble the good folks of Balize have made a levee or breakwater along the shore, so as to form a path, scooping up the mud from behind their house to form the said levee. Captain Taylor told us long and interesting anecdotes of Lafitte, the pirate of the Gulf, and of Du Puytren,[17] one who had the reputation of a sea-rover and whom he had [the] pleasure of stopping in his career some little time since. Captain Taylor took us to his dwelling place, regaled us with good cheer; his wife, who is young and with pretensions of beauty, charmed us with some pretty songs.

After supper one evening our host took us to his armory; it well merits this appelation. A house being built expressly for this end, wherein is a large and choice collection of Indian dresses, decorations, arms, and accoutrements—presents from Chiefs of various tribes such as the Cherokees, Seminoles, Choctaws, etc. To each present is attached some peculiar reminiscence which the gallant Captain relates with many interesting observations. But the most interesting collection here is the armour, arms, guns, flags with "deaths heads and bloody bones" that belonged to Du Puytren that the Captain captured at sea in a fine vessel not long since. Du Puytren was indicted for piracy, but after a long and tedious

[17] Bollaert spelled this pirate's name differently each time he used it in his journal. In an article published in 1852 on the pirate Laffite (see footnote 4, Chapter II) Bollaert calls the former Du Puytren, and states that "perhaps he was the last of the pirates in the Gulf area." An extensive search by the editor fails to produce any further information about him.

trial was acquitted. In the armory hangs the portrait of this would-be buccaneer, moreover the "Rules and Regulations" that were observed on board his vessel.

I now [Friday, June 3rd, 1842] left my privateering friends, and pursued my way to New Orleans in a "tow boat," visiting whilst there the "Austin," "Wharton," Texan Men of War.

The appearance of the "Crescent City" from the River is imposing; the immense number of buildings, the dome of St. Charles Hotel peering proudly above all; then the levee or embankment thrown up to protect the city from the inroads of the mighty mother of waters, when there is a rise in the river—on the levee being placed the stores or warehouses and in front of it the shipping. I arrived just as the busy season was closing, still the continual bustle in the principal streets and toward the River gave me some idea of the extent of business transacted in this city. (Now the trades and others were hurrying away to the north out of the influence of "yellow jack.")

The St. Charles Hotel is the "Monstre Hotel" of the South. Its exterior arrangements are upon a very extensive scale and managed with considerable skill and ability. The exterior of this edifice evinces the desire [on the part of] the New Orleans folk to have something classic, but with great deference to them it is not of an architecture appropriate to the character of the establishment or the climate. The Verandah and the St. Louis Hotels are more in character. The Exchange is located a short distance from the St. Louis Hotel. It is a very interesting building and contains some good chiaroscuro decorations.[18]

About 1684–5 Robert de la Salle left Canada, discovering and coming down the Mississippi, reaching the Gulf of Mexico. Thus France claimed what is now known as Louisiana. [In] 1699, d'Iberville was sent from France as Governor of Louisiana; the country he took possession of was from Mobile Bay to the Bay of St. Bernard in Texas. [In] 1717, New Orleans [was] founded by the

[18] [At the Exchange Hotel] are some fair Chiaro Oscuro paintings. Independent of the Hotels there are boarding houses and numberless "furnished apartments," and no want of churches and chapels for all denominations. The Banks are fine buildings.—Bollaert.

French. [In] 1762, [the] cession of Louisiana by France to Spain, through what was called the "Family Compact," but by private treaty, and was only given up 21st April, 1764. Mons. d'Abadie, the Governor, received orders from Louis XV to deliver up his command to the Spanish authorities. The idea of giving up so beautiful a gem of the crown of France preyed upon d'Abadie's mind and led him to a premature tomb. [In] 1800 [the] retrocession of Louisiana by Spain to the French (under Napoleon) but 20th December, 1803 Louisiana was given up to its present possessors, the Americans. I need hardly mention that [it] is since that period New Orleans has flourished. At present, times are dull, because cotton is low; yet a very considerable trade is carried on during the latter end of the autumn, winter and following spring all is alive in this city. Towards the middle of summer the merchants leave for the North, and traders for the interior. The foreign shipping has nearly all sailed with cotton principally.

"Yellow Jack" walks abroad but the native inhabitants lead a life of luxury and comparative indolence. But woe be to a stranger who has any *fear* of Yellow fever; if he has he will certainly catch it and in too many cases it is a "touch-and-go" with him.[19] I am happy to say that the disease is better understood than formerly and there is no want of medical men.[20]

An American from the North being asked his opinion of New Orleans moved his quid about and expectorating a stream of infusae nicotiana Tobacum—"Tis a funny country—almighty strange place—mother of rivers—all dream of dollar-dollar-dollar in the Crescent City."

I must not omit to mention one of the most interesting sights in the city—say the Bar Room of the St. Charles Hotel daily about 11 A. M., lunch time, where for the moderate sum of one bit (about

---

[19] "Yellow Jack" comes on after the very hot weather, and when vegetable decomposition is rapidly going on, the weather is said to be generally very beautiful and cool—the nights lovely, but then it is in some seasons that grim death stalks about seeking whom he may devour.—Bollaert.

[20] For at every other house "Doctor ———" is seen on the door—Chemist and druggists shops are numberless. Then comes the segar "Contiques," groceries, tailors, boot and shoe makers, etc.—Bollaert.

6ᵈ.)—you have eatables and drinkables, a choix even to delicacies from every part of the world—and—O ye aldermen of London's city, think on it—turtle soup into the bargain. Then the "tipples," or drinks, shall I ever forget ye—No! Mint julips, sherry cobblers, brandy toddy's, sangarees, lemonades, porterades, pig-and-whistles, Tom and Jerry's, cock-tails, etc., etc., and all for the small charge of a bit.

Fires are very common here, but the "brigades" to extinguish them are well organized. A night seldom passes, but one is woke from his slumbers by the cry of "fire" and the rattling along the streets of the engines and hose.

Amusements during the season are in abundance, even to an Italian opera. The English, French, and German plays are represented. The remnants of the Spanish population amuse themselves with their guitars and sing their beautiful melodies[21] and have their characteristic dances. Concerts and balls are always going on. A stroll through the excellent markets of a morning is an interesting promenade and after breakfast if one feels inclined to *voir les moeurs* a visit to the Recorder's office is interesting. The Recorder's office [on] Anglice Bow Street is situated near to the old Cathedral. About 10 A.M. the doors are thrown open, when a large cage-like piece of architecture is seen on the right, full of drunkards, vagabonds, and thieves taken during the night. The friends and acquaintances of the incarcerated, those who have them, are seen busily making known to "Counsel" the *real* state of the case. The Recorder takes his place—"Silence! Order in the Court! A book is opened—fatal scroll! It is the list of names of prisoners and their reputed crimes. According to their turn they are let out of the said cage and brought before the Recorder. Drunkenness and vagabondizing appear to be the principal crimes, and if the culprit cannot make out a pretty good case for his intemperance, he is fined, and if he have committed any particular excess, sent to prison at Baton Rouge. The Recorder I saw on the bench appeared a very gentlemanly man. He heard the cases with

[21] One I heard was an old favourite of mine I had learnt in Peru: "El tiempo fue de mis placeres"—In Other Times What Joys I've Seen.—Bollaert.

great patience, he remonstrated with the prisoners in a kind and parental manner, and was more satisfied to get a promise of future good conduct than to incarcerate the delinquent. The majority are generally let off. The Clerk of the Court, I may mention, looks out after the "fees."

I shall close my observations on New Orleans by a scene at the "Exchange" where slaves were selling by auction: young quadroon females selling for $250 and $300, elderly females for less, strong boys from $300 to $400, field hands $500 to $600, elderly men from $200 to $300.

"Hannibal, my boy, come up," said Mr. B——, the auctioneer. Up perched upon a stand the Negro in question, well dressed and looking most good humouredly about, rolling his eyes and showing his ivory teeth. "Gentlemen, I offer you this boy Hannibal— raised in Virginia and warranted free from all maladies and vices, *according to law*. He is a first rate field hand, shoes horses, good gardiner, and moreover *a very good boy*. Look up Hannibal. What do you say gentlemen—make me an offer—$200. Thank you Sir." In a few moments his price went up to $600 and Hannibal changed masters; down he jumped from the stand, was introduced to the purchaser, who said: "Hannibal, my boy, if you are a good boy, I'll be a good master to you, but if you are not, I'll whip you." The Negro replied, "I will be very good, Master." "Well, come along home."

The next offered was a young quadroon girl, almost as white, as one remarked, "as a Christian"—dressed very prettily; she gave herself great airs on being brought to the "stand." Her name was "Blanche," and merely was described as a good house keeper. "Not a picayune offered—O Gentlemen, Gentlemen, I am ashamed of you!" said the auctioneer good humoredly. An old planter from Opelousas bought her for 200 dollars. She appeared to know her fate, that of retiring from, to her, the gay world of New Orleans to a plantation in the wilderness, but she has one consolation— she will evade the vices of the Capital of the South. Among Southern people, it is not [that] they hold the Negro or slave in any great abhorrence, but they never speak of them. Indeed, it is considered a breach of good manners here to discuss the point of "slavery," but I must add with very few exceptions I have always seen the Negroes treated with kindness in New Orleans and more particularly in Texas—indeed, several Negroes have been given their liberty on account of their devotedness to their masters. Others have become free by purchase. The last applies only to New Orleans.[22]

To me, New Orleans was an interesting point, the more particularly as having been and was even then the hot bed for all operations regarding Texas. There, resources of all sorts for every part of the Union were centralized, and at every emergency there were always found parties in N. O. to assist in widening the breach in every possible way between the New Republic and Mexico.

There was a charm to me even as an old traveller in the rich expanse of the Gulf of Mexico, its lazy calms, gentle airs, fresh southern breeze, furious hurricanes accompanied with terrific lightning and wondrous peals of thunder—the freezing northers. Then it was the cruizing ground of privateers, of pirates of old

---

[22] The following clipping from a New Orleans' newspaper was inserted at this point:

Unlimited sale of valuable Negroes will be sold at auction on Tuesday, 16th inst. at 12 o'clock, all of whom are from one owner and can be well recommended, and sold for no fault, viz:

JIM, a likely Boy aged 12 years, house boy.
HARRIET, likely Negress, 15 years, child's nurse and house girl.
ELLEN,   "   "   , 13   "   "   "   "   "   "   .
AMERICA, "   "   , 15   "   , field hand, etc.
TABITHA,   "   "   , 16   "   , good house girl, washer, ironer,
                                          and sews well.
ETTY,   "   "   , 15   "   , nurse and house girl.
ANN, aged 20 years, field hand, and a house woman and her child
          aged 1 year.
JONAS, aged 22, field hand.
DANIEL, aged 25 years, field hand, and a good rope maker and spinner.
RYLAND, aged 26, field hand, and good waggoner and drayman.
CYRUS, aged 23 years, mulatto, good cook, waiter, coachman, and
                    first rate barber.

The above Negroes are very likely, and fully guaranteed against the vices and maladies prescribed by law.—Terms—cash.

sheltered in the lagoons and creeks of the coast, as Barataria, Sabine, Galveston, etc., etc., attracted by the richly laden galleons, etc. Then the strange, almost unearthly entrances to the thick and turbid Mississippi, its low mud shores, with vast quantities of drift wood, from the impenetrable forests inland unknown, and then the alligators sleeping in the water and looking like pieces of drift wood.

Ascending this mighty stream, this mother of waters, the land becomes a little higher. Steamers sailing vessels of all sizes began to ————. The recollection of the defeat of the British arms. Then approaching near to the Crescent City—its vast extent and forests of masts and still nearer the bustle and business carrying on on the levees or embankments which have been thrown up for its protection from the inroads of the river. Then its interesting and changing history was presented, but above all to me—without the existence of this great, rich, and powerful city—Texas as the abode of our race would not have been in existence. In fact, New Orleans was the Naval and military arsenal and treasury, wholesale and retail resources, and its citizens its arduous abettors and advisors, and at the same time formerly upheld in all these operations by the sanction of the White House of Washington on the Potomac.

It may be asked what was New Orleans to reap from Texas: In the first place, the belligerent excitement was in accordance with the feeling of the southern population. 2nd, by an extension of country south of them to be inhabited by their own race, for years to come N. O. would be its emporium and would thus reap considerable advantages from the produce etc. of Texas. 3rd, for a long period the principal land speculations of Texas would be carried on there; and lastly, (omitting other minor advantages) the occupation of Texas by the white race would open the door to the rich natural production of Mexico and doubtless there were some aspiring minds who did not consider it as very problematical to see the whole of the Great Empire of the Montezumas divided into a number of states and forming part of the Union. Onward, was and is their cry, and it is very difficult to say when or how it

is to be arrested—or if such is not the natural course of events—
which cannot be stopped by human means. These thoughts and
impressions were then but loosely hovering in my mind—but let
us for a moment anticipate and look at the present very awkward
position of Mexico as regards the United States.

[Additional Comments and] Impressions of New Orleans
It is said of the Americans that they are born in a hurry, live in a
worry, and go to New Orleans to die of yellow fever, and the
history of many of the inhabitants of New Orleans is the following:

Brought up in the North, they receive a fair and useful education. At an early age he goes into a counting house. In two or
three years he considers that he knows sufficient to become master
on his own hook, goes with a small assortment into the Western
States, perhaps among the Indians. Here he gets tired of being
his own master and a wandering life, when after various failures
finds his way to New Orleans as clerk of a steamboat—often soon
becoming its proprietor—then a merchant when cotton is high.
Cotton goes down, when he is ruined on account of injudicious
speculations. He does not despond, but takes a cool review of his
case—takes to clerking on the steamboat—all goes right again,
becomes ambitious, abandons trade for the study of law, goes
ahead—runs for Congress, serves his time—his funds are low and
his energies somewhat abated, talks more than he acts—marries
a rich widow whose "moral character" consists principally in having a plantation and lots of Negros, becomes a respectable member of society and "valuable citizen."

At the period which I visited it, times were dull, because cotton
was low. The end of autumn, winter and spring are the periods of
mercantile bustle. As the summer comes on the great bulk of
merchants and traders retire to the North and the more healthy
states of the Union, the foreign shipping leans principally with
cotton—then the Creoles of New Orleans, or native inhabitants,
and those who are acclimated, lead a life of luxury and comparative indolence. But strangers, should their views on life detain
them there, seldom escape the fever or "Yellow Jack," which

comes during and after the hot weather. It is generally beautiful weather and the nights magnificent—then it is at times that death stalks about seeking whom it may devour. The management of this terrible fever is pretty well understood, but the chief physicians and surgeons are foreigners, and there is no scarcity of the "Sons of Galen," for, at nearly every other door "Doctor ———" is written up.

In New Orleans and its vicinity vegetation is most prolific in the flower gardens. Exotics such as we have under glass in England are to be seen in great variety in the open air, particularly the Nerium Oleander forming groves. Of vegetables there is a great abundance and variety and [in] the markets of the city one of the sights. Poultry, game, and fish in abundance, but the beef and mutton may not be equal to that of more northern latitudes. That luxury of ice is well known and ship loads come from the North—selling as low as ½ to 1^d. per pound.

During the day, even the hotter parts of it, there is but little cessation from business, except in the height of hot weather, and towards evening the promenades, particularly of the levees, and excursions in carriages and horse-back take place, when one has an opportunity of seeing the beauty and fashion of the city of the mixed population of America, French, Spanish, and a pretty good sprinkling from every part of the world, particularly from Germany and Ireland. There follows every grade and color of the Negro race and a few Indians occasionally seen wandering about and begging. Those I saw were some of the conquered of the Seminole Nation.

Duelling, which was proverbally a pastime in New Orleans, is not so frequent as formerly, but now and then one hears that the "Colonel has shot the Judge," etc. There is a large quantity of drinking going on at the "Bars," but *drunkness* is principally confined to foreign sailors, as liquor is cheap and labour well paid.

On Sundays in particular may be seen congregated about the Post Office a short time ere the letters are delivered, crowds of merchants, their clerks, shopkeepers, etc., and there it is that the purchase of new books from the North commences, for here may be had the American editions of new works of Europe. I purchased *Zanoni*[23] for about 1/6.

Horse racing is a favorite amusement, but principally trotting matches. Rifle shooting is much practiced—and they have several watering places, the principal one Pontchortrain. Smoking and chewing *ad lib*, much singing and dancing and theatres.[24]

The houses are large and generally well furnished, but the mosquito bar is required for the bed rooms and a literary man I met with here had a frame work of mosquito netting under which he sat to write, so as to avoid the stings of this insect.[25]

Tuesday, June [*14th*] *1842:* About the middle of June I left New Orleans on the "New York Steamer." It is about 100 miles to the S. W. Pass of the Mississippi and from 30 to 36 hours in an average run across the Gulf to Galveston. It is invigorating indeed to get to sea after being pent up in New Orleans for any length of time and a delightful change is the residence on the Island of Galveston.

The British Brig of War the "Victor" (Capt. Otway) was anchored outside the Bar. C—— paid us a visit to know the particulars of blockades, and if the West Indian Steamers would be molested by the Texas Cruizers. General Houston, who was then in Galveston, replied in the negative. The French Corvette "Brilliante" has been here also.[26]

[23] A romance by Bulwer-Lytton, published in 1842.
[24] Each house has its peculiar amusements. The Italian opera, English, French and German plays—and the remnants of the Spanish population amuse themselves with their guitars, castanets, their dances and characteristic melodies. There is no lack of concerts and balls—public and private.—Bollaert.
[25] These comments appear in Bollaert's notes and were not included in the regular journal. "Bollaert Papers," File No. 86.
[26] Bollaert writes elsewhere in his notes that he arrived back at Galveston at 5 P.M., Wednesday, June 15, 1842.

VI

VISIT TO HOUSTON AND VICINITY

[June–July, 1842]

Friday, June 16th, 1842: A grant of land in the vicinity of Kennedy's[1] and Castro's[2] Grants has been made by the Texas Government to Messrs. Ducros[3] and Burgeois[4] upon same terms as to K. and C., for the introduction of 1,700 emigrants, of 3 million acres, a little more than 223 leagues (4,473 [4,428.4 in Texas] acres per league). Met Messrs. Ducros and Burgeois at N. Orleans on their way to France to prepare for the emigrants. (Saligny[5]

[1] William Kennedy and William Pringle obtained a contract from the Texas Republic in February, 1842, to settle 600 families south of the Nueces River. The boundary of the colony (which was never settled) is described in Appendix I.

[2] In 1842, Henri Castro, a descendant of Portuguese nobility, entered into a contract to settle a colony in Southwest Texas on the Medina River. The colony was established in September, 1844, including the present towns of Castorville, D'Hanis, Quihi, and Vandenberg, and might be considered one of the more successful ventures of its kind. Texas Colonization Papers (MS., Texas State Library).

[3] A grant of land has been made to W. L. M. Ducos and Burgeois of 3 millions of acres towards the West and in the Indian territory for the introduction of 12,000 [1,200] families of French emigrants—with reserved lands—moreover some lands bordering the Rio Grande and on the Coast.—Bollaert.

Bollaert's figures are inconsistent. Actually there were two grants made to Armand Ducos and his associate, one permitting the settlement of 1,200 families and the other 700 families, the former in the region of Uvalde, Frio, and upper Medina rivers, and the latter on the Río Grande. No evidence exists that the grantees ever located any settlers on either grant. Rudolph L. Biesele, *The History of the German Settlements in Texas, 1831–1861,* 71–76.

[4] Alexander Bourgeois d'Orvanne.

[5] Alphonse de Saligny was appointed the French chargé d'affaires to Texas in 1839 and built the so-called French Embassy in Austin, which is still standing. He got into many difficulties in Texas and returned to France a short time afterwards, thus temporarily suspending diplomatic relations. He returned to Texas for a brief period in 1842 and again in 1844, the latter trip for the purpose of preventing annexation of Texas to the United States. Joseph William Schmitz, *Texan Statecraft, 1836–1845,* 79–80, 228–30.

This gentleman had interested himself much in the rising fortunes of the Republic, but the affairs connected with the failure of the Franco-Texas [Franco-Texienne] Bill and moreover some colonization views of Felix Houston which seemed to jar with those of the said Bill—led to disagreeable reflections and M. Saligny found it necessary to return for awhile to New Orleans. The President La Mar being sick, the Vice President Burnett acted and suggested thro' the

may have something to do with it). I hear that a Mr. Gifford was here, supercargo of brig "Amanda," gone to Matagorda. Mr. Power tells me he is about some emigrating business and in concert with Mr. Castro—emigrants of Swiss principally. British Barque "Funchal" arrived with a few settlers. One of them from Brighton—acquainted with Old Boy.

The British Brig of War came off this port yesterday—The *Victor*, Captain Otway to see us and to know particulars of blockade—to know if our West India Steamers would be molested. General H[ouston] rec'd the officer sent on shore very kindly. General Houston said they would not, but a ruffian-like volunteer from the states insulted him. A French Corvette the *Brilliante* has been here. General H——, Anson Jones,[6] etc., etc. went to Houston to prepare for Congress.

Saturday, June 17th, 1842: Rain. Wind, northward—diminution of temp:—at 9 A.M. from 82° to 78°. General Hamilton[7]

Texan minister in Paris the removal of M. Saligny. This the French Government did not acquiese in, requested M. S—— to remain in Texas and sent him the grade of officer in the Legion of Honour.—Bollaert.

6 Anson Jones served as Houston's secretary of state during the latter's second term as president of the Republic. Jones helped manage Texas through many diplomatic crises; in December, 1844, he became the fourth and last president of Texas. Herbert Gambrell, *Anson Jones, the Last President of Texas.*

7 Through the unremitting exertions of General [James] Hamilton, Texas was recognized by England in November, 1840 and previously to this period the General had the honor of negotiating the treaties of recognition with France, Belgium, and Holland. It was hoped by these recognitions that General H—— would have been able to negotiated a loan for Texas, but the general financial crisis and some other causes prevented this, thus General H—— left Europe and passing through the United States, presented himself at Austin. The Congress was about adjourning as new President [Houston] and his administration now held power and altho' General H—— had rendered important diplomatic service to his newly adopted country—his not being successful in financial matters caused his reception in Austin to be anything but flattering. General H—— left Texas for Carolina to join his family, from whom he had been separated some time, with the idea of returning shortly to Texas where he should have arranged his private affairs in the states. It is said that some misunderstanding took place at Austin between General H—— and W. K[ennedy], that the General has sent him a challenge to England and has followed it.—Bollaert.

Success was almost in Hamilton's reach in obtaining the five-million-dollar loan he was seeking when Houston became president in 1841. Houston dismissed him and repudiated his work and put the Texas government on a program of economy.

gone to England. Adjutant Cruger[8] coming here with at least 100 men. According to Saligny's interpretation Mr. [Richard] Bullock wished to take a most extraordinary advantage over him in his Hotel bill. Mr. S—— was there only 5 days and Bullock insisted upon a month's pay— and other exhorbitant charges and even threatened to do him personal harm.

Tuesday, June 20th, 1842: Wrote to R[oyal] Geographical Society. S.K. and Wm. K. sent papers to Texan Legation. The *Frolic* Privateer came in from the Balize. She chased a Mexican trader, but ere the enemy could be got at she had slipped into the neutral waters off the Mississippi.

One of the Mobile Volunteers shot a brother volunteer yesterday. The sooner some of these are sent off the better to fight the Mexicans. Mr. S—— has been advanced a grade in the Legion of Honor puede ser que volvera a F. lluegase dejando aqui un encargado. . . . The Captain and Super-cargo of the prize *Marie Elizabeth* went by *New York* to New Orleans yesterday. They have abandoned the prize, but as yet an "interlocutory" decree has been given by Judge [Richard] Morris—and final decree postponed till August. There can be no doubt but that the cargo is Mexican property and that the vessel is likewise so. If she be decreed a "grand prize" she stands a chance to be eaten up with law expenses. (See Ducros and Bourgeois grant 3 Million of Acres—to introduce 1,200 families—with more lands on reserve if wanted toward Rio Grande—they have another grant on Rio Grande from Reinosa 10 miles up the R. then across to 10 miles above Pt. Isabel—then the coast and river up to Reinosa.)

Mons. S—— tells me that he discovered that Mr. Castro was but a Jew Adventurer and that he had been one of the managers of a bank in New York which was burned down suspiciously and

---

The latter (Hamilton) was never compensated for his expenses in behalf of the Texas government. *The Writings of Sam Houston,* II, 32, 428, 471, 486–87.

[8] Major Nicholas Cruger was ordered to proceed to South Carolina by President Houston, April 30, 1842, "to raise funds and men to an unlimited extent for the army of Texas." *The Writings of Sam Houston,* III, 42–43.

the iron chest in which the money ought to have been found deposited was found open and no accts. rendered and that from that period Mr. C—— had been in fine feather in Paris. This coupled with other circumstances led him to advise his government to refuse him his exequatur. His appointment from this government will be annulled likewise. Mr. S—— informs me that a Desafis was sent sometime since from a Gentleman here to Mr. K[ennedy] to meet General H[amilton] and now that General H—— has gone home the *difficulty* I suppose will be settled.[9]

P——[10] will not come out again, but may make over his grant to another party in Belgium. Another row amongst the Volunteers —a man shot. Count du Serin[11] not fortunate; his people sick— this may disgust him and he may slope[12] homeward.

Friday, 24th, 1842: Attended by invitation the Masonic celebration of the anniversary of St. John the Baptist, not being a Brother of their excellent fraternity.[13] They met at the Presbyterian Church. The prayer was said by the Rev. Mr. Hucking,[14] then followed that beautiful piece of music "Before Johovah's Awful Throne." The installation of officers, charge to officers and members of the Lodge, an interesting oration by Brother Walton, then the anthem "Avisson"—concluding with the prayer and benediction. We partook of an excellent dinner. On the cloth

[9] Bollaert uses the word "difficulty" frequently. He explains in one part of his notes that this word generally refers to a fight or duel with guns, pistols, or knives.

[10] Belgium sent an agent in the person of Captain Pierson to communicate with the government. This gentleman, after visiting Austin, made a journey through part of the western country and suggested that a colony of Belgians might be established on the Río Grande, in which the Texas government acquiesed. Captain P—— returned to Europe to give an account of his mission.—Bollaert.
   No evidence can be found that the Belgian colony was ever established in Texas.

[11] Count du Serin was the French nobleman who accompanied Bollaert on his trip to Texas and whom Bollaert visited on his plantation in Montgomery County a few days after writing the above reference to him.

[12] The word "slope" was a colloquialism that Bollaert picked up in Texas. It was a common slang expression of the nineteenth century, especially on the frontier. It meant "to run away," "elope," "disappear suddenly," or "decamp."

[13] There are already 20 [Masonic] Lodges in Texas.—Bollaert.

[14] This probably was the Reverend James Huckins, pastor of the Baptist church in Galveston in 1842. *The Handbook of Texas*, I, 857.

being removed, the band was put in requisition and among the songs the air of "God save the Queen," called into requisition as an accompaniment to a Texas national song. Brother Sam Williams in the chair.[15]

Saturday, June 25th, 1842: The Extraordinary session of Congress meets at Houston in a day or so. The "War Party" are for invasion of Mexico by sea and land, with what forces there may be in the country—that is, our own citizens and the U. States volunteers.[16] But the Treasury is empty and the government had no credit. Some of the "War Party," to use their own language, wish to "go the whole animal horns and all," and add, "Let us prepare for an invasion of Mexico in the fall—we will have 20,000 men in the field. Our brethren in the states are burning with desire to assist us and fix our boundary along the mountains." (Sierra Madre).[17]

The Texans talk of their "Main Army" as if they had 20,000 men under arms, when really there are but a few companies of volunteers, but in case of necessity all would turn out. General Houston has been so worried by the "War Party" that it is whispered about that his intimate friends have had much difficulty in persuading him to retain the Presidency.[18] Others say that he wishes

[15] Samuel May Williams operated a mercantile business in Galveston at this time with Thomas F. McKinney, and for many years he was prominent in banking and farming and other business enterprises in the Galveston area. "S. M. Williams Papers" (MS., Rosenberg Library, Galveston).

[16] Yesterday a battalion of U. S. Volunteers left for Corpus Christi—rather disorganized. They are a queer set of fellows. There is some squabbling at C. Christi amongst the Volunteers—too many wish to command. It is not judicious to have volunteers inactive—bring them into action—if not they add to the plagues in a country, viz: lawyers, doctors, parsons, politicians, and mosquitos.—Bollaert.

[17] But grub for these [will cost] from one to five millions of dollars. (Where is this to come from?) And then these invaders intend to "bring under this government" the whole territory of the mountains, etc., etc., etc. But let us see what General Houston's idea is and this we shall do in a few days. He has been vexed by many and keeps his own council. He, I believe, knows what he is about—the distressed state of the country, her inability to resist just now upon her enemy—moreover, Texas is and will become interesting to E[ngland], F[rance], and U.S., and these powers must protect her.—Bollaert.

[18] The following story is told relative to General Houston: During the period

Sketch of doctor's office from Bollaert's journal

"Professional men make heavy charges, and were their bills punctually paid they would soon be rich."

Bollaert's drawing

*"Visited the 'President's house.' It is falling to pieces,
and now the residence of bats."*

Reproduced from *Texas in 1840, or the Emigrant's Guide to the
New Republic,* 1840

*"On entering the city of Austin, Lo! Dreariness and desolation
presented themselves; few houses appeared inhabited
and many falling to decay."*

to annex Texas to the U. States, etc. etc. (Twaddle)

General Houston may resign, annexation to the States may take place—but Mexico will *never* count Texas amongst its provinces again. True Texas is at the present time without trade, without money, and little credit, but our population will increase—cotton will grow—corn will rise up—and with a little judiciousness on our part—and industry—Texas ought soon to be as bright a Star and one of no inconsiderable magnitude.

Read Marshall's *Life of Washington,* Cooper's *History of the Navy of the United States,* read [Samuel Lorenzo Knapp's] first volume of *Life of Aaron Burr.* He [Burr] was a man of strange passions—extraordinary, and might have been one of the greatest ornaments of society—but for the gratification of mere *libidinous* passion—love it cannot be called. Yet, when he married Mrs. Theodosia Prevost—from their correspondence he appears all constancy and propriety. The first volume finishes with the excitement for his or Jefferson's election for President and it does appear that Burr was too proud to truckle to party and promise places—which ended with Jefferson being appointed President. Had Burr become President, he would never have meddled with his scheme of revolutionizing Mexico or in anywise have annoyed the States—"Tis circumstances too often make or mar men—and desolate countries."

Tuesday, June 28th, 1842: Congress met at Houston. Not enough in the morning to form a quorum. A few Indians near

of his late re-election for President some of his most violent opponents declared that it would be well if the General could be "got out of the way." A stout fellow in a hunting dress leaning upon a long rifle begged to know what it was required to do with the General. When he was informed "it was to shoot him," the hunter said that he would shoot him or any other man if he were paid for it. His price was demanded—It was $1,500. The dollars were not forthcoming. The hunter sloped, and General Houston opened the Extraordinary Congress.—Bollaert.

Les documents relative to the Extraordinary Congress, the Presidents veto of the War Bill introduced by the opposition. Communication of Hon. J. Reilly Minister from Texas to U. States to that Gov^t. on the subjects of entrepot, repeal of duty on cotton, and drawback on goods foreign to the United States—This ultimately ended in the U. S. not coming to terms with Texas relative to a commercial treaty.—Bollaert.

Barton's Springs, west side of Colorado, killed a white man and a horse. [Mariano] Aristas' intention to have his H. Quarters at Mier of 3,000 men. Matamoras has 1,000 men—Camp of Volunteers moved shortly to the Nueces. Mexican marauders beyond St. Antonio killed Col. ———.

Thursday, June 30th, 1842: New York Steamer came in—no letters from home. Financial crisis increasing in New Orleans. . . . Commodore Moore arrived from N.O.—reports that the Squadron is in good order. General Houston arrived from Houston. All appears judicious and peaceable. Expenses of the French diplomatic establishment 2,930,000 francs, that of M. Saligny in Texas, 35,000 fr. that of Legation 6 to 10,000 frs. the French Ambassador in London 300,000 frs. Mr. Hall[19] complains much of W[illiam] K[ennedy] marking and cutting out articles in his collection of the *Telegraph* he took to England. From the s^d. *Telegraph*, published first in 1835, K—— got nearly all of his official documents. This is the most important file of papers in the Republic for the early history of Texas.

Friday, July 1st, 1842: Little rain during the night. 9 A. M. commencement of a norther, cloudy, black 78° clouds in the N. W. with occasional lightning and thunder—continued till 11 A.M. No rain. 3 P.M. 84° Calm, fine during afternoon squalls from N. W. 77° with lightning and thunder.

Saw General Houston. He returned to Houston. Has received his communication, will write to him, discuss his kind and affectionate regards and sends his letter to Govr. Smith to him. Some sharp discussions are expected in Congress, but all that can be done (without means) is normally to organize. Arista has resigned his command on 28 ulto. Commodore Moore went to Houston. He tells me that the fleet will be ready before it is positively wanted —and he will have sufficient force to compel a blocking of the Coast of Mexico.

[19] This was probably Warren D. Hall, who practiced law in Galveston in 1842 and who was prominent in the affairs of the Republic in the 1830's. Thrall, *Pictorial History of Texas*, 205.

The President's message appears judicious, temperate, and conciliatory and with the spare means he has at his command—must be looked upon as a masterly document.[20] Yucatan appears to want to maintain its sovereignty. They have paid $4,000 more they owed our Navy. General Isador Reyes has succeeded him "a weak man" and totally inadequate for the station. The Army of the North including 1,800 men in Matamoros—of 5,000 rank and file scattered over the villages of Rio Grande— of these 2,000 are new recruits.

Saturday, July 2nd, 1842: Man came from M. Seguin—says there are silver mines upon the 11 leagues of Garcia's[21] land— that he got silver out by smelting—to bring specimens shortly.

Sunday, July 3rd, 1842: Passed the morning with Judge Dor.[22] He was partner with General Houston as Lawyers—read correspondence between them—sound reasoner—elegant writer— jocose at times and in all his writings appears most affectionate. Judge Dor was a resident in Texas under the Mexican regime and his wife made the first Texas flag that was unfurled in the cause of Texas Freedom. Judge Dor has a tracing of the Sabine River some 500 miles up, but it is only a rough "reconnaissance." Pillan will get a lithography from Opelousas of a correct one.

[20] The full text of Houston's opening address to the Texas Congress (June 27, 1842) is printed in *The Writings of Sam Houston*, III, 74–83.

[21] Luciano García was a Mexican official in the Texas province during the 1820's. He acquired large holdings of land in the vicinity of San Antonio, and after retiring from the services of the Mexican government in 1826, he devoted the remainder of his life to stock raising. Bejar Archives (MS., Archives Collection, University of Texas Library.)

[22] John M. Dor was Houston's law partner at Nacogdoches before the outbreak of the Texas Revolution. He later served in several minor positions, as commissioner to treat with the Indians and primary judge of Nacogdoches, and conducted legal business in Galveston from time to time. His wife, whom Bollaert says made the first Texas flag, was the former Eliza Frisby of Nacogdoches. This might have been the flag that Haden Edwards raised in December, 1826, when he declared the Fredonian Rebellion, for it appears unlikely that Miss Frisby designed the first official flag of the Republic (December 10, 1836). *The Writings of Sam Houston*, II, 35–39; *The Handbook of Texas*, I, 514.

Monday, July 4th, 1842: Anniversary of American independence. The American Minister, Judge Eves,[23] invited his friends to a *dejeuner a la fourchette.* Considerable quantities of tipple swallowed today. Galveston Coast Guard kept it up. A Mr. Smith has been in Texas about a matter—sent out by the Earl of Derby to collect objects of natural history.

Tuesday, July 5th, 1842: Wrote to Wm. K[ennedy] by Power. M. Saligny left for New Orleans—may go home probably—*New York* sailed.

Wednesday, July 6th, 1842: 5 P.M. Left for Houston—8 A.M. crossed Fish Bar.

Thursday, July 7th, 1842: Got into Buffalo Bayou—like to a canal; the bottom wooded principally with Pine—owing to sandy soil—fine magnolias in flower. This is not the land for plantations —too poor. We gazed with some interest at the battle field of San Jacinto.[24] Passed Harrisburg, "a deserted village." Arrived at Houston; paid my visit to the President who[m] I found in a very small apartment surrounded by persons on business his private Secretary busily employed writing. Amongst other conversations he c——d the Volunteers, who, to get them out of the way he had allowed to go down the coast—and was fearful that they would bring on a fight on the frontier and then if they were all killed, why then he would be blamed for it.

In the afternoon I went to see Count de [Serin] with whom I

[23] Died at Galveston, June, 1843.—Bollaert.

Joseph Eve was appointed United States chargé d'affaires to the Republic of Texas on April 15, 1841. He was an admirer of Sam Houston and an ardent annexationist, but Secretary of State Webster recalled him in April, 1843. Eve remained in Galveston, where he died of tuberculosis on June 16, 1843. "A Letter Book of Joseph Eve, United States Chargé d'Affaires to Texas," *Southwestern Historical Quarterly,* Vol. XLIII (1939–40), 365–77.

[24] The Battle of San Jacinto was probably lost to the Mexicans, owing to the influence of a Mulatto Girl (Emily) belonging to Colonel Morgan, who was closeted in the tent with General Santana, at the time the cry was made "the enemy! they come! they come!" and detained Santana so long, that order could not be restored readily again.—Bollaert.

had come fellow passenger from England. He had located himself and family on the upper part of Buffalo Bayou, an excellent place for a Southerner and his Negros, but not for European emigrants. Instead of erecting log-huts at once, there they were under tents thro' which the sun rays were darting fiercely. All were attacked with chills and fever and the mother with a congestive, the European servants pale and wan, miserable and dejected. The result was that ere I left they told me that they were disappointed in the country and should return to France. This was the very best thing *they* could do. Had they known anything of farming operations etc. and were told, they should have gone off to the West, or up into Montgomery County where there were many European families comfortably settled, and this I subsequently found was the case.

I fear that this instance of failure is that my worthy friend did not know how to choose his ground, and not suited to the difficulties that arise, at least the first year that one is establishing himself. The picture that presented itself was distressing, people brought up in the luxuries of Paris and full of intelligence were now seen utterly helpless. Such like people have come to this country from all parts of the globe; they fail—they get disgusted—return to their native homes and curse Texas. Now that is [not] the case of the American settler, the English, Scotch, and German farmer. They know what to be after; the first year they work hard and suffer some privations, but then comes their season of enjoyment and ease. Their land costs them but little, and there is not much difficulty in getting a piece of land given to an industrious person. It is their own and their childrens, no proud lord to look up to, no tythes or taxes, no game laws, and to use an American expression, "One feels freed and one is free" and enjoying life and one's family, certain that want can never approach their door.

For a "poor gentleman" this is a bad country; the sooner he learns to work the better—nay, beg for something to do, if only as Paddy says "to be a Bricklayers Valet," thus he will learn habits of industry, and every labourer is well paid for his services, let them be what they may. Professional men make heavy charges, and were their bills punctually paid they would soon be rich.

Friday, July 8th, 1842: Visited the House of Representatives during a debate upon the War Question. Business was carried on judiciously and gentlemanly, considering the "excitement" of the question before them. The Government party appears to be in the majority, and the "War Party" in the minority. It is warmer here than in Galveston. There is not so much sea breeze, and thus agues are occasionally felt.

Houston is a large place, and carries on a good trade.[25] It is a central position for the Planters in this vicinity to bring their cotton to and farmers their produce, but the farming about here is not of great extent, plantations of cotton principally seem worked by Negro labour. A friend has given me the following as his opinion relative to the choice of land by emigrants: Say a straight line drawn from Belgrade[26] on the Sabine towards Swartwout[27] on the Trinity River through Montgomery County to Columbus on the Colorado River and its "bottoms"—outside this line or towards the coast cannot be recommended to European emigrants of the agricultural class. First, the produce is of a tropical character, such as cotton, tobacco, etc., suited rather to Negro labour. Second intermittent ague and bilious fevers are common on these low alluvial lands. It may be remarked that the ague, etc. are met with or contracted but in the woods or "bottoms"—the open prairies seem to be healthy, but there it is rather too hot for European labour. Inside of the line referred to, viz: the Cherokee lands, Red River, those above Austin, down to San Antonio and the West, are excellent for grazing cattle and sheep and wheat growing.

25 This is a large place and just now containing 2,000 inhabitants.—Bollaert.

26 Belgrade today is a ghost town, but it formerly was located in Newton County where the Coushatta Trace crossed the Sabine River. It was an important river port during the period of the Republic, but was by-passed by the railroads.

27 Swartwout was located on the Trinity River in southwestern Polk County at the site of the Alabama-Coushatta Indian village. It too was an important port town during the period of the Republic, but the discontinuance of boat traffic on the river some years later caused the settlement gradually to die out.

Visit to Houston and Vicinity

Saturday, July 9th, 1842: Left Houston and taking a S. W. direction towards the sun burnt prairie to Major B[ingham].[28] The next morning arrived at Colonel Austin's[29] on the Brazos Road at Oyster Creek. Cotton and corn look pretty well, although suffering from drought. The creeks on the prairies between the "timbers" are without water, thus the cattle suffer, if great care be not taken. At Colonel A——'s the wells are 18 feet deep, in a sand soil and good water. Game is plentiful generally but at this season game and birds are scarce. It is hot for travelling during the middle of the day, and a covered buggy is preferable to horseback. All through Texas the traveller can be accom[m]odated at the Farm Houses and "entertainment" for man and beast for a dollar a night—that is supper on arrival in the evening—bed—and breakfast the following morning.

The more opulent farmers and planters extend their hospitality with an unsparing hand, more particularly to the poor emigrant.

Sunday, July 10th, 1842: Returned to Houston. There are news from Corpus Christi that a large party of Mexicans are southward of that place at the San Gertrudes river [Santa Gertrudis Creek], thus many of the volunteers may be indulged in drawing their maiden swords upon the enemy. I was shown some fine specimens of gold ore from some 60 miles above Austin.[30] Silver ore is said to be found about the same spot. A few persons in Houston have associated themselves together, leaving in August to commence mining operations.

[28] Elsewhere in his notes Bollaert identifies "Major B——" as Major Bingham. This undoubtedly was Francis Bingham, one of Stephen F. Austin's Old Three Hundred, who owned a large plantation on Oyster Creek in Brazoria and Fort Bend counties. Bugbee, "The Old Three Hundred," *Quarterly of the Texas State Historical Association*, Vol. I (1897-98), 108-17.

[29] William Tennant Austin was a cousin of Stephen F. Austin. He participated in the Texas Revolution, serving as a military aide to Stephen F. Austin, Edward Burleson, and later Sam Houston. Austin owned a plantation in Brazoria County; in 1848 he was a merchant at Washington and later entered the cotton business in Galveston. *The Writings of Sam Houston*, I, 373.

[30] Gold and silver mining has never been extensive in Texas, although there were some mining activities during the period about which Bollaert writes. The region which he refers to probably was the Llano district, which has produced a small quantity of gold and sliver for more than a century.

Monday, July 11th, 1842: Attended Congress—discussion relative to the President having uncontrolled power—which he will get. 5 P.M.: Started for the Trinity. 1½ miles from Houston are the "Union Springs," said to have mineral properties. May this not become a Saratoga, Bath, or Cheltenham some day or other? We had left Houston rather late in the day and got benighted. We saw a light in the distance apparently in our track. We approached it, and crack went a rifle ball. We sang out lustily that although we were *dear*, we were not quite the sort of game to be taken in that way.

I need hardly say that the light we took for a house was a pan of pine sticks, burning by some deer hunters. In a word they had "shined" our horses' eyes, taking them to be those of deer.[31] They apologized to us and we pursued our way. The night was very dark, and we supposed from the distance we had travelled that we had rather overshot the spot we had intended to remain at for the night and neither of us had ever been this road before. As yet there are no sign posts. We held a "council of war" and finding that we had no provision or water, came to the conclusion to "camp out." My friend rode in a "sulky" and I was on horseback. We tethered our beasts, then got under the lee of the "sulky," were amused with an occasional howl from the wolves, but at last went to sleep.

Tuesday, July 12th, 1842: At day break in the morning we found that we were about three miles from the settlement we had intended to have slept at. Two travellers who turned out to be Canadians came up with us. We gave them a dram, but called "bitters" when taken in the morning. Canadian politics were discussed, but my ideas as a "Britisher" of that hubbub not suiting our companions, they dropped behind.

Now then for a domestic scene. The companion with whom I was travelling became very sedate and thoughtful, saying, "Friend,

[31] The general plan of fire hunting in Texas is to use the plain fire pan and the handle; but it is said that a lighted torch or candles may be stuck on the hat of the hunter with a small polished reflector behind the light. If this be correct, a lamp with a reflector might be used with advantage.—Bollaert.

I must confess that my wish for you to accompany me is selfish, but believe me most necessary for my future happiness and that of a young lady I am much attached to. To be brief, I have known her for some time, she is now staying on a visit with a family at Galveston. She has accepted me, but I think there will be a 'difficulty' in getting her father's consent. He is a Spaniard, he speaks hardly a word of our language, neither do I understand his, nor have I ever seen him. Now, I put the whole of this delicate business into your hands, carry it through for me, and I shall ever be indebted to you for your kindness. I will present by letter of introduction to the old Don—you must do the rest."

Accordingly, we rode up to the plantation. The letter was presented. I saluted him with *Buenas dias Caballero*. The old gentleman gave us a welcome, read and re-read the letter, for in it were detailed some particulars relative to my friend's wishes. "Pues," said he. "Es preciso que hablo con mi muger." (I must speak to my wife). He left us for an inner room; my friend sat on the edge of a box twiddling his "finger and thumb." I had taken possession of a large arm chair and in a "brown" study how to repel any unfavorable symptom of denial. The lover said, "I've made up my mind—yes—yes." "What will you do?" "I'll run away with her." "Patience, my good fellow, that is a *dernier resort*. Be quiet—here comes your future Papa." "The devil!"

This was the moment for a painter—the father entered, the mother, three sons, another daughter, and a young Spaniard, a visitor who had some intentions of becoming a suitor for the hand of the lady in question, brought up the rear. The old gentleman had no smile on his visage; the mother was in tears; the other members of the family look[ed] dull and heavy. I will try and put the principal part of this novel sort of matrimonial negotiation into English for the benefit of those who are not acquainted with the Spanish language.

"Gentlemen," said the old man, "I am glad to see you. It is now only that I am made acquainted with the cause of my daughter's long visit and delay. I have written to her repeatedly to return home. I love her very much, but she has stolen a march upon me."

"Sir," addressing my friend, "I have no blame to attach to you, but—but—but do you not think your acquaintance with my daughter has been of too short duration? I think so. I know what you will reply. Well, Sir—I will be candid with you. I have no fortune to give her, but should she outlive me, as there appears every likelihood, she shall have her share of my property. Now, Sir, tell me before this assembly. Do you really love my daughter?" (Here the father shed tears!) Silence was eloquent, and after some time the reply was, "Yes Sir." The father approached and embraced him, and shook me by the hand.

Whilst a "first rate" breakfast was preparing, the old Gentleman returned to his room; the rest of the family dispersed. We went into the garden and the disappointed lover saddled his horse and rode off to his home. After breakfast we brought the guitar into requisition, sang songs, sipped "gloria" and after dinner, continued our journey.

This side of Montgomery [we] put up at a wretched farm house. Regaled with bear's flesh and sassafras tea, not particularly invigorating after a long ride.[32]

Wednesday, July 13th, 1842: Off at daylight and crossed the San Jacinto (dry). It is but a small stream just now; got to L—— settlement about dinner time. On a traveller approaching he says, "Good day Sir, or Madam" to the inmates. "Good day" and a slight sharp nod is returned. "Can we stop here?" "I expect you can." After the horses are "fixed" by the Negro, and whilst the meal is getting ready, news and information mutually given: Sam Houston—taxes—Congress—particulars of the "runaway scrape" which appears to have been very disastrous. One woman lost her baby for 6 weeks—found by another who nurtured it—about that time the Mexicans were very sanguinarily killing lone women and children, whilst their husbands, sons and brothers were at the War. Mothers delight to tell how many sons they have and how they fought the Mexicans.

---

[32] The settlers about this part of the country do not patronize gardening—corn and cotton [are] their principal productions. Tobacco grows here well.—Bollaert.

4 P.M.: Started. 14 miles brought us to W—— settlement.

Here after supper we had a dose of snake stories. One was that a Mr. T—— a short time since had been bitten at this settlement by a rattle-snake and died three hours afterwards. Then came adventures with Indians, bears, wolves, panthers, etc. We were solicited to go to bed first, which we did. The moment we had turned in, out was blown the light; the daughters crept into a bed in one corner, the parents in another, and the brothers opposite to us. But they, the ladies, generally manage to escape very early in the morning, bless them. This is a badly arranged establishment.

Thursday, July 14th, 1842: 7 A.M. 10 miles to thick wood and cane break— brought us to a little rivulet put down as "Big Creek." It is a fork of E. branch of San Jacinto. 10 miles more— wood with fine magnolias brought us to Mr. Hubert's, 8 miles from Swartwout. Here for the first time from a height—one has a fine landscape looking east. Big Creek does not come up higher than 20 miles below Swartwout. 2 miles more to Colonel Tomlinsons. 3 P.M.: Started back and by a short cut by Mr. Cockran's, save 3 or 4 miles. Found our way by short cut to road or track by the "blazes" on the trees. In this way roads are conveniently made thro' forests—taking the direction from starting point by compass, "blazing" or marking the trees here and there—then continuing such a track for some time, a trail track and ultimately a road is formed. 4 miles from Mr. Winters is a deserted Indian Camp. 8 P.M.: Got to Mr. Winters'—put up for the night.

Friday, July 15th, 1842: During the night raining torrents. After breakfast it still continued to pour down so that not wishing to have a wet ride we remained, amused with our host's adventures etc. with the Coshatees [Coushatta],[33] Bidais,[34] Kickapoos,[35] Muskoougs [Muskhogean] etc., who inhabit these parts.

[33] Coshattes Indians [are] probably a remnant of the Natchez—they worship the sun and moon. Met a woman of this tribe yesterday on horseback—good looking and matronly—clean—hair in one plat behind—cotton dress, the upper part kept together by a large silver brooch. The principal part of them live in a village below Swartwout, are a quiet orderly tribe and respected by the settlers—grow

But few indigenous fruits have been found in this section of the country, save the wild peach and plum. Of timbers the principal are pine, black, white and post oak, hickory, wild China, mulberry, walnut, magnolia, and cane brakes. Then among the animals there are bears, wolves, panthers, deer, coons, opposums, leopard cats, pole cats, skunks, and then snakes.

The people of the Northern States are not the arrant Emigrant rovers as those of the Western and Southern States of the Union. Some emigrate to get away from a *"difficulty"*; others knowing the more westerly lands are rich and virgin, and many try and persuade themselves that they are going to a "land of milk and honey" when they come to Texas, and this is in a measure true— for stock raising is easy and wild honey in abundance. These new lands of Texas merely require "scraping" and a crop of corn or cotton comes up the first year. In the majority of locations, clearing the land is not necessary, for on the skirts of the "timbers" (where there is always water) the farmer is immediately rewarded; moreover, in the "bottoms" and in the woody country which extends from river to river, there are patches of open land sufficiently large for plantations and farms.

Under the Mexican "Empresario" system and since then up to the present time, with some modifications, grants of lands are given to emigrants come from where they may: thus all that was

---

corn. Their method of preparing deer skins is the following: (Done by women— the men only hunt). Soaked in water for a time, the hair scraped off—rubbed with the brains of deer and water—then dried with smoke of bark of trees. These skins are of a tawny, very soft and used principally for hunting dresses. Some of the Indian tribes make very smart dresses. The Coshattes move about—the reason I presume is that the White Man wishes to have their lands, but their principal villages are "Colete" (that is the lower Coshatte Village)—near Swartout there is another Coshatte Village and above this another called "Battist" [Batista]. They numbered 100 warriors some 10 years since—now about 30 or 40. Some "Muscovy" Indians live with them—these use the bow and arrow—but the Rifle is their principal arm in hunting.—Bollaert.

[34] Bidais live and hunt about Cincinnati and the prairies towards Lake Creek Montgomery—there are but few of these; less than the Coshattes.—Bollaert.

[35] Kickapoos—some are found between Swartout and Cincinnati. They are better than the former mentioned.—Bollaert.

wanted was to arrive in the country; say in the case of a planter with his Negros, and in a brief space, cotton crops appeared. The cotton found its way either to N. Orleans, Galveston, or Matagorda. In the case of a farmer, he brought his family and stock. His fields became laden with corn, his prairies with cattle and the good dame had abundance of poultry, and when they were an industrious and thrifty people a kitchen and even a flower garden was added to their settlement. When the Emigrants were educated people, the simple log house had, independent of every necessary comfort, oftimes objects of luxury. The American Emigrant would arrive in Texas, say by the Red River: he would take up the first unlocated land that suited him, or he might purchase land at a very reasonable rate. His party might be composed of himself, wife, sons, and daughters; the elder children on horseback, the younger with the mother in the "Jersey" waggon containing likewise their baggage, household, farming and carpentering implements, not forgetting the axe; moreover, a few pet pigs, dogs, poultry, garden seeds, etc.

The settlements they passed would be kind and hospitable to them; they would select a spot; their waggon would be their first domicile. The axe would now be called into requisition, the trees would soon be felled, a substantial log house erected, cook-house, stables, graneries, and the "lot" or small enclosure for cattle. The cotton and corn lands enclosed by a Virginia fence of long split rails, and should there be much timber on the plantation, they would just cut a ring round each tree so as to prevent further growth; in a short time the leaves fell off, the tree would soon follow, and thus the land became quickly cleared. All this for the American planter, or farmer, is nothing more than what he is brought up to from a child: and even for others of industrious habits they would find but little difficulty to carry such operations into effect.

Say for some of those of the over-populated countries of Europe, they would find a peaceful home, a plentifull table and in progress of time, if not for the first settlers, their children would have rich plantations and farms; wealth would roll into their coffers, when commercial city should spring up, as we have seen, as if by magic in the United States. Thus, a once unhappy starving, and degraded and dependent family in a few years would look around their own broad domain and find themselves possessed of a hundred-fold more land, stock, and produce, than the Lord or Baron whose humble tenants they had been. This is no imaginary picture, but what has taken place in the United States, and by no very abstruse train of reasoning will be seen in Texas. The little farmers about here cultivate or "raise" cotton enough for their own use, which the females of the family card, and spin for clothing and with deer skins the men make their hunting and working dresses.

Started and got to L[indley's] settlement, and next day to dinner where we had been regaled with the "Baars'" flesh and sassafras tea,[36] and then the same sort of repast was again set before us.

The heavy rains had swelled the creeks, and at Cypress Bayou, there being no ferry, had to amuse ourselves by swimming it. It being a hot day, the dipping was a comfortable bath.

Arrived at Houston in the afternoon. On the road met the courier or post man, or mail rider; he gave us a paper containing an account of the fight at Lipantitlan—which I cut out and present to my readers:[37]

Saturday, July 16th, 1842: Roads bad and rains. Noon, got to Mr. Smith's. Mr. Phipps took to the "sulky" and some 10 or 12 miles on the road it was broken to pieces and Phipps had a narrow escape of serious injury. Left the wreck of the sulky in the road to be brought on to Houston. Got a saddle for "Jerry" and got to Mr. Pilot's for the night.

Sunday, July 17th, 1842: 7 A.M. started. The prairies draining

[36] The Yaupon leaves—to my taste make a better substitute for tea.—Bollaert.

[37] Bollaert included two long, detailed newspaper accounts of the fight at Lipantitlán in San Patricio County on July 7, 1842, in his journal. Since the author of the journal summarizes the action in his narrative a few pages later, the articles need not be reproduced. Lipantitlán was also the site of a skirmish in October, 1835, when a Texas force under Philip Dimitt attacked the Mexican garrison there.

off—roads very wet. Had to swim Cypress Bayou. Roads bad to Houston. Arrived 2 P. M. Heavy rain. Swam the horses over Union Creek. We passed on a log. A few days since some 700 troops and Rancheros attacked some 200 of our Volunteers at Lipantitlan near San Patricio—they came off second best. Our Volunteers arrived, General Davis[38] killing a few and taking some prisoners. The enemy returned and it is supposed to be reinforced. We ought to reinforce likewise. There may be wigs on the green this fall.[39]

Monday, July 18th, 1842: Called on the President. [He] has had a letter from W. K. [William Kennedy], date 5th June. Congress at their vocations—squabbling today about the election of Judge Lipscomb.[40]

Tuesday, July 19th, 1842: Rain over. Weather getting warm. Some more summer rain and heat will cause vegetable decomposition and quinine will be in request. 11 A. M.: Left Houston per Steamer *Vista,* for Galveston small and uncomfortable boat. Saw at Houston some of Jeff Wrights portraits—There is one of Bowls of the Cherokee chief—and an unfinished one of G¹. Houston. G¹. Houston will forward papers to W. K. Came to anchor for a few hours above Red Fish Bar. Here once more I enjoyed the cool and grateful seabreeze. Things are looking very flat: "Poverty is staring us in the face, our imports exceed our exports this year, our difficulties very pressing."

Wednesday, July 20th, 1842: 9 A. M. arrived Galveston. Found letter from Sam K[ennedy][41] enclosing one from W. K[ennedy],

---

38 The Texas volunteer army at Lipantitlán was under the command of James Davis. By the last of June, 1842, Davis's forces had been reduced by desertion to 192.

39 Meaning "a free fight."—Bollaert.

40 Judge Abner Smith Lipscomb was former chief justice of the Alabama Supreme Court. He established a law practice in Texas in 1839 and was later appointed secretary of state by Lamar. He was not appointed to the Texas Supreme Court until 1846. *The Writings of Sam Houston,* III, 40.

41 Bollaert makes frequent reference to Samuel Kennedy, the brother of William Kennedy. For details, see the first paragraph of Bollaert's "Notes on William Kennedy" in Appendix II.

dated June 3 to him. Elliot[42] has left for Texas. Treaties to be exchanged in a few days. L[d] A.[43] acknowledges the Texan blockade of the Mexican ports. From a member of the French legation in Mexico—Mexico has no hope of success in invasion of Texas—that her army was a horde of naked beggars. Santana was threatened with overthrow by military rivals—says nothing on colonial affairs.

It is strange I have no letter from Sadie[44]—none since Feb.[ry]! Sanders is here. Pellegrini[45] has purchased some few thousand acres of land some 8 miles up the Colorado as a sort of depot for his introduction of 2,000 emigrants. *nous verrons!* Baron Philibocourt[46] has joined him as Major Domo.

Sanders intends to make a claim of $6,000 for self and partner Low for property sacked at San Antonio when Arista's proclamation came in. Houston will have as much power as he pleases. The fleet will be got in order—H[ouston] will raise money say on Cherokee lands[47]—and if peace is not made, we shall be at least on our frontier this fall. Poverty stares us all in the face. Our imports of necessity exceed our exports this year—but on the President our hopes we fix, and he appears the only man to extricate us out of our pressing difficulties. . . .

[42] Charles Elliot arrived in Galveston on August 6, 1842, as British chargé d'affaires for Texas. He became a personal and trusted friend of Sam Houston, worked for the abolition of slavery, free trade, and peace between Mexico and Texas. He was instrumental in securing the release of some of the Mier prisoners. He opposed the annexation of Texas to the United States and persuaded Mexico to recognize the independence of Texas if she would refuse annexation.

[43] George Gordon, fourth Earl of Aberdeen, succeeded Lord Palmerston at the Foreign Office, August 20, 1844.

[44] Bollaert doubtless refers to his sister, Jane Sarah Bollaert. He married Susannah McMorran soon after his return to England, November 22, 1845.

[45] Snider de Pellegrini made a contract with the Harrisburg Town Company under which he was to direct French immigrants to Harris County in return for banking privileges and land. The venture eventually failed because Pellegrini was unable to secure the needed immigrants. *The Handbook of Texas*, II, 357.

[46] See Chapter III, footnote 7, for details relative to Baron Philabeaucourt.

[47] The War Bill which Congress passed in July, 1842, provided that the President would sell ten million acres of land formerly belonging to the Cherokees in East Texas. Houston replied, in part, as follows: "The Executive does not possess the facilities requisite to convert these resources into means. To effect a disposition of lands, by sale or hypothecation in the United States, would not be practicable." *The Writings of Sam Houston*, III, 118.

General Houston is kept well informed from Mexico and acts accordingly. He is aware of their inability to do anything. The late affair was of a marauding character. It would be preferable could peace be obtained—even at this date by acknowledging a certain quota of Mexico's debt to England. This peace would facilitate all sorts of operations. Why not someone sent to Mexico à la coon to negotiate, say General G——.[48] I'm afraid he would not go. Offensive war would irritate and do no good. Defensive— when and if the marauders come they will be hung as sure as 2 and 3 make five. Reported that Mr. Packenham has been superseded by another minister in Mexico. Sent copy of Emigrating Contracts[49] to W. K[ennedy]!

Friday, July 22nd, 1842: "P——" came in from the West with some runaways and a few volunteers. When General [James] Davis with some 200 volunteers left Corpus Christi—they made their encampment at Lantiplan [Lipantitlan] some 35 miles from C. C. on the opposite side of the river. General Davis had timely information of General [Antonio]Canales's coming on with 700 men—500 cavalry and 200 infantry— where he had taken up his encampment was not a good position and he removed a short distance into a dell, leaving his baggage, papers, etc. This was injudicious. On the 7th [July] coming from up the river, the enemy attacked—were beaten back, losing 6 or 8 killed and 20 wounded and some prisoners—took all the Texas baggage, etc. This they would construe into a victory, altho' they lost some dozen or more and a few prisoners taken. The Texans [lost] *not one!* The enemy [retreated] to the other side of the Nueces and a few it is supposed towards C. Christi. They are in all probability some 5,000 soldiers and Rancheros on the frontier. Our Volunteers are

[48] This was probably in reference to General Duff Green, an advocate of the annexation of Texas and United States consul at Galveston (1844), or Bollaert might have been referring to Thomas Jefferson Green, who was second in command of the Somervell Expedition to the Río Grande during 1842 and later captured at Mier.

[49] A copy of the contract which Bollaert refers to here (dated February 15, 1842) is in the Texas State Archives: "Proclamations and Colonial Contracts," No. 48, President Samuel Houston, 1842–44. (See Appendix)

at Lamar, having been joined by some 260 who went from here some little time since. It is presumed that for the present Canales will remain at C. Christi.

What we shall do or what we ought to do, there is a diversity of opinion. Should the enemy advance, we I doubt not shall be prepared for them. Had we had 50 good cavalry, the Mexicans would have been well whipped. Ours were all new volunteers. The Congress has not adjourned yet, but all important business has been gone into. The War Bill,[50] with its amendments by the opposition, gives Houston more power than he requires and if it suits his book he may veto it on the score of unconstitutionality. This Coup I do not think he will do. So poor is the Government that the $6 per day cannot be paid to the members. Exchequer bills may be issued, but they are at 70% discount; this is bad.

I have no doubt but members might have been chosen who could have "paid their way." The majority are rich in land and stock—they should have sold some. Only consider—members of Congress going in debt for their board and upon the strength of their $6 per day fees—and now the Government knows not how to pay this!

When I left for up the country the *Amanda* French Brig came up from Matagorda with Mr. Pelligrini. Mr. P——says he is under the patronage of Mr. Guizot.[51] They will sell their "effects." There is no money, but may purchase land—wish them joy.

General Cañales who headed the late marauding party has long had it in contemplation to form a Northern Republic—to be composed of part of Chihuahua, Tamaulipas, and up to the Nueces. He has, or considers that he has, lands up to the Nueces and is

[50] The special session of Congress which met on June 27, 1842, passed a bill giving Houston authority to conscript one-third of the male population and to dispose of ten million acres of land in order to invade Mexico. It was an obvious attempt by the opposition to put Houston "on the spot." Just at this time the United States government was prepared to offer its services to Texas and Mexico to mediate the difficulty between the two nations. Also, England had just recognized the independence of Texas, and if the war bill were carried into effect and a full-scale war broke out, Texas could easily lose its present advantageous position. Houston had only one choice, namely to veto the war bill.

[51] François Pierre Guizot was a French historian and statesman, premier of France from 1840 to 1848.

aware that even now that by worrying our frontier, will prevent permanent settlements. But out of various military parties we ought to reap some benefit. All Mexicans or parties who are in commission with them must be narrowly watched, altho' they should appear and act as friends—? for instance—et des autres—

Since the late heavy rains the weather has been very warm. The temp: of a cool room was today 8 A. M. 84°. Noon 86°—3 P. M. 86°. Midnight 82°. Little or no breeze and myriads of large mosquitos—biting and stinging thro' one's clothes. All the cattle and horses driven from the prairies into the city by these unharmonous wizzing winged devils. All the summer one is obliged to sleep under a *Bar* or gauze or muslin. (In N. Orleans they have their bars—so large and fixed in a room like a tent so that a sofa, table and chairs can be introduced). At night it is pretty amusement to get under one's bar and pass the flames of a candle near their legs—burning them and then they fall and are easily killed. Last night I could not sleep and [was] obliged ere daylight to leave my couch and walk about. O for a good southerly breeze to blow them all to the devil. It makes a Northern Man wish to be out of the Tropics—now that I am writing it is midnight. The immense numbers of these whizzing animals keep up a continual din. It is almost impossible to write. *Paciencia!*

Saturday, July 23rd, 1842: General Cañales (a base traitor to Texas[52]—why don't he pay his debts in Galveston) who headed the Lipantitlan Marauders, had long had it in contemplation to form a "Northern Mexican Republic," but General Arista coquetted with him for some time and brought him to Santana's views. Cañales had it in contemplation to unite Chihuahua, Tamaulipas, and a part of Texas up to the Nueces, thus to form a "Dictatura" for himself—and is aware that by marauding the

[52] This has reference to the period when Jordan and many Texan volunteers were to assist him.—Bollaert.

Samuel W. Jordan, a former captain in the Texas Army, led 180 Texans to join the Mexican forces under Antonio Cañales in 1839 in the effort to establish the Republic of the Río Grande. "Diary of Adolphus Sterne," *Southwestern Historical Quarterly*, Vol. XXXI (1932–33), 63–83.

Texan frontier, will effectually prevent permanent settlements. This peace was made with Cañales to put Santana in a better position to intimidate Yucatan and or Texas.

Communication of Hon. J. Reilly,[53] minister from Texas to United States to that Government on the subject of entrepot, repeal of duty on cotton, and drawback on goods foreign to the United States. This ultimately ended in the U. S. not coming to terms with Texas relative to a commercial treaty.[54]

Sunday, July 24th, 1842: 8 A.M. 83°. Noon 95° in a balcony but exposed to sun's radiation of the streets and 87° in a room. President Houston has vetoed the Amended War Bill as unconstitutional and giving him too much power, even to dictatorial. At all events by his veto to the said Bill the "War Party" are somewhat perplexed to know what to be at. Congress has adjourned. Exchequer bills which are 70% discount will be issued to defray the expenses of the Representatives.

Monday, July 25th, 1842: 8 A.M. 78° Rain and cloudy. Noon 83°—cloudy. 3 P.M. 85°, 7 P.M. 82°. Last night the mosquitos were in amazing numbers—even in the bay, out of one's depth they were in myriads. Those who attempt bathing day or night are victimized. I was a sufferer.

Tuesday, July 26th, 1842: 7 A.M. 82°—noon 87°.

Thursday, July 28th, 1842: Wrote to Wm. K. and Sadie per Steamer *Merchant*.

[53] On July 13, 1842, James Reily negotiated a Treaty of Amity and Commerce and Navigation between the United States and Texas with Secretary of State Daniel Webster. The United States Senate failed to approve the treaty.

[54] The treaty failed for reasons other than those Bollaert gives here. Reily later reported that "the day after the report was made [Senate Committee report on the treaty], the news of our internal commotions, our dissensions and civil discords, coupled with our disasters, reached here, in all their glowing and exaggerated enormities, and, like a withering sirocco, blasted every effort of our friends, and paralyzed every movement in behalf of our treaty." Dudley G. Wooten, ed., *A Comprehensive History of Texas, 1685–1897,* I, 409.

Visit to Houston and Vicinity

Friday, July 29th, 1842: Mr. Cobb, French Consul celebrated the anniversary of *Trois Jours Glorieux*[55]—*dejeuner a là fourchette.* 8 A.M. 83°. Noon 87°—cloudy—air from S. and W.

Saturday, July 30th, 1842: United States Brig of War *Dolphin* arrived bringing news that the Santa Fé prisoners would be liberated in a few days, on Santana's birthday.

[55] "The Three Glorious Days" (July 27, 28, and 29). The July Revolution occurred during the closing days of July, 1830; Charles X, king of France, was overthrown and driven into exile.

VII

GALVESTON REVISITED

[August–September, 1842]

Monday, August 1st, 1842: Variable weather. Fresh gales occasionally from northward and eastward, and high tides—the water coming up into the town. The NE winds and rain this time of the year are not looked upon as healthy, as blowing from the low swamps of Louisiana. Yesterday the U.S. Brig of War *Dolphin* came in 6 days from Vera Cruz. The Santa Fé prisoners were liberated and would be here in a few days. It was said that Santana had an army of 40,000 men!—stationed in various parts of the country—3,000 at Vera Cruz and about marching upon Yucatan. The Mexicans had cut a vessel of War out of one of the ports of Yucatan. Santana would probably be President again—by the election of the bayonet. Mexican papers talk much of Texas invasion.

Fisher and Miller's grant.[1] This is not quite arranged—probably not convenient for the empresarios to go on. Orders have been issued regulating the formation of Independent Companies of Volunteers from each county for about 1,500 men.[2] When these march towards the Rio Grande they may *cross it*—to the dismay of the enemy. 10 bales of cotton came into Houston a few

[1] Henry Francis Fisher and Burchard Miller received a contract from the Republic on February 8, 1842, to settle 1,000 European immigrants on a three-million-acre tract between the Llano and Colorado rivers. By the end of 1845, both Fisher and Miller had sold all of their interest in the enterprise to others. Meanwhile, some settlers had arrived in Texas and taken up land in the colony, which they subsequently sold. Biesele, *History of the German Settlements in Texas*, 81–82.

[2] Orders were issued by Houston on July 26, 1842, to raise a volunteer army of 1,420 men, including 100 Indians, to retaliate upon Mexico. Two regiments were eventually raised and ordered to San Antonio, and on October 3, 1842, Houston ordered General Alexander Somervell to proceed to the Río Grande. His forces eventually numbered approximately 700 men, and, as subsequently noted, his expedition turned into a dismal military failure. S. B. Hendricks, "The Somervell Expedition Down the Río Grande in 1842," *Southwestern Historical Quarterly,* Vol. XXIII (1919–20), 112–40.

days since. The first 5 bales gets a silver cup (on 29th, the other 5, 31st). The first 10 bales a gold cup. Mr. Power[3] gives a silver cup for the first lot of cotton coming into Matagorda.[4]

Tuesday, August 2nd, 1842: 8 A.M. 74°—strong breeze from N.E. during night blowing hard from same quarter. Noon 82°— 9 P.M. 78°.

Wednesday, August 3rd, 1842: 8 A.M. 75°—strong breeze from N.E. This blows the water into the bay towards the Island. Some years since part of the Island was under water by such wind, but the wharfs, houses, etc., on Strand will now prevent this—the shore has risen 3 to 4 feet by buildings, rubbish, etc. Noon 82°— winds N.E. 9 P.M. 77°.

Thursday, August 4th, 1842: N.E. breeze at night. 8 A.M. 75°— wind acting on the water in the bay and coming into lower parts of town. This wind blows up much dirt and sand and not a pleasant wind, but not reckoned healthy as sweeping over the low swamp lands of Louisiana and Mississippi. We have no sickness here yet, being out of vegetable miasma, but at Houston it is sickly, owing to this and a clayey soil in which the late heavy rains remain. It is supposed that 15 to 17 inches of water fell during the last heavy rains of 15th, 16th, and 17th ultimo. This N.E. wind is filling the bayous; should it continue and the wind get round to N., then the wind would blow the waters out of the shallow inlets or bayous and overflow the lower parts of the Island. The Island runs E by N and W by SW. The eastern side is nearly [a] straight line. The western [is] indented or full of shallow inlets, some taking water enough as to form small lakes and this I presume is one of the causes of the formation of salt deposits and salt lakes on this and the coast between the Nueces and Rio Grande. (Get acct. of rise of Mississippi—Father of Waters—in the vicinity of

[3] Probably James Power. See footnote 11, Chapter III.
[4] 80,000 bales expected this year.—Bollaert.

plantations towns, and cities, where there [are] great rises, it must be fearful indeed.)

Within 4 years there have been a dozen newspapers started here. There is one now—*The Civilian*—quite enough at this time of the year.[5]

Wednesday, August 10th, 1842: Yesterday the *Boxer*, U.S. Brig, came from Vera Cruz bringing Colonel W. G. Cooke[6] and Capt. Houghton of the Santa Fé prisoners. Dr. Brenham[7] came up in the *San Bernard*. All the prisoners had been liberated—they got to Vera Cruz and ready to embark, when an order came from Mexico to press all vessels in port to transport troops against Yucatan. Even the vessel the Santa Fé prisoners had freighted was detained—so they may be still some time there. It was reported that Santana had serious ideas of doing a little "a la Iturbide" under the name of Antonio I, Emperador! and marching towards Texas with 15,000 men! Veremos!

The government of U.S. appears to be getting tired of the "mañana" system of Santana on account of several millions of dollars and if Mexico does not settle up, there will be a difficulty. Mail in from N.O.—Texas treaty signed, 28th May.[8] American

[5] The *Civilian* was published under several names, but at this period it was called the *Civilian and Galveston Gazette*. Its founder and publisher was Hamilton Stuart, a strong supporter of Sam Houston. *The Writings of Sam Houston*, IV, 420.

[6] William G. Cooke was a member of the civil branch of the Texan Santa Fé Expedition. He was released from a Mexican prison on June 16, 1842, and later served as adjutant general of the Texas militia. Harry Warren, "Colonel William G. Cooke," *Quarterly of the Texas State Historical Association*, Vol. IX (1905-1906), 210-19.

[7] Dr. R. F. Brenham, like William G. Cooke, was one of the three civilian commissioners who accompanied the Texan Santa Fé Expedition. Soon after his return from a Mexican prison, he was captured on the Mier Expedition and was killed while attempting to escape from Salado, Mexico. Patrick Ireland Nixon, *The Medical History of Early Texas*, 1528-1853, 254, 366-68.

[8] Bollaert is referring to the three treaties between England and Texas which were ratified on June (not May) 28, 1842. These treaties, pertaining to commerce and navigation, the public debt, and the suppression of the slave trade, were actually signed in 1840, but ratification was delayed for two years. Ephraim Douglass Adams, ed., *British Diplomatic Correspondence Concerning the Republic of Texas*, 1838-1846, 102.

boundary question about being settled.[9] Great rejoicing in Mexico about the affair of Lipantitlan.

Thursday, August 11th, 1842: 8 A.M. 86°. Storm from S and Westward during night. Noon, 80°—strong storm and heavy rains. 9 P.M. 82°. Bennett nearly bowie-knived on Tuesday. A German shot by W—— yesterday died today!

Friday, August 12th, 1842: 8 A.M. 85°. 11 A.M. storm from SSW with heavy rains—thermometer fell to 77°. Noon 79°. Fine. 9 P.M. 81°. Fine.

Sunday, August 14th, 1842: At no period did the political horizon of Texas look so clear, or its position among nations better. Treaties signed and sealed with U.S., F[rance], B[elgium], H[olland], R[ome], and lately with Great Britain—which last country will now necessarily pour in emigration and commerce. Altho' the country has for the last 6 or 7 years been under the influence of great excitements from the Mexicans, and emigration say from the states not gone on rapidly, yet it has gone on—produce has increased and the returns of Galveston from January to July gives: exports, $215,861; imports $201,487; $14,403 in favor of exports. Next years exports will be greater, particularly of cotton.

After the battle of San Jacinto there was no more use for the regular army—the majority of citizens left the sword for the plough. But many of those who came to Texas as military volunteers found it difficult to settle down in this country—returned to the U.S. A military party existed and when out of power were somewhat turbulent. The Navy generally found employment— and latterly in the assistance of Yucatan.

The *Outs* in Texas lived on excitement only, and violent opposition to the Executive (General H——), and on the entré of Arista's proclamation in the spring they found this advantageous

---

[9] This is in reference to the Webster-Ashburton Treaty (August 20, 1842), signed between England and the United States, establishing the present Maine-New Brunswick boundary.

to excite the people. But General H—— knew the precise position of the country and discountenanced, as much as he was able, belligerent demonstrations: first, that it was impolitic (considering what was going on diplomatically in the U.S., E[ngland] and F[rance]), and secondly, the treasury was empty. His political opponents construed General H——'s conduct as *treason*, etc., but within the last few days, all must see that the Executive was *right*. Party spirit may now—seeing this favorable turn to affairs—even try to thwart them and throw obstacles in the way of the well-being of the country. Veremos!

Wednesday, August 17th, 1842: Wrote to Wm. K[ennedy] and Sadie. At noon a slight storm from due N with heavy rain—temperature decreased—after rain, calm, and then it was sultry.

Thursday, August 18th, 1842: 8 A.M. 79°—82° noon—9 A.M. 80°.

Saturday, August 20th, 1842: The American Minister Mr. [Joseph] Eves received dispatches from Washington express to the Texan Government: "The hope that it may be deemed to comport with the interests of the Texan Government to suspend military operations which may be in contemplation against the Mexican Republic until it shall learn the result of the negotiations which Mr. Thompson[10] had been directed to undertake."

Sunday, August 21st, 1842: Vessel from N. Orleans 16 days out brings news that Captain Elliot, the British Consul General to Texas, had arrived in that city. A Brig with a white flag at her fore and Mexican at her Pique came in—bringing the Santa Fé prisoners under Colonel [Hugh] McLeod, from Vera Cruz 10 days. 14 men had died in Vera Cruz of black vomit. The Brig

---

[10] In July, 1842, Daniel Webster sent General Waddy Thompson, from Kentucky, as minister to Mexico with positive instructions to demand release of the Santa Fé prisoners who were citizens of the United States, and also to require that the Texas prisoners should be treated with humanity and not abused or put to slavish or degrading labor. *Comprehensive History of Texas*, I, 383.

came to anchor 3 miles below the town—calm—went on board. There were some 160 or more huddled together—it was dusk— thus little else than a sluggishly moving mass of sun-burnt visages and ill-clothed men could be observed. The effluvia on board was unpleasant. Then there were sundry reports of "yellow fever" being on board. A Captain Holliday[11] had died on the passage. They appeared will generally—some observed that "they had had enough of such expeditions," some "that they were ready for another." It is said that at least "one-third of those who formed this expedition have been killed by Indians and the Mexicans [or] died of sickness and fatigue."

Evening meeting at the "Tremont" to procure clothing etc., for them. 270 men formed the escort and about 30 more, making 300 [on the Santa Fé Expedition]. Some 50 or 60 killed and died (by Indians and Mexicans), some 50 have remained in Mexico, some 183 came in the Brig yesterday, 3 joined the Mexican services in Vera Cruz, 14 died of black vomit in Vera Cruz—the others liberated before and those who escaped made up the balance. The Santa Fé Expedition, if it were a judicious one—was too long preparing—thus Santana had time to give his orders and prepare for defense against them—their object being to revolutionize against Mexico and trade. Could they all have arrived in good health and spirits, and with their arms at Santa Fé, they might have probably prevented any serious attack upon themselves, but would have done but little trade. Then the majority composing the expedition were men who had little else to employ themselves—others for want of excitement and a very few with scientific views. They did not pursue the route they proposed—they got lost, bewildered, disgusted, etc. They separated or at least some went on the hopes of facilitating the aim of the expedition. They then finding they were opposed by armed forces, gave up their arms, and thus became an easy prey to the enemy. They must have suffered much in

---

[11] John J. Holliday was one of the few men who escaped from the Goliad massacre. Later, after remaining in the Texas army, he participated in the Santa Fé Expedition, and as Bollaert reports, he died en route from Vera Cruz to Galveston, August, 1842. Herbert Davenport, "Notes From an Unfinished Study of Fannin and His Men" (MS., Archives Collection, University of Texas Library).

crossing the country—more so travelling on to the City of Mexico —then working in chains in its streets for so long a time—and here are some 160 of them in a most deplorable state of poverty and wretchedness.[12]

Monday, August 22nd, 1842: 8 A.M. 76°—small rains—Noon 82°. 9 P.M. 78°—calm.

Tuesday, August 23rd, 1842: 8 A.M. 78°—D°.—D°. 82°. 9 P.M. 79°—D°. Santa Fé prisoners landed below the town; in a short time they got clothes—they appear a modest lot. From a gentleman lately from Mexico it is the bayonet alone that keeps Santa Ana in power. The priests rather cling to him—he occasionally confiscates them. His health is bad—his leg was badly amputated and troubles him—but will not permit another operation—*tiene galico* or probably secondary symptoms, *y es mui enamorado.* He strikes terror and governs by fear. Colonel Morgan[13] tells me that Wm. K—— has been appointed British Vice Consul to Galveston —in letter from Ashbel Smith.[14] Steamer *Merchant* came in, Captain Elliot one of the passengers. We Britishers made him a visit on board—his appearance and manners appears to take.

Wednesday, August 24th, 1842: Rain. 78°—noon. Duke of Orleans died from a contusion of the brain in jumping from his carriage which was being run-away by his horses. William Bryan[15]

[12] Santa Anna's speech to the Santa Fé prisoners on the day of their release from bondage: "Texans—the generous Mexican Nation whom you have offended —in recompense for her many favours—pardons you. And in the name of the Mexican people—always great—I restore you to that liberty which you lost by invading our territory and violating our domestic firesides. Return to your country, and publish to her people, that the Mexicans are as generous to the conquered as they are valiant in the field of battle. You have proved our valor, now prove our magnanimity.["]—Bollaert.

[13] This was probably Colonel James Morgan, who was prominent in many public and private activities in the Gulf Coast area and the founder of the town of Swartwout. James Morgan Papers (MS., Rosenberg Library, Galveston).

[14] Ashbel Smith at this period, 1842–44, was Texas chargé d'affaires to England and France.

[15] William Bryan was first appointed Texas consul in New Orleans by Lamar in December, 1838. He was relieved in February, 1842, and reappointed by Hous-

appointed Consul for N. Orleans—P. Edmund[16] resigned—
Lachlan McIntosh[17] late consul for England—Kennedy resigned.
"Yellow Jack" occasionally making his appearance in N. O. Dined
with Captain E[lliot] at MacDougals.

Thursday, August 25th, 1842: Morning sultry. 11 A. M. violent
storm and rains, lightning, thunder, temperature fell 3°, that is
to 80°. Mr. Hunt laid down course of Santa Fé Expedition—Mr.
Bonnell intends to write a lengthened report and probably will
give the course—Comanche Peak 5 or 600 feet high—Passing
Nolan R. prairie country is gone through laying between the
Upper and Lower Cross Timbers—then along to Big Washita,
some supposed that one of the S. Canadian Forks for Red River
which they had passed—Anjos turns laid down right on K's map
—made Prisoners at Anto[n] Chico on the Puercos St. Miguel or
the Puercos—Waggon road comes into St. Miguel—Three peaks
—The Centre peaked—the two other flat—Le Grand obs. s^d.
to be correct. Dr. Weideman (drowned in July or August, 1842),
botanist at San Antonio, sells his plants to [Ashbel] Smith.

Friday, August 26th, 1842: 8 A. M. 76°. Rain. Noon, 77°. Rain.
This rainy weather is uncommon at this period of the year and
will render the coast unhealthy. Dined with Dr. Desmond and
party with Captain Elliot at ½ past 6 P. M. William Dyke died of
congestive fever—he had had of late several rather severe attacks
of intermittent fever caused principally from perhaps too much
exposure to the sun, particularly when hay cutting—he being

ton in August, 1842. Bryan was appointed a commissioner in January, 1843, to
effect a secret sale of the Texas Navy. Alma H. Brown, "Consular Service of the
Republic of Texas," *Southwestern Historical Quarterly*, Vol. XXXIII (1929–30),
299–314.

16 This name is often found spelled "P. Edmonds." He served as consul in
New Orleans from January to August, 1842, and proved very inefficient in the
service. He abandoned the office without even the courtesy of a formal resignation.
The Writings of Sam Houston, II, 453.

17 This was George S. McIntosh, who was made chargé d'affaires to France
and England and remained in that position until superseded by Ashbel Smith the
following year. *Ibid.*, 115–16.

very much attached to his two horses, Jerry and Sally. He had been groom to the Marquess of Waterford.

Saturday, August 27th, 1842: 11 A.M. Mr. Goulborn and self as mourners, Reverend Mr. Henderson officiating. 8 A.M. 80° Noon 85° (in sun 108°) 9 P.M. 82°. It is asserted by some that where there are many rattle snakes, there grows a "weed"[18] that if taken internally (say a decoction) or applied externally as a poultice—will cure the bite! Veremos!

Sunday, August 28th, 1842: 5 A.M. heavy rains. 8 A.M. 76°. Noon 84°—fine. 9 P.M. 82°. Up to Nueces in a valley, sulphuret of iron found (have specimen). Near Franklin on the Brazos—near a mill are two curiously carved statues—something like to Asiatic carving. (See Mr. Kellogg) Mr. Tyball his nephew drew a picture of them (Dr. Kirchoffer at Crockett).

Wednesday, August 31st, 1842: 8 A.M. 81° with airs. Showers from N.E.—Noon 86°—9 P.M. 84. $100,000 or more will be collected this fiscal year   200,000 was expected as Revenue from Duties and Taxes—but will be obtained by duties alone. On Monday evening a meeting was held by the citizens of Galveston to express their thanks to R. Packenham Esq. H.B.M. Minister at Mexico and the Hon. Waddy Thompson, M.U.S., for their humane exertions in favor of the Santa Fé prisoners.

Duties on importations secured at Custom House, Red River District, from 1st February to 30th April and from 1st May to 30th June, 1842: Cash duties for gr[ain] ending 30th April, $2,175.00; cash duties secured in store, $1,843.72; total $4,018.72. Collector's salary and expenses, $207.11; net amount for April, $3,811.71. Amount secured from 1 May to 30 June (two months), $2,173.21. Net total from 1st February to 30th June—$5,984.92. There appears to be about $25,000 Exchequer bills remaining in

18 "The snakeweed plant resembles the blue flag [plant]. Its roots contain its healing properties, which are pounded and applied to the affected parts" as a remedy for snake bite. *Bulletin of the Antivenom Institute of America,* Vol. IV (1930), 72.

circulation and more to be paid for 60 days. Messrs. Waldeck and Leininger Westerburger arrived here from N. York via Velasco to see the country.

Friday, September 2nd, 1842: 8 A.M. 78°, 86°, 82°. Messrs. Borden,[19] Potter,[20] and Bache[21] proposed as candidates for the ensuing Congress. Borden a Houston man—Potter generally opposed to the views of President, Bache (a great grandson of Benjamin Franklin) an elderly man.

Saturday, September 3rd, 1842: Mr. Lawrence[22] for Senator, spoke very sensibly upon the position of political and other affairs.

Tuesday, September 6th, 1842: Gave Captain F—— packet for Geological Society [and] Louis Wache letters for Sadie, Plimpton, Jane. Mr. Crawford arrived here from Vera Cruz via New Orleans—Nephew to Consul at Vera Cruz. Potter and Lawrence elected. By letters from England the Government sympathizes much with Texas. 8 A.M. 84°. Noon 88°. 83°. Fine week.

Wednesday, September 7th, 1842: Mr. Harbord, who came down from Colonel [James] Morgan's some three weeks since suffering under great debility resulting from intermittent fever, appeared to be getting better—when from probably eating too much—produced congestive fever on Monday and died at ½

[19] Gail Borden, early-day Texas newspaperman, first collector of the port of Galveston and later the inventor of the process of condensing milk in a vacuum, left Texas in 1851 and ultimately founded the Borden Milk Company. Joe B. Frantz, *Gail Borden: Dairyman to a Nation.*

[20] Ruben M. Potter served as chief clerk, deputy collector, and collector of customs at the Port of Velasco, and as comptroller of customs at Galveston between 1837 and 1845. James H. Leach, "The Life of Reuben Marmaduke Potter" (M.A. thesis, University of Texas, 1940).

[21] Richard Bache, grandson of Benjamin Franklin, moved to Texas in 1836. In 1842 he was elected justice of the peace at Galveston and later represented Galveston County in the Texas Senate. *Biographical Directory of Texas Conventions and Congresses,* 47.

[22] William Lawrence, formerly quartermaster of the post at Galveston, served several terms in the Texas House and Senate during the period of the Republic. *Ibid.,* 121.

past 3 P.M. yesterday. 8 A.M. Reverend Mr. Henderson officiated at his funeral. Some 3 feet of water at bottom [of grave] owing to the present high tide. It has been blowing from N and E and continues. Should it increase and get more to N we shall be over-flowed. "Yellow Jack" at New Orleans. Treaty between England and U.S. signed. England obtained the right of search, but U.S. will keep a Naval force off the Coast of Africa. Bocanegra[23] has returned from office of Secretary of Exterior Relations, succeeded by Alaman,[24] who acted thus under Iturbide! Hurrah for Emperor Santana and his army of 80,000 to eat up the Texans. 8 A.M. 82° —Noon 86°—9 P.M. 82°. Hot, sultry, and disagreeable gales from E with very high trades overflowing the lower part of the town and a digging 3 feet water oozing in plentifully. Mosquitos in a most annoying abundance. When the trades rise high here, it is owing to easterly gales in the Gulf. Waters rising all day came up to front of Mr. Powers, the Market Place, and the lower part of the town under water—sailing and rowing in boats.

Thursday, September 8th, 1842: 8 A.M. 85°. During night gales from N and bringing fine airs from N.E. Sea broke in last night at the Bathing House.

Friday, September 9th, 1842: Noon 87°. 9 P.M. 83°. High tide gone down, squalls and showers from SSE. Wrote to Mrs. Harbord by "Funchal" communicating death of her husband, en-closed to Revd. Harbord, Trafford Chambers, South John St., Liverpool, England. Messrs. Elliot and Crawford went to Hous-ton. Captain E. functions as C. general, have ceased with the rat-ification and arrival of the Treaty, and is now Chargé d'Affairs. Graff Boos Waldeck[25] and Monsignore Leininger Westerburg[26]

---

[23] José María Bocanegra was minister of foreign affairs in Mexico in 1842. He held several positions in the Mexican government from 1829 on, and was known for strong anti-American views. Josiah Gregg, *Commerce of the Prairies*, 343–44.

[24] Lucas Alamán was the guiding spirit of the conservative party in Mexico in the first half of the nineteenth century, also a distinguished historian. *The Hand-book of Texas*, I, 21.

[25] Count Boos Waldeck came to Texas in 1842 as a representative of the

went to Houston. For some time past the only excitement we have had have been the elections. These are now concluded and it is asserted that Washington [on-the-Brazos] is to be the next place for the meeting of Congress.

Sunday, September 11th, 1842: 8 A.M. 85°. Heavy rains. 82°. Wrote to Pringle[27] to explain opinions of people leaving this country. Steamer *Merchant* from New Orleans—Mr. Teulon[28] arrived on her bearing the Ratified Treaty with England. Brought me a batch of letters.

Monday, September 12th, 1842: 82°. 86. 83°. Moderate and fine. Wrote to Sadie—Plimpton, Aunt—by Funchal—may get off to-day.

Tuesday, September 13th, 1842: 8 A.M. 78°—during night and morning, rains. Winds from S. 76°. (The map of Galveston Island[29] I have started on supposition that the range of circular holes were made by the Indians—I am assured that they are formed naturally so—say like *Pond Hobs*). Mr. George Knight Teulon who has traversed Texas in many directions—gives it as his opinion that, say a straight line be drawn from Belgrade on the Sabine on to about Swartwout, through Montgomery to Columbus and bottoms of the Colorado—inside of this line, or towards the Coast cannot be recommended to European farmers: 1st, the produce is tropical; 2nd, intermittent, bilious, or congestive fevers are common—and may be denominated low alluvial lands.

Adelsverein, an organization of German noblemen interested in purchasing land in Texas. Biesele, *History of the German Settlements in Texas,* 67.

[26] Count Victor von Leininger accompanied Waldeck to Texas in 1842 as the other representative of the Adelsverein. *Ibid.,* 67.

[27] Bollaert mentions William Pringle several times in his journals and notes. He was one of the principal stockholders in the Kennedy Colony and apparently never came to Texas.

[28] George Knight Teulon was the editor of the *City and State Gazette* (Austin), an anti-Houston, anti-administration paper. *The Writings of Sam Houston,* III, 532.

[29] Bollaert prepared a map of Galveston Island for the Royal Geographical Society.

Outside the above line—the Cherokee Lands—those above Austin and from there down to San Antonio he speaks highly of, as a grazing and wheat-growing country. Perhaps it would be a good way to get to K——'s colony by flat-boating it up the Nueces with horses.

Wednesday, September 14th, 1842: Raining hard all night. Raining all day. At no period has the exterior political horizon of Texas looked as clear (save as regards Mexico) or its position among nations better. Texas has been recognized by the U. States, France, England, Holland, Belgium, Rome and negotiations at this point are going on with the Hanseatic States. Now England especially when there shall be peace with Mexico, her manufactures and emigrants will pour in. Although this country has passed and is still passing through a painful ordeal, yet produce has increased and the returns of Galveston from January to July gives a considerable item in favour of exports. After the Battle of San Jacinto the majority of citizens sheathed the sword and took to the plough. Many of those who came from the U. States as volunteers found it not to suit them to settle down in the country, returned to their homes. Yet a military or war party existed and when out of power, they have been accused of acts of turbulence. The Navy of late found employment in assisting the Yucatecos. The *Outs* in Texas live on, and love "excitement," and their opposition partakes at times of factious violence. When the Mexicans entered San Antonio in the spring, the "War Party" were up in arms and "onward" was their cry. The President discountenanced, as much as he was able, violent belligerent demonstrations: 1st, there may have been good political reasons; 2. The Treasury was empty; 3. what credit had Texas None! The promised loans from France and England did not arrive. Still the "War Party's" cry for the invasion of Mexico.

Thursday, September 15th, 1842: Wrote Pringle, Sadie Harbord, and S[am] Kennedy. 8 A.M. 72°. Cloudy, breezes from NE. 74°–72°. This evening Mr. Phipps married. Passed evening jollily.

Friday, September 16th, 1842: 8 A.M. 73°. Cool and breezes from NE. Noon 78°. 9 P.M. 76°. Lately specimens of gold, silver, and copper from the headwaters of the Brazos have been sent to Houston.

The President has issued his Proclamation recalling his previous one of blockade of 26th March[30]—Thus to shew he wishes to be amicable etc.—signed 12 December [September].

Doran Maillard,[31] "Barrister at Law in Texas," somehow or another on his return to Europe after a short residence in Texas—(among his other operations was received as a Barrister; this honor he would in all probability have found difficult to obtain in his own country). He returns to Europe then writes *his* history of Texas, but not the History of the Country. The old Spanish proverb of "Dime con quien andas, yo te diré quien eres" explains at least to any enquiring person the reasons he had in concocting his work i.e. under the patronage of the Mexican Government. I mention here the subject of a communication by him not very favorable to Texas, read to the Geographical Society of London in 1840 and call to his mind the discussion that arose out of that production and the not very favorable personal remarks made to Mr. M. by a member of the Society. If he has forgotten this may bring it back to his recollection. I might fill pages in showing the untruths and vindictiveness contained in his work, but refer 1st to what he says when speaking of Texan Ladies. Mr. M. could never have been admitted into the Society of Texan Ladies, or he would not accuse them of smoking pipes. That Mr. M. might have seen some "gude auld wife," in the back woods whiffing at a corn cob pipe, I will not deny. Has Mr. M. ever travelled in

[30] Houston's reason for lifting the blockade (September 12, 1842) was his concern that further maintenance of the blockade would "embarrass the commercial intercourse of those nations which have recognized the independence of this Government. *The Writings of Sam Houston,* III, 156.

[31] Nicholas Doran P. Maillard arrived in Texas in January, 1840, and shortly afterwards became co-editor of the Richmond *Telescope,* but he only remained in Texas approximately six months. Upon his return to England he wrote *The History of the Republic of Texas . . .* (London, 1842). He not only was severely critical of Texas and Texans, but worked against the recognition of the Republic by England. Needless to say, Maillard became highly unpopular in Texas.

Wales, or in some parts of Yorkshire, to say nothing of auld Ireland, if not I beg to inform him that, I have seen farmers wives and others smoking their pipe in England.

Then in reference to the "Swab," I have never seen it used by ladies in Texas. I have in the West Indies, and a piece of the proper sort of wood makes an excellent apology for a tooth brush, but as to snuff being generally used—O fie on you Mr. M. Even if it had been so, where is your gallantry to the sex. (In a subsequent journey I noticed this case *once*).

Then with regard to the Hotels.[32] I confess that the accom-[m]odation occasionally met with is not quite so recherché as at Fentons or Longs, but in the principal towns I have been in such as Galveston, Houston, Matagorda, Swartwout, Austin, Brazoria, Gonzales, San Antonio, etc. etc. I have been perfectly contented with the accom[m]odation offered, and this moreover during a period that was not for the moment so flourishing as when Mr. M. was in the country. It was probably my good fate to make the acquaintance of hospitable planters and other persons in the country and whilst travelling I have uniformly received every kindness.

Then with regard to the killing of Indians. Mr. M. says 8,000 perished during the Mexican and Texas Revolutions. Preposterous! I beg to inform Mr. M. that the Mexican Revolution commenced about the year 1810. What number of Indians were killed from that time until 1831, when the Texas Revolution commenced, must be substracted at least from the 8,000. I suppose I must confess I am not sentimental enough to be ever repeating "O the Poor Indians! O the poor Red Man! The Natural possessors of the Soil etc., etc." But I may observe that for their own sake it is a pity they do not become agriculturally inclined—then a smaller quantity of land would administer more rationally to their wants; industry would assist in civilizing them. They would

[32] Maillard says this about Texas hotels (p. 222): "The Hotels and boarding houses in Texas are conducted in the most miserable way, being extremely filthy, filled with vermin of every description, and wretchedly supplied with food. Their charges are exorbitant, and after the description I have given of the people, the reader can easily imagine what the society must be."

no more be the arrant indolent wanderers, nor require so much territory for their hunting excursions.

The intercourse between them and the White Man would then be what it ought to be and the Red Man in time would become useful member of society. At present, they are mere hunters, and oftimes petty traders take advantage of them. Some of the Indian Chiefs in Texas are intelligent men, speaking English and Spanish and with proper management and in time many of the Indian tribes in Texas may be reclaimed from the Savage State. I need hardly mention here the progress towards a state of civilization the Cherokees in the U. S. are advancing. They were doing the same in Texas, had their farms and stock when the war commenced and moreover the Cherokees were found to be in communication with the enemy, which ended in the death of "Bowles,"[33] "Egg" and other chiefs and the dispersion of the tribe.[34]

Mr. M. says in another part that there are no roads in Texas (excepting natural ones). The old Spaniards, Mexicans, and the present occupiers of the soil have cut many roads, and at great expense. I have travelled from Houston to Swartwout on a carriage road, cut through pine woods. Is there not a carriage road from the Rio Grande through the whole of Texas by Nacogdoches into the United States? Roads are made through forests by, finding the direction by a compass from say from one town to another —then commencing on that line, cutting pieces off with an axe from the sides of trees in that line—this is called "blazing," and removing the intermediate trees. I must own that the Texan forest roads would be better for sundry stumps taken away, but the roads or traills on the prairies in dry weather are excellent.

---

[33] Chief Bowles was the chief of the Cherokee tribe that crossed the Sabine River into Texas about 1819. He and his followers settled on the Cherokee lands in East Texas. Because of their support of the Mexican government during the Revolution, Lamar had the Cherokees driven out of Texas, at which time Bowles was killed (July 16, 1839) in trying to resist. His lands were later seized by the Texas government. Hodge, *Handbook of American Indians*, I, 163.

[34] I may observe that of late treaties have been made with all the Indian tribes in Texas, excepting the Comanches and ere long it is expected to have a treaty with them.—Bollaert.

A friend of mine went the other day from Houston to Austin, then on to San Antonio and the Nueces and from thence to Galveston in a buggy. Indeed, with few exceptions the greater portion of the country can be traversed in pretty direct lines by waggons at least, or how could the settlers move onwards.

I have considered it a duty on my part to have made the above observations relative to Mr. M. view of things in Texas, and in conclusion will add that we must have seen through a different medium.

Sunday, September 18th, 1842: 8 A. M. 62°. Strong breezes from NE and blowing up the water out of the bay. The *San Bernard* Schooner is waiting for a fair wind to go out and join the *Austin* and *Wharton* to go down immediately to Vera Cruz and Yucatan. The *San Antonio* Schooner gone off there some 15 days since. The *Guadalupe* Horn Steamer from England appears to have arrived in Vera Cruz. If our fleet can catch anything Mexican, they will.

Every now and then the subject of California and the Oregon Territory is mentioned even here in Texas and affords points of interesting discussion. The unfortunate circumstances connected with the Santa Fé expedition have drawn the attention of some of the Missouri traders and trappers to Santa Fé and California in retaliation against Governor Armijo of Santa Fé and on account of the suffering of their countrymen. We are informed that the far west is a "glorious country" and, moreover, assured that if once the Americans get a footing in the N and NW Mexican regions, upon whatever be the pretext, there will be a "difficulty" to get them out.

A Mr. Warfield[35] has been some years travelling in the western parts of U. S. and considerably in California. He describes that

---

[35] Charles A. Warfield was authorized by Houston on August 16, 1842, to invade New Mexico via Santa Fé, to levy contributions from Mexican settlements, and to capture Mexican property, one half of the spoils to be delivered to the government of Texas and the other half divided among the members of his expedition. The venture turned out to be a miserable failure. W. C. Binkley, "The Last Stage of Texas Military Operations Against Mexico, 1843," *Southwestern Historical Quarterly*, Vol. XXII (1918–19), 260–71.

last country with its ports on the Pacific in high terms for stock raising, fur trade, and trade with the Pacific. His object in coming here was to get permission from the Government to march into Texas by the Missouri Trail with some 400 followers, or say by "Bent's Fort" into the vicinity of Santa Fé—upon a marauding expedition against those who behaved badly to the Santa Fé prisoners. This I think injudicious in our present posture of affairs with Mexico. Mr. Warfield told me that he had not obtained permission, but he has been in N. Orleans lately and asserted that he had—moreover, says he would not take $10,000 for his share. The opposition declaim against this proceeding and flatly call it a robbery.

11 A.M.: Went on board Schooner *San Bernard*—Captain [Downing H.] Crisp. The barometer stood at 29.40, temperature 77° Fah^t. Blowing from NE. The fluctuations in the Bar: do not appear to be very great—but no good observations have been made. See Purday on Mexican Gulf—Cadiz 6°–18' W. Long. of London—Northers this time of the year are unhealthy in N. Orleans, bringing to the city miasmas. Even here it is not very pleasant—blowing hard all day from NNE. We may call this an Equinoctial Gale, and moreover, it is full moon. Midnight, NNE Gale increasing.

Monday, September 19th, 1842: 2 A.M., blowing a regular hurricane or typhoon. The Town under water—dark wicked looking weather—lights here and there flickering about in the houses. We could just distinguish that some of the vessels have broken away from their moorings—that some of the houses on the Strand have been smashed, others giving way and the streets covered with rafters and wood-boats floating about. A baker's cart floated up to Mr. Powers, some poor people had to decamp with their children, their shanty having given away—about 4 A.M. the gale commenced subsiding—and at day light the Tide went out—but the Town of Galveston, particularly the Strand, one sad scene of destruction.

The Protestant and Catholic Churches wrecks, many of the

houses in its vicinity ruined—the stores all down town more or less injured—with their goods. The Exchange has suffered much, one-half of the flooring gave way. The whole of the Strand one scene of devastation and road strewed with rafters, timbers, and nearly all the houses slewed round one way or another and many gutted, particularly those on the sea-side.

The wharfs much injured. The Barque *Funchal* off the point has stood it out bravely—the *San Bernard* got on shore, the Brig *Atlantic*, after a severe bumping against McKinney's Wharf, got aground—the *Maria Elizabeth*, "Prize Schooner" on shore— Simpton's House washed away and his pilot boat foundered— Many smaller craft and boats smashed. This hurricane commenced blowing for some days past from eastward, then NE. Yesterday NNE, and this brought up this terrible gale. The strongest wind blew from NE and at 2:30 A.M., Bar[ometer] on board *San Bernard* stood at 29 inches—having fallen 4/10 since a few hours before. The easterly winds filled the bays with water and then the N and NNE blew the waters up over the Island. There is only one way to remedy this—by a leveé—but this we cannot afford to make. The houses must be built upon higher piles or brick piles. It is impossible to say what is the loss—but 60 or 80,000 dollars will hardly defray it, perhaps $100,000.

8 A.M.: 70° Weather fine and clear and fine airs from N.W. This gale has been as severe as the great one in October, 1837.[36] A few more hours would have prostrated the whole town. We fear now and with reason for the cotton crop, and moreover, Louisiana and Mississippi will be in a difficulty. Noon 78°. 9 A.M. 75°. Fine all day. Airs from NW. This gale did much damage to the Island of Cuba the 15th.[37]

[36] In 1837 there was a severe gale from about SE, perhaps E. It ran so high as to blow up the waters of the Mexican Gulf all over the Island, so that a schooner ran in from the Gulf—over the Island—and went up to Buffalo Bayou. This is to the credit of a resident here.—Bollaert.

[37] According to several newspaper clippings which Bollaert inserted at this point, the Galveston storm occurred on the evening of September 18, 1842. The editor estimates the damage wrought at $50,000. The disaster was not without its humor, and Bollaert also encloses the following from the *Civilian and Galveston Gazette:* "We are told that during the late storm, a worthy tailor of this city arose

Tuesday, September 20th, 1842: We have had very rainy, disagreeable and changeable weather of late, accompanied with some sickness in the shape of bilious fevers—yesterday the coast was visited by a tremendous storm or rather hurricane.

During the spring assizes, it was expected that there would be a very interesting trial, namely that of a woman for the murder of her husband. The case was that the husband had given her cause to be jealous upon which in a paroxysm of jealous rage—she shot him. The Coroner's inquest found her guilty of murder and she was incarcerated until the Assizes should open.[38] Judge [Richard] Morris opened the court—then followed the entry of Mexicans into San Antonio; the Judge, gentlemen of the bar, and the principal officers of Court were off to the Army. The woman who was about to be tried for murder, was *bailed.* She went up the country to her friend's and in all probability when called upon will be *"non inventus."*

The following occurred in Galveston lately—a most violent rascal of a fellow whose brother had been hung for murder in the U.S. and he himself had the reputation of one, was beating his wife early one morning. An industrious citizen was passing by on the way to his store, when the woman cried out for help to him as he was passing by, requesting him to go for the Sheriff. The husband immediately ran out, plunged a knife into the individual passing, some neighbors rescued him—a surgeon was sent for and dressed his wound. The wounded man, considering himself in

from his bed, and waded through the flood to his shop—a small building near the Strand. As he approached, he saw that the house had changed its position and was floating about at the mercy of the waves. He however discovered a light in the tenement, and making his way to the front window soon ascertained the agreeable fact, that his journeyman had placed all his cloths and other valuables, on the upper shelves beyond the reach of the flood. His fears were succeeded by merriment, when he discovered his faithful jour, steadying himself in the middle of the shop—up to the waist in water—his elbows elevated, and playing, "Over the water to Charlie," on a violin with all imaginable zest; a bottle of ardent occupied a nook in loving proximity to his *bow* hand."

[38] An auld Brig that had run ashore in a "norther" was the prison. The person who had charge of this died and no one was found willing to continue his office—thus we are without any place of confinement to the utter discomforture of our worthy Sheriff, who I have often heard say, "O Sir, the laws cannot be made to be respected without a gaol."—Bollaert.

danger, loaded his gun and kept it in his store in readiness in case the fellow should repeat his stabbing. The wretch approached the store to do more injury, when he was shot—he lay for some time in his gore in the street until a jury could be called—when he was acquitted almost immediately.

Attended summer assizes—the following case occurred: Commodore W—— indicted for the murder of John Pole, a man who had been his servant and cook. They had had words in the kitchen when [George Washington] Wheelright said that the deceased offered to strike at him with an axe. Wheelright retreated—told the difficulty to Mr. Rossignol [?], who put a loaded pistol into his hand. W. then went to the kitchen—shot the deceased—who threw the axe afterwards at him—died of the wound. Verdict, not guilty. Had W. awaited for the man and not gone into the kitchen, then it would have been justifiable homicide.

But in these warm countries (and those of the U.S.) a *friend* tells you, he will shoot you, or it is intimated by another friend that s⁰. *friend* intends to have a *difficulty* with you—if you wish to save your own life you must kill s⁰. *friend* as soon as you can—a jury will find a verdict of not guilty. I have seen a fellow rush upon his fellow-man with a villainous Bowie Knife, and by great good luck the knife was wrested from the assassin (A Captain of Volunteers). On being expostulated for this act—replied that he had been informed that the one he took for his opponent had said he "would shoot him." Some of the Southerners talk much of chivalry etc., then if they feel themselves insulted let them act as gentlemen by sending a *Second*, and not turn assassins.

In the trial related of today, there was a very gentlemanly man as Judge Morris. The District Attorney, as Prosecutor for the Republic—opposed by half a dozen lawyers—ready at speech and loads of references—from Magna Carta upwards. The Court was over a crockery store used on Sunday for a Methodist Chapel—the Judge, chewing his quid, thrown back in his chair, his legs thrown up on his desk—the District Attorney, chewing and smoking—the Council for the prisoner, D°. D°. and a small quantity of whittling—indeed I saw the weed in the mouths of some of the

lookers on. Order was kept in the court, but ever and anon a squirt
of tobacco juice on the floor. About two years since a Judge Tomkins[39] went thro' the country and hung two for murder and one
Nigger for breaking prison.

After late wet weather, and moreover since the late gale, fears
are beginning to be entertained relative to the cotton crop, particularly on the plantations on the Coast.

In the Southern Countries, the dead are soon enterred—a few
hours only in some cases after the vital spark has fled. It would
appear that a man in the town of Galveston named [Haskins]
had been seized with congestive fever. A medical man was called
in, who ordered, among other things in his prescription, some
opium, but pronounced the case to be a very bad one. At the
expiration of a few hours, the patient appeared to his friends to
be dead. The barber was sent for, shaved the corpse, and it was
laid out on a carpenter's bench, envelloped in a shroud. The
friends of the defunct retired to a lower room to recruit their
spirits with a "drink." They had done all that they were able, and
now awaited the arrival of the coffin. They recounted all the good
qualities of the deceased, for he had been in many a fight during
the revolution, and his death was not a very melancholy one, not
being a married man and his relatives not known to his friends.
A wag present could not help drinking him a safe journey to
Heaven. On this being drunk, a noise was heard in the upper
room, as if some one had fallen on the floor.

"By ———!" said one of the party, "David has fallen down."

"Fallen down!" replied another, somewhat scared. "How the
devil can a dead man fall about?"

A stifled groan was heard—all started on their legs, when pat,
pat, pat, something came down the stairs, when to their horror
and astonishment David ———, their friend whom they had supposed dead, stepped into the lower room wrapt up in his shroud
—looked at them most piteously, pointed to his parched tongue

[39] Augustus M. Tomkins was appointed district attorney for the Second District of the Republic of Texas in December, 1836. Later he established a law
office in Houston, but there is no official evidence that he was ever a Judge in the
Republic. *The Writings of Sam Houston*, I, 512.

with his left fore finger, extending his right hand out and in a weak voice said, "Give me some brandy and water." "Tis his ghost!" they all exclaimed, and ran out of the house. David ——— sat himself down and helped himself to the brandy and water and his own "funeral baked meats"; when after an interval, one by one his friends came to the door and saw that David was alive— he recovered perfectly and has been in good health ever since.

On the afternoon of the 20th news arrived in Galveston of the following tenor: San Antonio was completely surprised on the 11th inst. by thirteen hundred Mexicans under General Wall [Woll]. Fifty-three of the principal citizens taken. The Proclamation of the President headed "The Enemy Again" orders the marching forthwith of the Militia of Brazoria, Austin, Fort Bend, Colorado, Victoria, Gonzales, Jackson, and Matagorda counties against San Antonio; and the counties of the upper Brazos and Colorado to march to Austin, and the citizens of the other counties to hold themselves in instant readiness. The orders of the Executive are direct that in the event of the evacuation of San Antonio by the Mexicans that they are to be pursued beyond the Rio Grande and chastised as "their audacity deserves." In the event of a formal invasion the western counties are to hold them in check until the rest of the Republic can rally to the rescue.

P.S. When San Antonio was taken the Circuit Court was in session and the Judge and officers of Court were made prisoners.

It is likewise reported that could General Woll have crossed the Colorado, which he could not owing to the waters, he would have marched to Austin, taken away its inhabitants and probably destroyed the Archives."[40]

Houston's maneuvers throughout the spring and summer of 1842 were paying off, and the opposition was becoming less vociferous as diplomatic and political events were breaking in favor of the administration. However, at daybreak on September 11,

[40] This newspaper announcement, which Bollaert clipped and pasted in his journal, appeared in the *Civilian and Galveston Gazette,* September 21, 1842.

1842, a force of approximately twelve hundred Mexicans under General Adrian Woll took the town of San Antonio by complete surprise. Resistance was futile and a speedy capitulation resulted. Fifty-three prisoners were taken, including the presiding judge in the local court and all the lawyers in attendance. When news of the event reached the Chief Executive, he immediately ordered Brigadier General Somervell, the senior officer of the western militia, to concentrate the most eligible forces on the frontier, to repel the enemy, and, if it seemed possible, "to advance with a prospect of success into the enemy's territory."

Meanwhile, the militia from Gonzales set out to meet the enemy. The battle of Salado Creek, six miles from San Antonio, resulted in a setback for the Mexican forces, but the Texans lost some thirty-two men under Captain Nicholas Dawson. The enemy began its retreat from San Antonio on the eighteenth, laden with prisoners of war and booty. Somervell did not move in the direction of the Río Grande until November 18, when he set out from the Medina with some 750 men. After an unpleasant march, he reached Laredo on December 8. Two days later, the commander, realizing that he did not have an adequate army or sufficient equipment and arms, permitted those who desired to do so to return home. The remainder of the army, some 500 men, moved down the river, crossed the stream, and captured the town of Guerrero on the sixteenth without resistance.

Once again dissension broke out, and on December 19, Somervell decided to return to San Antonio. Only two hundred men accompanied him, the rest choosing to follow Captain William S. Fisher and resume their march down the river. On Christmas Day they captured the town of Mier, but were subsequently forced to surrender by a superior force. The story of the Mier prisoners is well known. Together with those recently carried off from San Antonio and Santa Fé, they added greatly to the burdens of an already overburdened and exasperated president of the Republic of Texas.

The news of the Mexican invasion shook Texas to its very roots. Coming on the heels of the great hurricane, confusion was added to confusion in Galveston. Bollaert chooses to describe the events throughout the last hectic days of September and early October through voluminous newspaper clippings inserted in his journal, which for obvious reasons need not be reproduced. But by the end of 1842 things had simmered down considerably: Mexican marauding expeditions had ceased, and Houston was silently and patiently stacking his cards for the jack pot prize—the annexation of Texas to the United States.

As September, 1842, drew to an end, William Bollaert continued to record the unfolding events in Galveston, both important and trivial.

Wednesday, September 21st, 1842: 8 A.M. 75°. Noon 80°. 9 P.M. 76°. Fine but cloudy.

Thursday, September 22nd, 1842: 8 A.M. 75°. Warm in the sun. Noon 82°. 9 P.M. 79°. *Merchant* left with letters for John Pringle, Sadie, Harbord, Sam K[ennedy] at 9 P.M.

Friday, September 23rd, 1842: 8 A.M. 76°. Warm in sun, airs from S and E. This morning awoke at 4 A.M. by a great huzzahing. I afterwards learned that it was occasioned by the breaking up of a jury on a case of trespass worth 20 dollars; they had been under charge of the officers of the court since 7 P.M. last night. Thus, a case of murder was decided in a few minutes and a case of trespass, value 20 dollars, took the jury 40 hours to deliberate upon! They could not settle it, there being one stubborn fellow. The defendant was Mrs. [Nancy Moffette] Lee [Lea], the President's mother-in-law, and the Jury was discharged.

Saturday, September 24th, 1842: Here we are all in excitement —the Mexicans are really in San Antonio and will fortify it. There have been some skirmishes and the best part of one Company that was alone was almost cut up. There does not appear so much enthusiasm here now as in the spring.

Monday, September 26th, 1842: The Barque *Grand Condé* [arrived] with some 40 or 50 emigrants—Mr. Pelligrini's folks. He has no plan arranged for them, but has purchased lots in Harrisburg. Until there is peace, there can be no emigration to the West. In the E and NE it can and is going on. 8 A.M. 74° 78°. 74°. Fine breezes from E—clear skies, thus the uncomfortable weather is over, but the late heavy rain has made the prairie lands wet and terrible roads with swarms of mosquitos—about 100 bushels to the acre.

Wednesday, September 28th, 1842: 74°. Cool—E breezes Noon 79°. 9 P.M. 78°. A small craft brought the subjoined this morning. If it be true about the shooting [of] the Texans taken at San Antonio, then little can be said about the eulogized humanity of General Woll, coupled with the cutting up of the Lafayette [County] band.[41]

Thursday, September 29th, 1842: 76° E breezes—2 P.M. 81° ENE breeze strong in the sun 112°, 9 P.M. 78°. By information today General Woll has fallen back on the Medina River. Here are some good spots for entrenching, etc. Why have the Mexicans left San Antonio? Do they fear us or wish to draw us away? They must take care of our rifles!

Friday, September 30th, 1842: 8 A.M. 74°. Strong breeze from NE. 2 P.M. 80°. 9 P.M. 79°. At 9 A.M. Company of Coast Guards went to battery near the Point. The severe gale and high tide had carried the platform and guns towards the sea—hauled the three 18 pounders up, cleared away the sand, and got it in readiness to place farther inland. Colonel Hockley[42] contemplates erecting a

---

[41] The Lafayette County band was the company referred to in the editor's narrative above. It was commanded by Nicholas Mosby Dawson, and during the skirmish at Salado Creek on September 18, he and his men were cut off and suffered severe losses. The event is known as the "Dawson Massacre." L. U. Spellman, "Letters of the 'Dawson Men' from Perote Prison, Mexico," *Southwestern Historical Quarterly*, Vol. XXXVIII (1934–35), 246–69.

[42] Colonel George Washington Hockley; see footnote 15, Chapter V.

good battery near the "Pass," putting *Ours* in good order and
erecting at least one more at the Bayou below the town. The NE
end of the Island has suffered some diminution from the great
gale. The winds blew the sand hills down and thus the sea broke
through, covering nearly the end of the Island. In some places the
sea comes in 50 to 100 yards inland. 10 P.M. Mr. Power landed
from *Bryant* from New York—they did not feel the gale we
had here.

All the news we get from Mexico comes trumpeting, that by
sea and land we may expect momentarily to be invaded. Should
this "consumation devoutly to be wished" come off—by land, the
Texans are ready for the enemy: Galveston Island is getting into a
state of defense under Colonel Hockley and the Volunteers of
the City. Nature has been kind enough to form natural trenches,
on the sea shore of sand. From behind these, should an enemy
land, there would be at least without any reinforcements 600 rifles
ready to welcome them, and no want of artillery.

VIII

RANDOM OBSERVATIONS

[October, 1842–August, 1843]

*From October 1842 to August 1843, Bollaert continued to use
Galveston as his headquarters, making short excursions to Houston and Montgomery County, farther north. His journal and
notes for this period are rather sketchy, with many daily entries
omitted. Undoubtedly much of his time was taken up with the
completion of the map and charts of the Gulf Coast area, previously mentioned. The narrative materials for the present chapter
are much more disconnected than previous and subsequent ones.
Indeed, the period itself was somewhat of a lull, in the activities
both of the narrator and of the Republic of Texas. Late in 1843
Bollaert would be starting out on a new and interesting adventure,
a journey to the Texas frontier. And Texas would be thinking,
talking, and moving in the direction of annexation.*

The last Congress offered the President almost dictatorial powers—he veto'd the bill to that effect as unconstitutional. Some
went so far as to say that the Congress wished to commit him. He
remained in Houston some time, oftimes personally suffering in
his finances. The President then for reasons best known to himself, removed the seat of Government to Washington on the
Brazos and went there with his Lady. The Secretary of War and
Marine, Colonel [George W.] Hockley, resigned, accepting the
command of Galveston. It is reported that the President has it
in contemplation, finding that the volunteer chiefs will not obey
him, to organize a standing army of 5,000 men to commence first
with 500–1,000. The cost of putting 5,000 men into the field will
be about $250,000 and then $150,00 per annum, the soldiers pay
$8 per month.

The American Minister Mr. [Joseph] Eves received dispatches
from Washington, U.S. expressing "the hope that it may be

deemed to comport with the interests of the Texan Government to suspend military operations which may be in contemplation against the Mexican Republic until it shall have learnt the result of the negotiations which Mr. Thompson had been desired to undertake.

Saturday, October 1st, 1842: 75°—Santana must have his hands full—his capital etc. to keep in *military* order, Yucatan to worry and tease, and lastly, Texas. From what I can make out of the present military promenade of the Mexicans under General Woll is that Santana believed him to be a smart officer, said to him, "Cross the Rio Grande with 12 to 1,500 men, go through San Antonio and make prisoners"—and unfortunately at the time the assizes, or courts, were sitting. We had no troops nor spies even on the frontier, and thus some 40 or 50 were captured. Woll now pushed on to the Colorado in the hope of crossing it, taking Austin for 24 hours, destroying it, and public documents, if found, and then retreating as quick as possible to Mexico, chanting victory. But the Colorado would not permit the enemy to pass. Then our brave volunteers, a handful of them, began to worry the enemy, in turn, under [Mathew] Caldwell, [Edward] Burleson, and [James S.] Mayfield, but not before the Lafayette Company of Volunteers from La Grange had been nearly cut to pieces— they being alone and some 50 or 60 of them only.[1] Woll got back to San Antonio with his wounded, leaving some 100 or 150 of his followers upon the field; after being there some days, it would appear he has retreated to the Rio Medina. Our forces [are] watching him closely. It is not the general impression that the long talked of "general invasion" is to come off this time.

Monday, October 3rd, 1842: 74° N. E. Dᵒ. 83°. NE 9 P. M. 80°.

[1] Killed at the Battle of Salado, 18th September (Sunday), 35 persons. Prisoners of Dawson's Company (The Lafayette Company), 15—prisoners taken at Bejar, 11th September, 52—these are at Sta. Rosa.—Bollaert.

Of the fifteen members of Dawson's company captured by the Mexicans, three escaped. Nine of the remaining twelve eventually reached Texas again after serving time in Perote Prison.

Reports that Caldwell and Mayfield with their men have been taken by the Mexicans,[2] who were reinforced with 2,000 to 3,000 men.

Captain E[lliot] surprizing me by telling me that he believes there are 30,000 Negros in Texas—moreover, that he has been informed that for 20,000 Negros capitation tax was paid—a year or two since.

Tuesday, October 4th, 1842: 74°. 83°. 70°. Winds variable from NE to NW. For some nights past, many meteors have fallen— course from E to W. For some time past Galveston has been unhealthy, owing probably to the late heavy rains. The "Strand" or lower part of the City, which is subject to overflows from high tides as well as the rains draining off by that locality, have assisted our present epidemic. All of us have had colds—these have in some cases produced nervous, bilious and congestive fevers and occasionally death. One or two persons from N. Orleans have died, said to be "Yellow Jack" they must have brought with them. Answered ——— Simons letters to Jamaica.

Wednesday, October 5th, 1842: 76°–85°. Airs from S. and E. Reports of [October] 3rd unfounded—some stupidity or other. General Woll has returned to Rio Grande—our fellows, many of them, gone home for awhile to prepare in 20 or 30 days to go to Rio Grande.

Saturday, October 15th, 1842: 10 A.M. crossed ferry—at Hards found some "Videttes" who are watching on the coast suspecting a Mexican fleet off here, but this supposition is founded only upon some vague reports from N.O. 2 P.M.: Arrived Galveston. Galveston has been sickly since my absence and some deaths.

Sunday, October 16th, 1842: 8 A.M. 70°. During night, cool. Things here look gloomy: General Woll's advance upon San An-

---

[2] Bollaert's information is erroneous: neither Caldwell nor Mayfield was captured by General Woll's forces.

tonio, with the capture of some 50 of the citizens—the cutting up of the Lafayette Company—and altho' Captain [Jack] Hays took 2 of their guns etc.—beyond San Antonio, the want of unanimity among the other officers—Burleson, Mayfield, and Caldwell in not joining Captain H——. The Mexicans got their guns back and all have returned, some, it is supposed, to Matamoras with the prisoners made at San Antonio, the rest probably hovering about the Nueces. Our few volunteers prevented Woll marching, say upon Austin, and the fight at the "Salado" was disastrous to the Mexicans. It is thought by some that a general invasion by sea and land is intended, and by others that we are only to look upon all this, the object being to worry us. This last has been effected and the whole of the West may be looked upon as broken up—to this may be added: 1st, the violent and ruinous storm at Galveston and generally along the coast; 2nd, the "army worm" having eaten some 60 per cent of the cotton crop; 3rd, a few days since only another "norther" with continued and violent rains rendering the country and roads impassable to haul the little cotton already produced—thus it will be some weeks ere this last can be effected.

Our good friends in N. Orleans have got some reports from Mexico that, this time it is a "regular invasion" and are not very anxious in coming forward to assist us. Probably their own affairs are in a bad way—with all this we have no steamers or other boats running—thus we are without news.

Monday, October 17th, 1842: Wrote to Pringle per S[am] K[ennedy]. My other letters went by this opportunity—[the "Santana" to N. Orleans].

Tuesday, October 18th, 1842: Received Austin *Gazette* from Teulon—that paper now opposes the President—for several reasons, but more particularly that of removing the seat of Government. Teulon has accompanied General McLeod[3] towards

[3] Hugh McLeod was made commander of the Texan Santa Fé Expedition by Lamar on June 17, 1841. Later, he was captured with his men and marched over-

Red River but will be with Burleson in November, has left politics for awhile—has written to Pringle giving him the "sub-rosa"
state of parties.

The President then found it convenient to slope, which he did,
with the government!!! consisting of the President, his wife, and
a waggon laden with their baggage and papers and one or two
clerks. (The Archives still at Austin). The Secretary of State,
Anson Jones on the Brazos—sick or playing his own game—The
Secretary of the Treasury [William Henry Daingerfield] in the
United States—The Secretary of War and Marine in Galveston,
having resigned accepting the Commandancy of Ordnance. Well,
the Government arrived at "Washington" and on searching for
quarters, the President was informed that it was requested to pay
the week's board in advance—his melliferous accents had no
effect here—and it is said he had ultimately to return to the plantation of a friend with his wife and government.

Saturday, October 29th, 1842: Neptune Steamer [arrived] from
N. Orleans. The folk in N. Orleans are scared at the position of
Texas, will send no goods. The *Austin* and *Wharton* [are] hard
up in a clinch there. Santana's forces gone to Yucatan and may
succeed, then he will come and worry us. To retake Texas is another affair, but our position is desolate. There is a report of a
loan of 1 million of dollars by France.[4]

November 1st, 1842: Many persons having families are leaving
Galveston, fearing that Galveston may be attacked.

November 7th, 1842: Letters arrived from Velasco at nightfall stating that a fleet of vessels with steamers in company was
supposed to have been seen off that port. All the volunteers obeyed

land to Perote Prison in Mexico. Upon his return to Texas he served in the House
of Representatives and in 1844 moved to Galveston. During most of his adult
life he followed a military career, serving as adjutant general of Texas and a
colonel in the Texas Infantry during the Civil War. *Biographical Directory of
Texas Conventions and Congresses,* 132.

4 This loan, like several others Texas tried to negotiate, failed.

the tocsin which was rung at the Presbyterian Church. The different companies formed under their respective officers, and the greater part of them occupied all night in getting Colonel Hockley's fort on the east end of the island in order in case there should be any truth in the report. Anxiously we watched the morning's dawn on the 8th. I accompanied Simpton, the Pilot, to the Beacon; he climbed to the top, waited there until it was broad daylight, but no signs of the enemy.

November 11th, 1842: The *New York* Steamer brought us news that the Mexican fleet, composed of 10 sail[s], had left Vera Cruz for Yucatan, with promises to come to Galveston after the rebel Yucatecos are brought to their duty. The Texan squadron is still at N. Orleans and without the means to get to sea. The summer has left us and it is getting cold. NW gales set in; now we have the commencement of winter.

The British Government has ordered home all the British officers and seamen now in the Mexican service—this act is a battle gained for Texas.

November 27th, 1842: The Mexican Government *talking* of settling certain claims[5] of the United States Government, so as to keep the Yankees quiet. Santa Anna was at his Hacienda of "Manga de Clavo" awaiting his time to return to the City of Mexico with the rod of iron and punish the malcontents—i.e. the Federal party or *Patriots*, but his excesses will not be very great, if his army is not successful before Yucatan.

Little or no business doing; thus all those who are fond of sporting and hunting have ample means of enjoying themselves.

[5] United States claims against Mexico were for supplies of money, arms, and other things sold by citizens of the United States to the Mexican government during the revolution against Spain, and for damages to property and persons of the United States during revolutionary disturbances in Mexico. They amounted to more then eight and one-half million dollars. Mexico began payment in 1843, but soon defaulted. This action, technically at least, was one of the major causes of the Mexican War (1846–48). Samuel Flagg Bemis, *A Diplomatic History of the United States,* 236.

December 6th, 1842: Whilst out hunting camped out at "Dollar Point," Galveston Bay. The weather has been warm for the last few days and at this spot passed "una noche horrorosa" on account of mosquitos.

December 18th, 1842: The English Yacht *Dolphin* (Captain Houston) arrived from England. Captain H—— intends to purchase lands and form a settlement; he has not decided upon the whereabouts yet.[6]

December 31st, 1842: It would appear that Generals Woll and Ampudia are hovering about our frontier, awaiting any opportunity to make incursions. The President at last (to keep the peace at home) has appointed General Somervell to command the volunteers in their march westward. But there is some confusion in our camp. The people or the numberless volunteer officers wish to command; the President thinks he ought to have something to say in the matter! At last our army started, capturing Laredo December 8th and Guerrero laid under contribution. Somervell believing his forces too inadequate to do more, wished now to return homeward. Fisher was appointed Commanding Officer over those who remained. Fisher entered Mier, but ultimately had to capitulate—having fought a terrible fight.

January 8th, 1843: We are great news-mongers and the arrival of the Steamer from New Orleans always causes an "excitement." Today we hear that "John Chinaman" has had to knuckle down and poney up 21 millions of dollars, etc. and moreover, the establishment of British Consuls in the "Celestial Empire."[7]

Sunday, January 15th, 1843: General Long[8] came to Texas in

---

[6] Apparently Captain Houston never purchased any land in Texas; at least, there is no record of his settlement.

[7] This is in reference to the Opium War (1839–42) between Great Britain and China. The Treaty of Nanking, August 29, 1842, forced China to cede Hong Kong to Britain, open several other port cities to trade, establish a uniform import tariff of 5 per cent ad valorem, and pay £ 21,000,000. indemnity.

[8] Dr. James Long was the last of the filibusterers in Texas. His ill-fated attempt

1819 before Moses Austin. His intentions were to revolutionize and thus get a footing in Texas, but Moses Austin had funds and pushed his views with the Viceroy and [agreed] that he should bring Catholic families, etc. etc. Moses was a smart man!

General La Mar tells me that after Lafitte left Galveston, there are no authentic records concerning him, but it is probable he is dead.

Monday, January 23rd, 1843: Captain Downing H. Crisp went home in *San Juan.* Captain O'Bryant went over the Bar with him —1½fᵐ water, but we were not in mid-channel. Commodore Moore[9] has not given the correct soundings generally of the Bars and the fault is that he has given too much depth of water. Saw Count Boos Waldeck—he has purchased a league of land from Robert Mills for 5 cents p.a.—$3,600 and goes today to N.O. to purchase some 20 Negros.[10] Thus to commence—a few respectable families will come out and if the thing succeeds, then they will introduce a considerable emigration. Introduced Mr. Seauel [?] about sale of 7 Negros, etc.—Today weather very warm— of late thick fogs and heavy dews. Yacht *Dolphin* goes out today. . . . There is great excitement in Galveston against "Old Sam." A storm is brewing and I suppose his opponents will not rest until they have a new expedition across the Rio Grande.

Friday, January 27th, 1843: Some days since H. M. Sloop *Electra* came with dispatches to Captain [Charles] Elliot. Foggy

---

to establish a republic in the Spanish territory of Texas resulted in his surrendering to the Mexicans and eventually being shot on April 8, 1842, while in Mexico pleading his case to Agustín de Iturbide. Warren, *The Sword Was Their Passport,* 233–54.

9 Commodore Edwin Ward Moore surveyed the Texas coast and made a chart which was later published by the British Admiralty. Bollaert borrowed heavily from Moore's work in constructing his own maps and charts of the Texas Gulf Coast. He was able to correct many of Moore's errors relative to soundings.

10 Bollaert is in error: Count Boos Waldeck bought the league of land from Robert Mills of Brazoria County (January 9, 1843) for seventy-five cents an acre. The total purchase price was $3,321. For an account of the results of Boos Waldeck's colonizing efforts, see Biesele, *History of the German Settlements in Texas,* 68–71.

weather came on; she stood out to sea for a day or two—answers
to them were given and she is now off to Vera Cruz.

Monday, January 30th, 1843: A norther from the NNE set in.

Tuesday, January 31st, 1843: Blew hard all day; fine.

Wednesday, February 1st, 1843: The lowest tide I have ever
seen. Pelican Island flat, exposed, and the water out to the channel—cold.

Sunday, February 5th, 1843: Mr. William Kennedy, G. B. Consul for Galveston and its neighborhood arrived in Steamer *New
York*. Occupied with him in getting a house and putting it in
order. Sent commission to the President.

Wednesday, February 22nd, 1843: Mr. Kennedy received his
Exequatur from Washington.

Thursday, February 23rd, 1843: Mr. Kennedy sailed for N.
Orleans in *Neptune* for Mrs. K——. I received letters from home
—Sadie, Plimpton, Pringle.

March 2nd, 1843: Anniversary of Texas independence. The
Declaration of Independence was publicly read in the Presbyterian Church by Mr. Stewart,[11] and an historical oration by Mr.
Merriman.[12] Public dinners and balls in the evening. Good news
from Yucatan—Mexicans getting whipped; among the killed the
son of Santa Ana. The Federal party opposing Santa Ana and wish
to come to some terms with Texas. Saw letter from Poor Calhoun
from Perote[13] where he is working in chains and likely to do so

[11] This probably was Charles Bellinger Stewart, one of the signers of the Texas
Declaration of Independence and holder of several minor offices during the period
of the Republic. Kemp, *Signers of the Texas Declaration of Independence*, 16, 23,
193, 330–36.
[12] F. H. Merriman was appointed district attorney of Galveston by President
Houston on February 5, 1844. Houston, *The Writings of Sam Houston*, IV, 245.
[13] Several photographs of modern Perote Prison, where so many Texans were
imprisoned by the Mexicans, are reproduced in the *Southwestern Historical Quarterly*, Vol. XLVIII (1944–45), 340–45.

for some time. Fisher and the prisoners of Mier are marched into the interior. Volunteers paraded.

Monday, March 6th 1843: Norther from NE continues—very cold. No one seen in the streets. Workmen stop at home; paint or varnish won't dry. Our cistern has been dug too low and to increase my dilema I can't borrow a wheelbarrow. Life in Texas!

Sunday, March 12th, 1843: Neptune arrived bringing Mr. and Mrs. Kennedy.

Wednesday, March 15th, 1843: 12:30 P.M. a violent "Simmon" [simoom] from NNW and black clouds blowing up the sand into eddies. It had been warm during the morning—the temperature changed to nearly freezing point. The white squall lasted about an hour—then a violent rain, the wind continuing for another hour. The wind got round to N; now a "clear norther" and stopped raining. Gale from N continued all night—clear.

Thursday, March 16th, 1843: 7:30 A.M. temp: 30°–23°; in my room top of house 28°. Clear sky—sun shining strong and wind abated. During the great blow of yesterday one of Dollard's Bar: stood at 29.75. Ice ½ inch thick. The coldest night this season. Clear all day.

Monday, March 20th, 1843: Sharp N wind with rain and cold. 8 P.M.: It is now blowing in strong, N and W—cold. We hope soon to have fine weather. Last year at the latter end of February it was fine and warm and spring was with us. This has been a very long winter.

Under this date I find amongst my notes an extract from an official communication from the Texan Minister to the Government of the United States, when speaking of the failure of entering into a commercial treaty with the United States[14]—the result

---

[14] That the treaty had failed—slander has performed its office! its work is complete—this is attributed to the "War Party."—Bollaert.

is that the Texan government has put *an additional* duty *ad valorem* of five per cent on all goods imported in foreign bottoms, with the exception of those foreign vessels which by treaty or act of Congress are permitted to enter on payment of the domestic duty. Thus, Texas having no commercial treaty with the United States is now obliged to pay five per cent more duty than England, France, Belgium, Holland and the Hanseatic States. Moreover, the tonage dues on the steamers from New Orleans we increased.

Tuesday, March 21st, 1843: Some days since Messrs. Andrews[15] and Lee came from Houston—they having been on a sort of "abolition crusade" on the Brazos etc.—they called a meeting in Houston, explaining that a great many planters (which does not seem to be the case) would emancipate their slaves, could, say English capitalists (the government or any of the Wilberforcians) purchase their freedom. At Houston this measure seems to have met with no opposition, but on the arrival of the said abolitionists their views met with no friendly "accueilli" and the majority of the mobocracy of this place (and who hold no slaves) threatened the parties with lynching and tar and feathering. Today (21), Gail Borden[,] Syndor etc. etc. wished to give Andrews a public hearing, but the glorious sovereign mob politely put Mr. Andrews into a boat and sent him across the bay to find his way to Houston. Mr. Lee had "sloped" up by the last boat. There is more in this question than meets the eye. Captain E[lliot] was accused of having something to do with it, but this is not true. British foreign employers are not to meddle with local affairs, and this one on the subject of abolition the "Southerners" get very mad upon. Bow-wow, says the Texan!

March 29th, 1843: Wrote to Sadie and Pringle.

[15] Stephen Pearl Andrews was a prominent lawyer in Houston at this period. Because of his abolitionist leanings, his home was destroyed by a mob in 1843, and soon afterwards he left for England. In 1847 he returned to the United States and settled in New York. He was a well-known linguist and writer.

March 31st, 1843: Put up papers for Pringle—Crisp. By *Dolphin* Captain Houston sails today by Havana to England. Viscount Cramayel[16] sails with Captain H——. Captain Elliot went up yesterday to Washington; Judge Robinson[17] likewise.

April 5th, 1843: Pleasant weather commencing. Gave letters of introduction to Major Sam Whiting[18]—for Evora—Huber—Sorgente—Leininger—Leckee go by the Bremen vessel to Europe.

April 15th 1843: Captain E[lliot] returned from Washington. The President *close* about his proceedings with regard to Mexico.

April 20th, 1843: Wrote to Mr. Leckee and home thro' Pringle, C. Plimpton by "Troubadour," Captain McDonall—for Liverpool. Under date of January 10th, Washington, U. S. Texas Minister Van Zandt[19] wrote to his Government that the treaty[20] has failed. Slander has performed its office! Its work is complete. This is the "War Party's doing." This same party—after its warlike

[16] Jules Edouard de Cramayel was French chargé d'affaires in Texas from 1842 until 1844, during the absence of Alphonse de Saligny. *The Writings of Sam Houston,* II, 443.

[17] This probably was James W. Robinson, formerly judge of the Fourth Judicial District of Texas. Robinson was captured by Adrian Woll on September 12, 1842, along with members of the court which was meeting in San Antonio at the time of the Mexican invasion. Santa Anna released him from prison and allowed him to return to Texas with terms for an agreement between Texas and Mexico. Robinson reached Galveston on March 27, 1843, and was probably responsible for the negotiations which resulted in an armistice of several months between Texas and Mexico. *Comprehensive History of Texas,* 215.

[18] Samuel Whiting was the founder and publisher of newspapers at Houston and Austin (1838–42). He broke with Houston over the removal of the archives from Austin, went to Europe in 1843, and did not return to Texas until 1849. He moved to California that same year. Joe B. Frantz, "The Newspapers of the Republic of Texas" (unpublished M.A. thesis, University of Texas, 1940).

[19] Houston appointed Isaac Van Zandt chargé d'affaires to the United States in 1842. During his two years' residence in Washington he worked hard for annexation of Texas to the United States. When this measure was assured, he resigned the office and returned home. He was one of the Republic's most farsighted statesmen. *The Writings of Sam Houston,* III, 113.

[20] The treaty that Bollaert is referring to was the one of Amity, Commerce, and Navigation, concluded at Washington on July 30, 1842, between Texas and the United States. It was turned down by the United States Senate because of the "internal conditions in Texas." See footnote 52, Chapter VI.

wishes were not countenanced—got up another excitement, "The Archive Party." The President, considering these precious documents unsafe at Austin, wished to remove them. This was opposed by the "Archive Party." Then we have the same individuals forming the "Seat of Government Party." Anyhow the worrying of the opposition! The *Texan and Brazos Farmer*[21] of 18th April shewing that Washington is constitutionally the seat of Congress—that locality, the government at Houston and Austin, was unconstitutional.

April 26th, 1843: Mr. Attorney General Terrell[22] dined with us—he has been some time on the "Indian Frontier" and has arranged a treaty of peace with many of the tribes. The Comanche appear inclined to peace now. Prisoners were exchanged—but two Indian women did not appear gratified to return to the woods.

Judge Terrell brought the Delaware Chief Saint Louis and Oahquash, the Waco Chief, to Galveston on a party of pleasure principally—to see the ocean and buy a few goods for them to take back, as they call it, to the "Wild Indians."[23] They speak English very well—intelligent—polite and gentlemanly. I accompanied one to make a purchase of 5 pounds of vermillion to sell to the "Wild Indians." It is curious that the "War Party" were against the Indians; thus they kept up their scalping, and all reason. Old Sam's plan is the best.

The Comanches would have come in but they were on an expedition taking 300 Mexican prisoners in to "exchange and ransom."

[21] The *Texian and Brazos Farmer* was published at Washington-on-the-Brazos from 1842 to 1843. The complete files of this newspaper are on deposit in the Newspaper Collection, University of Texas Library.

[22] George Whitfield Terrell served in the Tennessee Legislature from 1829 to 1836. He moved to Texas in 1837. He served as secretary of state of Texas under David G. Burnet, and was made attorney general of the Republic by Houston in 1841. From 1842 to 1844 he was Indian commissioner for Texas and as such negotiated several treaties with the Indians. Later, he served as Texas's diplomatic representative to France, Great Britain, and Spain. *The Writings of Sam Houston,* II, 366.

[23] See *Texian and Brazos Farmer* (April 15, 1843) for particulars and speeches of the Two Chiefs before General Houston at Washington[-on-the-Brazos] where they had come to see "The Great White Chief."—Bollaert.

They were unwilling to come in at first; they will not easily forget the killing of their chiefs at the Court House in San Antonio,[24] but by persuasion of friendly chiefs of Texas they may be made to be interested to come in. After all treaties of peace with Indians ought always be kept up by our having an armed force always ready to act rigidly with them when they are the aggressor. If we commence, we must not complain.

At last the Texan fleet, or as it appears to me, Commodore Moore's fleet, reduced to two vessels—the *Austin* and Brig *Wharton*—have left New Orleans with 500 "desperate fellows," having been assisted by Yucatan with some cash. It was said that we should see Moore off here—for what? It is more probable that he has gone direct to Yucatan. Now or never, Moore, for your own sake, you must conquer, or die, or take one of the Mexican steamers. Colonel Morgan[25] left this about 3 weeks since for N. Orleans with orders from the Executive to stop the sailing of the vessels to Yucatan, sell them or bring them here. If Moore is acting on his own responsibility, or backed by the U.S. Government or the N. Orleans folk in any way, and succeeds, then all will go right. Should he fail, there will be the devil to pay and no pitch *hot*.[26]

After Van Zandt's excellent letter relative to the non-ratification of the treaty, I can hardly think that the U. S. Government

[24] The Court House Fight (Council House Fight) occurred in San Antonio on March 19, 1840. About sixty-five Indians, including women and children, gathered at the court house for a council with a Texas delegation headed by Hugh McLeod and William G. Cooke. Three companies of infantry under the command of William S. Fisher stood by. A fight ensued when the white delegation disputed the Indians' claim of holding only one white captive. Thirty-five Indians were killed, along with seven whites. This action destroyed the waning confidence of the Indians in the Texan government, making future friendly relations almost impossible. Rupert Norval Richardson, *The Comanche Barrier to South Plains Settlements*, 109–11.

[25] Colonel James Morgan (see footnote 13, Chapter VII), with William Bryan, was charged with the secret sale of the Texas Navy. He became *persona non grata* with Houston after his defection to Moore.

[26] Moore persuaded Morgan to go to Yucatan and sell the vessels there—taking Morgan along, and in the event of falling in with any Mexican vessels to take them. [William] Bryan is associated with Morgan in the Naval Commission. Sam Williams was offered, but refused.—Bollaert.

would sub-rosa edge Moore on to anything that might compromise them. There are people in N. Orleans who say, "The Government of Texas is a joke and everything connected with that country is below par." Let the Yankees look at home at their own jokes relative to financiering and repudiation. Let us suppose the worst case, that Houston is a traitor: the cotton and corn will still grow —the stock will increase, and the men who have fought for so fair a land will not relinquish it to appease political party spirit. O no! The New Orleanites may think so, but they are very much mistaken birds—very fond of flying kites!

Saturday, April 30th, 1843: A few citizens gave a chowder party of some 7 or 8 of the heroes of San Jacinto, General La Mar happening to be here. The British Chargé d'Affairs, Captain Elliot— Messrs. (the Consuls) Kennedy, Klaener,[27] Cobb,[28] and a few invités assisting. The party was held at Hockley's fort in what was formerly used as the powder magazine. On our arrival at 3 P. M. some of the party were preparing the chowder—that is—they had caught some fish and these been well cleaned etc. First some fat pork and sliced onion browned in the iron kettle—these taken out—then layers of fish, potatoes, onions, pork and biscu[i]t, with plenty pepper and salt and a little water—all boiled for say an hour and then the "chowder" or an American version of *tuia-lai* with improvements ready for the table. During the height of the cooking, a drenching rain came on, nearly put the fire out. It soon cleared off. Each one appropriated a spoon and plate and having pretty good appetites managed to get through a tolerable quantity. There were plenty wines and liquors and the chowder party wound up by General Lamar giving a very appropriate sentiment for the occasion and drinking a mint julep—we then all tipped off to town.

[27] This was D. Klaenner, consul of Bremen for the port of Galveston in 1843. Diplomatic Correspondence of the Republic of Texas, III, 1578 (MS. in the Texas State Archives).

[28] Henry Adolph Cobb was vice-consul of France for Galveston and St. Louis. *Ibid.*, 1361.

The *Texas Times* is wound up[29]—I believe I am the only one who has a copy of the last Thursday's number. The "War Party" and "Malcontents" could not afford to subsidize any longer. Its politics were too wild for me, but [Ferdinand] Pinckard bestowed much pains upon the literary part.

May 1st 1843: May day festival at Galveston. Review of troops on the Island—all but the "Coast Guards." The young ladies of the town fetched their "Queen," Miss Martha Wynn, from her house to the place appropriated for the ceremony—with music and song. The four "Seasons" complemented her—she was then crowned and all had a dance round the May pole. A dance in the evening concluded the ceremony. This old English custom of the celebration of May day has been introduced of late years into the U.S. and from thence into Texas.

May 2nd, 1843: During a ride with Mr. Attorney General Terrell, he mentioned that he had been a successful competitor as a Representative in the U.S.[30] This made Crockett very sour with him. Crockett is a strange man—a mighty hunter, but rather "smart" than really good. He had little or no political consistency or honesty—and was not looked upon by his friends as a very brave man—wanting moral courage. With regard to the "Alamo" —when the inmates found that the hordes of Mexicans would not receive their flag of truce, then Crockett and the rest did their best.

A son of Poor David is a Representative in the U.S. and very highly spoken of.[31] The Coon Skin story is true.

[29] The *Texas Times*, a strongly anti-Houston paper, was published weekly in Galveston by D. Davis and Ferdinand Pinckard from October 12, 1842, to April 22, 1843. Lota M. Spell, "Samuel Bangs: The First Printer in Texas," *Southwestern Historical Quarterly*, Vol. XXXV (1931-32), 267-78.

[30] Terrell served in the Tennessee House of Representatives and not in the United States Congress as Bollaert's sentence implies. He was a Houston and Jackson man, which accounts for his political differences with David Crockett.

[31] David Crockett's son referred to here is John Wesley Crockett (1807-57), who served in the United States Congress from 1837 to 1841. From 1841 to 1843, he was attorney general for the Ninth District in Tennessee, then moved to New Orleans, where he became editor of the *National. Biographical Directory of the American Congress, 1774-1927,* 862.

Thursday, May 4th, 1843: H. B. M. Sloop of 28 guns—the Honorable Captain Elliot—[arrived] from Vera Cruz. Merida,[32] it is said, has capitulated and thus fallen into the hands of the Mexicans. The Yucatecos getting the worst of it just now. There has been treachery on the part of Iman[33] the commander of the native forces. But Moore is now off there by this time. His motto must [be] "sink or swim."

Wednesday, May 10th, 1843: Per *Neptune* news that the Mier prisoners had been decimated by Santana. There were 170 of them, thus 17 have been shot. This news [the "black bean episode"] has produced a gloom indeed here. In the escape of the Mier prisoners 5 Texans fell and 25 Mexicans killed; 113 took the road to Texas—they were ultimately obliged to surrender to a very large force, when Santana ordered them *all* to be shot. This was not carried into execution but they were decimated and 17 shot on the 25th March at the Salado near Saltillo.[34]

Wednesday, May 17th, 1843: Gun Boat *Republicano* 6 days from Yucatan with dispatches for the Government corroborates the news [of Commodore Moore's successes in Yucatán] and brings accounts of the *Wharton* having engaged the two steamers. Two salutes fired by the Galvestonians—all "excitement," brought letter from a Mr. Gordon dated Ship *Austin* corroborate the operations there.

Throughout the spring of 1843 Houston was bending every effort

[32] Merida is the capital of the Mexican state of Yucatán.

[33] According to Bancroft, Iman, a militia officer, raised the standard of revolt at Tizimin in May, 1839. After several unsuccessful movements made with untrained men, he was able, in 1840, to capture Valladolid. This success gave importance to the Yucatecan cause. "Iman was proclaimed provisional commandante general, and a governing council assumed charge until Governor Cosgaya entered office." Hubert Howe Bancroft, *History of Mexico*, V, 218, 218n.

[34] According to authoritative accounts of the Mier episode, 179 Texans were captured, 3 made good their escape, but 176 were returned to Salado. Seventeen men were selected for execution, and later Ewen Cameron, the leader of the break, was also executed. John R. Alexander, "Account of the Mier Expedition" (MS., Archives Collection, University of Texas Library).

*to prevent further belligerent action with Mexico which might
complicate matters and lead to trouble for the United States. The
latter was attempting to bring about a cessation of hostilities between the two southern republics. Meanwhile, Commodore
Moore was in New Orleans supervising the refitting of the Texas
fleet, now composed of the* Austin *and the* Wharton. *The Secretary of Navy wrote Moore (upon Houston's orders) that if he
could not refit to go to sea, he should return to Galveston.
But the Commodore, fearing that the fleet would be sold from
under him, ignored the orders and renewed negotiations with
Yucatán. Three commissioners—William Bryan, Samuel M.
Williams, and James Morgan—had been sent to New Orleans to
bring Moore back. But Moore talked them into letting him go
and, in fact, Morgan accompanied the fleet on its last cruise.
On April 30, 1843, the Texas Navy engaged two large modern
steamers of the Mexican fleet in an indecisive battle. Other engagements followed on May 2 and May 16.*

*When the President discovered that Commodore Moore, as
well as his commissioners, had disobeyed his orders, he published
a proclamation proclaiming the navy to be pirates and requesting
any friendly country to capture the ships and return them to Galveston. Ultimately the news reached Moore and he set sail immediately, docking at Galveston on July 14, 1843, where he was
hailed as a hero by Houston's enemies.*[35]

May 20th, 1843: The "War Party" meet to express their "admiration and gratitude to [Commodore] Moore, [Colonel]
Morgan, officers, and men" of expedition.

The important effects produced by Commodore Moore [are]:
1st. He has beaten off the Mexican fleet from before Yucatan—
causing at least much injury to the Montezuma—and daring them
to approach the coast. Had he had but one steamer to have

[35] See *Brazos Farmer* of—[for] Houston's Proclamation against Commodore
Moore under date March and letter to him of March 23rd and instructions to
James Morgan and Wm. Bryan, Commissioners. The opposition say it is all a
trick of Old Sam's, and that Morgan accompanies Moore to Yucatan of his own
free will to sell the fleet.—Bollaert.

brought him into action, the Mexican Squadron would have been taken. 2nd. Moore has raised the seige of Yucatan [and] he has given confidence to the brave Yucatecos. Medez has discovered the cunning and falsity of Ampudia and thus the Mexican general must capitulate. 3rd. Moore will have prevented the transports with reinforcements from joining Ampudia and will in all probability make prizes of them. 4th. Thus, we may look upon Santana's operations against Yucatan as having failed—and moreover, the most important point—no invasion of Texas at least by sea can take place.

It is suggested that all Mexicans taken in the War against Yucatan—will be exchanged for the Texans now in chains in Mexico.

Wednesday, May 24th, 1843: Anniversary of Her Majesty's birthday. Aged 24. At sunrise the French, German, and American Consuls hoisted their flags and the Texan flag floated over the Tremont in honor of Her Majesty. Ships in the harbour likewise. Mr. Kennedy hoisted the British flag. At 5 P.M. the foreign consuls, collectors, mayor and Mr. Low sat down to dinner—and a joyous party it was. It was after midnight when the toasts, songs, and plenty of the finest wine had been quaffed, the party broke up with blessings on the Queen.

In some parts of the U. S. when maiz has been scarce, wheaten bread was given to the Negros. They complained that they did not thrive upon it and a planter in Virginia had to send 50 miles for maiz for his Negros. The Negro it is said could not do his quantity of work upon wheaten bread. This may be so. I am not fastidious with regard to food, but hunger alone can make me eat the common corn bread. When milk and eggs are added, it is then more palatable—butter being added. Upon persons unaccustomed to corn bread it produces a relaxed state of the bowels. The effect was compared "as if one had a cargo of juvenile scrubbing brushes in one's stomach." It is probable that independent of the mechanical action, there may be some diarrhetic property in the maiz. When "chicha" (a fermented drink made from

171

maiz) is allowed to stand, a yellow oleaginous matter floats up to its surface, and of a slight aromatic odour. Vide Journal in Peru.

Steamer *New York* brings reports that Sam Houston had been burned in effigy in N. Orleans and that Santa Ana had sent a bribe of $25,000 to Old Sam. What twaddle! The few malcontents that now remain jump at such yarns and expuitions and magnify them extravagantly.

Saturday, May 27th, 1843: Disturbances in Mexico against Santa Ana. In Guadalaxara headed by General [Mariano] Paredes, in the South by [Juan] Alvarez and [Valentino]Guzmán —with [Nicolas] Bravo concerned in all. In the City of Mexico the principals are in prison.

Fear is entertained that the Apaches may even get down and pillage Matamoras. They have done so before—said to be 3,000 strong and supposed probable that Cameron[36] and some of the Mier prisoners are with them "ordered and assisting."

There are reports afloat in the U. S. that Seeger[37] and some of his officers have been killed and that the *San Antonio* may have turned pirate.

Monday, May 29th, 1843: 8 A.M. 70°. Airs NE, slight showers. When we have these beneficial rains—for water and our gardens —the air is cooled, and sometimes even in summer [we have] a clear "norther," but these are rare and not strong. 8 P.M. A dry norther set in; cool and pleasant.

Wednesday, May 31st, 1843: Weather fine—crops look thriving—but fears are entertained that the rivers may rise.

Under date of 20th April General Santana provisional President, or Dictator of Mexico notified to the foreign ministers in

[36]Ewen Cameron was shot on April 25, 1843, by orders of General Santa Anna. He could not have been leading a band of Apaches, as Bollaert suggests.

[37] In September, 1842, Commodore Moore sent William Seeger, in command of the *San Antonio*, to Yucatán to obtain money for the use of the Texas Navy. The ship never reached its destination and is presumed to have been lost in a storm. Hill, *The Texas Navy*, 162–64, 170.

Mexico that he will not answer the claims made in favour of foreign emigrants made prisoners by Mexican soldiers, that they would be treated as enemies and punished accordingly—moreover that Foreign consuls in Texas will not be allowed any other rights than neutral foreigners and even this Santa Anna calls a concession. The Foreign Minister protested against this, and the Texans look upon it as another specimen of Mexican bombast.

On June 1, 1843, Bollaert accompanied five British friends to New Orleans on the steamer New York. *The purpose of the voyage is not divulged in his brief and somewhat illegible account of the event. "During my stay in N.O.," he writes, "it was hot, then heavy rains and miserable weather. It is a real Babylon and unique . . . smart and melancholy." The day before Bollaert's return to Galveston on June 16, 1843 the chargé d'affaires of England in Texas had communicated to Houston the news from the English minister in Mexico that "the President of Mexico would forthwith order a cessation of hostilities, on his part, and the establishment of an armistice between Mexico and Texas, and requested that the President of Texas would send similar orders to different officers, commanding the Texas forces."*

Houston had been delighted with the prospect of peace at last, and promptly issued a proclamation declaring hostilities at an end. Nor did he pass up the opportunity, at the same time, of publicizing the fact that it was England, and not the United States, that had notified Texas that the armistice had been arranged with Mexico. At this time Texas agents were pressing for annexation, and Old Sam knew how to play off England against the United States.

Bollaert found Galveston, except for Houston's enemies, relieved over the news of the armistice. But he, like many other Texans, was bitter that the United States had done little or nothing to help Texas through the recent tribulations.

Tuesday, June 20th, 1843: Sam's Proclamation of Armistice with Mexico arrived. President Houston has had faith in the good offices of Old England—he has signed the Proclamation for an Armistice with Mexico (dated Washington[-on-the-Brazos] 15th June 1843). Neither Monsieur Cramayel[38] or General Murphy[39] can feel very much complemented in relation to it—the former particularly. But Jonathan ["Uncle Sam"] will be very sore, considering his Government's peculiar views at the present moment. Why did not the U.S. Government come out boldly and nurse its offspring? O no! that would not suit parties. Why did not the U. S. sign the treaty of Commerce with Texas as F[rance], E[ngland], and H[olland] has done? O no, always playing "possum"—in fact the Proclamation shews that old Grandmother England will at last get a peace for this country. The "Right down Easterners" and loafers already see the British Flag hoisted! that is the "War Party" (the remains of them) and as a matter of course condemn all Houston's acts.

French Sloop of War *Brilliante* arrived yesterday from Vera Cruz 8 days. H. B. Sloop *Scylla* fired a salute in commemoration of H. M. *Accesion*—answered by the *Brilliante*.

Wednesday, June 21st, 1843: Jones[40] arrived from C. Christi. One Sanchez, a Mexican, had set the Karonks on to kill Jones— they met in his craft laden with tobacco, etc., fired at him and two others, but steered off. The Comanches have been down about C. Christi and taken several persons into captivity and killed one man. The Comanches killed some Karonks. There are only some dozen individuals of the Karonks at C. Christi and another small remnant at Matagorda.

[38] Jules Edouard de Cramayel (see footnote 16 above) was probably responsible for Texas' failure to secure a million-dollar loan from France in 1843, because of his unfavorable reports on Texas to his government.

[39] William Sumter Murphy was appointed United States minister extraordinary to Central America and chargé d'affaires to Texas in 1843. He later helped promote President John Tyler's plan for the annexation of Texas, doubtless prompted by his belief that England was exercising too much influence over Texas and President Houston. *The Writings of Sam Houston*, IV, 233.

[40] This was probably one of the members of the firm of Frankland and Jones, which operated the largest mercantile business in Galveston in 1843. See footnote 41 below.

Thursday, June 22nd, 1843: H. B. Sloop *Scylla* left for Vera Cruz with Sam Houston's Proclamation of the Armistice with Mexico.

Saturday, June 24th, 1843: Weather fine and seasonable—not like last year. Crops look well and great plenty as well as peace expected—thus the emigrant will find beef, bacon, corn, etc. reasonable in the fall when there is no doubt but they will come in. Now [that] there is a chance of peace the beautiful West will be re-settled.

Monday, June 26th, 1843: Correspondence with Messrs. F[rankland] and Jones relative to *Caroline* and *Antoinette*. Mr. K[ennedy] suggested the propriety of stopping *Caroline*—which was acceded to by Collector of Customs. 9 P.M.: insolent visit of Mr. Jones to Mr. K——.[41]

Tuesday, June 27th, 1843: 8 A.M. arrest of *Caroline* removed. Mr. Jones sent Mr. K—— two insulting letters. Afternoon the *Caroline* under new name of *Sarah Barnes* left for N. Orleans. Heavy rains from SSE and SW during this month.

Northern people complain of the want of twilight in tropical countries, but how beneficent Providence has been about this—for if the nights in the tropics were not so long—the days particularly would be unsuf[f]erably hot—and probably unfit for the residence of man.

July 3rd, 1843: Under superintendence of Mr. Moss a series of small "Tableaux Vivants" produced by some of the ladies and gentlemen of Galveston.

[41] Frankland and Jones Company was a British concern which feuded with Kennedy during the latter's entire residence in Galveston. On May 29, 1844, Kennedy complained to Lord Aberdeen that this company was engaged in the illegal slave trade. Kennedy to Aberdeen, Galveston, May 29, 1844, as quoted in Ephraim Douglass Adams, ed., "British Correspondence Concerning Texas," *Southwestern Historical Quarterly*, Vol. XVIII (1913–14), 322–23.

July 4th, 1843: Chowder party at Point, near bank, building "Houston" fort; fired a gun from "Hockley's" fort, reached to the wreck of the *Cuba.*

July 8th, 1843: During night heavy rains and sultry. If this continues it will do the crops no good. For some days past we have had a few mosquitos and their persecutors, the "Mosquito Hawk" (Dragon Fly). I do not recollect meeting with this strange and somewhat beautiful insect in South America. It is about 3½ inches long—thick round head—coloured black, blue—deep and light green, a very large mouth or at least the trap to catch its prey, with two pairs of strong claws within it to kill the captive insect. The body is about 3 times the size of the head—rich brown colour and green stripes into which is inserted 4 long wings of more than 2 inches long of most exquisite workmanship. Then follows a long tail 2½ inches long—narrow and pipe like—black with green stripes across ways—at the end of the tail there is a protuberance, and moreover, two others like paddles sticking out —joined by a black web—this I suppose acts like a rudder. This insect has 6 long and strong black legs—fly with celerity through the air and sometimes make a slight ———— in the face if held in the hand without care—will bite, but leaves no mark or causes swelling or pain. The interior of the body is composed of thick yellow muscular matter.[42]

Friday, July 14th, 1843: Ship *Austin* and Brig *Austin* [*Wharton*] hove in sight off the bar at daylight from Yucatan. During the morning came to anchor off the town, the ship under Commodore Moore, *Wharton* under Louthrop.[43] The Volunteer companies turned out to welcome the arrival of the ships, when there was a considerable quantity of saluting. The Commodore and

[42] When mosquitos, flies, and spiders are caught and presented to the Mosquito Hawk, he eats them voraciously. Such is its formation that in flying through the air he falls short of his prey.—Bollaert.

[43] J. T. K. Louthrop was the commander of the *Wharton* in the battle off Campeche, and was later dismissed from the navy with a dishonorable discharge along with Commodore Moore. Hill, *The Texas Navy,* 185.

principal officers and Colonel Morgan came on shore, when the sherry cobblers, mint julips, etc., went to work. The whole of the Mexican forces have left Yucatan—so Santana's campaigns there have been fruitless. Moore is still under the ban of the President's proclamation, and I hear he has given himself up to the Sheriff. Some say he will get hell and scissors others that he will get through it.

Sunday, July 16th, 1843: Dined on board *Austin*. She looks in good sea trim and her crew quiet and orderly. Col. C. touched upon the hanging of the 3 mutineers and murderers of the *San Antonio,* observing that M[oore] had the power, but did not explain.[44] The Commodore, among other things, shewed me Don Tomas Marin's (the commander on board the *Guadalupe* Steamer) bombastic challenge to go out and fight him. Whenever the Texans had a chance they went out, but calms and light airs is not the way to try sails versus steam—with a snorting breeze the *Austin* and *Wharton* would have in all probability taken the steamers. The Yucatecos are very poor, consequent upon the long war with Mexico, yet they behaved well to Moore—they repaired his damages, and gave him some money—2 or $3,000—to pay his men off, which will be done in a few days. The new men he shipped he paid $20 bounty and took them for 6 months. At the period he shipped his men the U. S. Navy was paying $75 bounty. Moore speaks well of his crew and the orderly behaviour of those which I witnessed is creditable indeed—saw some without arms —poor stumps.[45]

The great quantity of firing on board *Austin*—4 guns being placed in the cabin—did not affect the chronometers (Arnold and Dents).

Sunday, July 23rd, 1843: H. B. Sloop *Scylla*, Captain Sharpe,

[44] In February, 1842, while the *San Antonio* was being refitted in New Orleans, a mutiny occurred. The crew, led by a marine sergeant, armed themselves and attacked the officers, killing one. The mutineers were quickly captured by United States authorities. Three of them were hanged by orders of Commodore Moore. *Ibid.*

came to anchor in the evening outside the bar. 11 P.M., Mr. Gifford, H. B. M. Vice Consul for Matamoras, came on shore from the Sloop on his way to that place expecting to find probably some opportunity from this.

Monday, July 24th, 1843: Captain Sharpe brought dispatches from Mexico from H. M. Charge there to H. M. Charge here for the Government of Texas.

Tuesday, July 25th 1843: President Houston burnt this night in effigy by the remains of the malcontents and Moore's friends for this day. Commodore Moore received thro' Bryant [William Bryan] and [William C.] Brashear (Navy Commissioners) a "dishonorable dismissal" in which he is accused of murder (hanging the mutineers who killed Lieutenant Taller), disobedience of orders, and piracy. Moore and Morgan have written defences of their conduct.[46]

Wednesday, July 26th, 1843: A court martial was called by the Secretary of War and Marine to assemble the evidence by 1844 for the trial of Commodore Moore and such others as may be properly brought before it. The court to consist of [Sidney] Sherman, [Alexander] Somervell, [Edwin] Morehouse, [Robert James] Calder, [James] Reily, [William] Hardin, [William B.] Hamilton, and [Daniel] Montague.

Wrote 25th to Sadie and Pringle—preparing to start to San Antonio.

August 6th, 1843: The *John Barnes*, formerly the *Antoinette*, property of Frankland and Company of Galveston, the first vessel with Texas colours that has sailed to Liverpool.

August 7th, 1843: Left Galveston for a tour in the interior.

45 There will be no pensions.—Bollaert.
46 See *Houston Morning Star*, July 25th, 1843.—Bollaert.

IX

AUSTIN AND BACK TO COLUMBUS

[*August–September, 1843*]

August 7th, 1843: Having explored the Coast and part of Eastern Texas, I started for the West. Leaving Galveston and being ferried over to Virginia Point;[1] it is only low prairie to Houston. A new road is now forming by Richmond on the Brazos River to the western country which is nearer than that by Houston. In the prairies large horse flies and mosquitos were in abundance which must be very troublesome to the stock. There are a few farms on Dickensons, Clear, Jim's and Bray's Creeks. "Austina" and "San Leon"[2] are marked on the map as towns; they do not exist as yet.

August 8th, 1843: At Houston. When this place was the seat of Government and Congress held here, it was a gay and bustling place. Now the Capital has been turned into an hotel, but where a good piece of roast beef may be obtained for dinner. Some of the trade of Houston has been taken from it, by the establishment of commercial houses on Trinity River, and the navigation of the Brazos by a steamer, yet there are cotton planters and farmers enough in its vicinity and even out of it who will bring

[1] Virginia Point is on the mainland side of the West Bay in Galveston County; it is located at the west end of the old Galveston causeway. A small village containing one store and a population of twenty was still there as late as 1950. The route which Bollaert pursued to Austin followed a well traveled road from Houston, via Richmond, Columbus, La Grange, and Bastrop. Most of the Houston-to-Columbus road paralleled present United States Highway 90. From Columbus to Austin, the road followed present State Highway 71.

[2] Austinia was in Galveston County on the north side of Galveston Bay. It was reputed to have a railroad in 1839 which ran to Bolivar on the Brazos, although Bollaert makes no mention of any railroad in existence in Texas during his travels. Presumably Austinia was a town for a few years, but no evidence of its remains exists today. San Leon did materialize, although it was washed away in floods of 1900 and 1915. According to the 1950 census it contained a population of one hundred people. It is located in northeastern Galveston County. *The Handbook of Texas,* I, 90; II, 557.

their cotton and other produce to Houston. Cash is very scarce, barter is nearly the only medium of trade.

August 10th, 1843: Left for Columbus on the River Colorado. Some 18 miles of low prairie, with the timbers of Buffalo Bayou on the right; forded the bayou (creek). During and after heavy rains these creeks are not fordable and in some parts of the low country, what with the water in the bottoms swamps and creeks, the roads are rendered impassable for weeks. Buffalo bayou from here takes a S.W. course a considerable distance, with timbers on either side. Continuing my journey onwards over prairie, passing "Pine Island"[3] and some small settlements the vicinity of the Brazos River is attained. I put up at Mr. M——'s on Marsh Creek, at a snug farm but rather low in case of heavy freshet in the Brazos. The land all about here is very rich, but like many of the "bottoms"[4] subject to overflows; when these take place stock, plantations, and families suffer much; people are lured to this very rich soil, but it would be more judicious of them to settle more towards the prairie or on high land; where they would escape fever from miasma engendered by the almost tropical heat, causing decomposition of vegetable matters. My host, Mr. M.,[5] gave me a graphic and interesting account of the late Captain Holliday's miraculous escape from the Mexicans,[6] during the massacre of Fannin and his party. His adventures were of the most strange

[3] The term "Island" is often given to clumps of trees in the prairies.—Bollaert.
Pine Island in north central Jefferson County, boasted a post office in 1840. The town never amounted to very much because of its proximity to Houston, and today it is little more than a conditional flag stop and siding on the Texas and New Orleans Railroad.
[4] The alluvial soil on the margins of rivers.—Bollaert.
[5] Mr. M—— was going part of my route with two gentlemen from Mississippi to purchase lands on the La Baca [Lavaca] River, of which part of the country they had had a good report. Their intention was to get suitable locations, and then return for their families.—Bollaert.
[6] Captain John J. Holliday was one of the approximately two dozen men that escaped from the famous Goliad Massacre in 1836, by swimming the river and concealing himself until the departure of the Mexicans from the area. Bollaert's notes on his subsequent adventures and death are correct. Herbert Davenport, "Notes from an Unfinished Study and Fannin and His Men" (MS., Archives Collection, University of Texas Library).

and at times comical nature; he ultimately got to Velasco. He had joined the Santa Fé Expedition, had been imprisoned in Mexico some time and died of black vomit on board a vessel a few days ere he reached Galveston, after his liberation with the rest of the Santa Fé prisoners.

August 11th 1843: Ferried over the Brazos River, which has a pretty good width and depth.[7] On the western side stands the remains of San Felipe de Austin; it is now a "deserted village." One or two families reside here only; weeds and bushes have grown up in the streets and unoccupied lots, so that one has a difficulty in tracing his way to the main road on the opposite side of the town. To the right of the town is seen where the Father of Texas, S. F. Austin[8] resided, and doubtless the locality of the maturing of his patriotic measures for a fine country he and his father had called into existence and of inviting to it as a home his countrymen and the stranger.[9] The house appeared to be in good repair, the fields full of corn and cotton and apparently a good orchard, and it was rendered picturesque, standing on a bluff and surrounded with trees.[10]

The prairies are now higher and have an undulating character, the pastures improve and the land only awaits the farmer and planter. We camped for the night under some trees on the west branch of the San Bernard river; just now it is a mere rivulet and takes its rise in these prairies. Saw a few silicious pebbles in the

[7] At this place there is nearly a complete skeleton supposed to [be] that of a mammoth found at that ferry about 1837. The vertebrae and fore legs are very large.—Bollaert.

[8] "Stephen Fuller Austin, the father of our country; the patriarch that led us on, and watched with more than paternal care, our infant steps; to whose untiring zeal and unerring judgment we are indebted for our safe passage through the perils of 'settlements' and the storms of wars. He who combined in a most eminent degree, all the virtues, that elevate and adorn the human character. Animated by the soul pure and spotless as heaven descending snow, before it meets earth's pollution; the strength and ornament of our land; the pride and glory of all." (Branch T. Archer. July 4, 1840).—Bollaert.

[9] When the tyranny and military oppression of Santa Ana drove the settlers to make choice either to leave Texas or fight the good fight for their rights.—Bollaert.

[10] Occasionally silicified wood is dug up in this part of the country, more particularly in the bottoms.—Bollaert.

bed of the stream. The night was beautiful, the great heat of the day was past and the cool and refreshing breezes from the south were invigorating indeed. A fire was soon kindled, the coffee pot was called into requisition, each cut a twig and broiled his strip of dried beef and with corn bread and cheese, *et voilà! notre souper*. Each took his pipe, the evening chat was soon over, our horses watered and then hobbled, buffalo robes and blankets spread and now, good night. We saw a few centipedes and snakes during our day's journey, but passed them almost unheeded.

August 12th, 1843: At day-light started over more prairie, passing through the scattered timbers of the Colorado, then its thickly wooded bottom. We ferried over the Colorado River and ascending its steep bank entered the town of Columbus,[11] formerly designated by the name of Montezuma. Ere we reached the town we met a traveller and asking him if there were any news in Columbus or from the West.

"Why, a day or two since there was a 'difficulty'[12] in town."

"What about?"

"Why whiskey arrived, some tippled too much, and Jim ———— had his head almost broken. Father Mathew[13] ought to pay us a visit!"

The Colorado bottom has very rich soil, and gets higher as it recedes from the coast. Sumach [sumac] begins to be seen here, affording a very fine tan—fewer horse flies and mosquitos, and

[11] This historic town was settled in 1823 by members of Stephen F. Austin's colony and was named after Columbus, Ohio. Steamboats operated up the Colorado River to Columbus in pre–Civil War days, but the town never grew to become a city, possessing less than 3,000 people in 1950.

[12] The term "difficulty" is used to express several contretem[p]s such as shooting, stabbing, dueling, etc. etc. etc.—Bollaert.

[13] Father Mathew was the Reverend Theobold Mathew, a famous temperance leader during this period, from Ireland. When Sam Houston was a member of the United States Senate, he introduced a resolution to admit Father Mathew within the bar of the Senate, but Southerners objected on the score that Mathew's description of poverty in Ireland was aimed at comparison with slave areas in the South. This was known as the "Father Mathew Affair." Llerena B. Friend, *Sam Houston, The Great Designer*, 201.

although very warm in the shade—90° during the day—the southern breezes cool the air.

At Columbus I partook of the hospitality and friendship of Mr. ———, an English merchant settled here. The wells at Columbus give water at 30 feet below the surface; after passing through thick soil, the rest through silicious pebbles.

Barter is the present system of trade. Cotton for sugar and coffee, and bacon for boots—corn for calomel quinine and whiskey—beef for brandy, etc. etc. Thus a Columbus trader's books would be an interesting M. S. for the British Museum; but times will soon change and then cash payments will enliven the hearts of buyers and sellers.

August 15th, 1843: Accompanied Senator Smith[14] up the eastern side of the Colorado River to La Grange. To this place there are gentle slopes down to the river, interspersed with open country or prairie and the woodland of the bottom; the lands are very rich, but at present there are but few plantations and farms worked; the roads are choked up with the wild sun-flower and weeds, so much so that other roads are made by the side of the old ones, for the little transit there is in this direction: viz.—a very few travellers and the "mail rider."

The sun-flower roads are called "Sam Houstons" and the comparative desolation of this and the western part of Texas is attributed to his removal of the seat of Government from Austin, thus suspending in a great measure the former trade and traffic. It is asserted by the Western People[15] that had the City of Austin remained the seat of government, the Western country would have become settled rapidly instead of being "broken up," and in all probability the Mexicans would not have annoyed Texas in the spring and autumn of 1842, but this was not Houston's

[14] John William Smith was three times mayor of San Antonio: from January, 1837, to March 30, 1844. He represented Bexar County in the Texas Senate from 1842 until his death in January, 1845, at Washington-on-the-Brazos. *Biographical Directory of Texan Conventions and Congresses*, 172–73 .

[15] Western people—War Party—Archive War Party, and the Opposition.—Bollaert.

opinion. As it is, the West has been paralyzed and can only recover with prospects of peace.

August 16th, 1843: Three miles from Mr. M——'s brought us to Rutaville[16] over a pretty undulating country; only awaiting settlers to take advantage of its gifts and resources. This picturesque town was founded by the Reverend Martin Ruta in 1833, a most benevolent man, "the pioneer and first general agent of Methodist Missions in Texas."[17] It is more to the right than laid down on the map,[18] and a Methodist Almanack I found here gives it in Lat^d. 29° 56′ 30″ N and 96° 56″ W. How far this may be depended on I cannot say. One of the principal roads from the West to Washington, the present seat of the Government, passes through La Grange and Rutaville. The plantations of cotton and corn are scattered over undulating land round Rutaville for miles. The town is built of wood with some view to regularity, and the houses have "rock" chimneys. This rock is merely sandstone indurated with lime, which is quarried all about this part of the country and found associated with the general alluvial covering, accompanied at times with silicious pebbles.

This place boasts of a University, and a very respectable female academy, both being well attended by the youth of both sexes.

Five miles from Rutaville is La Grange[19] on the Colorado; the

16 Rutaville [Rutersville] is in central Fayette County, six miles northeast of La Grange. The town boasted of the first Methodist, and first Protestant, college in the Republic, which operated from 1840 to 1856. It called itself the "Athens of the South," but fell far short of living up to its boast. Approximately 100 people still reside at the old settlement, but the town was never the same after the closing of the college established by Martin Ruter. Julia Lee Sinks, "Rutersville College," *Quarterly of the Texas State Historical Association,* Vol. II (1898–99), 124–33.

17 Bollaert's error in referring to Martin Ruter as Martin Ruta was probably due to the error on Arrowsmith's map (see footnote 18 below), which he had in his possession. The map put the town down as Rutaville, instead of Rutersville. Martin Ruter did not come to Texas until 1837, and the town was not projected by him until the following year. During his brief stay in Texas, the Reverend Ruter established twenty Methodist missions. He died on May 16, 1838. *Ibid.*

18 When I speak of "the map" I mean the one compiled by [John] Arrowsmith for Kennedy's *Texas* from the best maps that are extant of Texas.—Bollaert.

19 La Grange was situated at the Colorado crossing on the old La Bahía Road. It is one of the oldest towns in Texas, possessing a trading post as early as 1819. Its population in 1950 did not exceed 3,000 people.

descent to it is enlivening and it appeared a busy place. Canvassing for Representatives was going on; a large keel boat was building to take some 2 to 300 bales of cotton down to the "raft"[20] and from thence it would be carted or hauled to Matagorda; the stores had a gay appearance and there was an air of comfort about the place; but, the removal of the seat of government from Austin, and the inroads of the Mexicans, had almost put a stop to improvements.

I was invited by my companion, Mr. Senator [Smith] to remain at his residence, which was on the other side of the river at Colorado—this town only comprising three or four houses, and moreover, to attend a Barbecue[21] or public dinner to be given to General La Mar, in a day or two; and this gave me an opportunity of looking about the country.

Bluffs now appear on either side of the river at intervals covered with timbers and having springs, sloping down towards the open lands or small prairies most eligible spots for locations. In this vicinity reside at present many of the families of those who have removed from San Antonio, after their fathers and relatives were made prisoners and now kept in chains in Mexico. Likewise, the widows and orphans of those who fell with Dawson at the "Mott" [mesquite grove] near the battle of the Salado was fought between [Mathew] Caldwell and General Woll.

August 19th, 1843: For some days past La Grange has been in bustle and activity, preparing a public dinner or barbecue in honor of General Lamar. He is in the opposition and consequently sympathizes with the Western people. Beeves, pigs, venison, and poultry have been slaughtered in numbers and early this morning commenced the roasting and cooking of the victims by large quantities of wood burnt in piles and then put into long fosses, across

20 A "raft," as Bollaert refers to it here, means an accumulation of driftwood from fallen trees in a river, lodged and compacted so as to form an obstruction to navigation. Most of the Texas rivers in the 1840's, particularly in eastern Texas, contained these rafts at their mouth, which made it extremely difficult for steamboats to get in or out of the interior of Texas.

21 *Barbecue* in Virginia is a frolic of all the neighbors for miles round; they go fishing in the rivers or bays and cook the fish upon the spot. This is called a chowder party in Texas. An ox roasted whole is said to be *barbecued.*—Bollaert.

which the viands were roasted. Heaps of corn cakes, sweet potatoes, beet-root, tomatoes, butter, etc., but no inebriating fluids—
barrels of water to supply their place.

The Barbecue was held in a large open space; the table [was]
of a right-angular form with seats on each side, and to keep the
company from the scorching sun, thick canvass overhead; this
was absolutely necessary for it was a very hot day. Early in the
morning the company began to assemble, coming in from the
different parts of the country: planters and farmers with their
families, on horseback, buggies, and jersey-waggons. Under the
shade of the large and magnificent live oak might be seen groups,
not merely "village politicians," but men who had fought hard
for their adopted country and now discussing the merits and de-
merits of "Old Sam." Some called him "traitor," others of a
calmer nature "would give him another trial, believing that he
was the only one to get them out of the 'scrape' and arrange an
armistice or a peace with Mexico." The ladies and children remained in the houses of the town until the arrival of their dis-
tinquished guest. About noon a salute was fired and General
Lamar rode into the town attended by a number of gentlemen on
horseback. He was introduced to the concourse by a venerable citizen in a speech full of kindness in regard to the one ex-president
of the Republic. General La Mar returned thanks for the great
honor done him, and entered into a narrative of the various acts of
his administration, complaining somewhat of vindictiveness of the
part of those now in power. He thanked those he saw around him,
and was very happy in some compliments to the ladies present.

[The gentleman who introduced the General to the assembled
citizens stood up saying, "Three cheers for General Lamar."
Whether it was the suffocating heat of the weather or any other
cause, there was no response.] The good things of this life were
speedily put on the tables, all appeared to enjoy their dinner, and
the remnants that remained would have given a good meal to a
thousand men. After the repast there were many speeches from
rival candidates for Representatives for the county and ere Sun
down all were moving homewards.[22] [Although this dinner was

got up by General Lamar's political friends, he did not appear to
have many at the Barbecue.]

August 20th, 1843: Left Colorado—journeying now on the
western bank of the River. "Noon'd it" at Grassmeyer's landing;
but, before arriving at this spot, I passed through a small but
romantic valley in which were several bricked up graves, and others
fenced in, of early settlers. About 3 P.M. continuing my journey,
came to the plantation of Mr. H——. His crops of cotton, corn,
sugar, tobacco, wheat, and crops of vegetables [were] most plentiful. He told me that next season he only wanted to grow coffee
and then he should be perfectly independent in case of blockade
of the coast. He had flocks of sheep and goats and they were in a
thriving condition, but for sheep he observed that the musquit
grasses and clear streams of the West was better than the part of
the Colorado he resided on. Spinning cotton and wool was going
on and the loom likewise was busy.

The river today has commenced rising rapidly, owing to rains
in the mountains, and a freshet is expected. There are hills about
here averaging from 100 to 200 feet from the prairies, composed
of gravel rounded silicious pebbles, and masses of indurated sands
containing much oxide of iron. This is used for building, particularly for chimnies and walls; the good folk adhere yet to the frame
and log houses; now if they would build entirely with this rock,
they would have cool houses in summer and tight ones in winter,
but all this will come about in time.

August 21st, 1843: The ferryman sick at what is called Hardman's ferry, and he lives on the opposite side, so the boat cannot
be got over. Three travellers were going my way and we concluded

[22] Not long after this General Lamar's only daughter died in the United States,
when he left Texas for Georgia.—Bollaert.

After his daughter's death in 1843, Lamar was plunged into melancholia and
sought relief in travel. From then until his death in 1859, he devoted his time to
travel, writing poetry, and collecting material for his proposed history of Texas.
He served in the Mexican War as a lieutenant colonel under Zachary Taylor. In
1857, he went to South America, where he served as United States minister to
Nicaragua and Costa Rica. Asa Kyrus Christian, *Mirabeau Buonaparte Lamar.*

to continue our journey on the western bank to Bastrop, crossing the Colorado there.

The very sudden rise of the River had filled the creeks with "back water" 30 to 40 feet in depth; we managed by putting our saddle bags and clothes over our shoulders to swim our horses over Cedar Creek, it being narrow and its banks not very steep.

We "headed" or got round Walnut Creek, after considerable difficulty, but the banks of one of its forks was so steep and the fork so full of water and just now of considerable width that we did not deem it prudent to swim our horses over, we being mounted on them, for fear of "bogging," sticking in the mud.

I was kindly received at Mr. M—— and seldom I think his hospitality had been more timely given, for I had not often been so fatigued and had not eaten anything all day. An excellent supper and a good feather bed put me all to rights.

August 22nd, 1843: Early in the morning a young Tonkeway Indian came to Mr. M——'s, begging for milk and some meat. My host was just going to morning prayers; he motioned the Indian to wait; down he squatted on his haunches by my side, his gun between his legs, only being encumbered as to habiliments with the girdle round the loins and a long narrow strip of cloth hanging before and behind; his face painted with vermillion, presented a pretty good picture of an Indian.

When Mr. M—— commenced praying, I put my hands over my eyes, the Indian did the same, but peeping through his fingers apparently to watch my motions; I put my other hand up to my face, the Indian did the same; I made several other movements, and he imitated them immediately. I must not be considered irreverent doing this at prayers, but it was to see what manoeuvers he would be after. Poor fellow, he had no idea we were rendering our morning thanks to an eternal bounteous Providence.

He obtained a bullock head, the pluck and entrails, upon condition that he was to make a *cabresto*[23] during the day for Mr. M——, but before he left he begged some tobacco of me.

[23] A cabresto [cabristo] was a rope generally made from the mane of mustangs. The Texans called it "cabris."

"Cambalache," said he to me (Will you barter?)

"No," I replied. "I am not a trader."

"Si, si, cambalache moccassins, alla' come." (Yes, yes, do give me something for a pair of moccassins, they are in my tent, come).

I promised that after breakfast I would pay him and his party a visit, which I did, he doing the honors of introducing me to the Chief, Campos. There were only four or five families of them there, all busily employed drying over slow fires venison and beef, so as to preserve and render it more portable for travelling. They were pretty good looking, but somewhat dirty. Campos asked me if I was a "Capitan." I explained to him that as yet I was only a Sergeant in the Texas Volunteers. "Soldier," said he. "Yes," I replied. "Si, si, Sergeant, same as Capitan," he continued. "Sam Houston, great Capitan. Burleson, La Mar, great Capitans." He then drew from a sort of helmet what appeared to me a bundle of rags; he began unfolding it and after some time produced parchment testimonials of brave conduct in the field, signed by Generals Houston, La Mar, and Burleson, but in recommending that the settlers should treat them kindly when they came amongst them to sell buffalo robes, deer skins, etc., not to let them have any whiskey. Campos shewed me a shield, gun and spear he had taken from the Comanches. Campos and his tribe are but lately from the Mountains where they have been buffalo hunting and he told me he would go and visit the coast this summer to see the ocean and hunt mustangs and deer.

This tribe, as well as many others, are hated by the Comanches and such Indians with whom the Texans have no treaties and would kill them could they get hold of them, thus the friendly Indians keep generally within range of the white settlements for protection.

Got over the Colorado to Bastrop[24] in a canoe, not safe yet to ferry horse across. Under the old Spaniards, the road from Nacogdoches to San Antonio passed through this place. This appears to

24 About two miles from Bastrop in a prairie was discovered the horns, jawbone, and teeth of some mammoth of which history gives no account. The horn [was] six and a half feet in length, nine inches in diameter; also part of a tooth, say one-third of it weighing sixteen or eighteen pounds.—Bollaert.

be a likely spot to thrive, and was doing well whilst the government was at Austin. It is situated on a high prairie, and towards the East, the Colorado Hills are only distant two or three miles and covered with timbers, being composed on the surface of alluvial matters of a silicious character with pebbles; in the neighborhood much indurated sand may be found and might be used for building. Silicified oysters, ammonites and other shells have been met with. It is considered healthy and every species of vegetation comes up most luxuriantly. There is only one store for dry goods in the town, and this was full of Tonkeways, bartering their buffalo robes, deer skins, moccassins, etc., for powder, cotton stuffs, beads, and such like finery for their squaws and an occasional bottle of whiskey from the tippling shop. This last is against *executive orders*. One of the Indians was a very ugly likeness of Mr. Macready,[25] the actor. At Bastrop, I found a countryman, Mr. N——, for whose attentions I feel obliged. I had the honor of an introduction to the Vice-President of Texas, General [Edward] Burleson, who invited me on my return from Austin to pay him a visit.

August 23rd, 1843: Left Bastrop by the upper road to avoid the deep parts of creeks. Noon, arrived at Webber's Prairie.[26] To the eastward is seen the Colorado Hills, gracefully clothed with groves and containing springs for the stock.

Wells here 30 feet deep. I was informed that in digging a well in this prairie lately, a large leg bone[27] like that of the buffalo was found at the depth of 21 feet, and in digging another well hereabouts mussel shells were met with at some depth. I have found in many of the Rivers and streams of Texas live mussels and have

[25] This was William Charles Macready (1793–1873), famous Shakespearian actor, whom Bollaert doubtless had seen perform at Drury Lane.

[26] Webber's Prairie, now called Webberville, was founded by John Webber in 1839. The town is a rural community in eastern Travis County. By-passed by the railroad, it failed to grow, and today has a population of approximately fifty people.

[27] Leg bones, probably of mastodon, very large, found by Mr. [John] Webber about a year since on the Colorado River 16 miles below Austin. The bank of the river had caved in and thus brought these bones to light.—Bollaert.

eaten them. I met here with a gentleman who had just arrived from the N.W. who mentioned that on the tops of the mountains on the San Gabriel River there were to be met with silicified or calcareous oyster, mussel, conque, clam, etc. My host shewed me a large specimen of ammonite from the San Gabriel, it was of calcareous matter and had small oyster shells adhering to it. I was likewise informed that the country between the Colorado and Brazos Rivers, in a N.E. direction from about Austin, is most eligible for settlers, indeed; it is called the "Land of beauty." It has been but slightly explored, but the "backwoodsmen" have begun to settle on the San Andres, or Little River,[28] and its tributaries. This section of country will undoubtedly become of great importance to Texas. It has the navigation of the Brazos, very many falls, from which mill-races can be easily constructed; it is free from local diseases, and moreover, a fine small grain growing country; game is in the greatest abundance and is at present one of the favorite hunting ranges of friendly Indians.

On Little River a forge was discovered not long since and sundry excavations which has led to the belief that either gold or silver mines had been worked.[29] Not long since a Tahuacany [Tawakoni] Indian girl who had been made prisoner by the Comanches and was afterwards re-taken by a party of Texans, told her liberators among other things that when travelling with the Comanches by the Mission of San Saba, she heard them say that in the ruins of the mission there was much *white and yellow metal.* This was interpreted by certain parties who live in this vicinity as gold and silver. It is well known that some years ago the Comanches came down upon the Mission of San Saba in great numbers, killing nearly all the residents, and it was supposed that from the report of the Indian girl that much precious metal might be still at the Mission. Accordingly, these good folks formed themselves into a *treasure-trove association,* they wished, moreover,

[28] The San Gabriel River is formed by three forks which rise in southwestern Williamson County and unite at Galveston. About fifty miles northeast of Georgetown, the San Gabriel joins Little River in central Milam County.

[29] 1844: I hear that Colonel [Jacob] Sniveley has re-commenced operations here, and that some quantity of silver has been extracted.—Bollaert.

to have a "frolic" and see the upper country. After six days travelling from Austin they arrived at the old and ruined Mission of San Saba, having in their transit up the valley seen many Comanche Indians.

The greatest labour and difficulty they had was to clear away the brushwood and weeds. This being done, they fell to digging and routing up the ground, and after many days labour, they only disinterred a large quantity of human bones; but my informant, who was one of the party, told me that they made only a partial exploration, and it was his intention at some future period to return with a larger party to continue the search, but more particularly to discover the position of the mines, from whence the old Spaniards dug the ore, these mines supposed to be only two or three miles from the Mission and in the mountains. Several forges were discovered in the woods round the mission.

The general height of the ruins of the Mission was estimated at fourteen feet, across it a hundred and eight steps, circumference about four hundred steps and the walls very thick.

The San Saba valley is spoken of as being very beautiful, in some places seven miles wide and with prairies of musquit grass sloping down to the river. Timbers are in abundance, principally the peccan and oak, the last being found very large in places and large quantities of Flax met with. Game is in abundance and large droves of prairie dogs were seen.

In the afternoon left Webber's Prairie. The road to Austin becomes pleasingly diversified with hill, dale, and timbers, passing Walbarger's[30] and Walnut Creek. The approach to it (Austin),

[30] Mr. Walbarger [Wilbarger] lives here, and has a fine plantation; this gentleman was wounded severely by some Comanches and left for dead, when he was *scalped;* after this cruel operation, he had strength enough to rise and get to a settlement.—Bollaert.

Josiah Pugh Wilbarger was a member of a surveying party which was attacked by Comanche Indians near Pecan Springs, about four miles east of present Austin. He was scalped but was still living when he was found the next day. He never completely recovered from his wound, although he lived for some twelve more years. Wilbarger County is named after him. Frank Brown, "Annals of Travis County and the City of Austin" (MS., Archives Collection, University of Texas Library).

which stands on the site of a town in embryo called Waterloo,[31] is very pretty. The cotton plantations, the fields of corn and cattle and horses grazing; with the hilly and mountainous scenery was a treat for one who like myself had been residing some time in the lower country and on the coast.

Bollaert's stay in Austin was relatively brief, and anyone who has ever been in that beautiful, but hot, city during August can well understand his reasons for not tarrying very long. Although he was impressed with the natural beauty of the surrounding country, his description of the town itself as it looked in 1843 is anything but flattering. Perhaps the Englishman was thinking of Austin a hundred years hence when he enclosed the following entitled, "The City of Austin."

[The City of Austin] has many advantages of location not immediately discernible to the traveller who does not look beyond the spot itself for the mines of wealth destined to contribute their riches for the enlargement and decoration of our new Capital. It is located at the foot of a spur of the Cordilleras mountains, terminating in the valley of the Colorado. From this place the great road of the traders to Santa Fé will be laid out through a rich and well watered country, abounding in game, and bees as numerous as the swarms of Hybla, and blessed with a climate fit to yield the Hesperian Fruit, which may here be gathered without the fear of the "sleepless dragon." Its proximity to the provinces of Mexico, on the north and west borders of the Republic, with the aid of capital, which will soon find its way here, must attract all the valuable trade at present carried to St. Louis and Matamoras. Its distance from the largest trading towns on the Rio Grande

---

[31] Waterloo was on the north bank of the Colorado River at the approximate site of the Congress Avenue Bridge in Austin. Joseph Harrell, a hunter, erected a tent on the river bank in 1835, and two years later he was visited by Mirabeau B. Lamar. President Lamar decided that the spot was an appropriate site for the capital city of the Republic of Texas. The Texas Congress adopted the name of Austin for the settlement when the capital was moved there in 1839. *The Handbook of Texas*, II, 869.

does not exceed four or five hundred miles—one third of the distance of the route at present travelled by the caravans from Missouri and Arkansas. We are barely permitted to glance at these advantages, satisfied that those interested in that valuable trade will soon turn their attention to this country.

It is difficult to give a full and just description of this spot with its surrounding scenery. If Rome was celebrated in song for her "seven hills," Austin may well boast of her "thousand mounds," covered with bowers equal in splendor to the Arcadian groves. The native beauty of the Colorado is not surpassed by any part of North America. Its mountains, its vales, its hills and its dales are ever before the eye; and when we tire gazing upon the one, we can turn with new delight to the other. Every shade of the majestic and beautiful can be traced in the wide prospect, where the brightest, sunniest spots slope gently to those of shady luxuriance; and, towering above all, are the tall, frowning pinnacles of the Cordilleras, "where the blossoms open 'mid darkness and gloom," while the sun of heaven smiles brightly on the landscape below. These gloomy recesses remind us of the mountains of Scotia, where castles were built in rocks for the retreat of Celtic chieftains, the history of whose lives, as exposed to every peril, have been so eloquently described by Scott. A view from the mountains is unequalled for its variety and magnificence. The lover of native scenery may stand upon the rugged brow of one of these cliffs, his head encircled by the brilliant arch of the rainbow, and behold among the distant hills of the San Saba "the Enchanted rock," worshipped by the children of the prairies and supposed by them to be covered with "gems Richer than sparkle on diadems." . . . Whilst the prairies below, in their boundless extent, are dotted here and there with numerous groves of live oak, round which are verdant lawns, carpeted with the richest grass, and spangled with the most brilliant of Flora's gems, and intersected with perennial springs of the purest water.

We cannot believe that this wonderful prodigality of Nature's bounties, the rich profusion of minerals which lie embowelled in the hills of the San Saba and the Piedra Pinta, the soft furs of the

Pasigono and the Incoqua in all their "silky pride"—the forests
of "rich gems and spicy health," where the lemon, the lime, and
the orange, "their lighter glories blend"—the "rocks rich in gems,"
or "mountains big with mines," will be permitted to waste their
wealth and luxuriance in the vast and untrodden wilderness. The
tide of emigration is rapidly propelling the car of enterprize to
the West, and we shall soon see the waste country above this city
"bloom and blossom as the rose." Where now the savage burns
incense to his idols, invocations shall arise to the only true and
living God. Where now ignorance and supersitition darken the
mind, learning and the truth of science shall illumine the path
of life. Where now is pealed the shrill cry of the wild rover of the
prairie, will be heard the hum of industry and the noisy din of
commerce. These are not creations of the fancy which fall like
thin flakes of snow and are seen no more, but they are the reasonable prognostics of events which have occurred in other portions
of our country, and may be anticipated, with equal certainty, of
the beautiful region beyond the mountains of the Cordilleras.

Of the population of the Colorado we may be permitted to
speak in terms of eulogy, as they have never failed in any one of
the duties of patriotic citizens. Industrious and thrifty, notwith-
standing the heavy losses they sustained during the revolution
and subsequently by their exposed situation on the frontier, they
are now independent and prosperous. They are generous and
brave, ever prepared to defend their own firesides, and equally
willing to aid their neighbors against the incursions of the savage.
They are moral in their habits, and just in all their dealings. Of
such a population, Texas may well be proud![32]

[*Here Bollaert resumes his narrative.*]

On entering the city of Austin, Lo! Dreariness and desolation
presented themselves; few houses appeared inhabited and many
falling to decay. The "Legation of France" empty, its doors and
windows open, palings broken down and appearing as if it would

[32] Bollaert introduces this article into his journal without comment, except for
a marginal note: "A. Gaz. Octr. 30. 1839!!!!" [Austin *City Gazette*].

be soon in ruins. The President's house looked gloomy, the streets filled with grass and weeds and the western people say all this "through the vindictiveness of Old Sam."

I found my friend, Mr. T——, with an attack of chills and fever. There has been much sickness this year on the Colorado, Brazos, and other rivers having much "bottom" land. Chills and fevers principally, some congestive and bilious, but very few cases have proved fatal. A large party of the convalescent (from chills and fever) inhabitants have just started for the mountains buffalo hunting to recruit themselves.

August 24th 1843: Latitude of Austin said to be in 30° 19′S. The hills and mountains of this section are a species of limestone, containing magnesia and traces of sulphur. The "soft rock" of Austin is easily quarried, it indurates quickly, but afterwards in wet weather cracks, thus care should be had in building with it. Fossils of the ammonite and fossil bones are found when quarrying, likewise sulphuret of iron. Common salt it is said has been discovered not far off. There are no traces of coal.

Here I had an opportunity of examining some small specimens of minerals from the San Saba mines; the gangue was of quartz with traces of copper and iron, but I could not without analyzing them properly determine as to their containing any of the precious metals. According to report, gold was the metal extracted there.

At night there were a few mosquitos, but they are seldom seen. Some wild cattle came from the mountains, they got amongst the stock in the prairie outside the town and then commenced a furious bellowing.

What are called "creeks" from Bastrop to Austin and about this part of the country have in many places the character of deep gullies. The elder is in fruit and flower, wine has been made from it; likewise from the mustang and other grapes, but from the want of knowing how to make wine properly, not much can be said for the latter. Vines are now being introduced from France and there is little doubt that under proper management they will succeed.

Austin will be the head of navigation without there be extra-ordinary freshets; for three miles from it there are falls of 4 or 5 feet. Two miles from Austin across the river are Barton's Springs. (Mr. Barton[33] is generally called the Daniel Boone of Texas, a true backwoodsman, and when he hears of any one settling near him becomes truly unhappy). "The falls consist of rapids 4 to 500 yards in extent," which will impede navigation upwards unless during great freshets. Three miles from these falls another of greater extent, and farther up other falls.

Mount Bonnell[34] is the highest peak of the range of mountains around Austin and from its summit a very extensive and interesting view of the country and the river is obtained. The summit is said by Mr. Bonnell to be composed of "coral rock, oyster, and other marine shells." "The foot of the mountains abound in iron ore."

High up on the Colorado, commences a series of table lands, or prairies with good pastures, and the margins of the streams well timbered. Honey Creek[35] according to Mr. Upshur is placed on the wrong side of the Colorado. Messrs. Upshur and Holden found in said creek an old forge, and the ground appeared to have been dug up as if for Lavadero gold. About this line of country the rocks put on a harder character than about Austin. There are large quantities of wild hemp about Austin, but not worked as yet.

[33] William Barton moved to present Travis County and built his home near the springs, named after him, in 1837. He was a skilled Indian fighter. He died on April 11, 1840, and for several years his body remained buried at Barton Springs before it was removed to Round Rock, Texas. Brown, "Annals of Travis County and the City of Austin" (Archives Collection, University of Texas Library).

[34] George W. Bonnell moved to Austin in 1839, where he established the *Texas Sentinel* a short time later. He was a member of both the Santa Fé Expedition and the Mier Expedition. Although he managed to escape when the Texas forces surrendered to the Mexicans, he was later captured and shot by a Mexican soldier. "Memoirs of Major George Bernard Erath," *Southwestern Historical Quarterly*, Vol. XXVII (1923–24), 46–49.

[35] There are thirteen creeks in Texas by this name. The one that Bollaert refers to in his journal doubtless is the intermittent stream rising in south-central Burnet County (northwest of Austin) and flowing southwest for four miles into Hamilton Creek. Arrowsmith's map has Honey Creek on the correct side of the Colorado River, but shows it flowing into the Colorado instead of Hamilton Creek.

Last year Mr. H—— showed me specimens of gold ore from mines of the Llano River, which is situated above Austin, but the inroads of the Mexicans and the general unsettled state of the country has prevented him and his companions from prosecuting their labours, but by next spring it is supposed there will be some amicable arrangement entered into between this country and Mexico, when a large party will proceed to the Llano mines and work them.

About Austin there is a great field for the Botanist; just now there are but small plants in flower but very pretty ones. No Botanist as yet has visited this part of the country. The inhabitants as they pass by the plants that are in flower name them according to their resemblance to any they may have seen in the United States. This is a good time to collect seeds, and I am much indebted to Messrs. T—— and U—— for sharing with me seeds they have collected this year.

August 25th, 1843: Visited the "President's house." It is falling to pieces, and now the residence of bats. The Capitol is the abode of bats, lizards and stray cattle. These buildings having been built of green wood and run up with great expedition, the timbers have dried, and become loose, the plaster peeling off, and the "Austin soft stone" cracking. If these buildings and others in the city are not repaired in a short time Austin will be a heap of ruins. In the flourishing times when Congress was held here I am informed that there would be at times 1,500 people here; at present I hardly dare mention the number of the resident population. Alas! Poor Austin, thy seven hills are nearly deserted, exposed to the marauding of the Comanches, and this year visited by considerable sickness, until then it was proverbally healthy; the balmy southern breezes tempering the heat of summer, and the high mountains behind shielding it from the frigid "northers." I could not have seen Austin and this section of Texas, as far as regards the social position of the inhabitants, at a more unfavourable period. Those cling to the spot who assisted to rear it, for they have their property there. They hope for better times and this year have occupied themselves seriously on their plantations and farms. There is a weekly newspaper published in Austin, the *Western Advocate*[36] and the organ of the opposition.

Evening, left Austin and slept at Webber's Prairie.

August 26th, 1843: At noon arrived at Bastrop. My countryman, Mr. N——, had a fine piece of roast beef on table for dinner, but from pains in the limbs and continual gaping, and other symptoms, I became too sick to partake of his good fare. Started in the afternoon for General Burleson's plantation on my way by La Grange to Columbus. Whilst at supper and discussing the merits of a roast squirrel, *the chill* came over me. I could eat no more, and wrapping myself up in my *poncho* sought the kitchen fire; the chill increased, when I thought it advisable to go to bed. Fever and profuse perspiration followed.

August 27th, 1843: Took a dose of quinine and journeyed onwards. At noon whilst resting and awaiting the heat of the day to pass over, took another dose of quinine. I am getting very sick and weak. Lost my road and found myself near to Rutaville.

August 30th, 1843: Since I have been here my chills and fever increase and I suffer with pain in the head. Left Rutaville with the intention of going on to Columbus, but when three or four miles on my road I became so enfeebled as not to be able to sit my horse. Fortunately the plantation of Mr. M——, a gentleman I knew, was near, who very kindly received me. Fever increased, excruciating headache and failure of sight. The medical attendant of the family had the lady of the house as his patient and calling to see her, I begged he would bleed me; this almost immediately relieved the pains in the head and I fell asleep. He prescribed and left me powders composed of calomel, Dover's [ipecac and

---

[36] The *Western Advocate* was a semi-weekly paper published in Austin from February 18, 1843, to July, 1843. It was revived in September, 1843, and continued to the following February. It was edited by George K. Teulon, previously identified as a strong anti-Houston man, and was virtually a continuation of the Austin *City Gazette. The Handbook of Texas*, II, 885.

opium], ipecacuhana, and camphor—and infusion of Valerian to keep down nervous action.[37]

August 31st, 1843: Heavy thunderstorms with rain.

September 2nd, 1843: Being sufficiently strong to sit my horse, started in the afternoon. Got to the upper ferry at Columbus, but the river running very rapidly and only one man there; had to remain till morning. Violent chills and fever all night.

September 3rd, 1843: Got to Columbus at last. From the quantity of calomel I had taken, slightly salivated. I really do not see the use of calomel in chills and fever, but it is the almost universal medicine of some of the American practitioners. I commenced taking small doses of quinine two or three times a day and by the help of rest and chicken broth "broke the fever," but remained very weak so as hardly able to walk. The only disease I have met with in Texas chills and fever (intermittent [tertian or quartan malaria] and remittent [estivo-autumnal malaria] bilious fevers) and congestive fever produced by exposure to the sun.

In the western and towards the mountain country, chills and fever are not known, and those who have been debilitated by it go to the West "in search of health," and a residence in San Antonio for a short time reestablishes them. With all due deference to the practice of the medical profession in Texas I would recommend in the case of European immigrants being attacked, say with chills and fever or terciana ague, to take 3 grains of tartar emetic or 30 grains of ipecacuhana the intermediate day after

[37] Bollaert was suffering from what is known today as malaria. It was not known in 1843, of course, that this disease was associated with mosquitoes. He, like most Texans of the period, attributed it to overexertion, exposure to the sun, and unwholesome food, as well as infectious material and noxious effluvia supposedly arising from stagnant water or vegetable decomposition in the lowlands. Malarial fever (ague) was expected as a matter of course to ravage the Texas and southern settlements each summer. Newcomers were especially subject to severe attacks. The fall and summer of 1843 were particularly difficult for the settlers along the Brazos, Guadalupe, Colorado, and Trinity rivers. William Ransom Hogan, *The Texas Republic: A Social and Economic History*, 225-26.

the chill, then about six or eight hours before the chill is expected, 5 or 6 grains of quinine in cold coffee and this will generally stop the fever. Should however the ague come on again, two or three doses of quinine of say 4 grains every 4 hours for 12 hours will be sufficient. Beware of quack medicines!

Congestive fever: this is produced by exposure to the sun and commences with chills. Take 10 grains of calomel at most, combined with 10 grains of rhubarb, and should the fever increase, bleeding may be resorted to. Afterwards a few small doses of quinine which will act as a tonic and strengthen the patient.

Bilious fever: take an emetic of 30 grains of ipecacuhana, or 3 grains of tartar emetic and a powder containing 8 grains of Calomel and 8 grains of Dover's powder. Should the first powder not clear the stomach, the calomel and Dover's powder must be repeated at the end of 24 hours, and re-repeated every 24 hours until the bile is thoroughly discharged.

I have met occasionally with persons who having had chills and fever upon them for some time for want of proper medicine, complain of an affection of the spleen and pain in the left side, this may be removed by the use of gentle aperients and Blue Pills. Beware of quack medicines! Dr. Vancouver's Powders have been introduced into Texas! A medical man informed me that they are composed of powdered peruvian bark, cayenne pepper, and magnesia. Dr. Champion's Pills and Thurston's ditto [Unrivalled Antifever] are favourites, they being composed principally of quinine, may be of some use.

In 1838 Dr. T[heodore] Leger of Brazoria wrote an essay on intermittent fevers, in which after treating the subject with much attention, says that the most opportune moment for taking the Sulphate of Quinine is the period of intermission about three or four hours, before the return of the access and when the patient is fasting. Sometimes it has been necessary to administer a second dose, but seldom a third. The dose of Sulphate of Quinine is from 10 to 15 grains dissolved in two ounces of liquid—at times administered in French wine. Sometimes made into pills for delicate stomachs.

Dr. L[eger] likewise observes: "How often do we not see our self-styled Doctors hurry to pour down their incendiary drugs, to administer purgatives, vomatives, bleeding and cupping, and bring into play all the resources of their pharmaceutic arsenal? Calomel and Blue-pills form their heavy artillery; then advance in second rank, Jalap and Rhubarb; Epsom-salts and Castor oil bring up the rear."[38] And to borrow the words of Moliere, "*Si la maladia non vult guerire repurgare, resaigare, recalomelisare.*"

Bollaert remained in Columbus for a little more than a week before starting a return trip to the frontier on September 11, 1843. Meanwhile, he wrote a brief summary of his recent journey from Austin back to Columbus, describing in rather gruesome details his painful experience with ague. His comments are prefaced with the following note: "Refer to this for romance of trip to Austin and return to Columbus. More truth than romance in it."

In August, 1843, I left Galveston for the interior of Texas to see and examine the country. The Weather was changeable, heavy tropical rains, a burning sun during the day and occasionally bad roads. I travelled westward, and then pursued my way up the ——— [Colorado] River towards the mountains, but some very heavy rains having fallen, the rivers swelled with freshets and the back water filled the deep creeks or ravines. I met with three travellers going my way and we agreed to journey together. We came to a creek full of water even to the overflowing of its bank, expecting to find a canoe at a settlement hard by; the canoe or "dug-out" had been washed away and we concluded to "head" or go round the creek.

After hours of riding through the brush and briar we found that on reapproaching the creek it was not fordable, being some 30 feet deep and no other resource left us but to swim it. Two of my companions could not swim, thus the aquatic arrangements were

[38] The title page of Dr. Leger's essay on intermittent fever proclaims the author to be "Late Professor of Midwifery of the Faculty of Paris, Member of the Medical College of Mexico, and Ex-Vice-President of the Medical Society of New Orleans." Reproduced opposite p. 285 in *ibid.*

left to the remaining one and myself. There were some Tonkaway
Indians on the opposite bank, they seeing our dilemma, made
signs that there was a large tree on their side which might be
taken to the other, when our companions, saddles, etc., could be
easily floated over. We took to the water, a red muddy stream, not
being quite satisfied as to the non-existence of alligators.

We got safely over, and with the assistance of the Indians succeeded in detaching the fallen tree from the bank, when my
swimming companion fastened one end of his cabresto to the
tree and putting the other in his mouth swam to the opposite side.
The horses being unsaddled were driven into the creek and in a
few minutes I had them on *terra ferma* secured. Our non-swim-
ming companions placed saddles, etc. on the frail bark and then
seated themselves across it and soon we had them over. When
we had concluded saddling up and about starting, black clouds
began to roll about in the heavens, heavy gusts of wind from N.E.,
accompanied with forked and sheet lightning and the "biggest"
thunder I had ever heard. The Indians wished us to go to their
camp, for heavy drops of rain were falling, but we had lost so
much time in "heading" and crossing the creek that we feared
if we did not push on, we should not get to our destination and
have to sleep in the woods and moreover we had no provisions
with us. We had not gone a mile when torrents of rain fell, with
heavy gusts of wind, lightning and thunder, and it became almost
dark with black clouds. The wind amongst the trees roared like
the tempestuous billows dashing on a rocky coast and now and
then was heard the crash of a tree falling. This continued about
an hour, when this tropical visitation cleared away, the sun shone
out and rain-bow after rain-bow appeared. I must not omit men-
tioning my "Mackintosh," for whilst my companions were wet
through, I was comparatively dry. For an hour or more we wandered about among the groves of live-oaks, undulating prairies,
now and then starting a deer, but without a track or trail. The
compass was resorted to and knowing that the ——— "bottom"
or timbers of the ——— River must lay in an easterly direction,
we took that way. We soon fell in with a track which conducted

us in to a valley and from some Negros we found on a plantation we found we were only some eight miles from our destination; but, this we did not attain ere nightfall. On approaching the ferry we found that the river was running so rapidly that it was impossible to cross.

I solicited hospitality at a small log house for the night, where a genteel woman appeared with several children round her. "Ah Sir, I could have done it a few months since and glad would I have been to have done so, for you look fatigued and the storm will do you no good. But pray Sir, where are you from?"

"From Galveston."

"From Galveston! Then you surely can give me some account of the San Antonio prisoners. My poor husband is one of them. His name is S——. I have lived on hope so long, that I am now sick and ill and I do not think I shall ever see my husband more."[39] Here she shed tears, in which the children joined, "Pray tell me your opinion, your sincere and candid opinion."

"Well, I do believe they will be liberated and from certain negotiations going on between Texas and Mexico and England, we shall soon have peace."

"If England takes it in hand there are hopes. You Sir, I presume are an Englishman. My father was a Canadian and that is the same thing. I will accommodate you if you like, but I would advise you to go to . . . [part of the sentence torn off] stable. But mind, come and talk to us tomorrow."

I accordingly took her advice—was well received and after a good supper slept in a *feather bed that night.* After waiting a couple of days I got across the river and pursued my peregrinations alone up to the foot of the mountains, examining the land, the geology, botany, collecting seeds etc. etc. But dearly had I to pay for swimming creeks exposing myself to the sun and at the same time under the influence of the miasma of the valley.

On returning down the valley I paid a visit to General Burleson and whilst at supper discussing the merits of a grilled squirrel, I felt a peculiar sickness, pain in the head and then a slight chill

[39] In the spring of 1844 he returned to his family.—Bollaert.

followed. I had during the day suffered from pain in the back, this I attributed to fatigue and continual gaping. I wrapped my mantle round me and betook myself to the kitchen fire. The chill increased, shaking the whole system, the hands got cold, the finger nails blue, and the tip of the nose cold.

I went to bed, heaps of blankets being heaped upon me. The shivering continued for half an hour and then fever followed, and during the night profuse perspiration. I was now a victim to chills and fever or intermittent. I took a dose of quinine the following morning and thought it prudent to make the best of my way to ———, which place I had made my head quarters, for there I could obtain medical assistance and be with my friends. The day was fortunately cloudy, but sultry. Riding on until noon I put up at a small farm, the property of a Methodist parson, who united in his person other functions of lawyer, judge, or magistrate and farmer. He "was down" with fever and his doctor had put him into such a state of salivation that the room in which he lay was perfectly pestiferous.

I threw myself down on an apology for a bed until late in the afternoon, when I joined a traveller going part of my way. We had not been long on the road when it commenced raining and continued until dusk. Some six miles from where I intended to stop for the night my companion left me. I proceeded alone; it was getting dark and I was nearly worn out when I came up to a settlement and I found I had taken the left hand trail instead of the right. I told them I was very sick and begged they would, if they had no convenience in the house, to let me throw myself down under the shed in front of the house. They told me that all were sick with fever and they could not conveniently render me any assistance. I was about throwing myself on the ground for the night, when they told me that ——— was only two miles off and that there was an inn. This gave me courage; on I went, but a longer five miles I never travelled. I went to the inn; it had been shut up some time, thus again I was disappointed, but recollecting that when passing through this place some time previously I had been introduced to a family here, I went to their dwelling and begged refuge for the night. They made a bed up for me on the floor, when I fell almost senseless on it. The following morning my chills and fever returned, with redoubled force; the little medicine I had brought with me from Galveston I had shared with the sick I had encountered on my journey and my last dose of quinine I was about to take. The medical man of the puritanical, temperance, and not very hospitable village I was in, had gone to a "camp meeting." (Camp meetings are a disgrace to society) and it was not certain when he would return. My fever having abated towards evening I found my hostess by my side in tears and looking somewhat frantic with a letter in her hand.

"I am grieved," said she, "that I cannot treat you better—we are poor indeed—my boys and girls are sick with fever, they cannot go for corn and other things our good neighbors on the other side of the river would give us, but I have killed my last chicken for you. The people here are selfish and have no feeling for the unfortunate. Wretched wife—unhappy Mother! When will my husband be liberated from his vile captivity in Mexico? Yes, they took him like a galley slave from San Antonio—and here he tells me in this letter that it is uncertain when they may leave the castle of Perote. Yes, once we were happy, I thought San Antonio a paradise, a fine climate, every thing in abundance, my poor husband doing well, my children joyous. Now we are beggars." Then casting her eyes up at two fine portraits of her self and husband, she burst into tears. "Look at our good furniture, all to pieces, and poor Elinor's piano ruined." I tried to console her as well as I could, but ever and anon she would come and add to my fever by the sight of her unhappiness. My fever and debility appeared to increase, but after some four days I tried to procure a cart and driver to carry me onwards; this I did not succeed in and left on horseback this poor family to proceed on my journey. *This was the only distressed family I have met with in Texas.* I had only strength to ride about six miles, stopping at a settlement, the owner of which I knew.

Here I lay almost insensible for a week, for independent of Intermittent, I was attacked with congestive fever. The medical man who attended the family was sent for, he gave me some medicine, but the fever increased and what to do with me was now the question. Several things were proposed, but from the distracting pain I had in my head and sight failing, I begged to be bled immediately. There was much consultation on this point, Doctor —— not appearing to think it orthodox practice. I was bled, found considerable relief and went to sleep. The bleeding took away the congestive and serious character of my attack and in a day or two afterwards I proceeded on my journey. The following day I reached my headquarters, where with proper medical attendance, quinine and chicken broth, I got rid of my chills and fevers, remaining very weak. I accompanied a friend to San Antonio, where in a few days I appeared to be completely recovered, but exposure to rains, northers, and travelling in the mountains, brought back four or five times chills and fevers, but of a mitigated character, only producing debility.

X

SAN ANTONIO DE BEJAR

[September–October, 1843]

September 11th, 1843: Left in company, by the road that goes through the settlements, and not by the main one,[1] with Mr. L——. Five miles on our way crossed Skull Creek,[2] which takes its name from a desperate battle that was fought here between Austin's first settlers and the Tonkeway Indians. The Indians were beaten and their skulls and bones remained at this spot for years. In crossing the western fork of Navidad River, we discovered a chaly-beate spring running into the stream. There is some pretty country on the Navidad, sufficiently timbered and well suited for corn, cotton, and stock. In it and its small tributaries there is trout, perch, and cat-fish; of game we saw deer, wild turkey, prairie hens.

September 12th, 1843: There are thunder storms daily, some rain, but the nights are fine. Put up for the night at Mr. F——'s plantation on Nixon's Creek, which runs into the Navidad. Mr. F—— has a race course on his land and a great amateur in horse flesh. He has a very fine settlement and good cotton and corn plantation; hundreds of his cattle roam about. He has some 80 Negros and not one appears to have been sick this season; they looked clean and comfortable, hearty and gay particularly the little ones. They spin and weave all their cotton and woolen clothing on this plantation and make the bagging and rope of cotton, for baling upon the cotton for market. It has been mentioned by some one who has written upon this country and repeated by

[1] Bollaert meant by the "main road" the eastern leg of the Old Presidio Road, which extended in an almost direct line from Columbus to San Antonio, by-passing the settlement of Gonzales, a few miles to the north.

[2] Skull Creek is an intermittent stream which rises in central Colorado County and flows southeast eighteen miles into the Colorado River. The stream was named after it cut into its bank and exposed a grave in which several skulls were found.

others, that the Irish potato planted in Texas becomes in time the sweet potatoe (is the convolvulus battatata—the other a solanum). This I will not vouch for, but Mr. F—— planted the white pea (large quantities of it) 3 or 4 years since, and it is now the small yellow pea.

September 13th, 1843: Continued our journey. Six miles from this on the La Vaca River[3] the wells are 50 feet deep, in some places going through clay and indurated sand.

We met with Captain Hatch[4] at the farm we stopped at; the evening was beautiful indeed and after supper we sat ourselves under a clump of live-oaks when Captain H. gave us an account of his being made prisoner at San Antonio by General Woll, the sufferings experienced by himself and some 50 or 60 fellow-captives on their journey to the Castle of Perote in Mexico, the inhuman treatment whilst there, his escape with Mr. Morgan[5] from prison, their difficulties and dangers ere they reached Vera Cruz, their getting on board an American vessel in that port bound for New Orleans and safe arrival in Texas, where the gallant Captain once more clasped dear wife and fond children to his bosom. He is now peaceably attending to his plantation on the Colorado River.

September 14th, 1843: Resumed our journey over undulating prairies by Ponton's Creek, rendered melancholy memorable for

[3] The Lavaca River rises in the southwestern corner of Fayette County and flows eventually into Lavaca Bay. The name in Spanish means "the cow," and was originally used by the Spanish explorers to refer to the buffalo. This stream was the first western boundary of Stephen F. Austin's original colony.

[4] This was George C. Hatch, who was captured along with fifty-one others by General Woll on September 12, 1842, in the Plaza of San Antonio. His name appears in General Woll's report of his expedition into Texas in 1842. Adrian Woll, "Brigadier General Adrian Woll's Report of his Expedition into Texas in 1842," *Southwestern Historical Quarterly*, Vol. LVIII (1939–40), 533.

[5] This was either Joseph C. Morgan or David Morgan. Woll's report contains the names of both men. In a letter written from Perote by Richard A. Barkely to H. G. Woods (quoted in Spellman, "Letters of the 'Dawson Men' From Perote Prison, Mexico, 1842–1843," *Southwestern Historical Quarterly*, Vol. XXXVIII [1934–35], 250), Barkely describes Morgan as "a noble fellow and spoke the Spanish language well."

the murder of Mr. Ponton,[6] an early settler, by the Indians—probably the Tahuacanies [Tahuunde] in 1835. We arrived at the "Big Hills,"[7] a high ridge running through part of these prairies, from which elevation, towards the W. and N.W. an immense extent of country is seen of hill and dale with herds of deer, woodland, and in the distance, the Guadalupe Mountains.

It is a picture, and well worthy the pencil of the artist, who could give an idea of the beauty of the country; it intimates to one that he is approaching the "Beautiful West."

At a short distance from the "Big Hills," the road through the settlements meets with the main one to Gonzales, still there are many plantations to the left. The pastures have been moderately good on our road, and in the creeks and hollows sufficient water for the stock.

Put up for the night at Mr. B——, myself and friend Mr. Low[8] had been sick with ague and still debilitated, so that riding through the sun for many hours would rather add to our weakness, and though fatigued, we could not sleep. We rose from our excellent beds and roamed about; the night was clear, the stars shone brilliantly, the moon was just rising[9] and shedding its silver hue over the trees. The stillness of the scene almost tempted one to meditation and reverie. After a long walk we returned to our room, where we found books, and not having any inclination to repose, commenced reading; Mr. L[ow]'s hand lighted upon *Pickwick*, mine upon *Elkswatawa, the Prophet of the West*.[10] The prophet was a brother to Tecumsee [Tecumseh], an Indian warrior famed

---

[6] William Ponton was a member of Green C. DeWitt's colony and was killed by the Indians, near the creek that bears his name, in 1834. *The Handbook of Texas*, II, 392.

[7] Big Hill derived its name from its location in Gonzales County on the highest of a series of rolling hills. The region today still bears the name, although it is only a farming and ranching community and not a town.

[8] This probably was Richard Low, originally from Chambers County, Alabama. The 1850 census (United States) shows a Richard Low a resident of Colorado County, Texas.

[9] The Moon shines so brightly at times that travellers camping out at night, play "Yuca" and Whist.—Bollaert.

[10] *Elkswatawa, the Prophet of the West* was written by James S. French (New York, 1836), in two volumes, and enjoyed about the same popularity during this period as the works of Cooper.

in the annals of the United States for his patriotism and bravery. The work is well written and will give the reader much information relative to Indian and frontier life, the sufferings of our glorious ancestors as pioneers in the new-world, for whom we ought to have unbounded veneration; and the history and persecutions of the Indian by the white man and his fearful retaliations. Alas! too often upon the innocent.

About this part of Texas and not many years since Indians hunted and camped, probably the Tahuacanies and Tonkeways, and many were the fights between them and the first settlers; the rifle has made havoc, and driven the Red Man off; the bow and arrow and tomahawk have been fatally used, and many a Pale Face lies buried in these woods, "not a stone to mark their graves," but their scalps preserved as heirlooms among the Indians!

The buffalo and mustang visited these woods and prairies in great numbers; the former has fled with the Indian to the interior, the latter, small droves are seen daily scampering about the prairies. Since settlements have been made, the howlings of wolves have diminished. The hunter can always find profitable amusement in the chase of the deer or bear, or he may trap the latter animal and the wolf also; and an inveterate votary to St. Hubert[11] may get a crack at a puma, jagua[r] (lion and leopard of Texas), leopard cats, wild hogs, etc. etc. etc.

September 15th, 1843: Wells here 20 feet deep, but a fine creek runs through the plantation (Peach Creek). Ten miles travelling brought us to Gonzales. It is situated on the eastern bank of the Guadalupe River and an excellent position it is for a town. This part of the country formerly formed part of De Witt's Colony.[12] Mr. De Witt is dead, but his family resides in the vicinity.

11 Saint Hubert, the Hunter's Patron Saint. He is allowed five feast days annually by some hunters, viz.: 3rd November, April, May, September, and December, but those of May and November are the principal feasts.—Bollaert.

12 Green C. DeWitt, from Kentucky, obtained a contract from the Mexican government on April 15, 1825, to introduce 400 families into Texas and settle them on the Guadalupe, San Marcos, and Lavaca rivers. Gonzales was the center of the DeWitt Colony, where DeWitt moved his family in 1828. He died on May 18, 1835. *Biographical Directory of Texan Conventions and Congresses,* 76.

In 1835, 2nd of October, there was a fight here under Captain [John H.] Moore, who commanded the Texans—the Mexicans were under General Castoñada [Francisco Castañeda] the Mexicans had to retreat. Previous to the commencement of the War, the Mexicans had furnished frontier towns, in particular, with artillery. But afterwards they wished to take such arms from the settlers. Ugartechea, the Mexican General, who had his head quarters at San Antonio, sent 200 men to Gonzales to return the artillery. They encamped on the western bank of the river and sent orders to Captain Moore, who had only some twenty men, to deliver up the cannon. His reply was "Come and take it." For a week or more General Castoñada diplomatised, but receiving a few rounds of grape and cannister from the Texans, returned to San Antonio, reporting to his superiors "that it was utterly impossible to carry his orders into effect."[13]

Gonzales was burnt by order of General Houston on his retreat in 1836, with a view to prevent Santana taking up quarters or finding refuge there; it has been partially re-built and only awaits peace to rise like the Phoenix from its ashes. Situated on so beautiful a stream, probably navigable to this place by small steam boats, surrounded by so inviting a country and on the main road to the West and Río Grande, with such advantages, Gonzales will become an important point.

On the map Seguin is placed too near Gonzales and ought to be placed as if at the apex of a triangle, the distance of Seguin from Gonzales being 35 miles and from San Antonio, 34. Gonzales was founded in 1827 [1825] and named after a Mexican General [Rafael Gonzales], was incorporated under the Mexican regime and consists of four leagues, laid off as town land, divided in blocks etc. and contained some 4 to 500 inhabitants. The corporation, I am informed, are willing to make donation of a certain

[13] The battle of Gonzales is generally described as the "Lexington of the Texas Revolution," or the first battle in the struggle for Texas independence. Captain John H. Moore and J. W. E. Wallace were in command of the Texas forces; their white battle flag was reputedly a rough banner with a picture of a cannon and the words "Come and Take It" written on it. The forces at Gonzales eventually marched on to San Antonio for the siege of Bexar a few weeks later.

quantity of town land to merchants, artizans, mechanics, and enterprizing people who might choose to settle here. Or town lots may be purchased for the corporation payable at the convenience of the purchaser. In many other places in the Republic, the same, I have no doubt, would be done.

September 16th, 1843: We started, rather a large party, from Gonzales for San Antonio, for still some fear is entertained of Comanches lurking about, particularly in the vicinity of San Antonio. Our party was composed of Old Texan warriors, hunters, traders, etc. Three miles from Gonzales, came to the San Marcos. This river and the lands on the upper part of the river are spoken of by those who have visited that part of the country with raptures. The road up the bank at the point where we forded without much difficulty was at a gradient of about 80°. Many of us had not seen a clear stream for some time, and we enjoyed copious draughts of it. We rode leisurely along. The weather was fine. Many plants in flower and the pastures improving.

I may mention here that capsicum or Red Pepper grows abundantly in Texas, particularly an indigenous sort called Chiltipin and is found in great quantities. It is about the size of a pea, of colours red and green. When dried it makes a very hot cayenne pepper, and when put into vinegar, gives it a fine flavour; there is a river named after this plant on the coast.[14]

It was after sun set before we crossed the Guadalupe[15] at that part known as the Capote, the settlement of Major E——; we found many travellers going to and from the West already "camped down," their fires gently blazing, the coffee pot on, and venison roasting. Mr. L—— myself and some of our party were accomodated by Major E—— for the night.

[14] There are two creeks in Texas that take their name from the red pepper plant which the Indians called *"chiltipiquin"*: Chilipin Creek rises in San Patricio County and flows into the Gulf at Copano Bay; the other, Chiltipin Creek, starts in Duval County and eventually reaches Agua Dulce Creek. The former creek is most probably the one Bollaert was familiar with.

[15] Here I first met Castro and the Lipan Indians—their appearance and encampment realized something of Indian life.—Bollaert.

213

September 17th, 1843: Strolled about the banks of the "Murmuring Guadalupe," its stream clear as crystal, the flowers and vegetation new to me and the gaudy "Cardinal" flitting about. The Capote Mountain is a conspicuous object, being isolated and elevated above the prairie 350 feet, and said to be composed of indurated silicious matter; it is covered with small timbers. Travelling some 10 miles up the Guadalupe we re-crossed it, it being nearer to do so than continue on its western bank owing to a bend in the river; and a short distance below Seguin "noon'd" and had dinner under the shade of some trees that surrounded a farm. They supplied plentifully with milk, buttermilk, and on our asking if they could bake us some corn bread a very pretty lass undertook to supply our wants. Caught cat-fish, trout, and buffalo fish in Guadalupe. One mile from our resting place crossed the river again at "The falls."

Now we fell in with fine pastures, particularly the musquit and gama grasses, and tree of same name (a species of acacia or mimosa), a plant looking like clover, moreover a cactus—the opuntia, I think. Camped for the night on Santa Clara rivulet;[16] this runs into the Cibolo River.[17]

September 18th, 1843: Crossed the Cibolo where was an opportunity of observing the geological formation of these prairies, seen to be about two feet mould, then rounded pebbles of limestone. Deer are beginning to be seen in great numbers and not shy. Three or four miles from the Cibolo saw in the road large specimens of fossil shells apparently of the oyster genus, in calcareous stuff.

One and a half miles east of the Salado River is the "Mott," a small clump of trees where Captain Dawson unfortunately got surrounded by an overwhelming force of Mexicans with artillery

[16] No such rivulet appears on the map which Bollaert was using, Arrowsmith's Map of Texas, 1840. Nor is such a stream listed in *The Handbook of Texas*.

[17] *"Cibolo"* was the word used by the Spanish explorers to mean "buffalo." There are at least three creeks in Texas which bear this name; the one that Bollaert has reference to is the present stream that forms portions of the county lines between Bexar and Comal, Bexar and Guadalupe, and Guadalupe and Wilson counties.

under General Woll last September. I am informed that when
Dawson saw his unprotected position and that he could not effect
a juncture with Caldwell, who was on the Salado, his advice was
to fall back upon [Captain Jesse] Billingsly's company, which
was safely posted in a hollow. But Mr. S—— and others cried out
somewhat vauntingly, "We came here to fight." "Then let us
fight," answered Dawson calmly. They commenced with their
rifles; the enemy began to play upon them grape and cannister,
accompanied with vollies of musketry; this firing was kept up for
some time when Poor Dawson and most of his company fell. Some
escaped and a few taken prisoners, amongst the latter was Mr.
S——. The graves of these citizen soldiers are in the "Mott" and
the bones of the Mexicans they killed lie around bleaching in
the sun.[18]

The next day after the affair with Dawson, was fought the battle
of the Salado under Caldwell; his brave band had pretty good
cover on the eastern bank of the river, each man took to his tree.
General Woll and the Mexicans were on a height in front of them.
Major H——, I believe, brought off the fight. Then the enemy's
infantry came up to within thirty or forty yards of the Texans, let
fly vollies of musketry—which produced no fatal effect; but each
rifle shot brought its man down. Now was the time for the Mexicans to charge, but they did not, they were panic struck to see so
many of their comrades either killed or wounded, and could not
be forced on, although their officers tried to force them to it at
the point of the sword. The rifle continued to annoy them, there
was confusion in their ranks, when General Woll considered it
prudent to retire and leave a handful of farmers and backwoodsmen masters of the field. The loss of the Mexicans is variously
stated, but to be within bounds from 100 to 150 were killed and
wounded; and only 1 killed and 4 wounded of the Texans. Many
Mexican skulls and bones lie in the valley of the Salado. The hero

[18] Bleached and gastly [*sic*] looking, a craniologist might probably find some
information here. Yesterday, the 17th [September 18, 1842] is the anniversary of
the battle of the Salado. I received many interesting details of the fight from one
of our travelling companions, Captain Ackland, of whom is told many daring acts
of bravery.—Bollaert.

of the Salado, Colonel Caldwell, died a short time afterwards and is buried at Gonzales.

In February, 1813, a desperate battle was fought here between the Mexicans, assisted by Kemper[19] and his brave associates, and the Spanish Royalists, to the discomforture of the latter. Four miles from the "battle ground," now and then the missions of Concepcion and San José seen down the valley, brought us to San Antonio de Bejar. As we approached we caught glimpses of the ruins of the *Alamo*, the towering steeple of the church and houses on the other side of the river through the dense foliage in the valley beneath us. Entering the town[20] by the eastern suburbs, the sparkling waters of the river from a thousand springs was easily forded. Not long since there was a bridge above the ford, but some heavy rains undermined the stone work at the ends, and now even it is inconvenient to foot passengers. After crossing the river, the main street of the town presents itself and the *plaza*, or great square, easily attained.

The arrival of so large a party created an unusual stir. Each soon found the abode of his friend or acquaintance, where he was hospitably received. The sun was sinking into the western horizon, the vesper bell tolled—the pious romanists went to evening prayer, we, as they call us *heretics*, to our suppers and then to rest.

The town of San Antonio may be said to be in ruins, but repairs are slowly going on. It occupies a fertile plain on the western bank. It is regularly laid off in streets, crossing each other at right angles, with an oblong space in the centre, about midway in which stands the church and other public buildings, divided into two equal

[19] Bollaert is referring to the battle near Rosillo, eight miles out of San Antonio, which was fought between an army of filibusterers led by Samuel Kemper and José Bernardo Gutiérrez, and a Spanish force of 1,200 men under José Manuel Herrera. The engagement took place on March 29, 1813, and not February, 1813. Warren, *The Sword Was Their Passport*, 48–49.

[20] [San Antonio de Bejar] from Conde de Bejar or *Bejar* in Spain, or *Abeja*, the Spanish name for Bees, and in all probability the first.—Bollaert.

Bollaert's first assumption seems to be the generally accepted one. The Spaniard's full name was Balthassar Manuel de Zuñiga y Guzman Sotomayor y Sarmiento, second son of the Duke of Bexar, who in 1716 was the ruling viceroy of New Spain. *The Handbook of Texas*, I, 155.

divisions of eight acres, the eastern denominated the civil, the western the military square. Around these *plazas*, or squares, are erected a continuous walk of flat roof'd stone houses, resembling fortifications.

There are other buildings of *adobe*, or sun-dried bricks, and lastly huts of the *Rancheros* erected of thin crooked muskeet[21] logs, placed endwise in the ground, the crevices "chinked and daubed" (filled with clay), without windows, flooring and thatched with prairie grass.

The San Antonio River is formed by numberless springs, three or four miles above the town. Besides affording an abundance of water to supply the numerous diverging canals, or *esequias* [*acequias*] for irrigation, it still sweeps on with a bold current, and with its flowery banks and its meandering channel winding gracefully through the city, may be considered its most valuable and interesting ornament.

From early evening until the soft hour of twilight the inhabitants flock to the river to bathe; and then the bronze-like forms of southern nymphs may be seen joyfully gamboling in the limpid stream, with their arch looks and their dark hair floating over their shoulders.

The population of San Antonio may be divided into several classes, as *Rancheros*, or herdsmen, a rude uncultivated race of beings, who pass the greater part of their lives in the saddle, herding cattle and horses, and in hunting deer, buffalo, or mustangs. Unused to comfort, and regardless alike of ease and danger, they have a hardy, brigand sun-burnt appearance, especially when seen with a slouched hat, leather hunting shirt, leggings and Indian moccasins, armed with a large knife, musket, or rifle, and sometimes pistols. To this class belong the peons or labourers, who in Mexico are little better than slaves.

The second is a link between the Mexican Indian and Spaniard, are somewhat civilized, superstitious and have less energy than the *Ranchero*. They reside in the city and its suburbs, cultivating

[21] There are several acceptable spellings of "mesquite," all of which Bollaert uses, with a few original forms of his own.

their beautifully situated *labors* [177 acres] or farms on either side of the gently running river, appearing to be perfectly independent and contented. Their usual dress is a broad brimmed hat of a reddish colour, or white, the band ornamented with silver ornaments or coloured beads, calico shirt, wide trousers, with a fancy coloured sash or girdle about the waist and the jacket thrown carelessly over the shoulder. Early in the morning they go to mass, work a little on the *labores*, dine, sleep the *siesta*, and in the evening amuse themselves with tinkling the guitar to their *dulcinea*, gaming, or dancing.

The females of this class are kindly and agreeable; they dress plain and tastefully and know how to develope the elegant proportion of their persons, particularly when tripping to matins, or vespers, their hands and faces coquettishly covered with the black mantilla or silk shawl—these are the votaries of the *Fandango* for which San Antonio is so justly distinguished. Nightly, while yet fresh and buoyant with the exhilerating effects of the siesta or bath, they flock to the scenes of mirth and music, conducted with decorum and without the restraints of announcements, bows, and introductions.

In *society*, the fandango is not introduced, their dancing is called *Bayle*, or a ball—there only is to be seen the *Madamas* of the city. Originally in the Fandango balls, the National, or Zapateos were danced, made up of a series of rather voluptuous movements, rather than dancing—but the waltz, quadrilles, and reels have of late been introduced. Spanish is the language generally spoken, but English, French, German, etc., may be heard.

Of Old Spaniards, or *Gauchupins*, there are none, and of their descendants, very few indeed; added to all these, there are a few American and foreign storekeepers who supply the Mexican traders or smugglers. The city officials are the mayor, justice of the peace, sheriff, constable, etc. The days of the Governador, alcalde, and Regidor are gone—gone for ever.

The inhabitants of Hispano-Mexican origin in San Antonio are of more abstemious habits than the Americans and foreigners. They adhere to the *Tortilla*, bread made of Indian corn, and each family has its *metate* for grinding it into a pulp, from which they make their bread in the form of thin cakes, something like a pancake which is baked on a heated piece of flat iron. The "metate" is of hard stone, such as granite. They soften the dried maize either by steeping it in a lye made of lime or from wood ashes. A sort of stew made of beef, chicken or any other sort of meat, with pumpkin and a large quantity of red pepper is one of their favourite dishes. Both sexes indulge largely in the tobacco in the delicate form of cigarrito, of finely divided tobacco, rolled up in a shuck or leaf which envelopes the head of the Indian corn. The never failing *metate*, a hide stretched upon a rude frame in one corner of the rancho, a copper or brass pot, a few earthern jars, *xorongos*, or Mexican blankets (called Poncho in South America) and a few small articles constitute the worldly effects of the Ranchero.

San Antonio has been the theatre of so many revolutionary scenes and skirmishes, that not a house has escaped the evidences of strife. The walls and houses on all sides are perforated by balls, and even the steeple of the church bears evidence of rough usage from cannon shot.

In September, 1842, whilst the Court was in session at San Antonio, General Woll pounced upon them, made them all prisoners, judge, jury, and councillors, sending them to Mexico to work in chains, the greater number being there still—thus, members of the legal profession have not thought it *convenient* to visit San Antonio since that period. On this account I was solicited to act as interpreter and adviser in the following case:
Calange v[s]. Clauzel

Mons. Clauzel, a French resident and merchant here, begged of me to go as interpreter with him to the Magistrates Court (his vice-consul Mons. Gilbeaux being absent)—presided by Judge McMullen[22]—for he asserted that two nefarious cases that had been brought *against* him—would go *against him*, one for $60 and

[22] This probably was John McMullen, formerly a partner in the McMullen-McGloin Colony, which received an empresario contract in 1828. Later, McMullen moved from San Patricio to San Antonio, where he served as alderman from 1839 to 1844. "Translations of Empresario Grants" (MS., General Land Office, Austin, Texas).

the other for $120. I will not enter into particulars of the cases, but mention that after the Judge had read over the plaintiff's deposition on oath, I asked if I might be Clauzel's legal adviser; this was granted. I observed that ere we could go into the case, we wanted to have the Plaintiff present. The Judge thought not. I shewed him Article 536—"Judgements and Costs" of Louisiana code of practice and afirmed that in Common Law that in the absence of the plaintiff or his attorney—I claimed a *non suit*. The Judge opened his eyes, put on his spectacles, looked into his law books and found that I was right. He then commenced turning and re-turning over the leaves of a book containing the Statuary [*sic*] Laws of Texas, and ultimately persuaded himself that his court had a similar attribute as the District Court of staying actions, say for 10 days. I admitted this point, being persuaded that the plaintiff in all probability would not appear, it being a queer transaction.

The next case was a claim against my client of $120, part only of which was admitted, but my client presented another account of $620 (which he never intended to claim had the plaintiff not concocted his). The items are curious—

1 bottle of whiskey per day for 240 days at 50 cents	$120
1 loaf of bread per day for 240 days at 50 cents	120
240 days grog drinking at the bar at Clauzels—	
$1 per day	240
Rice, pepper, salt, coffee, sugar, etc. etc. etc.	140
	$620

My client brought forth witnesses, one of whom substantiated to the above bill en masse, and the judge seemed *now* to coincide with us. There was much examination and cross crimination, and recrimination. He being a Spaniard, the other a Frenchman, there was considerable quantity of discussion, both talking and appealing etc. etc. etc. The Judge and self got them to order, and we, the J. and self, proposed, that the affair being of a *curious* character, should be settled by arbitration—this was growlingly acceded to—and they mutually cancelled their claims, the plaintiff *bearing costs*—thus we gained our suit.[23] My client liberally supplied my quarters with champagne and we had a good laugh over my first legal success.

In the good old times the Alcaldes were the judges, juries, etc., etc. and [decisions] *went by favour*, and any one who had money and no *influence*—he was fined or had to pay, without being permitted to defend his cause.

September 19th, 1843: I took up my quarters at Antonio Lockmar's, a native of Trieste, married to a Mexican lady, who resided on the outskirts of the town up the river. It is rather a low situation near the river and owing to the unusual visitation of mosquitos, could get no sleep. Bars or gauze mosquito curtains not being used so far west. There was another nocturnal annoyance in the shape of large numbers of small bats flitting about during the night. These animals particularly infest the town, owing to the number of houses in ruins.

A number of Mons. Castro's emigrants are here, several of them sick owing to their injudicious march up the country in hot weather. Many have died, and the greater part who are left, are about returning to France with the hopes of getting Mr. Castro to return them the 100 francs he made each pay to him ere they departed from Europe.

Santa Anna passed the Rio Grande on the 12th day of February [1836] with 8,000 men—the 23rd halted before San Antonio. Travis and some 130 took possession of the *Alamo*, fortifying themselves, having but few great guns. Travis appears to have repulsed the enemy on the 25th in two attacks. Now there commenced one of the most sanguinary assaults upon record, even the bloody Duke de Alba,[24] who was engaged in religious wars in the Low Countries, can be compared to this. Travis's letter dated

[23] Bollaert resorted to a practice sometimes used by clever lawyers in frontier courts, but today considered highly unethical.

[24] The Duke of Alba (or Alva) was sent by Philip II of Spain to suppress the Dutch revolt in the Netherlands (1567). His campaign was marked by extreme cruelty.

3rd March should be looked upon as a glorious specimen of unequal patriotism.

Poor Travis was killed on the 6th and at that period only 7 Texans were left. The Mexicans entered the Alamo, murdering those who remained, excepting a woman and a Negro, who were brave indeed—Bowie [and] David Crockett "If for the right, go a head"[25]—and who has not heard of David!

The bodies of the slain were burnt, some partially so! in revenge for the number they had killed with their unerring rifles, some say 1,000 to 1,500 men. I was shown the spot where their ashes are interred under some peach trees a short distance from the Alamo. An artist some time since finished a monument to the memory of the "Heroes of the Alamo," hoping that the Government would purchase it, which it did not do. The artist was exhibiting it about the country. It is constructed with stone of the ruins of the Alamo.[26] Many things have been made of same stone, but pipes principally for smoking. The deeds of such men will be recorded in the hearts of every patriot, their sufferings draw the tears and those who pass the Alamo and the cold grave where their ashes now rest must say "Oh! Liberty, how dearly thou art purchased." Much good poetry has been written on the "Fall of the Alamo."

In the evening a party was made up to visit the Alamo, passing the wooden bridge which is out of repair owing to a swell in the river. The sanguinary histories connected with this spot we all knew, but we met with an old Mexican who, as he traversed this

[25] This is what he told a young man who came courting David's daughter. —Bollaert.

In addition to Mrs. S. A. Dickinson (wife of Lieutenant Dickinson, who fell in the defense), other survivors were her child, a Negro servant of Colonel Travis, and two Mexican women of Bexar. Bollaert's account of the siege is fairly accurate, although the number he lists as slain, 130, is far too low. The number is considered to be 188. *Comprehensive History of Texas*, 240.

[26] This is the work of Messrs. Nangle and Co. It is intended to have the battle of San Jacinto, Goliad, etc., commemorated in a similar manner.—Bollaert.

William B. Nangle, an Englishman, completed this stone work in 1841. The monument can be seen today in the basement of the Old Land Office Building, Austin, Texas.

sacred pile of ruin with us, showed us where Crockett, Travis, Bowie, and others fell, recounting to us the brutalities of Santa Anna and his followers. One thing in particular our guide expatiated upon, namely the execution Travis did with "his gun" upon the Toluca regiment.

The church of the Alamo[27] must have been a very fine building. The front has still some fine scroll work. Over the door-way is to be seen a coronet and underneath it a shield with "Año D 1758,"[28] the period probably when the church was finished. The images of saints that occupied the four niches are non-inventus. From the top of what is left of the church there is a fine and extensive view.

The Alamo Church, the Presidio, barracks, or military post, was built by the Indians. On leaving the Alamo we strolled towards the "Alameda," formerly a public walk, and in the ruins of a house and in a garden, now choked up with weeds and full of snakes, thereabout found the statue of San Antonio decapitated, that of San Fernando sans nose, an eye pocked out and otherwise injured. The mutilation and destruction of the Alamo, the breaking up of the bells weighing some 5,000 pounds and throwing them into the River, and all connected with it, may be attributed principally to the Mexican General [Vicente] Filisola, when he retreated from San Antonio after the Battle of San Jacinto.

September 20th, 1843: On going to the Alamo to make sketches, an Old Mexican woman kindly brought me out a small chair and table. She had lived near the "Alamo" from a child and had known nearly all those who had fallen in the wars. "Yes Sir," said she. "I knew them all. Poor Travis! What a tiger Santa Anna must have been. I shed many a tear during that siege. He can have no peace." Whilst she was recounting the horrors of the siege, I

[27] Alamo or cottonwood.—Bollaert.
[28] The site was selected for the Alamo chapel in 1724; the cornerstone was laid in 1744. Amelia W. Williams, "A Critical Study of the Siege of the Alamo and of the Personnel of its Defenders" *Southwestern Historical Quarterly*, Vol. XXXVII (1933–34), 157–84.

was sketching and sympathizing with her, when she looked over my shoulder. "Ah Señor, had you but seen the Alamo on a Feast Day, as I have seen it, not like it is now, in ruins, you would have been delighted and I would not leave my Old Rancho here for the best house in San Antonio." She flattered my drawing as it went on and resumed her observations: "Then did I go every morning to Mass with Old Aunt Carmelita, who was one of a very few who escaped the "matanza" by the Comanches at San Saba (she only died a few years since), but now I only go into town on Sunday and great feast days. Ah! Señor, the front of the church was so beautiful. On one side of the door way stood San Antonio, on the other San Fernando with other saints. The bells rung a merry peal; they were broken up and thrown into the River, some say 50 quintals weight (5,000 lbs.), the enemy not being able to melt them into bullets. I never look into the ruins of the Church without shedding a tear; not half the walls are now to be seen and those grown over with weeds, moss, and even shrubs growing out of the cracks in its walls and what numbers of bats and snakes, but I have seen the Texas flag float over the poor old walls. It was then all walled in. There were large barracks for the troops and gardens with fruit trees vegetables and flowers in the *labores.*"

The old lady stopped her lamentations and looking at the sketch: "Ah, there is nearly all but the old walls and ruins behind. Well, well, I am glad you love the Alamo; here, I'll give you a crucifix made from the stone. Tis but ill-done but will serve as a remembrance of the Alamo." On my return I shewed her the sketch of San Antonio. "Very good, but you see it is in ruins and will remain so—*hasta quien sabe* until who knows when!"

Visited the church of San Antonio. It has been twice accidentally burnt down; the walls of the interior are very bare, and very poor apologies for altars, considering this is a roman catholic country. The Sacristan or vestry clerk was polite and communicative; he told me they were in a "difficulty," not knowing exactly to whom the church was dedicated, San Fernando, or Our Lady of Guadalupe, or San Antonio.

Towards sun-down accompanied Major Hays[29] a few miles from town down the river to his encampment preparatory to starting westward. Here we found the Major's "Spy Company" busy preparing supper—plenty fine beef, corn bread, coffee, and with the luxurious addition of sugar. Over our pipes a few songs were sung, the blanket was spread and then to sleep.

Major Hays is from [Wilson County] Tennessee; he has been in command of the Western Rangers for a long period and lately the government has given him very extensive powers as regards the frontier. The Major is young, amiable, and exceedingly modest, and beloved by his followers. He has the reputation of an Indian fighter and good backwoodsman. Many have been his encounters with the Comanches and Mexicans. A few weeks since Hays and 16 of his company fell in with Antonio Perez and some eighty Mexicans prowling on the waters of the San Miguel: when this small body of Texans drove them off.[30]

September 21st, 1843: Our camp in movement for a start, crossed the San Antonio at the Nogal, below the Mission of San José, and when fairly out in the prairie had a fine view of San Antonio, Concepcion, San José, La Espada, and down the river. It is reviving to the European, to behold in the far West of the New World, edifices partaking of the character of the sacred buildings he has left behind him; and we cannot withold our praise from the Spanish ecclesiastics who designed and reared with the assistance of the Indian the churches, dwellings for the Indians, etc. forming the Missions on the San Antonio River. The styles of these churches is light and of a mixed modern, Italian,

[29] John Coffee Hays became a captain in the Texas Rangers in 1840, and was charged with the protection of the frontier from Indians and Mexicans. He participated in several engagements with the Indians, later served in the Mexican War as a colonel in charge of the Texas Mounted Volunteers. In 1849, he moved to California. He remains one of the most famous Texas Rangers of all time. James Kimmins Greer, *Colonel Jack Hays.*

[30] The incident which Bollaert describes occurred in August, 1843, between Hays and Manuel Pérez. The latter was defeated and chased across the Río Grande, along with his superior force of a hundred men. Pérez had hoped to sack San Antonio and exact vengeance upon the few Anglo-Americans there. *Ibid.,* 91–92.

and Spanish. The statues of Saints, angels, ornaments, particularly the scroll work, was of a superior character. If the destructive hand of the Hun, Vandal, or Goth has not been here, that of the volunteer has made sad havock with the various ornamental parts of the several missions and generally manufacturing pipes for smoking out of say the nose of some saint, or the foot of a Virgin Mary —feeding their horses out of a beautifully carved font, etc., etc.

After leaving the San Antonio River we entered the Llano (Prairie or Plain) del Leon, which is some seven miles across; somewhat of the hog-wallow character with musquit trees, but affording good pastures of the excellent musquit, or muskit grass.[31] About this country grows another fine grass called by the Mexicans, "Mocallo," which is green all the year round. This prairie and the adjoining ones were formerly full of cattle and horses and a few sheep. At the present time nothing of the sort is seen.

In crossing the Llano del Leon, on the left is seen the undulating lands of the lower part of the Medina River; on the right, ranges of hills, which run through the whole country, their vallies full of fine pasturage, cedars, elms, cypress, etc., etc. Out of these ranges of hills rise peaks, one in particular called La Culebra (The Snake),[32] bears W. 10°, N. and 15 miles from San Antonio. The Tetillia Peaks, N.E. of the Salado, are likewise seen.

Passing the dividing ridge between the Leon and Arroyo del Medio[33] and travelling five miles brought us to the Arroyo, or stream, where we camped. The country alive with deer and hares. Of timbers, there is abundance of musquit, post-oak, hackberry,

[31] As the growth of cane and peach are the signals to the planters of cotton, sugar, tobacco, etc., so is the musquit [mesquite] tree and musquit grasses to the herdsman and shepherd in the selection of lands. The Indians are said to eat the seeds of the musquit tree, which is a species of locust; the Mexicans feed their hogs on them. It is something like the blue grass of the United States. Beautiful furniture has been manufactured from the musquit wood, and it might be made a valuable object of exportation. The natives in their admiration of this wood call it Texas mahogany.—Bollaert.

[32] There is a creek by the name of Culebra, which is an intermittent stream which rises in northwestern Bexar County and joins Leon Creek about seven miles west of San Antonio. Culebra Peak apparently now has another name.

[33] Medio Creek rises in the western part of Bexar County. It flows southeast approximately fifteen miles to empty into the Medina River.

elm, etc. It had been very warm during the day, but the evening was fine and the air cooled by the southern breeze.

From the Leon to the Medio, the surface of the land covered occasionally with small silicious pebbles, but the soil said to be rich.

September 22nd, 1843: A guard was kept all night, for there is still a possibility of Comanches being in the neighborhood; but from the very severe lessons they have of late received, there is not much to fear from them.

Went with Major Hays to the Medina River over undulating land three miles distant from our encampment. The river was very low; at times it rises 12 or 15 feet. The "bottom" is well timbered with many sorts of wood, and many pretty settlements might be formed with fine ranges in the prairies for stock. Nearly all the best land on the streams in this section are located, but not settled upon.[34]

Afternoon returned to San Antonio with Major Hays, Mess[rs]. A. & R. Mons[r]. Jean Bonnian of Angouleme in company; on reaching that place found that monsieur had the reputation of being "Un peu fou," so if he persists in going to Mexico Major H. will make some safe arrangements for him. In the evening I had the pleasure of going with Dona J. M——, one of the belles of San Antonio and the whole of her family to see the "Maro-

[34] Here a page is missing. The following takes up the narrative: wallet on the ground, and offering us a bottle of whiskey and in an imploring tone commenced "O mes chers Comanches—no no—Messieurs les Mexicains je vous prie d'avoir pitie de moi—je suis un pauvre français, je suis venir chercher fortune en Amerique, mais je n'aime pas la nouvelle Orleans laisse moi partir pour la Mexique pour l'amour de Dieu—Voulez vous mes cher messieurs prendre du Eau de Vie." On our telling him we were neither Comanches or Mexicans, but Texans and mustering up all our french tried to quiet the fellows apprehensions. He did not appear to be in his right senses, when Major Hays concluded to take him back to San Antonio[,] ascertain if possible something about him, and moreover if he was bent on going to Mexico with his wallet containing pins, needles, pomatum, thread and such like things to get some of the traders to allow him to accompany them: He had travelled by land from New-Orleans had been treated kindly by the settlers on his route, and was now about traversing alone, unarmed and with only some half dozen small loaves of bread, the uninhabited country from San Antonio to the Rio Grande, but we could not make him believe that the chances were against him of being made captive by the Comanches, but the more likely thing he would get out of tracks or trails, be lost and must perish.—Bollaert.

meros," or Provincial rope dancers and actors! the company consisted of a comical Payaso, or clown, three young men and one female. The performance was *al fresco* in the court yard of a house in a public square. At the foot of the tight rope was made two large fires, this being the only illumination for actors and audience. The rope dancing over, tumbling commenced, this being finished, upon a rude stage, a comedy and two farces followed, the three pieces occupying about twenty minutes. I cannot speak favourably of the polite composition of the dramas represented; it was indeed very *low comedy*.[35]

September 25th, 1843: Visited the Springs that form San Pedro Creek,[36] the waters gush out in great quantities from the "rotton limestone" rock, which said rock appears to have been formed from probably primitive limestone of the interior. Fossil shells of the Ammonite and other species are said to have been found in the San Antonio River. Some twenty-five miles from San Antonio there are very extensive sulphur springs which are in considerable repute for scorbutic patients, the principal spring bubbling up with such force, and although very deep, a person throwing himself in can only sink up to his waist.

The majority of *labors*, or small *lots* of land around San Antonio, [are] full of weeds. In former times they were in a flourishing condition. An emigrant having one or two *labors*, say of 50 or 60 acres, could farm all he needed and graze any quantity of stock and sheep in the adjoining prairies and upon the very best pastures.

Money is very scarce here, even the curate is obliged to receive for his different duties, cattle, corn, etc., which he barters for what he may require.

[35] Zebulon Montgomery Pike passed through San Antonio in June, 1807, en route from Mexico to the United States. His observations on the Mexican rope dancers and acrobats performing on the Plaza were as follows: "[They] were no wise extraordinary in their performances, except in language, which would bring a blush on the cheek of the most abandoned of the female sex in the United States." Zebulon M. Pike, *Expeditions. . . . ,* II, 694.

[36] San Pedro Creek rises in central Bexar County from springs in the city of San Antonio and flows south two miles through an artificial channel into the San Antonio River.

September 26th, 1843: Visited the springs, or head waters, of the San Antonio River three to four miles distant from the town. The numberless springs form three or four principal streams which soon unite and form the pretty rivers. The waters issue from the springs with considerable force out of the limestone rock and are somewhat tepid. All round the springs is a thick and almost impenetrable underwood, with large timbers of all sorts, on the branches of which saw flocks of wild turkey, called by the Mexicans Gujalotes. When peace with the Mexicans and Comanches shall have been made, these springs will be a most excellent spot for Barbecues or Pic-nicks.[37]

On our return to town found Major Howard,[38] the sheriff, and others starting in pursuit of Comanches. A young Mexican had just come in wounded in the leg and reported that a few miles down the river he had been shot by Comanches. During the day we discovered that the said youth was very much in love with Doña ———, and had been loitering too much of his time, in the opinion of his father, upon his young beautiful mistress. His parent desired him to attend to some business at the farm and that immediately the love-sick youth left the city brooding upon self-destruction, but upon second thought, shot himself in the leg, hurried into San Antonio reporting that the Comanches had shot him. The young lady, on being made acquainted with the real state of the affair, was so ashamed of him that she *cut him.*

Major Howard was kind enough to conduct me to the court house in the plaza and give me an account of the fight with the Comanches there in March, 1840. By some this occurrence has been called a "massacre," by others as a most just measure. I will not comment upon the particulars but give the official document connected with it. There are a few Comanche children in San Antonio; on asking one, a boy who was assisting a stone mason

[37] Bollaert was a prophet indeed. This spot today is the famous Brackenridge Park, which is not only a picnic spot but also contains one of the largest zoos in the Southwest.

[38] This was George Thomas Howard, who served Bexar County as sheriff from 1843 to 1845. Major Howard distinguished himself in the Council House Fight. *The Handbook of Texas*, I, 852.

in the Plaza, how and when he came there, he replied, pointing to the Court House, "My father was killed there"; but, he appeared gay and happy.

September 30th, 1843: For some days past there has been very heavy rain, accompanied with lightning and thunder and strong breezes from N. E. Although agues have visited Texas from the Sabine to the Colorado pretty extensively this year, there has not been one case of chills and fever here. Monsr. Castros emigrants many of whom travelled up to this section of country during the heats of summer fell sick and several have died. Some of them believed the rigid diet was the best course to pursue, this debilitated them, when they ought to have lived generously, say upon good corn bread, milk, game, beef, of which there was and is plenty of here; they preferred a small quantity of wheaten bread and cabbage soup.

Sunday, October 1st, 1843: Fine weather again with southern breezes. The Maromeros, or Mexican rope dancers are jumping about this evening. Although San Antonio is governed by Texan laws, Mexican customs prevail; rope dancing, tumbling, and plays on a Sunday!

We have now fine weather. The N. E. winds and rains appear to have left and balmy indeed is the air, the few clouds floating about prevent the sun's rays from being oppressive. Low and self passed a good night—took 3 grains more of quinine. This was my fever day, but thanks to care and quinine it did not come on.

The evenings are pleasant and still, save near the river and esequias (aqueducts for irrigating the land) where [there are] a very few mosquitos, but they meet with their never failing enemy, the mosquito hawk. But about 1 A. M. one is often awakened by the roosters (cocks—one must not say cock in these diggings) in the vicinity, when one has for half an hour the pleasure of hearing their discordant notes. About 3 A. M., this is repeated with the barking of dogs. And ere daylight the roosters recommence a furious crowing, much harsher than in Britain.[39] About sunrise roosters, hens, chickens, squally children, and scolding mothers commence and then it is advisable if one is not sick to seek quietude in a walk—but not too far, for a Comanche might scalp you or Mexican robber kill you. But with all these little difficulties, one, were there a peace, might live very comfortably here.[40]

Monday, October 2nd, 1843: Accompanied a party to visit the "Old Missions." The Mission of Concepcion [is] 2½ miles from San Antonio on the eastern bank of the river. The walls round it are in ruins, but the church is in pretty good order still. It bears the date of 1754 over the door way.[41] The interior of the church is crowded with bats' nests and the body of it covered in some places with the excrement from these animals a foot thick, giving out no very pleasant odour.

A few hundred yards from the church is the battle ground of the "Grass Fight,"[42] on the 28th October, 1835, under Bowie and Fannin. There were 92 Texans against 360 Mexicans. Of the

[39] One is summoned to breakfast, not long after sunrise in these parts by the blowing of an ox's horn. In more populous towns by the ringing of a bell, but at New Orleans and other places in the United States by the striking on a Chinese *gong*, thundering its vibrations to a great distance.—Bollaert.

[40] Goods can be got from the Coast to San Antonio at about a cost of 25 p. c. The shop-keepers here formerly expected 3 to 400 p. c. Now some are contented with from 100 to 150 p. c. There is little or nothing to be done in San Antonio at the present moment in really a mercantile line. The very few picayune shop-keepers supply the smugglers who come in from the Rio Grande, these bring seldom more than 3 to $500 and the talking and chicane to be used and heard is perfectly disgusting. Were there a peace and commercial regulations arranged between the two countries, one English Agent—I will not say *House*—would at moderate prices and *no credit* swamp the whole of the *would-be merchants*, who are jealous even of each other.—Bollaert.

[41] Concepción Mission was moved from East Texas and established in San Antonio on the San Antonio River in 1731. C. W. Hackett, "The Marquis of San Miguel de Aguayo and His Recovery of Texas from the French, 1719–1723," *Southwestern Historical Quarterly*, Vol. XLIX (1945–46), 193–214.

[42] The so-called "Grass Fight" was fought one month later than Bollaert indicates, November 26, 1835. San Antonio was occupied by a Mexican force under General Martín Perfecto de Cós, while outside the town a revolutionary army of less than one thousand men, under General Edward Burleson, was camped, guarding the approaches to San Antonio. A detachment of Mexican troops went out to gather grass for the Mexican cavalry. The Texans, seeing the Mexicans and believing them to be reinforcements, made a charge which resulted in about fifty of the enemy being killed. *Comprehensive History of Texas*, 192–93.

Mexicans there were killed and wounded 100 men, whilst on the part of their opponents only one killed, named Andrews, who unfortunately exposed himself too much.

Three miles further and on the west bank of the river stands the Mission of San José,[43] the church of which is still in good preservation, built of stone—the limestone of the country—but the images of saints and other ornamental parts have been sadly mutilated by the soldiery during the wars. The ornaments on the door way and window of the sacristy or vestry still show much exquisite work and labour that had been bestowed upon them. On the tower of the church is the date of 1781, probably the year it was finished. There is only one bell left and that is split. The Church is full of bats' nests, but mass is occasionally said to some 8 or 10 Mexican families who live within the walls of the mission. The missionaries who superintend this establishment were those of San Francisco, who resided at the *oriel* end of the church in a fine suite of rooms, shaded by a broad corridor.

This as well as the other Missions were walled in so as to protect the sacred teachers and those Indians they were reclaiming and who were instructed in agriculture etc. by the pious fathers from the attacks of Comanches, etc. Independent of the rich lands this Mission had on the river and around it, eleven leagues of pasture lands were donated to it, commencing at the Loma del Paderon, 12 miles east of San Antonio and running 7 or 8 miles west of the Medio Creek. This land is now in litigation, [John] Mac-Mullen versus certain land speculators who have located on part of it.

One and a half miles is the Mission of San Juan, on the eastern bank of the San Antonio River. It is in ruins; part of the belfry and walls only remaining; here reside a few Mexican families in

---

[43] Massive and rude as are these half Gothic edifices, they produce an agreeable interruption to the sameness of the surrounding hills; and that of San José may be esteemed as possessing claims to symetrical architecture and sculptural beauty. It appears that as many as 1,200 Indians were employed in its building, who were forced by whips and by the gloomy dread of certain death, if resistance was manifested, to pack upon their shoulders the ponderous materials from a quarry several miles distant."—Bollaert.

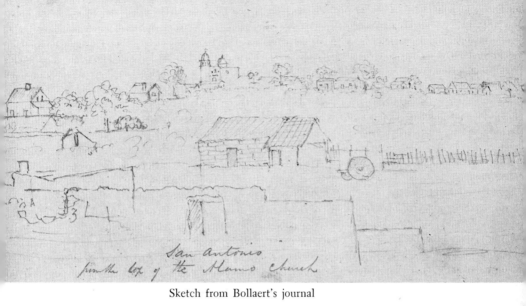

Sketch from Bollaert's journal

San Antonio from the top of the Alamo Church.

Broken Bridge over the San Antonio River.

Bollaert's drawing

Bollaert's drawing

Texan Farm in Montgomery County.

their favourite mud ranchos. Having recrossed the river, about a mile brought us to the Mission of La Espada de San Francisco; it is not quite in so ruinous a state as that of San Juan; here were a few Mexican families.

There are no more Missions I believe on the San Antonio river until Goliad is reached;[44] the mission was on the eastern bank; the fort and town on the western settled in 1716. But when this country was under the Old Spaniards, there were many Haciendas, or large farms, on the San Antonio, each of which had a chapel. The old Mission of Refugio is near Copano Bay,[45] and there was another near San Augustine.[46]

By a law of Congress of January 13, 1841, the Alamo church, that of San Antonio, Concepcion, San José, San Juan, La Espada, Goliad, Victoria, Refugio, with some portion of land, and the church lot at Nacogdoches were ceded to the Roman Catholic congregations.

Our party returned and put up for the night at San José in the sacristy where after a good supper prepared by our Mexican friends, we passed the evening very pleasantly.

Tuesday, October 3rd, 1843: Our party enjoyed themselves much in the *sacristy* last night—the glass went round, the song was sung, but not one from the Americans of the party. They are very fond of convivial parties, but add little, more than tippling and smoking. Morning raining but obtained a sketch of the mission. Returned to San Antonio—raining and unpleasant for travelling, making the roads very heavy. It would appear that such

[44] The Spaniards moved the mission Nuestra Señora del Espírito Santo de Zuñiga and the presidio Nuestra Señora de Loreto, the popular name for both being La Bahía, to present Goliad in 1749. Previously, Goliad was the site of an Indian village. *Comprehensive History of Texas*, 47.

[45] The mission at Refugio, Nuestra Señora del Refugio, was established in 1793, the last of the Texas missions. W. E. Dunn, "The Founding of Nuestra Señora del Refugio, the Last Spanish Mission in Texas," *Southwestern Historical Quarterly*, Vol. XXV (1921–22), 174–84.

[46] This was the mission of Nuestra Señora de los Dolores de los Ais, built in 1716 and permanently abandoned in 1773. E. C. Buckley, "The Aguayo Expedition into Texas and Louisiana, 1719–1722," *Quarterly of the Texas State Historical Association*, Vol. XV (1911–12), 1–65.

changeable weather is hardly in the recollection of the oldest inhabitants. 5 P.M.: Heavy thunder storm and rains. The town and roads a perfect quagmire. From sundown to 10 P.M. "a considerable up street tall rain."

The principal tribes of Indians subdued by the earlier missionaries were the Tehas, Tejas, or Texas Indians[47] (I am informed that two or three of these still exist), the Xaramenes,[48] and the Adaes, or Adaices.[49] The last roamed about Eastern Texas. At the Mission of Concepcion a few Apaches were occasionally brought. The Indians when got into the missions were comparatively pacific, sometimes they would try to escape to their wilds, and to make them cultivate the lands about the missions oftimes coercion was necessary. They sometimes rebelled against their spiritual masters, then the military of the Presidio del Alamo was called in to quiet and intimidate them.

The Missionaries were generally Francisans and others of the order of Our Lady of Guadalupe of Zacatecas. About 1800, the missionaries left Texas, but ere that period there were no more Indians in the Missions, they having died off. And in a mutilated record belonging to San José, more than 1,200 deaths of Indians are noted down. The three tribes of Texas, Xaramenes, and Adaes Indians, are now extinct, thus this would go to prove that the sort of civilization introduced by the missionaries did not tend to increase their numbers.

[47] Tehas is the Comanche name for the residence of happy spirits in the next world. Thus, the Spaniards from Tehas formed Texas, which means the "happy hunting ground," or the elysium of the Comanches. The following satirical couplet gives the etymology of the name, as at present received in the Western States of the Union:

> *When every other land rejects us*
> *Here is the land which freely takes us (Texas)*.—Bollaert.

[48] The Xarame Indians must have constituted a very minor tribe, for they are little known or associated with the early history of Texas. The great authority on North American Indians, F. W. Hodge, says that they probably were a Coahuiltecan tribe, originally from the vicinity of San Antonio.

[49] The Adaices formerly resided about Nacogdoches. There was a Spanish town called Adais, Indian name, between N[acogdoches] and Natchitoches, and formerly the residence of the Spanish Governor of Los Texas.—Bollaert.

The various missions supplied the garrison of the Alamo with the produce of the soil and cattle, for which the holy fathers were paid. The Spanish Military were a proud domineering class and considered themselves lords of creation and many are the acts of oppression attributed to them. Their main occupation was to guard the frontier and the missions from inroads of the Comanches. It is known that many were the encounters between Spanish troops and the Comanches, but the following partakes somewhat of cool-blooded revenge. For years the parties in question had been at war, when after certain arrangements made between commissioners from either party, it was concluded that the principal Comanche Chiefs should assemble at the Mission of La Espada, a feast and presents should be given to them and a treaty of peace and perpetual friendship entered into. On the day appointed two thousand troops were secreted in the Mission of La Espada, and when three hundred of the Comanches came to make the treaty, they were surrounded by the Spanish soldiery and all killed.

Notes for a History of San Antonio de Bejar

A complete history of San Antonio from its foundation about 1716, or perhaps before that period, up to the present time would indeed be interesting. About 1716–18, the Marquis de Aguayo offered his services and fortune to the King of Spain to prevent the French colonizing Texas; France then being at war with Spain. To the Marquis was entrusted the regulating of the different settlements around the frontier of the colonies, correctly considering the place an excellent trading station, both for the people dwelling along the Rio Grande, and the populous tribes of northern Indians, numbers of whom, by this time, had been converted to romanism, and reduced to labourers and cultivators of the soil. Aguayo petitioned the King that four hundred emigrants might be sent to San Antonio de Bejar: that two hundred of these emigrants should be selected from the Indians of Tlascala,[50] the

[50] According to Hodge, the Tlascopsel (Lacopseles) was a tribe of south cen-

remainder from Galicia in Spain and the Canary Islands, confer-
ring the rank or *hidalguia* upon such families as would embark in
the undertaking. Of the four hundred families, it appears that
only sixteen reached their destination and these from the Can-
aries, the expense of whose transportation amounted to 72,000
dollars, which was mainly defrayed by the indefatigable Aguayo.
This attempt having so far failed, it is said that the Marquis be-
sought that the prisons of Mexico be emptied of their inmates,
who were sent to supply the deficiency.

The emigrants first settled at the head of the San Pedro Creek,
about a mile W of the town, but soon took up or removed to the
present site, naming it "La Villa de San Fernando, capital de los
Texas en el reyno de las Nuevas Filipinas." (Town of San Fernando, capital of Texas in the Kingdom of the New Philipines);
the presidio asiento, or military station, of the Alamo[51] on the
other side of the river [was] under the tutelary care of San Antonio de Austria. The emigrants from the Canary islands were
ennobled, or made *hidalgos*, and much form was observed in their
municipal arrangements; documents up to 1756, I have had the
perusal of, relative more particularly to the partition of lands upon
the river San Antonio. After the establishment of the Alamo and
the town or city of San Fernando, the various missions on the
river were formed, for the civilization of the Indians in the lower
country, and many Spaniards and Creoles of Mexico settled in
this frontier town and it is reported that in its flourishing times
the population amounted to as many as 10 to 12,000 souls.

Louisiana belonged then to the Spanish Crown, and there was
a road from that place across Texas by San Antonio to Mexico.

tral Texas, probably Attacapan. They undoubtedly were descendants of the Tlascalan Indians from central Mexico, brought into Texas as soldiers and slaves of
the Spanish in the sixteenth and seventeenth centuries.

[51] The Alamo Mission was originally referred to as San Antonio de Padua, or
San Antonio de Valero. During Mexico's war for independence from Spain, a
company of Spanish soldiers from Alamo del Parras, Coahuila, occupied the then
abandoned mission. The name Alamo probably originated from this association,
although Bollaert (as well as some historians) maintained that the name was
derived from a grove of cottonwood trees growing on the banks of the *acequia*.
(See footnote 28 above.)

A line of forts were likewise established from the Pacific Ocean through California and Texas, probably by San Saba, where mines were worked, San Antonio, and Goliad, and terminating at Refugio on the Gulf of Mexico.

After the extinction of the Indians of Texas, many Mexican Indians and Creoles made arrangements to work the prolific lands on the San Antonio; then this part of the country may be looked upon as at its height of prosperity.

Napoleon's conquests, which put the Old World somewhat out of joint, shook the political frame of the new, and although the colonies remained loyal for some time, there were spirits who soared above the mass of the people and declared for independence. A few Mexican patriots assisted by some daring Americans in 1812 commenced their opposition to regal power. They took Goliad, the Battle of Rosillo[52] followed, the Spaniards had to retire from San Antonio. The patriots drove their opponents from their strong hold of the Alamo, capturing the military chest and other valuables; they gave the Spaniards battle afterwards on the Alazan Creek, but this time they were unsuccessful and had to retreat. Some years afterwards General [James] Long, an American in conjunction with the Mexican patriots, harassed the Spaniards considerably on the northern frontier. Then came the Mexican Civil wars, and lastly the Texan wars, all of which tended to prostrate and ruin San Antonio.

But for nearly a century, things went pretty smoothly on in this "Vale of Avoca,"[53] between the proud soldiery of the Alamo, the rich Spaniards and Creoles, their quasi slaves, the peons and *tame* Indians, who attended to agricultural operations and the large herds of stock, and the missionaries, friars, and other ecclesiastics. The Comanches would occasionally descend from the mountains to rob, kill, and scalp; then the military would sally forth and

[52] It is said in San Antonio that Bernardo Guiterrez [Gutiérrez], the revolutionary commander, after the battle had six of his principal prisoners' throats cut. These are known as "Los seis gobernadores," this sanguinary operation being performed by one Juan Vasquez, who is still alive.—Bollaert.

[53] Avoca, or Ovoca, is the name of a valley and river in Wicklow County, Ireland, celebrated in one of Sir Thomas Moore's songs.

punish them. There is a record of a great fight and overthrow of the Comanches by the Spaniards under Colonel Uvalde [Juan de Ugalde] in a valley N.W. of San Antonio, which from that occurrence bears his name. The valley is said to be most picturesque, and moreover fine lands for settlements. The Comanches subsequently have entered San Antonio [January, 1790] and demanded tribute of the residents!

In referring to the year 1812 when one Bernardo [Gutiérrez] was the revolutionary chief in command, the Royalist troops were defeated with great loss at Rosillo not far from Goliad. Bernardo in one account is said to have had seventeen Royalist officers (his prisoners) killed. Six more of the prisoners who were known as the "Six Governors," he ordered to have their throats cut! This sanguinary order was entrusted to Juan Vasquez, who executed it to the letter. Yesterday this same Juan Vasquez, who since the period of the Mexican Revolution has led the life of a brigand, was met by a person some twenty miles down the San Antonio River.

Vasquez: Is it the road to San Antonio?

Traveller: I know you. Why do you ask such a question?

Vasquez: Do you take me for a thief?

Traveller: Why you have been a thief and murderer all your lifetime.

Vasquez: Draw and defend yourself.

Vasquez drew a pistol. At this moment a Mr. F. came up, and seeing Vasquez about firing at his opponent, levelled his rifle, but missed the brigand. Mr. F. and the other, after some time, made Vasquez prisoner, and in marching him to San Antonio, Mr. F. saw a deer; he dismounted to shoot it. Quick as lightning Vasquez "broke" and ultimately escaped.

Juan Vasquez has for some time been connected with a gang of Horse and Cow thieves.

In 1819, there was a famine in San Antonio, many of the inhabitants retiring to the Colorado and occasionally after very heavy rains the river rises and does much damage to the farms.

Iron and coal, it has been reported by some to have been found near San Antonio—this is an error.

We have no positive information, but it is suspected that the Texas Commissioners, if they have started, have gone by way of Matamoras.[54] In the East it is believed that there will soon be peace, in the middle counties they *hope* only, but it excites them —but it is rather expensive amusement. In proof of this, even when Woll came on in the following autumn, there was no pillaging, and had not the citizens been taken within arms, he would not in all probability [have] made them prisoners: i. e., the Perote prisoners. His object was to prevent the West from becoming settled, to intimidate the foreign residents and scare, if possible, the Americans; and if there was a chance of getting to the then almost depopulated Austin, which was then the nominal capital of the Republic and w[h]ere the Archives were, either to have destroyed these records, or have taken them to Mexico, and to have trumpeted for victory. It is only 3 days march with an army to Austin, but his orders were to go beyond San Antonio, and I think the Colorado River was high, and ere he could have done much damage to the defenseless *capital*, the *brush* all round would have poured forth its hundreds of rifle balls, and *every one* would have told. Indeed, I know that Woll was censured by Santana for going out to the Salado, posting himself where he did, even with 1,100 men, and here a handful of Texans in the narrow bottom *whipped* him. Probably two things combined to save him from disgrace—1st, the entry of the Texas citizens into Mexico and prisoners; 2nd, the slaughter of Dawson's Company and the par-

---

[54] Bollaert is referring to George W. Hockley and Samuel M. Williams, whom President Houston appointed as special Texas commissioners (September 26, 1843) to meet those of General Woll, at some point on or near the Río Grande, to agree upon the terms of the armistice. The Texas commissioners met with two Mexican officials at Sabinas, on the west side of the Río Grande. After some difficulties, the negotiation was cut short by information of proceedings in the United States and Texas in regard to annexation. But an armistice was eventually signed on February 18, 1844, in which Texas was referred to as "a department of Mexico." It was promptly rejected on the part of Texas. *Comprehensive History of Texas*, 420–24.

tial backing up of the West—but as a set off he had 150 killed and wounded.

Wednesday, October 4th, 1843: Rain all night, morning cloudy. Last night supped at Mr. Lagnis, heard Mr. Chevalier give an account of his hair-breadth escapes, after being taken prisoner (when out spying with Mr. Dunn) by Mexican *"scouts"* who preceeded Vasquez. He described the *break* from San Antonio from the Mexicans when on his *parole,* knocking one of the soldiers down, etc. making for the head of the river, the guard after him—getting up into a tree; whilst there Mexicans and Indians (Cherokees) for three days upon his trail, and often under his hiding place. At one time he heard voices speaking English; now he thought he might descend, but on looking before he leaped, he saw it was a Mexican with a lot of Northern Indians who spoke English on the look-out after him. Had to play 'possum again. After a sufficient time had elapsed, he descended, got into the bed of the river, waded up it some distance, got out upon some rocks, so that his trail might not be traced, and with a blanket only, made his way E, toward the Salado, and soon met some of his friends returning to San Antonio. It was generally believed that Vasquez's party was the advanced guard of a large force that was coming on, and even when many of the foreign merchants were told to the contrary, they in their *excitement* must "slope." Some were ruined and others put to considerable expence and loss. But some of my Texan friends love confusion.

Colonel W. G. Cook[e][55] was good enough to shew and explain to me particulars relative to the capture of San Antonio in 1835, in which he took a very prominent part, and many inter-

[55] Colonel Cooke, who was principal commissioner [of the Texan Santa Fé Expedition, 1842] tells me that he advised that waggons should not be sent—in case of a difficulty. General Lamar hoped during his administration that with the few that he ultimately permitted to go, would have been able to have revolutionized Santa Fé in favour of Texas and thus had a direct trade; and as Texas claims the Rio Grande as its boundary, he fondly hoped to have had it soon enrolled as a Texas city. But there would have been difficulties with the U.S. traders, for had it succeeded, it must have curtailed their trade. But a much better trade awaits the Texans—viz: the Rio Grande and onwards to Chihuahua.—Bollaert.

esting observations relative to the "war-worn" [Ben] Milam. He was from Kentucky and fought against England in 1812–15. He joined the Mexicans against the Royalists. He was imprisoned by Iturbide,[56] but rescued by the people. In 1828, he had a grant of land in Texas. He was imprisoned by the Mexicans but escaped and joined the Texans in the capture of Goliad. Milam fell at the glorious assault of Bejar, 7 December 1835.

Thursday, October 5th, 1843: Had as comfortable a rubber of whist at Antonio Lockmar's on the bank of the San Antonio as if we had been in Grosvenor Square. Sipped hot toddy—had a snack and then to bed. We have news just brought in that there are some strong outposts of Mexicans on the Nueces, one of these was attacked some little time since by the Tonkeways, some Mexicans killed and their military trappings taken away. This I do not think is very judicious.

Some months since a party of Mexicans, scouts or spies, came upon the Medina and there was nearly a fight with Hay's Company. About this time it was intimated to Hays from General Woll that if he continued to or did molest any Mexicans—that Woll would get him watched narrowly and hang him, and recommended him *as a friend* to leave his command. Probably General Woll would like him to take service in his army!

[56] Agustín de Iturbide was emperor of Mexico from May, 1822, to March, 1823. He was overthrown by Santa Anna after his brief but extravagant and arbitrary regime.

XI

THE VALLEY OF THE GUADALUPE

[October, 1843]

Friday, October 6th, 1843: After dinner joined a small party of six for a trip into the mountains to hunt bear, bees, and fat bucks. Found we wanted for some few groceries, etc., and an axe [and we] sent in a Mexican. We camped for the night near the eastern springs of the San Antonio River under some fine peccans, profitably amusing ourselves shooting wild turkies as they would come to roost for the night. Last year the peccans [were] in abundance —this year they will be scarce. This is a pretty general rule. Sallied out into the woods after wild turkey; the moon is near its full and lights our way. Saw none. There was a remarkable stillness in the air when we lay down, but at 11 P.M. a very strong norther came on, and very cold—could not keep myself warm.

Saturday, October 7th, 1843: Very sick—vomiting—could keep nothing on stomach. Started, but obliged to stop the party on one of the branches of the Salado, 9 miles from our camp, and lie down. With some toddy, sleep, and coffee—much better. A buck shot and "fat ribs" roasting. About half-way today in a prairie saw a cave supposed to be deep and branches off—but too sick to make observations. Country pretty—plenty of deer, but want of water; good musket grass for cattle. Afternoon better— Dunn went out hunting; he fired several shots in rapid succession. Robson[1] thought Indians had got round him. Off we sallied, but

---

[1] Bollaert was closely associated with Colonel Robert Robson from the time of his journey to San Antonio in October, 1843, until he left Texas the following year. The 1850 United States census shows Robert Robson living in Colorado County at that period. His age was given as forty-six, and he was still listed in the 1860 census, but not in the 1870 census. Robson owned a plantation in Montgomery County and another one in Colorado County, which he considered his home. The Montgomery estate was called the "Scotch Hermitage," where Bollaert spent considerable time late in 1843 and early 1844. The Englishman sometimes referred to it as a "hunting lodge."

Robson was a man of considerable wealth, and from indications in Bollaert's

found he had two deer and another wounded in the brush. We only want the skins now to make *botas* to put wild honey in. Meat is left on the prairie for the "t[urkey] buzzards." The buzzards will follow hunters and Indians for a great distance for what may be left. Hunters seldom, without pressed with hunger, eat other than the "fat ribs" and tail, sometimes the head and other tit-bits.

The country about here is undulating, with post oak timbers, and strewed with "rotten limestone" with occasionally silicious pebbles; and flints are often met with.

Sunday, October 8th, 1843: Night beautiful and clear—full moon, heavy dew, calm, and cold, probably about 40°. We are now approaching the mountains and about 450 feet above the level of the sea.[2] 6 A.M.: Left camp—a short distance Davis turned off to the right with the idea of meeting them [the other members of the party] in the next valley. They were not there, neither could we find their trail; had to go back thro' brake and brier and at last found it. This was about 10 A.M., and from that hour until 4:00 we had a precious job to reach the Cibolo (Indian l[anguage] for Buffalo). The distance from San Antonio is 7 or 8 leagues—24 [miles],[3] but we put a pretty good *yapa* ere we found our companions. Deer getting tame in the wildness. I shot a buck at about 50 yards. Only stopped to tear his skin off—leaving the body to be devoured by buzzards and carrion crow. The country we tra-

notes he must have been one of the stockholders in the Kennedy Colony. He was born in Dumfries, Scotland, and came to Texas around 1840. Sometime around 1850, he built a large mansion on his plantation in Colorado County which was known as "Robson's Castle," a showplace of the entire area. The castle covered a fifty-acre plot; it was made of homemade lime and gravel, and was built on the south bank of the Colorado River where Austin surveyed the site for his headquarters, and was surrounded by a moat and had a drawbridge. This was probably the first building in Texas to have a roof-garden and running water. A severe flood on the Colorado in 1869 did considerable damage to the castle, and it was finally torn down in 1883, and a beef processing plant was built on the site. "Scrapbook of Colorado County," University of Texas Archives.

[2] Bollaert is very much in error relative to the elevation of the country which he was approaching, the Edwards Plateau. The elevation is closer to 2,400 feet above sea level. It is difficult to understand how he could have made an error of approximately 2,000 feet unless by a slip of the pen.

[3] The hunting party must have been somewhere in the vicinity of present Leon Springs, Texas.

versed today was undulating and hilly—trees small of live and post. The land is covered with large quantities of the tertiary limestone and in some of the gullies it is seen stratified horizontally, with an E declination. From our camp this morning on the Cibolo, 400 feet more the stream running about 2 miles. It has been higher a few days since, owing to rains. When these are down, then the Cibolo is a very small stream. The land we have traversed today appears *just now* to be only fit for grazing.

Monday, October 9th, 1843: Awakened very sick—commenced retching but brought nothing up—saddled, retching continued—about 2 miles here I became very ill and weak and settled into chills and fever—took an opium pill and 3 calomels and rhubarb. 4 P. M. moved on 6 miles to the "esequia." Hays passed here when after the Indians.

Davis believes that he is never lucky whilst hunting without he has a piece of gold or silver in his pocket, Robson, that we lost our road by his having fired his gun on Sunday—his rule being not to do so, but there is no resisting a fat buck.[4] But Davis' piece of superstition is the first I have met with in this country.

Tuesday, October 10th, 1843: 7 A. M. started towards the Sabinas,[5] not so rocky and rising a little as we get to the heads of the streams—pastures covered with little musquit grass, small timbers of post and live oak, black jack. Occasionally wild cattle

---

[4] Robson is a Scotchman. He loudly protests against hunting on a Sunday, but he could not resist yesterday, although it was the sabboth, to have a "crack."—Bollaert.

[5] On the map there is a creek called *Sabinas*. There are two, 1st and 2nd *Sabinas* (Cypress Creeks) owing to the number and beauty of these trees, and what is called "Verde Creek" is a continuation of the Guadalupe River, according to our hunters.—Bollaert.

There are a total of twelve creeks in Texas today named "Cypress Creek" (none by the name of *Sabinas*). The two creeks which Bollaert refers to here undoubtedly were Cypress Creek, an intermittent stream rising in northern Kendall County and flowing southeast about nine miles to drain into the Guadalupe River; Cypress Creek, an intermittent stream rising in northeastern Kerr County and flowing southeast about nine miles into the Guadalupe River just across the county line in western Kendall County.

met with about here. Saw some but they were off before we could get after them.

When wild cattle is met with, and it is the intention to rope or lasso them, no guns must be fired or they will all be off. Our party separated again, Dunn and the Mexicans. We had a hunt after them, but gave them up and made for the Cibolo higher up; approaching the river here it is prettily timbered and some good little prairies—when the very good lands are settled a great deal of the Cibolo will have its graziers and hog raisers. Noon camped —Phelan[6] and self got fire under way and mush in the coffee pot —for our absent friends have the principal cooking apparatus— bread, etc. Davis and Robson went into the woods, and soon returned with a young and tender buck. I contented myself with a kidney and made some venison broth. Our lost companions, had crossed the river, and espied us—leaving the baggage on the other side made for us and came in time for dinner. Crossed the Cibolo to a good camping ground. Rocks on either side in layers, almost horizontal. If there were a few more navigable streams in Texas, what a country it would soon be, but its peculiar resources will be turned to account some day.

Four species of grape generally is known: the summer, winter (the small), fox (largest) and blue grape (between F. and W.). Davis and Dunn went across the river and in the bush—in less than ¼ acre—they gathered the summer and winter grape, black-walnuts (smaller than ours, which is the W.W.), black and red haw, 2 sorts of persimmon—peccan, mountain plum, etc. The grapes were small—the summer ones sweet—the winter grapes ripen when the first frost comes on.

Wednesday, October 11th, 1843: Sunrise—up camp, got to the source of Las Sabinas. Many springs from the hills forming this rocky stream. Here large cypress line the steep banks—up here the rock of the hills puts on the appearance of—probably waters retiring and leaving—a series of shelving on either side of the vallies. Large trout in river. On our arrival had a severe attack of

6 Phelan, my old Portuguese comrade.—Bollaert.

chill and fever, which lasted nearly all day; could not move off my blankets. For the last two days we have been on Indian ground and have to keep a good look out for Comanches and Tawakonies [Wichitas]. We are rather too few for a fight with any numbers of them. One is never safe in the Indian ranges with some 10 or 15 well armed, and in an advantageous position.

All very hungry. Dunn went out and shot a hen turkey, just as they and their gobblers had roosted. The inner bone (from the second joint) makes a very good turkey call. Fever did not leave before 4 P.M.

Thursday, October 12th, 1843: Shot another turkey for break-fast and with mush, honey, and coffee, made a good meal. Started for the Guadalupe Valley and camped about 3 or 4 miles, but just as we approached one of the tributaries of the Guadalupe, fell in upon a fresh trail—then a camping ground. Then in a small prairie, with the continuation of said trail, council of war held. It was decided that some 20 Comanches had been down about 3 days since, had hunted, and scared the wild cattle and perhaps the bears and had moved off towards the Guadalupe and then to join their tribe in the upper vallies. Very pleasant for amateur bear hunters and shews that a party should not be less than 15 or 20 well mounted—for several reasons.

The hunter should be habited in the tanned hunting shirt and leggings or trousers,[7] armed with spear, holster, pistols, and rifle, Bowie[8] or hunting knife and a smaller pocket knife—to be com-

---

[7] In warm weather cotton drawers and cotton shirt—in winter, flannel shirt and drawers. Summer, moccasins will do, in winter stout boots, particularly when the mornings are damp, rainy, and much dew. Hat, colour of dress, high and broad brim—for wet weather, covered with oil skin.—Bollaert.

[8] There are three or four brothers, Jim, Razin [Rezin], Pleasant, and another. Razin Bowie had been one of a party of 4 on each side in a duel at Natchez. Two or three of the party lay dead, and Razin badly wounded, when one of the victors made a pass with his sword, with the intention of running the wounded man through. The sword passed in one side of the body—this gave Bowie time to draw a small *couteau de chasse* or Bowie Knife (made for him by one of his brothers) and insert it between the (two to the right) ribs, turning the knife round and severed the heart, so that when the man's body was opened, the heart was found loose and dislodged. The Bowie Knife now came into fashion, and was followed by a similar sort of weapon called the "Arkansas tooth-pick." (Dr. Wooster)—Bollaert.

fortable divided into mess of 5, each mess having a camp kettle and iron pot, frying pan, coffee pot—each his tin cup—or half a gourd will do better, for then one can drink with[out] burning oneself, and thus be a match for the backwoodsman, whose mouths and throats are insensible to the feeling of heat.[9] When in Indian country dark horses are preferable, for they are not so easily seen at night by the Indians. During the day horses may be allowed a pretty wide range, but at night brought into camp. Saddle and saddle bags should form the pillow—the bridle at one's head. Blankets placed so that they may be laid hold of in the dark and if necessary, horse saddled quickly. The arms, if fine weather, may recline on the tree one lies under—if wet, rifle and pistols laid along side you under your blanket. There should be one guard during the night for 1 or 2 hours and if there be apprehensions of Indians, make but a small fire to cook by and that ere sun down. No firing or hunting—and put fire out after cooking.

2 P.M.: Up camp— got into wild cattle trail—heard one bellowing, camped on a little stream (2 miles) that runs into the valley of the Guadalupe. Up here the valley is broad, full of fine little tributaries, running thro' lands full of good grass, and the cypress taking the head among its timbers. The grape we picked as we rode along, but our attention was directed after wild cattle and bear. Saw but few deer up here, perhaps it is getting a little too cold for them. The Guadalupe hunters went out but could not catch them. Went bee hunting—found some in the hollow of a cypress tree. Bear and buffalo tracks seen, formerly large herds of the latter animal inhabited these spots; they appear to have migrated more northerly. We are a little too soon for bear, but as

---

[9] Indian corn meal is the best for bread-making—a little venison fat put in the frying pan and when melted, put in the meal and water. It soon cakes; turn it and the bread is made. *Mush* is good also. Even when a pack mule is not taken along, bread, dried beef, coffee, sugar, salt, pepper, tea, may be carried in the saddle bags. In the pouch which may have two compartments for bullets, punk for kindling fire, or a piece of rag rolled up and the end rubbed with powder—then with flint and steel, fire can be soon got by putting the (amadou) punk or rag into some dry grass—whisk it about, the grass takes fire, then a few dry sticks and *voilá fuego*. —Bollaert.

yet bruin is luxuriating and fattening upon acorns and in the thick timbers and brush bottoms. In the evening went out and a fine black bear was our prize.

Friday, October 13th, 1843: Night cold and distribution of blankets would have been acceptable. Up camp and 1 mile brought us to the picturesque Guadalupe River—not fordable in parts—banks of limestone perpendicular in places—at others little prairies reaching down to the stream.[10] Phelan sighted a young black cow—off went D——, crack went his rifle—but he required four or five to bring him down.[11] Robson and self down with chills. About 3 P.M. I got over it and just strong enough to make these few notes—the rest busily at work cutting it up a lò Mexicano so as to dry it and thus we shall have meat for some time. Quantities of cypress on the bed of the river at the sides— at sundown the wild turkeys (Juajalote-Mexican) roost on them —and black walnut is in no scarcity, and the armorers (Mr. Goodman an Englishman an armorer) in San Antonio does not wish for any better wood for stocks. I have seen stocks and furniture made of this wood and with a little age takes a fine dark colour. I am too weak to go into the thick woods, but I have seen enough of the small trees.

Sunday, October 15th, 1843: Cold during night, heavy dew. We are about 50 to 60 miles from San Antonio—Robson taken down with a chill after breakfast. It was my chill day and I nearly brought

[10] The travelers were now in the vicinity of present Kerrville, Texas.

[11] We thought to have got sight of the bison, or buffalo, about here, but it appears that they are just now some distance N and N.W. of us. A party not long since left Austin and anticipated to come upon the buffalo, after two or three days' travelling. The buffalo comes down occasionally into the low country of Texas, and there are a few at times to be met with near the coast. All the Indians are great buffalo hunters, preparing the skins with great care for "robes." It was a brown-bull that was exhibited in England some years since as "The Bonassus."

I am not able to discover the etymology of the word "bison," but buffalo I think I have made an approach to it. A day or two since we crossed a river called the "Cibolo." Now the Indians call the buffalo "cibolo," and formerly about the head waters of this river there were numerous herds of the animal—then again, it may be that the Indian has accom[m]odated the word buffalo to "cibolo."— Bollaert.

it on by turkey shooting. Our hunters rather unlucky—but we have fine weather and drying our beef.

Anecdotes: An American farmer seeing his family increase, and altho' himself and wife were very industrious, they could not get on. One day whilst working his corn field he observed to his wife: "Nancy, go to the house, I smell a snake—when I come, I shall come with a rush." He then clandestinely left for Texas and is now living here.

A settler was struck all of a heap, that he wanted a wife, and knowing that a rich but ignorant neighbor had a daughter to dispose of with considerable "moral"[12] conduct, saddled his horse early one morning. He arrived at his neighbor's and found that the damsel in question was in the pen milking the cows, to which locality he repaired, to observe, etc. She had just filled her pail, when the cow kicked it over. She re-filled her pail and returned to the house—saying, "Dad, what do 'ye think?"

"What Sal?"

"Why old Brindle kicked the pail of milk hell-west."

This was enough for the would-be Benedict, and he sloped home, observing to himself (he having some knowledge, as a surveyor of the compass): "Hell and scissors, I've boxed the compass many a year, but never heard of such a point as 'hell west'!"

There is at present a family in Texas, one of Austin's settlers, but there are few such—neither the father, mother, children, and a son-in-law know how to read and write, yet by dent of industry, arising out of his league and *labor*, he the year before last branded

[12] In the Southern states of America, a *gal's moral character* or fortune is generally in Negros and land, in the Northern States "bank stock" and notions and whether or not the Papa is likely to become a bankrupt shortly; sometimes there may be cash.

"Why don't you marry, neighbor?"

"There is time enough for such a difficulty."

"Neighbor B. has a likely daughter. Have you no use for her?"

"How stands her moral character?"

"Why, when she marries, the Old Man intends to give her ten Niggers, stock, and a good slice of Caney land down there by the creek."

"How does she favour?"

"Not the handsomest gal in the world, but mighty smart, clean limbed, and can milk cows first-rate."

"Let's ride over there tomorrow."—Bollaert.

2,700 head of calves, and drove 1,100 head of beef cattle to New Orleans, for which he received $18 per head *in silver*=$19,800. His capital when he started was 2 cows and calves, 2 horses, a colt, a jersey waggon, a wife, and some young children. A respectable man begged the hand of one of his daughters and was refused on account of his knowing how to read and write.

Deaf Smith was taken very ill on the Medina and made up his mind to die. He called Davis to him, and begged that Davis as a dying man's request—should dig his grave some 6½ feet and put him down head foremost—the reason he gave was that he had come into the world feet foremost, and thus had been unlucky, but hoped that going out of it head foremost, he would meet with a better fate.

Monday, October 16th, 1843: Night cool but fine. About here in the bends of the river, fine hunting preserves might be enclosed which ultimately would become stock raising settlements, and by judicious management even the Comanches might in time be conciliated. There are parts that might be cultivated— plenty grazing land for cattle—but just now it is only a hunting country. There is one great disadvantage for navigation about the rivers in and toward the mountains: during the freshets caused by heavy rains, the rivers run torrents; the rains over, they dwindle down to small streams.

8 A.M.: Broke up camp with our dried beef etc., on our way to San Antonio. Crossed the two Sabinas Creeks; at the second is a very rocky path up from the stream—*escala*. Got into the Pintas trail and journeyed on over several ranges of hills (dividing ridges) then thro' a fine prairie for stock and came to about 1 league from the Cibolo—few deer seen today. Found some grapes occasionally. Dunn and Melchor killed a bear, and Davis a very fat buck. Evening—star light and the air balmy.

Tuesday, October 17th, 1843: Robson very bad all morning with chills. I had no chill or fever, but had to lay up, suffering much from debility. Coffee without sugar, no bread or meal, and meat only—with pretty heavy dews—are not quite the thing for sick people. We had to remain in camp—our companions out hunting. Game very tame and fat. 4 P.M.: Up camp; 3 miles crossed the Cibolo 6 miles above where we first crossed it; 5 miles more came to the Pintas Spring at the foot of Loma del Pinto. Night rather warmer than we have had it.

Wednesday, October 18th, 1843: On our route today the country was alive with deer. Some good locations might be made, if the settler would be contented with springs, small streams, and good prairie pasturages. Nooned at the Olmos Springs,[13] the waters from which run into the San Antonio. Here are excellent hunting grounds.

In the evening on our approach to the ancient capitol of Texas, firing as if of musketry and shouts were heard. On our gaining the summit of the ridge known as the "Indian Lookout," two miles from the ancient capitol of Texas, the valley of San Antonio was seen in great perfection; the cupola of the church, the houses and dense foliage made it a perfect picture. The "Indian Lookout" is used by the inhabitants to see over a large tract of country and to observe if there be any Comanches about. The Indians likewise come to this spot and should there be any horses in the valley, they soon find their way into the Comanche camp.

As we approached San Antonio, we heard shouts and firing as of musketry. There was a halt—council of war held, which occupied a few seconds only—unanimously decided to enter the town. If the enemy had arrived during our absence, they could shoot us if they pleased, or take us to Mexico, if they caught us. In a few minutes our views relative to a probable sojourn in the castle of Perote underwent a change; for in a *labor*, or field, we perceived a Mexican family busily employed eating water mellons. We smiled at each other. The firing we had heard was occasioned by the town sportsmen partridge shooting.

[13] Olmos Springs form the headwaters of Olmos Creek in north central Bexar County. The stream flows south about fifteen miles into the San Antonio River in the town of San Antonio.

Bollaert and his hunting companions undoubtedly were very much fatigued from their expedition up the Guadalupe Valley. There are no entries in his journal or notes again until October 24, 1843, except for the following brief notation in Spanish for Saturday, October 21, 1843: "My birthday. It may be that my Sadie will remember me this day. Today my fever should have taken effect, but it appears that I will have the pleasure of passing this day without great difficulty."

A brief essay entitled "On the Different Sorts of Hunting and Species of Game in Texas" might also have been written at this period. Although it contains no specific date, and is unattached in the notes, the subject is relevant to Bollaert's recent experiences.

On the Different Sorts of Hunting and Species of Game in Texas

Deer—1st: (Deer have been met with with 36 points on antlers or 18 on each side. Deer shed their horns, and every year a new point comes out). By merely shooting them down in day light with the rifle; this is deer-stalking and hunters generally get up to the game from 80 to 100 yards—others fire when they can discover plainly the eye of the animal. When game is scarce, then dogs are employed to scent them. Deer, if not badly wounded, will run and dodge about, then dogs are useful to catch them, particularly in the woods.

2nd: By fire hunting. This is performed by one person carrying an iron pan basket filled with burning pitch-pine with which they *shine* the eyes of the deer, and thus are enabled to shoot the deer in the darkest nights.

3rd: To watch near their trail as they go to water.

4th: To hunt them with stag or fox or grey hounds—the hunt seldom exceeds two hours.

5th: To shoot them by making a "salt lick." For this purpose the hunter fills a small hole with salt, which entices the deer near their drinking places, and whilst they are licking the salt, the hunter from his ambush, which is generally from up a tree near him, to prevent the deer scenting him, shoots them down.

6th: To have a pet doe with a bell attached to her neck, when sent out into the woods, entices the bucks to the house.

It is generally recommended to aim at the neck, or thro' the shoulder, so as to ensure a dead shot. The elk is seen and very large in NW part of Texas, as well as the antelope.

Bear: This animal is generally found in thick cane brush, he is hunted with dogs, shot with rifle when in distance, and speared at times. When the bear is a large one, and has not been mortally wounded, the hunter must look out, for "he's the boy for a fight!" But in all difficulties with a bear, and when he prefers close quarters, the Bowie Knife may then be resorted to with success. The black bear is the only one known in Texas. They are sometimes trapped, at others made to shoot themselves, by wires placed across the path they may take, which wires are connected with the trigger of a rifle. The largest may weigh 1,200 pounds—but generally 6 to 700 pounds. Four friends of mine unarmed fell in with a bear; they only had their Bowie Knives with them—they went to work and killed him.

Mexican hog, or peccary: These are found generally in the low hollows of trees and shot; the meat is very good.

The *Grey Fox* is in great abundance; he is much smaller than the English fox, but its habits are nearly the same. He is hunted with dogs, and generally after a two hours run, the fox takes up a tree, when if the hunters are fatigued, they pop a bullet thro' his head. This taking up a tree appears to be on account of wolves hunting them, thus the wolf being unable to climb trees, has the mortification of losing his prey. Dogs often will go hunting on their own hook, they go regularly to cover, scent, and start the fox, give tongue, chase him. When Reynard is hotly pursued, up he scrambles a tree; the dogs, when the fox is treed, alter their tongue, then if any hunters be near he makes for the dogs—crack goes the rifle and down tumbles the fox, and then he gets an awful shaking.

Opposum: Burrows in the ground or in the hollow and old roots of trees, and is a slow travelling animal. He is seldom seen in the day time, and the Negros hunt them at night with dogs. The opposum takes to the tree, when the tree is cut down and the dogs catch him. The flesh is good.

Coon: He is hunted like the opposum; the meat is good, and the skin gives a good fur.

Skunk or pole-cat: They are several colours; they are very slow in their movements, and can be shot from horseback, but the fetid odour they exude when chased generally prevents their being taken, except by Old Hunters or Indians. When the stink being removed and its hair singed cleaned and broiled, the meat is like young pig, but rather darker.

Panther: or American lion is generally met with in the river "bottoms" or in the cane breaks and peach thickets on the margins of rivers. He is hunted with dogs and brought down with the rifle. The skin is valuable.

Leopard (spotted) the *Jagua:* Its habits and manners of taking same as the panther. Skin is valuable.

Leopard cats: Same as above. Grey panther cats, colour like the panther.

Squirrel: Grey, black and fox—generally shot on the ground and in trees. There is a "flying squirrel," having a membrane like a bat. All are eaten; gives good fur and leather for shoes, gloves, etc.

Ground hog: Small and burrows—it is something like the opposum, but does not climb. This animal will fight hard against dogs, ere he gives up.

Wild hog: This is the common hog run wild—hunted with dogs and shot—makes fine bacon.

Wild cattle: is good hunting and fine meat.

Buffalo: The habits and hunting of this animal have been so often described that I omit to say more than there are immense droves in Texas.

Wolves: There are two species. The large black wolf and the prairie wolf. They are hunted and shot. They destroy young cattle.

Hare, rabbits, minks, otters, and beavers in abundance. Of feathered game, in abundance, and the rivers and bays are full of fish, and not omitting to mention the alligator.

Mustang, or wild horse of Texas: When residing on the coast I heard much concerning the numbers, excellence, and beauty of the mustang from some people, whilst the observation of others went to shew that the same animal was not what it was "cracked up to be," being very wild, difficult to catch and break in, and above all, full of "mustang tricks," such as running away when an opportunity offered and "taking to the woods," dangerous to bridle and saddle etc., etc.

The Texas mustang is not like the wild horse of the Pampas of Buenos Ayres, as regards its blood, numbers, or beauty, and these and other desirable characteristics, it must not be expected from them, considering their origin. The wild horse of Buenos Ayres has descended from a better and purer stock, the best sort of Spanish horses from the Barbary or Jennet. He has had and still has boundless prairies of 1,000 miles broad and 2 to 3,000 miles in length and only occasionally hunted for his hide, and this by the white man, being seldom harassed by Indians excepting by those who dwell to the S and W of Buenos Ayres, who consume their flesh, particularly that of mares and make use of the hides. Thus, in crossing the Pampas of Buenos Ayres to Mendoza or towards Salta, very large bodies of wild horses are met with scampering along with the fleetness of the deer, the manes and tails distended with the wind and revelling in sweet liberty.

Now the mustang of Texas is of Mexican descent. As a mustang he cannot trace his history very far back and ere he found his way over the Rio Grande, either by running away from the vicinity of the Sierra Madre, or from the Apaches or Comanches, etc. one of whose great delights was and is to steal horses from the Northern Mexican frontier, or horses escaping from the "Missions" or in the fights with the Indians. The mustang of Texas may be considered a sort of mongrel.[14] One of the best proofs of his indifferent qualifications is that the Indian horse robbers, Comanches, Apaches, etc., seldom catch them except it is to eat the young ones, generally the dried flesh and for hides, making "cabrestos"[15] of their tails and manes, preferring a Mexican or an American horse. The breed of the mustang may improve if not hunted too much by the Indians: Lipans, Tonkaways, Tawacancis [Tawakoni] etc., who, when they approach the Coast in the summer, hunting them for their meat, jerking or drying it, and for taming so as to use them to carry their camp equipage, themselves, and families. (It is said that droves of mustangs rove about the NW part of Texas). These and other Indians will give great prices for very common American or Texas horses, but the Indians generally do not know how to take care of a horse: he has no corn for him, and all grass and no corn, when the animal is worked by long journies, makes a horse very thin and often one Indian journey does him up.[16]

The pure Mustang is easily taken, but when they have been accompanied by American mares or horses, they get very cautious, difficult to catch, but their size and breed is improving. Thirteen hands high is given for the pure mustang. The general way of catching the mustang is to get them hemmed in and noose them with the lazo. They kick and struggle for a few minutes, but finding a tight rope round their necks and strangling them, take not Hudibras idea of life and death not to continue the wish of run-

[14] Some authors on Texas I think have considerably overrated the mustang, but they are useful animals.—Bollaert.

[15] Cabristo—a long rope made of horse or cow hair.—Bollaert.

[16] Feeding of horses: morning, noon, and evening—10 or 12 ears of corn and fodder; in the West muskit grass only.—Bollaert.

ning away, but give themselves up to be civilized and thus become useful members of society. Another plan of securing the mustang when he "takes to the woods" and there is a difficulty in lazoing him, is to get pretty near to him and "crease him;" this is done by shooting him with a ball just under the mane about the centre of the neck; when this has been done by a steady marksman, the animal generally falls, when he is then easily taken (the wound soon heals) and then broken in, and if refractory, his first schooling is very severe. Should, however, the "crease" have been made too far down, then his hide, tail, and mane is manufactured into cabrestos, his flesh a feast for the "turkies with a surname" (buzzards) and carrion crows. I have seen fine mustangs taken, and docile in a few days. I have seen mustangs full of dangerous tricks, and with "mighty" wicked eyes, being ever on the look-out to give a bite, kick, shying and running the rider up against trees; but travelling in Texas is mostly performed on American horses, or bred from them. The English stallion or two have been wafted over the great waters—"Smoke," etc.

Tuesday, October 24th, 1843: It was expected that Messrs. [Samuel M.] Williams and [George Washington] Hockly, the commissioners for treating with those of Mexico in regard to the armistice, would have passed through San Antonio on their way to Laredo on the Rio Grande, but they went by water from Galveston to Laredo, via Matamoros.

Trade is very dull, the only purchasers are smugglers from the Rio Grande, who rarely bring with them more than 500 dollars each. Manufactured goods and groceries are at moderate prices, but there is little or no cash. The following are offered as specimens of "trade" or barter:

"Señor, buy this wild turkey?"

"What do you want for it?"

"Mother told me to ask for 1 lb. of coffee and 2 lbs. of sugar."

"Will you take half a pound of coffee and a pound of sugar?"

"Mui bien Señor" (badly pronounced Heñor). "Very well Sir."

"Señor, quiere mercar gallinas y huevos?" ("Will you purchase chickens and eggs?")

"Yes, what do you want for them?"

"Some coffee, sugar, candles, and some printed calico stuff."

"Señor, don't you want a cart load of fodder and some sacks of corn?"

"Yes, if you sell reasonably."

"Then I want some tobacco, salt, coffee, sugar, and some velveteen for a pair of trousers."

But let this country be blessed with a peace, this system of things will change, and *cash, cash, cash,* will once more be seen.

About noon this day we left San Antonio de Bejar for Columbus and the eastern part of Texas by the lower road to Gonzales which is uninhabited. Five miles from the "Powder House" a good view of the Alamo and town may be obtained. Five more to the 10 miles "water hole," here we nooned. Twelve miles more to a creek and camped, being ½ mile from the Cibolo. Country wooded, post oak principally and no scarcity of deer. The evening beautifully clear and calm—prognostications of a change. Midnight, cold norther and then pretty heavy rains. Oh! MacKintoshes thou art great fellows—to keep wet off.

Wednesday, October 25th, 1843: Cloudy, cool, and wind NE. Robson killed rattlesnake 5 feet—circumference 6 inches. How he did rattle and jump ere he gave up life. Robson takes his skin to make a cravat of! 7 A.M. started—cold NNE, temp: 45°. Nooned about 12 miles from Cibolo—over 8 or 10 miles of a Sandy Road. Post and live oak and hickory—many grasses and pretty flowers, plenty deer, fine bucks. Started 14 miles over sandy road, with occasional indurated iron sand, camped for the night.

Thursday, October 26th, 1843: Slight rain during night—along this road there are no regular creeks just now but sufficient water in what is called "water holes." We are journeying by the old [Presidio] road. It is 10 miles nearer than that by Seguin, the one generally used, as being more settled. Formerly the Cibolo had settlements. We had a very cold ride of 12 to 14 miles to the Guadalupe. Strong norther and rain. Took a snack, hoping to be able to swim our horses over ourselves, and saddles get passed in canoe. Norther increased and altho' we fired vollies, the ferry-man on the other side could not hear us. We had to locate ourselves in a small log cabin—one room—the man[17] his wife and child in their bed. R[obson], L——, and self stretched on the ground. 6 P.M.: Norther subsided—night clear. Lewis camped at River, having sent his horse over.

Friday, October 27th, 1843: During night very cold, below freez-ing point—had but few blankets. 7 A.M. took our coffee. When I got a severe chill, obliged to stop at a log cabin. Companions went over to Gonzales to wait for me. Noon, fine clear sky—sun out—and quite another climate. These "northers" come very severe upon convalescents and residents of the Coast. Depth of water of river here—25 feet; it may rise at times as much again. Flat boats with produce go down, but as yet do not pay. River wants surveying. Corn 4 bits a bushel (a flour barrel with shucks or 125 heads). The lands about here have a good name and it is a pretty country. Got over to Gonzales in a small canoe or "dug out." Fine evening—cool.

Saturday, October 28th 1843: Frost during night—morning fine and clear—bright sun. Afternoon left for Mrs. Jones', 7 miles, but only ½ mile from the Guadalupe.

Sunday, October 29th, 1843: Chills and fever came on at break-fast. Obliged to stop all day—shaking, fever, sweating, and de-bility. Evening blew hard from NE and rain. Mr. Anderson,[18]

[17] Mr. DeWitt—son of [Green C.] Dewitt the empresario. Saw widow of late Mr. DeWitt. She told me that they had had so much trouble, wars and other diffi-culties, that they had become contented to raise enough to live on. And many fam-ilies, who could they return to the States, would do so. Even young men. I told her I thought peace would put all in order. Our grandchildren may live peaceably. —Bollaert.

[18] This probably was John D. Anderson, who practiced law in Gonzales County at this period. He was a member of the House of Representatives from Gonzales in 1847. *The Handbook of Texas,* I, 45.

lawyer, married to Miss Jones, is very gentlemanly and intelligent. Wheat grows well here.

Monday, October 30th, 1843: Left Mrs. Jones'. Missed our road and took the direct one instead of by the settlements, came to the Lavaca, but made across the prairie to cut Eggleston's trail, which we did about 5 or 6 miles. Got to Egglestons; about Lavaca much wild indigo and used for dying; took a cup of coffee and 6 miles more brought us to Mr. Foley's the plantation of our good friend, on Nixon's Creek.[19]

Tuesday, October 31st, 1843: After breakfast—chill, fever & perspirations came on—could not ride—Year before last, there was a great drought and even the Colorado in some places stopped running—but in the winter season there is water enough for flat-boats and small steamers. Much may be done with the Texan streams, in waiting for the freshets—The cotton plant is small about here and staple is small, but good colour.

[Wednesday], November 1st, 1843: Left Mr. Foley's and with a pretty good share of rain, lightning, and thunder reached Columbus on the Colorado.

[19] There is no such creek as Nixon's Creek in Texas today. However, John T. Nixon owned a ranch near the Wilson and Gonzales county lines in 1843, and doubtless the stream herein mentioned was named after him. *Ibid.*, II, 281.

XII

FROM COLUMBUS TO MONTGOMERY

[November–December, 1843]

Monday, November 6th 1843: For some days raining and cold weather. Ferryboats washed away. A few flat boats with 200 bales of cotton from Lagrange stopped at Columbus for more. The flat boats take their cargoes to the raft near the mouth of the river, from whence it is hauled to Matagorda.[1]

Tuesday, November 7th, 1843: Left Columbus in company with Mr. R——. Owing to heavy rains, the Colorado River was very high, its waters for miles covering the "bottoms" inland, and doing much damage to many plantations. We could not cross at the ferry, but had to pull the flat-boat up the river two miles by holding on to branches of trees. Having attained the eastern bank, we travelled over muddy roads to within four miles of west branch of Mill Creek.[2] During our ride passed several thriving German settlements located in pretty undulating country with sufficient timber.

Mr. Byrne Junr.'s[3] father has given him a league of land 3 miles from La Grange fronting the River Colorado. A creek runs thro' it and he thinks that farmers might find eligible selections with river front of say 2–4 and 600 acre farms—at $2 per acre. I have

[1] Matagorda—from *mata*, a bush, and *gorda*, thick or stout.—Bollaert.

[2] According to Arrowsmith's map, which Bollaert had in his possession during all of his travels throughout Texas, Mill Creek is a small stream flowing from the northwest and emptying into the Brazos River a short distance above San Felipe de Austin.

[3] This must have been the son of James W. Byrne. The latter was born in Ireland and came to Texas (1835) where he acquired a tract of land on Lookout Peninsula. In association with Robert Hall and George Armstrong, Byrne founded the town of Lamar, Texas. His only son, and the one Bollaert refers to in his journal, was named William Odin Byrne. Records show that he died at Lamar on September 10, 1862. The Byrnes were interested at one time or the other in numerous transportation projects in Texas, including railroads, none of which appear to have materialized. *Biographical Directory of Texan Conventions and Congresses*, 61.

been over the land, there is plenty of fine timbers and plenty prairie at back for range of cattle. Mr. Byrne Junr. and others have it in contemplation to cut a canal from La Mar to San Antonio; when peace is established there will be no difficulty about funds. The idea is to bring out Irish labourers and allot them on the canal portions of land, which when necessary can be irrigated. A treaty has been insured to the Canal Company 6 miles on each side of the canal, where farms and plantations may be formed. Mr. B. Senr. has a good corn farm on St. Joseph's Island, where he removed to from his property of La Mar in 1841.

Wednesday, November 8th, 1843: Stopped at Mr. York's,[4] 20 to 23 miles from Columbus, 25 from San Felipe de Austin, 2 miles from Mill Creek and 1 mile from La Grange Road—2 miles from *Industry*. There are several small creeks running into Mill Creek. Boos Waldeck near 1½ Cummings Creek—gone to Galveston for his health.

We were 2 hours going 1½ miles in flat boat pulling ourselves up by the branches. Stream running rapidly, but falling—the bottoms full of water. On our way up eat the winter grape, small but sweet—care must be taken not to eat the fruit of the poisoned oak, which is somewhat like the winter grape.

Thursday, November 9th, 1843: Crossing[5] Mill Creek arrived at the town of Travis,[6] which is well situated. Travis and its vicinity is in a thriving condition and this section may be recommended to European emigrants, and particularly as laying between the Brazos and Colorado Rivers. From Travis to Jacksonville[7] 14

[4] John York came to Texas in 1829 from Kentucky and settled near San Felipe de Austin at the future site of Industry, Texas. He led several expeditions against the Indians before participating in the Texas Revolution. In 1846, he was elected one of the commissioners for newly created DeWitt County. *The Writings of Sam Houston,* II, 53.

[5] Had to *tote* our "traps" over a log.—Bollaert.

[6] This town probably was named after William Barret Travis. Bollaert reported that it was in "a thriving condition" in 1843, but it must not have thrived very long. No such town (except one in western Falls County) is recorded as being in existence today.

miles, rolling country and thickly studded with plantations and farms. We had to swim a branch of New Year's Creek[8] and intended to have remained for the night about 1½ miles on the other side, but found it was inconvenient to receive us, the family being sick. It was now past sun down, but we pushed on through a dense woods, having been informed that we could be accom-[m]odated about three or four miles off. We came to another branch of New Year's Creek and owing to a large sycamore that had fallen into the creek and the darkness of the night, got out of the road, or rather trail, and could not find it again.

Now then commenced our difficulties—pitch dark—high and steep banks—creek full of water—quick-sands—thick brush full of spiney briars, etc. My companion dismounted, waded up and down the stream in the hope of finding an outlet—not even a cattle trail could be seen. I had made up my mind to light a fire and camp down for the night, for we had with us some dried beef for our supper; when we heard the distant bark of a dog, we concluded we could not be very far from a settlement. We hollowed "like mad" for half an hour, when we were responded to by human voices. Three gentlemen from a plantation about ¼ mile off kindly came to our assistance and with much difficulty, extricated us out of the "brush," taking us to their habitation. A good supper was prepared for us and we all had a hearty laugh at the late "fix" we had been in. This was a corroboration of advice often given to us that "when in a strange country, without the traveller is a backwoodsman, not to travel of a dark night if it can be avoided."

Friday, November 10th, 1843: Here we found the bonnet-gourd in great perfection—two feet long, green exterior, when split seen to be full of black seeds imbedded in fibrous and mucilaginous matter, the latter being washed away, the seeds fall out and a

[7] Jacksonville (Washington County) was named for Terrell Jackson. The abandoned settlement was listed as a ghost town in 1936. *The Handbook of Texas,* I, 902.

[8] New Year Creek rises in east central Washington County and flows southeast twenty miles into the Brazos at the Washington-Waller county line. It was named by several of the Old Three Hundred, who camped here on January 1, 1822.

slightly yellowish tissue of fibres remains which bleaches white by exposure to the sun, when it is made into ladies bonnets, hats, mats for the table, and lastly "cup cloths and dish-rags."[9] Ten miles over thickly settled country brought us to Washington, on the western bank of the Brazos, and the present seat of Government. President Houston and his cabinet had been at Galveston and Houston for some time, but we daily expected [them] to return for the forthcoming Congress. A[nson] Jones now in Mexico. At an anniversary of Santana's at Tampico, a British Jack was placed as a trophy—this Doyle[10] has resented and they are in discussion about it. General [William Sumpter] Murphy gone to Mexico; there were some discussions with the President and Murphy, but all is arranged.[11]

The upper part of the Brazos from general report appears to be a very fine country, particularly the lands watered by its western tributaries, such as the San Andres or Little River, San Gabriel, etc. On account of the many falls in the upper part of the Brazos, I am informed by a gentleman who has lately explored that part of the country, there can be no better place for erecting flour, saw, and other mills. Not long since the steamer *Mustang* from Galveston came up the Brazos to Washington and even went higher up to within 20 miles of Nashville,[12] discharged her freight, and returned with a cargo of cotton.

[9] Indigo was prepared here from the *wild* indigo plant. I am informed that the Spanish indigo has already been introduced into Texas and succeeds very well. The Indigo plant is boiled, (instead of the former way of fermenting it), strained, then agitated or churned for some time; lime water "or the juice of some very astringent vegetable is added to it, and it is left to precipitate or settle to the bottom, the liquor is drawn off, and the blue mass or indigo left to dry."—Bollaert.

[10] Percy W. Doyle was the British chargé d'affaires to Mexico, 1842-43. He had great sympathy for the Texan prisoners, and did all he could to make them more comfortable and to alleviate their suffering while they were confined to the Mexican prison in Perote Castle. *The Writings of Sam Houston*, VI, 94. (See also footnote 25 below, for the results of the incident).

[11] The "discussions" which Bollaert refers to here might have had something to do with President Tyler's plans at this period, or slightly later, for the annexation of Texas. General Murphy was an active promoter for annexation. He gave Houston an unauthorized promise of military protection for Texas at the time of the negotiation of a proposed treaty of annexation. Murphy's confirmation as chargé d'affaires to Texas by the United States Senate was ultimately rejected. *British Diplomatic Correspondence Concerning the Republic of Texas*, 208.

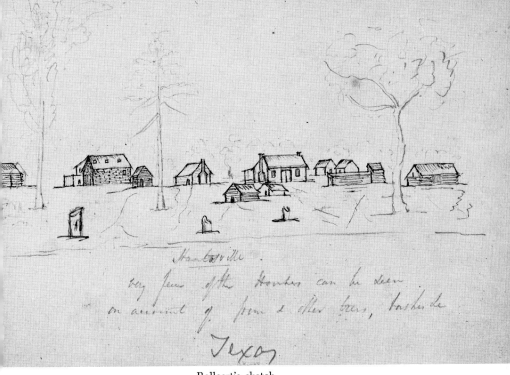

Bollaert's sketch

*"Three miles brought us to Huntsville,
situated on a pine height."*

*"We arrived at the 'Scotch Hermitage,' the residence
of my excellent friend and companion, Robert Robson Esq."*

Bollaert's drawing

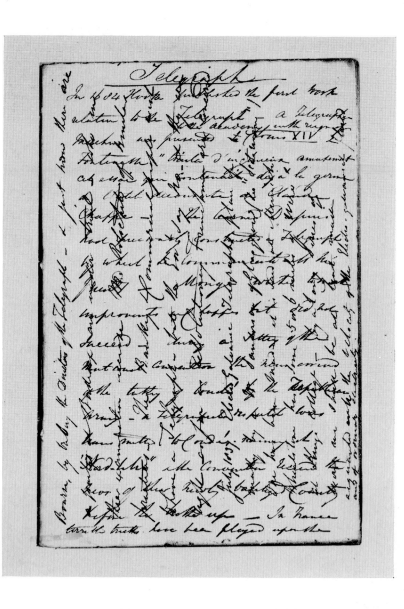

A typical page from Bollaert's journal.
He wrote over his own writing to save paper.

The Brazos River was very high, which obliged us to go up the Navasota River a couple of miles. The rich lower lands between the Brazos and Navasota are overflowed, and the Brazos bottom in many places covered with water for a distance of five miles inland. Roads very fatiguing for our horses, being over muddy prairie country, and unfortunately lost our track this evening again—put up for the night at an unfinished log hut in a pine wood, as yet not "sealed" or boarded inside and no fireplace "fixed." The inmates a young man, his wife and child had only moved in the day before, and although every thing was in confusion, they did all they could to accom[m]odate us.

Saturday, November 11th, 1843: Before sunrise started and by a trail got into the main road and 5 miles brought us to Mr. Senator Grimes[13]—16 miles, or half way to Montgomery.[14] All this part of the country pretty thickly settled and appears a good farming country. Last summer some sickness in the shape of chills and fevers, from probably the effluvia of the Brazos bottom, Trinity, and the woody country about here. Mount Vernon County seat of Washington County about 16 miles from Washington. From Grimes' to Colonel [Jacob] Shannon's—9 miles undulating Country and full of settlements—dined at Col.'s[15] fine plantation

[12] Nashville, 65 miles from Washington and its surrounding country eulogized much by [George W.] Bonnell as one of the finest settlements in Texas—rich prairie, as well as bottom lands.—Bollaert.

[13] Jesse Grimes came to Texas in 1827 and settled on Grimes Prairie in present Grimes County. He was active in local affairs and participated in the formation of the Republic in both a civil and military capacity. He represented Washington County in the Senate of the First Congress of the Republic (1836–37). Subsequently, he served several terms in the House of Representatives and the Senate in both the Republic and the state governments of Texas. Kemp, *Signers of the Texas Declaration of Independence*, 92.

[14] The town of Montgomery was formerly the county seat of what are now Grimes, Walker, Madison, and Montgomery counties. It was created in 1837, and named after General Richard Montgomery of American Revolutionary fame. The town failed to keep pace with its early start, and in 1889 the county seat was transferred to Conroe. Discovery of oil gave it a new lease on life in the 1930's; its population according to the 1940 census was 750. "Montgomery County Scrapbook," University of Texas Archives.

[15] Colonel Jacob Shannon was an original land grantee of the Republic of Texas. Along with James Montgomery, he built the first house in 1830 on Town Creek, about a half mile north of the present site of Montgomery, Texas. *Ibid.*

—cotton, corn, tobacco, sheep, stock, etc.—y una hija hermosa. Don Juan L[ewis][16] recien salido de la escuela nos fatigé con su sabiduria! una curiosidad!

Two miles brought us to the bridge over Lake Creek and 6 miles more to Montgomery—full of farms and plantations and some comfort. Before we arrived at Lake Creek, passed a large plantation belonging to Colonel Julian Devereux.[17] He has all his slaves together forming a "Nigger Village." After passing Lake Creek my companion shewed me what he thinks is continually going on—viz: say when the pine seeds get into a post oak forest and they take root and grow up, whilst so doing they will destroy the oaks and die and fall, then another oak forest springs up and destroys the pines and thus it appears to go on successively. This may account for the post oaks not being large.

There are great trees in the country, particularly the cypress, sycamore, walnut, peccan, and they must be of great age. The pine grows in this country to a great height, say 150 to 200 feet. Cotton tree is the shaking ash, a species of poplar, spongy wood, and not much used, but cedar is the favourite building wood.

Two miles from Montgomery put up at Squire H. We were too late to go to Robson's Hermitage. In passing through Montgomery, saw two large stills, as yet not put up. We have come from Columbus without the voyage having cost us a bit, because we said we did not have it, but we have to pay $5 in order to cross the Colorado and the same for the Brazos. We travelled as Illustros Mendicants.

Sunday, November 12th, 1843: Morning raining, but we arrived at the "Scotch Hermitage," the residence of my excellent friend and companion, Robert Robson Esq., about two miles from Montgomery, situated in one of the numberless "pine barrens"[18]

[16] This must have been the Colonel J. R. Lewis, Matagorda, Texas, whom Bollaert briefly identifies in a note relating to this period as an "agent for purchase of lands for Mr. [William O.] Byrne."

[17] Julien Sidney Devereux, from Georgia, settled in Montgomery County in 1841. He soon became a successful planter and at one time owned approximately ten thousand acres of land and eighty slaves. *The Handbook of Texas,* I, 494.

that occur in this country. We found ourselves in a "difficulty," Mr. Robson having left his keys at Columbus.

Messrs. Hassel and Lewis passed afternoon with us and we had some 4 or 5 editions of "cracks"—plenty grey fox, coon opposum, squirrel, bear, deer, panther, leopard cub and leopard etc.

Monday, November 13th, 1843: In the eastern counties nearly all the plantations are on lands cleared from the bottoms—in the western counties and between the Colorado and Brazos in prairies.

Mr. R.'s Negro shot a sand-hill crane of very large proportions —whole length, 5 feet and 6½ inches—beak 8 inches—length of neck from breast to top of bill, 27 inches, weight 13 lbs., length of leg 36 inches—colour of bird, lead grey—good eating, like duck, if well stuffed it would be excellent.

Tuesday, November 14th, 1843: Mr. Lewis came for us before daylight with his dogs—started but did not come up with other hunters. We anticipated a fox-hunt, but they only had a deer in chase this we knew by their rapid change of position and great distances run. The fox (grey and small), when he breaks cover, dodges about and when hard pressed by the dogs, trees it—that is, he climbs a tree, but has to descend, for that position is not comfortable to him, then the dogs take him. Raining hard all day —bad cold and fever. Kept bed all day; took aperient pills— very weak.

There is daily hunting for fox, deer, opposum, etc., in these pine woods. Some of the planters have a few good dogs. The late rains have rendered the woods impassable, thus the planters cannot haul their cotton to Houston. There are some flat-boats building on the San Jacinto River to convey cotton and other produce to Lynchburg,[19] and from thence the steamers can take it to Galveston. It would appear that more rain falls in eastern than in

[18] Pine barrens, or oak openings, are "lands partaking of the forest and prairie." —Bollaert.
[19] Lynchburg is in eastern Harris County at the point where Buffalo Bayou flows into the San Jacinto River. Nathaniel Lynch established a crossing known as Lynch's Ferry here in 1822.

western Texas, and the reason given is that the former section being more timbered is less exposed to those winds that carry off the rains towards the Gulf.[20] Up to the end of the month, but very indifferent weather, but at times good enough for hunting.

Bollaert's siege of malaria must have kept him in bed for several days, for he does not make another entry in his journal or notes until November 23, 1843: except for some random comments on prices of land and goods, emigration, peace with the Indians, and Negroes in Texas.

At San Antonio Indian corn was at two bits, or 25 cents, the bushel in the shuck. The bushel is the contents of a flour barrel. On the Colorado, something less. At Montgomery:

Corn: 18 to 25 cents per bushel, or 100 bushels for 18 dollars (30 to 50 bushels per acre).

Steers (for beef): 5 to 6 dollars, or 1 cent per lb. in small quantities.

Cow and calf: 6 to 8 dollars.

Pork: 1½ to 2 cents per lb.

Bacon: 6 to 8 cents per lb.

Sheep: 2 dollars, rather small, but very good.

Sow and litter: From 3 to 6 dollars. This will depend on the breed.

Oxen (pair): From 20 to 50 dollars. *Buffalo robes,* 2 to 5 dollars. *Dressed deer* skin, 50 cents. *Saddles,* 5 to 10 dollars per tree.

Wheat: 2 dollars per bushel. *Oats:* 3 to 4 dollars per bushel. *Barley, buck-wheat,* and *rice* as yet only grown in small quantities.

Horses: From 25 to 100 dollars. Racers, up to 3,000 and 4,000 dollars.

Fodder: 50 to 75 cents per hundred weight.

[20] It apparently did not occur to Bollaert that the heavy vegetation in eastern Texas was the result of more rains, rather than the cause. It is common knowledge today, thanks partly to television weather reports, that the warm moisture-laden winds from the Gulf do not extend beyond the 98th meridian as frequently as to the eastward.

Tobacco: 25 to 50 cents per lb.

Eggs: 12½ cents or 1 bit a dozen. Texas *sugar,* 10 cents. *Cotton,* 4 to 5 cents. All 1843.

Butter: 12½ cents per lb.

Indigo: ——— *Peas* (Black-eyed) 5½ to 6 cents.

Cow hides: 4 to 6 cents per lb.

Chickens: 1 dollar per dozen. Other poultry in proportion.

The dollar is 4s 6d English currency. The dollar is divided into 100 cents. The bit 12½ cents. A dime 10 cents. The above mentioned articles may be purchased for less if *cash* were paid. The general system at present is "trade," or barter.

The term for granting head rights to emigrants expired 1 January 1841,[21] but a bill is now before Congress for the continuance of free grants of land. It may be observed that very nearly all the land on the rivers and their tributaries has been located for some time past, commencing from the sea up to the Indian country. But lately President Houston has concluded treaties of peace with all the tribes excepting the Comanches, and there are hopes that during this year some arrangements may be entered into with them. For some years past emigrants from the United States, bring in their Negros, have been in the habit of purchasing lands from old settlers with farms and stock upon them. Large land-holders are willing to give from 2 to 500 acres to any industrious farmer, or person of capital at a very moderate price and to be paid at

[21] The term for granting headrights to immigrants expired on January 1, 1840 (not 1841). On January 4, 1839, Texas passed a law that all free white persons who had immigrated to Texas since October 1, 1837, or who might immigrate to Texas before January 1, 1840, would be entitled to a conditional grant of land. Additional acts were passed on January 4, 1841, and February 5, 1842, authorizing companies to reeceive contracts to introduce colonists to settle on unappropriated lands of the Republic. Dissatisfaction arose over the colonization in 1843, and Congress passed a bill for the repeal of all laws then in force which authorized the President to grant colonization contracts. Houston vetoed the bill on January 10, 1844, on the grounds that "it directly impaired the obligation of existing contracts." Congress successfully overrode his veto. This action prevented the Kennedy Colony, in which Bollaert was vitally interested and for which he came to Texas in 1842, from ever being established. Department of State *Records,* Republic of Texas, Vol. XL, 299. Bieslie, *History of the German Settlements in Texas,* 70.

the convenience of the emigrant. The following bargain was obtained a week or two since in Montgomery County: 800 acres with good farm house, out-houses, stables—all well enclosed, 40 head of stock, 600 bushels of corn, some cart loads of potatoes, and 200 pigs. Titles for a league of land to be located and 500 acres of located land. All this was offered for £160, or 800 dollars cash, not above 3 or 4 months since; and a few weeks ago was sold "in trade" for 1,400 dollars £280, but paid in a Negro boy valued at 600 dollars, and a note for the remainder at a long date.

Great bargains in land may be had all over the Republic. A large land-holder offered to give a friend of mine, an independent gentleman, 2 or 300 acres of good land, and build him a house, if he would remain in the donor's neighborhood. Near San Antonio 1,000 acres of fine land were sold for 120 dollars, 500 acres for a pretty good horse, etc. Should there soon be a peace, lands will rise rapidly in price and doubtless there will be much ruinous speculation.

In dry weather emigrants from the United States enter Texas by the N.E. boundary, supplying themselves with groceries—bacon and such things—ere they leave their former homes. Deer, buffalo, and wild turkey etc. will keep the party in fresh provisions. It is more com[m]odious to travel with waggons as far as regards the little comforts of life; but the journey of a small party on horseback in spring or in autumn is quickly and pleasantly performed. The party will not have to "camp out" without they please, for there are many farm houses considered as houses of "entertainment," or inns, particularly in the eastern counties. Many prefer camping out when they find good pastures and enjoy the beautiful nights. At the inns the charge is from 1 to 1½ dollars for supper, bed, and breakfast and stabling for the horse; but the majority of farmers will not receive payment. In the cities or large towns when there are hotels, the boarding and lodging [varies] from 15 to 20 dollars per month. In the country, 10 to 12. Under no circumstance is a traveller rich or poor turned from the door. Two families from Alabama, about fifteen in number, with three waggons, fifty Negros, oxen, horses, and mules—their expences on the road to Montgomery were about 120 dollars, a considerable portion of this paid for ferries and repairing waggons.

An acre of land will generally produce 2,000 lbs. of "seed cotton," which yields—after being ginned or the seeds separated—about 600 pounds of cotton ready for baling. The bagging and rope for each bale costs two-and-a-half dollars. When a planter has no "gin" on his estate, he has often to give 1/8 or 1/10 "toll" for the separation of the seed from the raw cotton. The overplus seed that is not required for the next crop is thrown out upon the land and acts as a manure. If low prices for cotton continue, it will not pay if the planter has any great distance to haul it in waggons.

Some few planters have shipped cotton on their own account to Europe, but they have been surprised at the *charges etc.* It is much better for the planter, when he has confidence in his merchant, to get his supplies from the merchant on the spot, and let him have the cotton. Some 2 or 3,000 bales of Texas cotton annually goes by Red River to New Orleans, much of which passes for American cotton. If it goes in as Texan produce, a duty of three cents per pound is levied on it; but [the duty] is returned if shipped to a foreign port within three months.

Negroes

Generally speaking throughout the Republic the Negroes are well treated, and I can bear witness that they are not over-worked, or ill-used. In the eastern counties they are principally "family Negros," or brought up by their owners, and when they get old are kept upon the plantations and not sold to an indifferent master. A good working hand in fine weather will pick 1,000 pounds of cotton per week. The Negro is allowed Saturday after 12 o'clock until Monday morning to arrange his or her own domestic affairs, but if they choose to pick cotton on Saturday afternoon, they are remunerated for it, and on some plantations all the cotton they thus pick is given to them and may amount to 30 dollars for the season. On well-regulated plantations, each Negro family has its log house, half an acre of land behind it for a garden to support some stock, pigs, poultry, which the Negro consumes or sells on his own account.

Negro Nursery

During the busy season when the Negro men and women go to their labours in the field, they intrust their young children to the care of old "aunty Suky," or on very large plantations there are several of these old Auntys who look after them until their parents return to their meals.

The "nursery" is a large log-house and the collection of juvenile blacks of all sorts, sizes, and colours—their cryings and scream-ings, the bawlings of "Aunty" and the what she won't do to them if they don't "quit" crying, her admonitions at their favourite pastime of eating dirt, which is only prevented by giving them a lump of fat bacon, is very amusing.

It is said in Texas and in the U. S. by many as a serious *fact* that if a Negro child be kept clean and well clothed it will pine and often die; but if allowed to roll and play about in the dirt there is no fear of its thriving.

Some of the small farmers who may not be possessed of Negros, will give any white man half of their cotton or corn to assist them in getting their crop in, and board him at the same time. Thus, all sorts of manual labour is well paid in Texas; in the large towns cash is paid, in the country by part of the produce: Wood cutters for shingles, rails and logs, carpenters, blacksmiths, bricklayers, masons, millrights, sawyers, and in the towns, painters.

It is the general opinion that the low lands of the coast and a considerable distance inland can only be worked profitably by Negro labour, for the white man, even those of Mississippi and other southern states cannot for any time stand continued ex-posure to the sun and miasma from the rich and wooded lands, which bring on agues, other fevers and great debility, whereas the Negro is but seldom attacked. In the interior, towards the moun-tains, and western Texas (passing the Colorado River) the coun-try is proverbially healthy and if so much cotton cannot be grown there, as on the coast and in the East, another article for exportation may be raised, namely, wool, for in the West the pastures are of the richest character, no boggy lands, clear running streams and luxurious climate.

Thursday, November 23rd, 1843: Heavy showers during night and blowing a gale from S.S.W. Morning cloudy—wind strong. We do not feel it much, being surrounded by high trees. 10 A.M.: Violent gusts of wind from S.S. West, howling among the forest trees, shaking them, and at times like the sea-waves beating upon the sea beach; then the falling of large trees, cracking as they broke away from the roots. These gusts of wind cleared away thick heavy leaden looking clouds, and at noon as was—stilled and fine. 8 P.M.: New moon, and beautiful evening followed. Sunset 5 P.M. —sunrise 7 A.M.

Friday, November 24th, 1843: During night a pretty strong "dry norther," but as we are surrounded by tall pine and other trees we do not feel the whole force of the wind, yet at 7 A.M. it was 40°—fine and clear. In a S direction there is nearly 40 miles of pine forest, the E. is rolling prairie and woodland intermixed, to the W some 20 miles of pine, and in a Northern direction, high rolling prairie and woodlands. 12 P.M.: 63°. The dogs in this part of the country go hunting by themselves. They run about in the woods, start a fox, run him until he is tired, the fox takes to a tree —the dogs commence barking, out goes the hunter, and their sly Reynard is up a tall pine; a ball is put through his head and "voilá Reynard," a victim at your feet. Just now plenty quail.

Saturday, November 25th, 1843: Morning cool, cloudy, and airs from S.W. sprinkling of rain all day. Dined with Mr. ———, a planter in the vicinity; all appears to go on well with him; he understands his occupation and is industrious without incommoding either his Negros or himself. His wife, tho' young and apparently delicately brought up, bustled about, *amused* herself weaving and kept the Negresses at their spinning. We sat down to an excellent and most palatable dinner, and served up very well, true we did not sit over our bottle and discuss politics, but the time is not far distant when, hot Toddys will be introduced after dinner in winter, Foreign and Texan wines, or Sangarees in Summer.

After dinner we adjourned to the corridor, when the segars of home manufacture being lighted, Mr. ——— commenced a most melancholy account of our moral and political position. I must mention, that he was of the Western, War, or Archive party, which at present does not exist, and only now and then met with, moreover, he wished to hurry to Houston with cotton and the badness of the roads, owing to so much rain, gave him some trouble, at times having to yoke 11 oxen to one waggon. He should have waited until the waters had drained off, or like our host, built a boat, and in that way, got it to Lynchburg by the San Jacinto to Galveston.

"Yes," said he, "Old Sam has been down preaching and throwing dust in the eyes of the Houston and Galveston people to conciliate them to his measures. He knows how to palaver them."

"No," replied Mr. ———. "He has been enlightening them on such points of his policy, he considered judicious, and explaining, as I believe most satisfactorily, that his acts for some time past have not originated in what is called his 'vindictiveness,' but that his doings have been such as was called for, moreover, that the War Party has done much harm to the country abroad by their organs of the press, and thro' their friends in the U.S. You talk of the country being broken up—the West only is in that position, but at San Antonio even good crops have been made this year. We have seldom had the crops such as this year. I admit that the unprecedented quantity of rain will spoil some of our cotton, but we have sufficient already to meet our merchants bills. Corn we have in extraordinary abundance, stock, poultry, and game more than we can consume. What more is wanted?"

"Peace," was the reply.

"And that the President *will assuredly* bring about. Why this morning I received news from Galveston, and such was the information, that I intend to act immediately on the information and build me another large room and make other improvements. I had already sent my 'force' Negros into the woods to saw plank."

And such is the fact, there will be a lengthy armistice, which *must* lead to a peace. The President is accused by his political opponents of trying to embroil Texas, get it annexed to the U.S., and run for President of the U.S.! He is likewise accused of being in treaty with England, to throw Texas into her arms, abolition of slavery would necessarily follow and President Houston would be a British Viceroy! with a salary of £5,000 per annum! Formerly Houston was accused of treason, being in correspondence with Santana and wishing to come under Mexican supremacy again as the price of peace! etc. etc. etc.

After dinner went to Montgomery. No mail in. After tea or supper, passed evening singing. Wife and a couple of pretty nieces present—piano, albums, and carpeted parlour.

Sunday, November 26th, 1843: All night gusts of wind and occasional rain from S.W. 8 A.M.: Same, and cloudy, air warm but damp.

Monday, November 27th, 1843: From *Vindicator:*[22] the Queen [Victoria] closed parliament 25 August. Atmosphere Rail way going on in Ireland successfully.[23] Burton [?] says 150,000 slaves are annually taken from Africa, 90,000 of whom are taken to Brazil. Houston's trip to the Coast *arrangera ses affaires*, invited to a barbecue at Houston. General Murphy gone to the U.S., but all right with Old Sam. German settlements in Austin and Colorado counties getting on well, many who only arrived pen-

[22] The *National Vindicator* was published at Washington-on-the-Brazos between 1843 and 1844. It was a pro-Houston paper, edited by Thomas Johnson. *The Writings of Sam Houston,* VIII, 142.

[23] An atmospheric railway is one so constructed that the motive power is derived from the pressure of the atmosphere acting on a piston working in a continuous iron tube of uniform bore laid from one place to another, the pressure being created by exhausting the air from that end of the tube toward which it is desired that the piston should advance, or by forcing in air behind it, or both. The system has been found suitable only for the conveyance of letters, telegrams, and light packages. Paris still uses the system, but it is most commonly applied to department stores or business houses (pneumatic tube).

niless a few years since have 3 to $5,000 each. Government gave them a league of land, which they could not then locate, owing to the troubled times, and have made themselves independent upon small tracts they purchased *on credit*. The "Kentucky Colony,"[24] is prospering; 200 left Louisville for the Colony last September. *Mustang* Steamer [is] running from Galveston to Washington-on-the-Brazos. Mr. Doyle has suspended relations with Santa Ana and sent to the West Indies and home—this is good for Texas. I do not believe that an English flag was taken from the Texans, but some retaliation of Santana's, owing to the sympathy he believed E. has for Texas.[25] All this is "nuts" for us. Yucatan Commissioners ordered to leave Mexico, thus if Santa can raise forces, there will be more fighting there. Wheat is very abundant at Austin and Bastrop; hogs will be fed on it for want of consumers. Corn is 12½ cents a bushel.

8 A.M.: 70°. Noon 80°—and warm in sun, no breeze. Went to Montgomery—a bag or two of letters and papers arrived all wet. A long letter in the [Houston] *Telegraph* of November 8th —signed John Adams, addressed to J. Q. Adams, Secretary of State in U. S. in which annexation is supplicated, for fear Texas should fall into the hands of the British. I think it is by Judge [David G.] Burnett. Since his Vice-Presidency under La Mar, he has only been playing "possum" in the woods and now comes out with his strange epistle—hoping that he may find supporters.

Tuesday, November 28th, 1843: 8 A.M. cloudy, breezes from S.W. more temperate and seasonable. Evening fine, not a cloud to be seen. 10 P.M. wind chopped round to N.W. with heavy rain.

24 Bollaert makes several subsequent references to the "Kentucky Colony." It is better known as the W. S. Peters Colony, although most of the settlers in the colony came from Kentucky. Peters and his associates received a total of four contracts from the Republic (1841–43) and succeeded in establishing a number of settlements in present Grayson, Collin, Denton, Tarrant, and Dallas counties. Peters' Colony File (MS., Texas State Archives).

25 The *Civilian* states that the Carancahua Indians had procured the "Jack" from a wrecked vessel and in a skirmish of the Mier Volunteers with the Indians, the "Jack" was found and preserved amongst their baggage. Thus it fell into the hands of the Mexicans, but was never hoisted. Proclamation for 8th Congress to be held at Washington 4th December.—Bollaert.

Wednesday, November 29th, 1843: 8 A.M. 50°. Rainy and breezes from N.W. The sudden change of temperature gave me a touch of chill today. In 1841 provisions were scarce in Texas and consequently high in price; then it was that the settlers carried on the "fire hunting" to a great extent. A party of three or four would in a day or so shoot down some 20 to 30 deer. The best way to go "fire hunting" is that the hunter be assisted by a Negro to carry the fire or pine wood. The hunter being on foot or horseback, carries the fire pan full of lighted pine wood over his left shoulder, left handed people the reverse, proceeding cautiously through the woods. Should there be any deer about they look towards the pan of fire, and in a moment the hunter sees a reflection of the light in the eyes of the deer. This is called "shining the eyes" and this in the line of his shadow, which shadow is elongated by a depression of the pan, and vice versa. Deer's eyes may be shined at a 100 yards or more, then they look like a horizontal streak of dim light, but on nearing the deer both eyes will be seen distinctly of a bright light bluish colour. Horses, cats, or human eye did not succeed with us.

The hunter generally approaches to within 40 or 50 yards of the game, so managing his pan of fire that he preserves "the shining" on the eye or eyes; he then draws the long wooden handle of the pan forward and makes it a rest for his rifle; aim being taken, the animal seldom escapes. A good hunter can shine a deer's eye 100 yards. In this same manner other quadruped may be taken, even a hawk's eye may be "shined."

Thursday, November 30th, 1843: 8 A.M., 47°. Heavy rain all the morning. Noon 44° and rain. Heavy rain all night. Wind N.W. Roads will be rendered almost impassable again.

Some planters are so injudicious as to plant more cotton than they have hands to pick, and if they do not plant early the autumnal and winter rains set in, then no picking can go on and it is after Christmas ere they can take their crop to market. Plant early—no more than you can pick—pick, gin, and bale quickly—

and get the cotton, particularly if there is a long way to haul, to market—ere the rains come on and the roads bad.

Friday, December 1st, 1843: Norther and deluges of rain all night. 8 A.M. moderated—temp. 37° but it must be at freezing point in the prairies. Wrote to W. K[ennedy]. Noon, temp: 40°. 8 P.M. 40°. Rain abated and norther going down—in bed all day with chills.

Saturday, December 2nd, 1843: 8 A.M., temp. 27°. White frost over the ground and ice ¼ of an inch. Noon 64°—light airs from N. not a cloud in the sky and warm in the sun. When cotton is separated from the seed by the hand, as is the case sometimes in India, about one pound per day. The first "gins" used are thus described "comprised of two or three fluted rollers set in motion by the foot in the manner of a turning-lathe, and by its means one person may separate and cleanse sixty-five pounds." The "gin" at present employed in the United States and Texas yields about 2,000 pounds of bale cotton, or 4 bales of 500 lbs. each.

I once attended a course of lectures "on the Evidences of Design in Creation" and I think these lectures were intended to show that all causes and effects were for some benevolent purpose. Now we all know that animals of superior prowess will attack, kill, and eat other animals of an inferior sort, and man in some parts of the world is not over particular in doing the same. But to my story—the poultry in many parts of Texas is sadly persecuted by the fox, wild cat, opposum, coon, skunks, etc., and of the class of quadrupeds, but this seldom in the day time, and poultry roost generally on the boughs of trees 30 and 40 feet from the ground; but in the day time the hawk takes a position in a tree near the walk of poultry and when he sees a chance, he dashes with his greatest rapidity at a chick or young chicken, and off he is with his prey. Then it is that the most melancholy and heart rending and unmusical half-smothered crows of roosters, painful chuckles of the hens are heard, and this commotion does not cease for some time, and often the hawk is back for a second victim ere the poultry is quiet. One hawk I have seen carry away four chicks in a fore-noon. But retribution occasionally awaits this destructor of chickens—the Black Cook may be at the kitchen door, she sees the hawk dart in amongst the chickens, she screams out to Zip to bring the gun, she continues screaming and shakes her petticoats. Zip takes aim and down comes the hawk. Now in those countries where the hawks are numerous, the only plan is to erect a covered poultry house, to be constructed with laths, or very open wood work, thus up against a wall or side of a building. The poultry might be let out occasionally. If this plan be objected to, where there is much poultry, then a smaller open wood work frame might be erected for those hens who have broods of young chickens.

Sunday, December 3rd, 1843: Daylight, white frost on the ground 8 A.M. 40°—morning fine breezes from S. but occasionally cloudy. Noon 63°. Went to Montgomery—the late rains have swelled the creeks and roads again impassable even for travelling for white man; Comanches might do it, but I doubt it would be too cold for the Indians.

Monday, December 4th, 1843: 8 A.M. 60°. Cloudy and slight rain. Noon 64°, rain. 8 P.M., 62°—rain.

Tuesday, December 5th, 1843: Rain all night. 8 A.M. 55°. Heavy rain—N.E. winds or airs var. Noon 60°. 8 P.M. 60°— moderate.

Wednesday, December 6th, 1843: 8 A.M. 46°. Raining very hard all night. Noon 48°—8 P.M. 42°. Clear and fine. Great freshets in 1833—last year and this pretty heavy. This will be like 1833. Last night in February, 1829, after fine warm weather, snow commenced and continued on the ground a week. Six or 7 persons have just removed from the Brazos bottom, on account of the late rain and over-flows to this vicinity. All the land near the rivers and low land on the coast is under water; farms will be ruined, stock will be drowned, and the corn and cotton not housed will be lost. A gloom is beginning to come over the settlers on the rivers.

Thursday, December 7th, 1843: 8 A. M. 40° fine. Noon 54° and fine (moderately). 9 A. M. took a ride to race course, cold N air caught me and brought on chill immediately, had to return to the Hermitage.

As mentioned before, that previous to the Mexican Revolution and even up to the settlement of Texas by the Austins, the mustang and a few indifferent Mexican horses were the only horses in the country. The settlers, many of whom brought into the country their saddle horses, a few for breeding and lastly when the Texan Revolution broke out some good horses found their way from U.S. to Texas for the use of the cavalry. After the battle of San Jacinto, cities and towns were founded with rapidity, and amongst other public improvements races and race courses were established, for amusement and for the bettering the breed of horses. At Galveston there is a very good course with stand and stables. Houston has its course, other towns have followed these examples and moreover the principal planters and farmers have formed courses on their lands, thus affording pleasure to the settlers and the means for improving the breed of horses.

Friday, December 8th, 1843: Today accompanied my kind host to a horse race about a mile from the Hermitage. The race was for 500 dollars a side, Diddle versus Moll-row, American horses, or what in England would be called ponies, not standing more than 14 or 14½ hands high. The distance to be run, 600 yards; this is more like the South American distances than English, and the race will thus be gained in some measure by the jump horses are taught for this short distance, than hard running. The race-course being so wet, the 600 yards being measured off, two parallel tracks of some 3 to 4 feet were hoed out concavely, about a foot deep in the centre and about 12 or 15 feet apart.

600 Yards

This is considered rather a crack race, but the coldness of the weather prevents "the aristocracy and their families" being present. But, under a clump of live-oaks some two to three hundred persons were collected, their nags fastened to the branches of trees, making their bets; cash being somewhat scarce—cow and calf vs. cow and calf; horse against horse; Negro against Negro; land against land, etc. are the valuable considerations for their bets. In the rear stood a table, on which appeared to be hot coffee for the concurrents, and hard by a barrel of whiskey. It was expected, as is sometimes the case, that there would be commotion and disturbance at the betting stand—the stump of a tree—but, all was order and decorum. I saw no rifles, pistols, or bowie knives (and the only person rather the worse for his liquor was the owner of one of the horses). Diddle appeared to be the favourite, but a few knowing ones seemed to think that Moll-row would "shave Diddle." After waiting some time the horses were brought from stables, situated at some distance from each other, walked up and down in their blankets by their respective riders. Diddle on being stripped, looked pretty well—rather short and skittish. He was then saddled, and his rider prepared himself for the contest, by first tying a "kerchief" round his head, taking his coat, trousers, stockings, and shoes off; merely riding in his shirt and drawers; this is somewhat different to the elegant and "crispy" turn out of a Newmarket or Epsom jockey. Diddle's jockey having cleaned out his hoofs from mud, was *comparatively* ready. Moll-row's jockey stripped, but kept his trousers on and was to ride without saddle, being above the stipulated weight; he cleared away the mud from his horse's hoofs and greased them.

The jockies mounted; and it was a considerable time ere Diddle appeared to relish running in the track. It was thought by some that this skittishness and jumping about was allied to "jockeyism."

During all this time a very old and dark looking man, wrapt up in a Mexican mantle, might be observed riding up and down on one side of the course absorbed in thought, speaking to no one, and with looks that told that his heart was fixed upon the result of the race—he was the owner of Moll-row. Madly galloping about, now stopping short and pulling up, now starting off again, he might be seen making for the whiskey stall (and ere the race was run he was *drunk*). This was Diddle's owner.

At last they were preparing to start; some remaining at the starting post, others on either side of the course, whilst many crowded round the winning post, their thoughts absorbed for the fate of their cows and calves, land, Negros, etc. The horses *start!* and in about 20 seconds the race is over, the favourite *losing*. Huzzah for Moll-row. (Tomorrow morning when Diddle's owner awakes from his painful and stupified night's rest, his feelings upon this occasion will not be of the most blissful character).

Moll-row's master and jockey went quietly off the course, perfectly satisfied. Diddle's owner must bear his loss philosophically.

A voice: "Squire, I'll send for the cow and calf tomorrow."

Squire: "All right—go a head! This is the last time Diddle diddle's me."

General: "Sheriff, you may send the Niggers over when convenient."

Sheriff: "Ay-ay, General. By the —— D—— on the race."

Captain: "Why Colonel, I hope you'll have better luck tomorrow, long races—none of these jumps. Zip will come for the Black Mare in a day or two."

And in this way, they settled about their bets until the course was clear. Some said there was jockeying, for when Diddle had got to half-course he passed Moll-row and shot a head, but the "Judges of the Course" were unanimous as to Moll-row's superior speed and decided victory.

Bollaert's entries in his journal for the next six or seven days are very brief, other than daily temperature readings. On Tuesday, December 12, 1843, he observed that the current norther "makes 14 northers great and small we have had this winter." And on the following day he wrote: "There appears to be a battling between N and S airs—if S predominates, then we shall have rain." The south winds won, for on December 14, 1843, "cold torrents of rain" came again. "I get slight chills occasionally," the Englishman recorded, "and they will not leave until I get a change of climate—say the sea air of Galveston Island."

XIII

FROM MONTGOMERY TO HUNTSVILLE

[December, 1843–January, 1844]

December 14th, 1843: At 3 P.M. left the "Court House." It soon commenced raining and pine forest in winter does not afford the best of shelter. Reached the farm of Mr. Dunlap, who is married to the daughter of the celebrated "Horse Shoe Robinson."[1]

December 15th, 1843: We had to go many miles out of our direct course owing to the late rains rendering the fords impassable, but at dusk put up at Mr. H——'s plantation. On all the creeks observed many farms and although this part of Montgomery has a[n] undulating sandy soil, there is no complaint of a scarcity of produce. On our road today, in passing a log house belonging to a chair maker, my companion, who was about commencing housekeeping, entered into an arrangement with the artizan to give him "pigs and small claims upon some of his neighbours" for chairs.

December 16th, 1843: Three miles brought us to Huntsville,[2] situated on a "pine height." This town was commenced in 1836, but made but little progress until 1842, when Mr. MacDonald[3]

---

[1] Bollaert mentions "Horse Shoe Robinson" two or three times in his journals and notes, but never identifies him by his real name. There were several Robinsons conspicuous in the history of the Republic, but the editor has been unable to find any clue as to which one went by the name of "Horse Shoe." A guess would be that the one referred to was William Robinson, who served as county surveyor for Montgomery County upon its organization in December, 1837. Prior to that date, William Robinson served in the Texas conventions of 1832 and 1833. According to the *Biographical Directory of Texan Conventions and Congresses*, page 161, Robinson was listed on November 8, 1850, as a farmer and stockman in Montgomery County.

[2] [Named] after Huntsville in Alabama.—Bollaert.

[3] Bollaert never identified "MacDonald" by his first name. In a note in one of the boxes of Bollaert materials the following comment is found: "Mr. Mac's father was quartermaster in the Glengarrys, or MacDonnells, Regiment, 800 strong, in Ireland and was in the Battle of Vinegar Hill and wounded there—so

gave an impetus to building etc., thus making it a convenient market for the neighboring planters and farmers. On entering the town is observed "Planters Exchange," Gibb's Grocery,"[4] "Huntsville Hotel," etc., etc. Mr. MacDonald, besides a very large and comfortable residence, has built a brick store, the upper part devoted to a masonic lodge. A large brick building for girls and boys schools[5] is now building and many other improvements going on.

The town is supplied from good springs, and wells at twelve feet supply abundance of water. On one side of the town there is a sulphur spring; indeed, there are many of this character in the county. Game is in abundance, but on account of the dense pine woods, the hunting is more difficult. Three miles from this and at forty feet in depth, a small fossil horn and fossil bones have been found. Mr. MacDonald has from 50 to 60 of his drawings of Texas scenery.

Found at Huntsville the "celebrated" Captain Barclay's[6] *Agricultural Tour in the United States and Canada*, 1841. He crossed the ocean with an idea of giving an opinion to a bunch of relatives on the purchase of property, and gave the preference to the U. S. Canada was too black, rocky, and woody—but the Captain deplores much the general system of U.S. agriculture—particularly as regards the land-owners who do not erect farms and *lease* them, being contented to take half crops. Then to prevent the impoverishing of lands, Captain B. presses the interchange of

---

was my father. After the rebellion in '98, the Glengarrys fencibles were disbanded, after 8 years service and many went to Canada. . . ."

4 This was the store of Thomas and Sanford Gibbs, established in 1844, and continuing today as the First National Bank of Huntsville. *The Handbook of Texas*, I, 867.

5 The town consists of more than 200 houses, a portion of which are built of brick. The female academy ["Brick Academy"] which is now built, is of brick, also Mr. White's store. There is likewise a good boys' academy. All sorts of artizans. Building is going on and sound of the anvil and hammer heard continually. —Bollaert.

6 The "celebrated" Captain Barclay was Robert Barclay (1779–1854), a British officer and pedestrian. He once walked one mile in each of 1,000 successive hours, a feat which gained him world recognition. It is doubtful if anyone else has ever tried it.

crops and taking more care of stock, etc.—manuring the land, which manure they could get in abundance if they housed their cattle in winter, and the cattle would not be having skeletons in the Spring.

Note: 10 bales of cotton, raised near Huntsville and shipped for the planter on his own account to Liverpool—sold for £79.17.9, or at 4ᵈ per lb. The freight from Galveston was £15–10—duty in England £6.8.7, and other charges left £48.16.1, which equals $216.91. $41.15 freight to Galveston, $3 per bale.[7] The farmer received $175.76.[8] This system with its charges would not suit the farmer, [since he would receive only $17+ per bale]. If cotton was high, say 12 to 15 cents, then the farmer or small planter would be remunerated, but with the present low prices, the planter loses by his crops, particularly those who are near some of the rivers and whose lands are subject to overflows. It is better for the planter when he can repose confidence in his merchant who supplies him with bagging, rope, groceries, etc., etc. to sell to him, rather than ship on his own account, for many reasons. The merchant also has to take care that the planter be a good man.

Generally speaking Scotch and English farmers followed the transatlantic plans—and the Captain only made one convert to the Scotch and English mode of farming who intended to put it into practice upon his estate. This subject leads me to say a few words on the agriculture of Texas. Generally speaking, the lands do not require clearing of timber without it is required that the plantation should be in the "bottom" where the very richest lands for cotton are.

In the West there is no occasion for clearing, but in the East and in some of the rich lands of small rivers, some *clear.* There arises in a few days the habitations of logs for Master and Negro— then the Virginia fence of split rails. Then according to the land a heavy or light plough which is turned up with ease. The cotton seed is sown (hand cast) and when it is about 2 or 3 inches, it is

[7] Cotton this year can be taken per steamer to Galveston [from Huntsville] for $2 per bale.—Bollaert.

[8] Unless there were other charges which Bollaert did not list, the farmer should have received $186.91.

thinned—a very great many cotton plants are pulled up and what remains appears to have been planted in rows. Cotton seed being of no object, all the super-abundant acts as manure, but it is hardly wanted. Cotton can be planted earlier by 2 or 3 weeks in Texas than in Mississippi and picking season continues later. Corn is planted in rows about 3 or 4 feet apart. Two seeds are generally put into each hole. On Trinity last year 40 to 50 bushels of corn to the acre. Cotton—about 2,000 pounds, but this is a high average for this County. Those fields near a gin are often strewed with cotton seed to get it out of the way and it acts as a manure, but not absolutely required.

Much more planting, particularly of cotton, would go on if there was more "force" (hands); as it is, many of the planters and farmers plant more than they can gather in or pick—which is blown about by the first norther, or nipped by the first frost. Tobacco is grown in some quantities, and on the Colorado and the Coast sugar is becoming a considerable article of manufacture. Grain of all sorts, rice also thrives well, and garden stuffs in abundance. And with care and attention orchards would do very well. All the southern plants, vegetables and flowers grow with great luxuriance in Texas. Northern and European seeds generally require care and watching for many of a small growth in the "Old Country" become almost shrubs in this climate.

There are two great and important things in the agriculture of this country in particular: 1) a rich and virgin soil; 2) such a temperature during the greater part of the year that to use an expression I heard the other day—"If you put ten-penny nails in the ground you will have a crop of iron bolts." Nevertheless, it is to be hoped that when emigration from Britain takes place to Texas, the farmer will not follow the modes he will find in use, but according to circumstances introduce more economical methods; thus, less land will be required to the worker, than is at present, and there will be more for pastures for the stock.

With regard to stock in Texas, it is a mixture of American and Mexican; in the West they revel in the musquit grass and get very fat and afford fine beef, but as one approaches the lower part of Eastern Texas, pine woods appear and even in the prairies the grass declines in goodness. Cattle is never housed and must suffer by the northers and the frosty weather that follows these frigid winds. Of horses, only the very best are housed, the others remain out all the winter and get shelter in the woods.

Wednesday, December 20th, 1843: A mail has arrived from the West and the Coast. Among other news the president's message dated Washington, December 12th.[9] As yet the election of officers only had occupied the House of Representatives and Senators. The President's message was little more than a repetition of his speech at Houston.

I am informed by a settler who has been more than twenty years in this country (the eastern part) that at an early period cotton would fetch 30 cents at N. Orleans, but occasionally Mexicans would cross Texas to the East and purchase cotton at 50 cents *in cash*, which was made up in small and convenient bales, so that a mule could carry two of them.

In a few years my informant, from being very poor, had a fine plantation and a considerable number of Negros, and Negros he considers the best property a man can have in Texas. A few years since only Negros sold for 1, 2 and 3000 dollars. At present 2 and 300 dollars cash and less. Everything is done by barter, or as called here *trade*.

Afternoon fine—made up a hunting party; the overflows in the rivers and creeks have drawn the bears out, who have been feeding and fattening on *mast* in the bottoms and low lands. The bear after a short chase took to a thicket, but soon became a victim to the rifle. He was a fine fat fellow, and black as a coal. On our way homewards the dogs started a fox and after a pretty run, Reynard took to an inclined tree. We had no time to spare to bother with him, and he soon had a bullet whistled through him. A fine fat buck was another victim.

[9] Houston's message of December 12, 1843, summarized the happenings of the previous few months, particularly relative to dealings with Mexico, Indian affairs, and finances of the Republic. *The Writings of Sam Houston*, III, 459–75.

We came by the head of Huntsville Springs, which has evident indications of a sulphurous odour and whilst admiring the Magnolias there, the dogs had found an opposum and he took to a gum tree. This was really "possum up a gum tree." After amusing ourselves sometime, he became a victim of the rifle.

During our chase saw many plants and trees new to me, but we scampered over the ground excited by the game we had started, that my companions thought of nought else but the chase; yet there was one plant which I got some information about, the persim[m]on. It is a small tree and yields an orange coloured fruit about the size of a very small crab apple; when the juice of this plant is fermented with a small quantity of sweet-potatoe, a very pleasant beverage results, called by the settlers "persim[m]on beer." From the sweet-potatoe another drink is made, by baking them, then mashing them up with water, and after fermentation has taken place it gets the name of "potatoe beer." There is no drink made in this country from Indian corn, like the chicha of the Peruvians.

Thursday, December 21st, 1843: Some years since the settlers about the Trinity came to the determination of circumscribing the range (which was of very little extent for an Indian who hunts and necessarily ranges a good deal) of the Coushattas, Muscovy's, etc. The reason given was that the said Indians robbed cattle, set fire to fences, etc. etc. This does not appear to be the case exactly, but some of the settlers wished for the lands the Indians were on. Many of the Coshattas and other Indians have gone over the frontier into the U. States and it is probable the rest about this part of the Trinity River will follow.

Accompanied Mr. and Mrs. MacD—— and a party some two miles into the pine woods; roads very bad, step by step only could we proceed on account of the mud which was of all consistencies. On our approach to the residence of the bride, we met many parties like ourselves going to the wedding; and on our arrival found that many had already congregated—their Bucephalii (horses) filling the "lot" and others attached to trees. All were in their best, with a sprinkling of fashionables.

My friend Mr. F. commenced by introducing me to the ladies —Mr. M—— to the gents, and in a few minutes I was at home. By sun down some 150 to 200 persons, i.e.: men, women, boys, girls, and babies, had congregated.

The Mammas with their chicks huddled round a blazing fire, then the "ladies" (young ladies) those connected with the ceremony, dressed in white, the rose of youth still upon their cheeks. One there was who looked the "lily sweet"—she was beautiful; but chills and fever of late had rendered her delicate, but gave at the same time a melancholy loveliness to her features, and rendered her particularly interesting. There were many other interesting females, one in particular, Widow N——, about 18 (no family, considerable moral character, Negros, lands, etc.)—But Willie [Bollaert] thy name is constancy! I thought of Sadie; from these wilds of the Red Man, to the gentle glades and placid stream of this abode, my thoughts wandered; my heart did beat, but it was for thee. I will not say all were happy here, but all tried to smile joy to the bride. I essayed too, but fond remembrance would come over me and the half smothered sigh gave a temporary relief.

A shout is heard: "Here he comes"—when the bridegroom, escorted by a squadron of his old companions on horseback, arrived in front of the log house. He was almost hauled off his steed by those in waiting to receive him; when I am sure he had to shake hands with a hundred persons. "Courage," said they with a smirking smile. We are now formed ourselves in one room of the log house, the minister, standing opposite the door the bridal party had to enter. In a few minutes there was a silence full of expectation—a rustling was heard in the passage, and then the bridegroom with the bride under his arm, supported by their necessary attendants. The bridegroom put a pretty good face upon this his present "difficulty." The bride with considerable pretentions to prettiness droopingly hanging on her to-be-husband's arm, occasionally taking a peep up at the company.

The Minister without any preamble or ceremony, commenced the marriage service extempore. The "I wills" were not audibly pronounced; the ceremony of the ring was not introduced, and from the moment the happy pair entered the room until the minister finished, they moved not. Having legally become man and wife, they now received the congratulations of the company. Supper was now announced in No. 2 Room, consisting of all the good things of this life; this took up a considerable time owing to the number of guests. After supper there was a cry for the music, but ere a good fiddle could be obtained, two hours passed; the interim filled up by singing.

At last the fiddle, after sundry snaps of strings, was announced, when cotillions, or "contra-dansé" were commenced, varied by reels and an occasional variation of "roaring river." The more venerable part of the concourse, Mammas with their *babies* and a few others, "sloped" about midnight, it being dark, when a very pretty scene presented itself. Negros running to and fro catching and saddling horses, each with a flambeau of "light wood" (pine) and those who left the bridal scene, their Negros ahead with the fire pan (that used in deer hunting) which sheds a very considerable light and over a great extent. The glare and smoke from the fire pan, the party on horseback, now a bonnet seen, then a cavalier riding up along side of a young lady doubtlessly whispering soft nothings into her ear, the dense pine woods, and lastly the horrible roads of mud and slush at midnight and a young norther blowing its ungentle airs—made the trip home *a scene.*

But the juveniles [who stayed behind] kept it up till nearly morning and when fatigued with dancing, who play at forfeits, "grind the bottle," "fish stalk," "Lennor says 'come to taw!'." When breakfast was nearly ready, many young gentlemen were discovered "in among the cotton, wrapped in the arms of Morpheus," and it was with some difficulty that Mr. S—— could be found, but was ultimately discovered by his herculean whiskers. After a good and substantial breakfast each and every one left the bride and bridegroom to enjoy the solace of matrimonial bliss undisturbed. Father Mathew would have revelled in extacy at this marriage feast—there were no spirituous liquors introduced—its place supplied with coffee or water—*a choix;* but some few who were votaries to the jolly god, had sundry bottles of whiskey.

Friday, December 22nd, 1843: Mr. Mac gave a dance. Fine airs.

Saturday, December 23rd, 1843: Fine and warm airs.

Sunday, December 24th, 1843: Slight frost during night. Fine and warm as a summer's day. 11 A.M.: Started for Cincinnati[10] with Mr. and Mrs. M—— and Mr. and Mrs. Cole. The heaviness of the pine woods relieved by an occasional small prairie. Land undulating, with a rise ere the Trinity bottom is attained; there is a ridge 150 to 200 feet above Huntsville. Roads pretty good considering the late bad weather, but with here and there some "pretty considerable sloughs." Mr. Black's[11] plantations are the principal ones on this road. On our arrival at Cincinnati, between 1 and 2 P.M., found that the V*esta* Steamer had started about an hour. This was treating Mr. Mac badly, for it had been previously arranged to wait until the afternoon or evening of today. So we had to return very much disappointed to Huntsville. Cincinnati is situated on a bluff on the W. side of the river, surrounded by "bottom" and woodland, and comes in for its share of agues. The principal store belongs to the firm of Frankland and Company of Galveston, supplying the planters and farmers in this section; and taking in payment purchasing their cotton. I cannot say much for this vicinity for emigrants. Some Germans went up the Trinity a few days since and others are daily expected under the

10 Cincinnati is now a ghost town on the Trinity River in Walker County, approximately fifteen miles north of Huntsville. It was once a well-known river port, but a yellow fever epidemic practically wiped out the settlement in 1853. The town was founded in 1838 by James C. DeWitt. *The Handbook of Texas,* I, 347.
11 This reference doubtless is made to John S. Black, who came to Texas in 1830. He received a headright in present Grimes County (formerly a part of Montgomery County), where he settled and eventually acquired several plantations. In 1843 he served as an Indian commissioner on the frontier with Thomas I. Smith and George W. Terrell. *The Writings of Sam Houston,* III, 348.

guidance of Baumgarten of Galveston. It would appear that the ferryman at Washington will clear more money this year than many a planter in Texas. He may take $6,000—$3,000 of which will be his share, it being a partnership. I paid 2½ dollars to cross 9 months since. Twenty-five cents is the regular price, but 75 cents have been charged during the past wet season.

Christmas Day, 1843: Egg nogs, the favourite beverage this morning (made of the white and yellow of eggs, beaten up separately, the yellow with sugar, then both mixed with whiskey, brandy, and new milk to thin it—somewhat pleasant, but of a bilious nature). Visitings amongst the neighbors; dinner and merry makings.

At this time of the year the Negros have their week's holiday, bedecked out in their best, they visit each other, the evening ending in singing and dancing. I am informed that in Virginia and two or three states about it, the Negros are very much attached to their masters in whose family some generations of Negros have been "raised;" that they are easily managed, and whippings are seldom resorted to.

It appears that as plantations approach more southerly, such propensities are discovered amongst the Negros, and when whipping is found to be of no use, they are sent to Louisiana and Mississippi and from thence to the New Orleans slave market. It is from the Louisiana and Mississippi that most of the Negros now in Texas (the older ones) have come, and must not be looked upon as equal to the Virginia Negros. But the great secret is to know how to manage them.

When they become cooks and house servants, they give themselves great airs, but the most serious objection against them is the wilful waste of everything they meddle [with] in the way of cooking, without they are very narrowly watched by the "guide" housewife. Moreover, one "maid of all work" in Western Texas or in the interior, out of part of the influence of southern suns, would do the work of three Negro women, do it well, and in a cleanly manner. But Texas is but a young country, and it is a matter of astonishment and admiration that there are so many necessaries and comforts.

Nigger Parady on a Methodist Hymn

Ven dat celestial day shall rise,
And all the Army shine
In robes of victory troo (through) *de skies*
De glory shall be mine. What!—
I walks and I talks vid my Jesus
Hallam—Hallam—lu-ja—
I walks and I talks vid my Jesus
Vid de glory of my soul—Hum (four times)
Hallam Hallam—lu-ja (four times)
I walks and I talks vid my Jesus—
    Hum (four times) *Oh! Oh!*
Vid the glory in my soul.

Ven dat celestial day shall rise
And de moon goes down in blood,
You Nigger you run to de mountain high
To hide your selves from God. Chorus.

Ye hiperam-crits, and conquerambines
Who lib (*lives*) *amongst the swine*
You go to your God, wid your teef (teeth)
    in your mouf (mouth)
And your sins you leave behind.

Camp meetings and conferences of the Methodists are flourishing in the Eastern counties. There is a conference a few miles from this; some 40 to 50 ministers have assembled and divers Methodist communicants. The planters and farmers in the vicinity have to accom[m]odate the holy and reverend men, who have considerable power over their flocks, as the following will shew:

Minister: "Friend—we never see you at meeting."

Friend: "I read my bible at home."

Minister: "That's well, but, but, but,—it would be better to attend meetings and if it be true what I hear that you intend running for Congress next year, if you do not mix with your Methodist friends you will not be elected. They all know you to be generous, well to do, and a man they like, but not being satisfied with your non-attendance at public worship, they will oppose your election, and probably some one may get the votes over you, who may do us all great harm in Congress. My Christian friend, consider this, and I'll do much for you with the brethren and ministers."

Friend: "I will take your views into consideration, and will attend meeting next Sunday."

Tuesday, December 26th, 1843: Fine airs from N.W. thermometer at freezing point. When the sun gets up beautiful and fine, even warm—fine and bracing. In 1840 there were two months of this delightful winter weather.

Attended an amusement called "candy pulling." Some 50 or 60 lads and lasses congregated to assist at this sport. A quantity of molasses is boiled down until it becomes thick; it is then poured out into dishes and plates, each one taking a portion in their hands and commence "pulling," or elongating it until it gets cold, when it takes on a yellow appearance and hardens, but the great fun and sport is to approach slyly those persons whose candy appears to be well pulled and snatch it from them, this produces great hilarity, and for the first time since I have been in Texas, this party made me think of the Christmas gambols at home—indeed, with the excitement of "candy pulling" the stiffness of the American character one sees in Texas was thrown on one side.

Dances and music in the evening. Quadrilles are called cotillions, and the contre-dance, a reel. Waltzes not patronized yet. A ball is soon arranged in these parts; if such is wished for, let the room be large or small, it takes place, some friend playing the violin, but for the cotillions the figures are "called out." "Roaring River," "Piney Woods," "Killicrankie," "Harper's Creek," "Bully

Thatché's," [Bull et chassé] "My Wife's Dead," and "I'm a
Widower" etc. are favourite reels.

Wednesday, December 27th, 1843: Frost during night—fine.
"For some days I have been ill with the ague and sad as can be.
My memories and thoughts about the future have about finished
me, and I cannot enjoy the society here, even though it is happy.
I believe that it is a very general observation that small and thin
women are without exception very capricious and devilish, at least
I have found them so, and they have made me suffer because I
have not been sufficiently independent to stay away from them."[12]

Saturday, December 30th, 1843: Last night it was cool and a
parcel of neighbors were huddled round the fire. The "village
politicians" were thrown into the shade by the Texas politicians,
some of whom had fought the good fight for their adopted country. They had but little sympathy for the Western War Party,
for they believed in "Old Sam" and his acts and views. Many of
the Eastern people, amongst others, had disobeyed General Somervell's orders—gone to Mier with Fisher and Green, some had
performed prodigies of valour, had injudiciously capitulated when
they were really the victors. They had trusted *once more* to Mexican honour—but were made prisoners. The blood of the Saxon
rebelled against this treatment, they rose upon their guards, killed
some of them, but effected only a temporary liberty. They were
re-taken, *decimated* by Santana and the rest kept as prisoners
and in chains.

It is the duty of the historian to study both sides of the question
and as far as in him lies to put the history of transactions in as
true and unbiased a light as he can.

---

[12] Bollaert at this point had dropped into Spanish, as he occasionally did:
"*Hace dias que estoy enfermo con Terciana—y triste hasta no poder mas—Mil
recuerdos, y pensamientos sobre el avenir me acaba y no puedo gozar de la sociedad
aqui aunque esta alegre. Creo q^e es una observacion mui general q^e las mujeres
chiquitas y flacas, son sin excepcion mui caprichosas y endemoniadas—a lo menos
yo lo he hallado, y me han dado a sufrir, porque no me he hallado sufficiente inde-
pendiente de zafarme de ellas.*"

When La Mar was succeeded in the Presidency by General Houston, La Mar and his friends became violently opposed to the new President, condemning with great violence his policy and acts. Houston's policy favoured amicable arrangements with Mexico, and on this point he believed that the United States, E[ngland], and F[rance] would interpose their good offices. The opposition now took the name of "The War Party," and was for calling to its assistance volunteers from the U. States (who would know but little of the real political state of Texas and her relations with foreign powers) and idlers and loafers who would like a campaign for many reasons. Standards would be unfurled with "Liberty," "Remember the Alamo," "Let us revel in the halls of Montezuma" on them. And it was hoped by the opposition that with a successful campaign across the Rio Grande to the Sierra Madre etc. Santana would sue for peace, and thus Houston and his peace policy would be swallowed up in the vortex of their glory. Circumstances at this juncture favoured the "War Party" by a military promenade of Vasquez and some 2 to 300 Mexicans entering San Antonio, distributing a proclamation calling upon Texans to return to *their obedience*. This promenade of Vasquez was construed by the President's enemies to be "an invasion." The party appealed to their friends in the U. S. against the wishes of the President. Volunteers arrived in Galveston ready for anything, and they were told by Houston very politely that they were not wanted. Some took the hint and returned to the U. States, others remained, hoping to bedew their virgin swords in Mexican blood and "revel in the halls of Montezuma." The War Party exerted every nerve to commence belligerent operations, but Houston's sanction was necessary; this he withheld from them as he supposed such a line of conduct would retard the peaceable settlements of the question with Mexico, particularly as the friendly powers to Texas had been solicited to assist Texas in a line of policy that did not suit the "War Party," but one in which the Executive had faith.

Violent indeed ran party spirit after some time, and Houston *treated* the hot blood of the U. S. Volunteers who remained in

Texas and the *fighting* adherents to the War Party to an amateur campaign, the history of the surprise of them and skirmish of Lipantitlán was no bad sequel, and was enough for the young warriors.

Santana sent General Woll with a considerable force into Texas, believing that such was the political and military disorganization of the "rebels" that there was a chance of recovering part of Texas, and moreover, preventing emigration. The War Party had lost some of its energy, by the steady line of the Executive's conduct, but it is true emigration was stopped and many of the settlers in the West left their homes.

Woll marched into San Antonio, but was glad soon to retreat over the Rio Grande after the "whipping" he got at the Salado River; although a host of the Mexicans managed to surround Dawson's Company in a "Mott" and slaughtered nearly the whole of them. The War Party's cry was "Texas will be invaded by sea and land—prepare we for them." But it was much cry and little wool—for the principal part of the War leaders were on a summer trip in the U. States and the Executive saw that Woll's entry would be a sufficient excuse for retaliation, pacify the fighting men, and make soldiers of the rising generation. Much time was passed in getting together some 700 or 800 men, making Bejar the rendezvous. Now had Houston a difficult card to play—he appointed General Somervell to the command, who doubtless could be depended on by the President in the executing of his orders and views to the letter. The War Party wanted General [Albert Sidney] Johns[t]on to be in command: La Mar, Felix Houston,[13] etc., etc., etc. these would have been *untractable* and might have upset the peace policy. Houston at most wished to make a military demonstration on the frontier, march into their towns as victors and then would have been very glad after this pacific retaliation, for the army to have returned to Texas and each to his home. Before or after the taking of Laredo some individuals hoped

[13] Felix Houston [Huston] is famous in Texas history for two things, namely: he was a bitter enemy of Sam Houston's, and he wounded Albert Sidney Johnston in a duel in 1837, when the latter was sent to relieve him as commander of the Texas Army.

that the operations of Somervell would be considered too apathetic and that he would be deposed from the command by the citizen soldiers and another put in his place—this did not happen —intrigues for command caused a general disorganization, when in the end the minority under [William S.] Fisher and [Thomas Jefferson] Green crossed the Rio Grande contrary to Somervell's orders, they got to Mier, they fought valiantly, but were trapped by the Mexicans. Somervell and the "law abiding" people returned to their homes. General S. is now enjoying the office of Collector of Customs at Aransas, his obedient followers their peaceable fire sides—the War Party cooped up in the prisons of Mexico.

Sunday, December 31st, 1843: Yesterday and during the night wind S. E.; showers. 8 A. M., cloudy but fine. Sun down, a shower and wind chopped round to N.W .Last night, through the kindness of Mr. Mᶜ., the Negros of this vicinity had their Christmas ball in his unfinished store. (The upper part destined for a Masonic Hall). It was late ere all arrived, many of them having had to come several miles. It was a "subscription" ball and the unfortunate Negro who could not raise a couple of bits (about 1s) was not admitted at the commencement of the ball, but Black hearts wax soft and as midnight approached and the strains of music sweet, the excitement produced by dancing the door keepers became benevolent and it was a public ball.

As the company arrived they were cordially greeted [with] bows and shaking of hands and introduced by the names of their masters and mistresses and young masters and mistresses. Thus was announced Mr. and Mrs. McD——, Mr. and Mrs. E——, Miss Mary E——, Master Joe E—— (Sukey, Fanny, Mary, Charlotte, Jim, Silas, Ned, Phil, Bob, Tim, Meg, Dinah, Miss Mary K. etc. etc.). They were well dressed and most orderly. Now and then a sable gay Lothario on bended knee soliciting the hand of one in whom was centered all his hopes for the dance—she would remain a few moments, coquettishly undecided, then put forth her "lily black paw" and concede to him his request. Gladness sparkled in his eye, decorum of carriage forgotten, every limb would be in movement, the truly joyous and hearty laugh would resound thru the room and the yagh! yagh! as finale truly indicative of the Nigger. About midnight they had supper and to it they went until daylight, when they returned to their respective homes, their Christmas holidays having terminated.

Congress is going on orderly and amicably at Washington[-on-the-Brazos]—with sobriety too[,] observes the *Vindicator*. The customs duties maintained the Government for the past year. Ad valorem duties anticipated—indeed, with such an administration as Houston has established, the Government of this country can be maintained at as low a rate as any republican could wish. Mr. [Frederick W.] Ogden,[14] by leave introduced a joint resolution for the annexation of Texas to the United States; referred to Committee of Foreign Relations. An Act read 2nd time to extend donations of land to emigrants—referred to Committee of Public Lands—claims of British subjects to empresario lands—President gave correspondence upon this.

Monday, January 1st, 1844: The "Village Doctor" in the U. States and Texas unites the characters of physician, surgeon, apothecary, etc., etc. etc. and has often to travel many many miles to visit their patients. They are gentlemen of education and from their appearance and manners would seem to be better suited to "town" rather than "country" practice. This may be accounted for by there being no "peasantry," but all over the country a similarly educated and politically constituted people; a people who consider themselves second best to no nation upon earth. When the Doctor is sent for, say 10 or 20 miles, off he goes with saddle bags so constructed as to hold such medicines he judges from report the patient may require, and dispenses them after seeing the sick man. This year has given a good harvest to the Doctors. Their charges will depend upon the distance they may have to

[14] Frederick W. Ogden served one term in the Texas Congress (the House of Representatives in the Eighth Congress) from San Augustine. *Biographical Directory of Texas Conventions and Congresses,* 146–47.

go, the circumstances of the party, etc. etc. and when cash is scarce, the medical man will be paid in cows and calves, horses, pigs, cotton, etc. etc. And it often happens that the Doctor is at the same time a small planter and farmer, so such payments are equal to money. I am speaking now of the medical practice in the interior of Texas. When population shall increase and there be a cash or a healthy note circulation, then the Physician will take his *fee* and the druggist dispense the medicine, as at Galveston, Houston, etc. Sometimes the Physician is in a sort of partnership with the chemist and druggist.

With regard to diseases in Texas, from personal observation, they appear to be very limited. On the Coast and along the margins of the greater rivers, agues prevail when there are overflows; and congestion and bilious fevers caused by continued exposure to the sun.

But I may remark, that although these attacks may be severe for a short time, the convalescence is very rapid compared to similar cases in the Northern part of Europe. During one of my peregrinations in the interior of Texas, I saw painted on a board outside of a log cabin (one small apartment only) "Doctors ———— and ————." I was introduced to them and found them two of the most gentlemenly men I had met with; highly educated, of fashionable exterior and carrying on a very good practice, turning their payments of pigs, cows and calves, horses, corn, land, etc., into cotton, sending this article to New Orleans and when sold the cash put to their credit. This to an English physician would appear most incongruous, but it is so; they are making money, they are enjoying themselves, and probably will marry in the vicinity where fortune has smiled upon them, they may become planters, members of Congress, and in a few years may grace the Presidential Chair if they choose to be nominated. With regard to civil honours, one is an alderman, the other a Major.[15] I will

---

[15] Of the medical profession, many fought the battles of the Republic. The present Secretary of State, Anson Jones, was a physician, and he is now a candidate for the Presidency. Ashbel Smith, the Texas minister to England is an M.D. Of the legal profession many have distinguished themselves in battle, and General Houston, when he first came to Texas, practiced law at Nacogdoches. K. L. Ander-

give an idea of their residence, which is a log-cabin, and description of the contents of it.[16]

Tuesday, January 2nd, 1844: Attended the marriage ceremony
of a run away match. The bride and bridegroom had ridden some
15 miles full tilt, the bride was deposited with a friend; the bridegroom posted off to the deputy county clerk for a license which
cost only 1 dollar; and now behold them before, or rather by the
bed side of Judge K——, who is almost bed-ridden. A certificate
was handed to the Judge by the Deputy County Clerk, purporting
that she was *over* eighteen; she took the oath to that effect, when
the Judge, after examining the marriage license, asked them if
they wished to be man and wife, and then after asking them this
separately, to which they nodded assent, the Judge concluded that
"What God hath joined, let no man put asunder," and they were
married. In a few minutes the married, and I hope, happy pair
mounted their horses and off they were to the log cabin of the
bridegroom.

Not long since in —— county, there was an amusing runaway match. Mrs. N——, a widow, had an only daughter, F——,
of course beautiful, as all young and unmarried ladies are, or as
they are reputed to be, was courted by Stephen J——, was accepted and received as the lover by the lady's Mamma. No difficulty whatever appeared to prevent the anticipated union, more
particularly as "they loved each other" and moreover their fortunes were equal. Time passed on. Stephen was happy; he attended with the greatest diligence to his plantation, turned his
old log residence into a kitchen, the former kitchen into store
houses, built a frame house and furnished it appropriately for
the reception of F—— when she should be his wife.

---

son, Esq. a few years since was speaker of the House of Representatives. He has
become Secretary of the Navy, and now a candidate for the Vice Presidency.—
Bollaert.

16 Bollaert includes a pencil drawing of a log cabin, representing the office and
residence of two Texas physicians. An additional sketch shows the interior of the
establishment, some twenty feet square, with beds, medicine shelves, stove, a table,
and two chairs.

A brother of the widow's unexpectedly died, and his plantation (which was only some few miles from her own), Negros, etc., became her property. The day of grief and mourning being over for *so good a brother,* the widow commenced counselling her daughter to look somewhat "higher in life" and for a person of more property than "poor Stephen," in whom, now the widow could discover many defects and with whose alliance certain very disadvantageous circumstances might arise. F—— combatted like an honest loving girl her mother's views, but the mother was inexorable, and as she wanted a year or more of eighteen, she thought it prudent to, apparently submit. Stephen was broken-hearted, but his faithful girl assured him that sooner or later she would be his and his only, and that the addition to her prospects only made her love him the more. The widow suggested several young men as "suitable" for her—a deep sigh, a heaving bosom, and downcast look was her only answer.

F—— has just passed her eighteenth year and her mother believed that her daughter had become dutiful and forgotten Stephen, when one morning Mamma found it requisite to go to the plantation left by her brother, leaving F—— at home. Now F—— had a faithful Negress about her own age, and "raised" in the family. She was dispatched with great secrecy to Stephen, informing him to repair immediately to a part of the "timber" hard by F——'s residence well mounted, to bring his sister "along" and a spare horse. All turned out well to the letter and off the three were to a neighboring town. The house servants shortly discovered that young "Missy F's gone and dat old Missy kill all de Niggers on the plantation when she come home." "Come home indeed," cried an old Negress. "If you wish not to be killed, run to old Missy and tell her young Missy gone—and tink runaway vid Massa Stephen." Off went one of the fleetest Negros to the widow. She rode home as fast as she could, dispatching her Negros in all directions, even to Stephen's plantation. Leaving the Mamma to bewail over the absence of her daughter, we will return to the runaways.

On the arrival at the town of ——— Stephen obtained the

license from the County Clerk, he presented himself and his faithful F—— before the Judge, and in a few minutes they were man and wife, when Stephen, now the happiest of mortals, "took her home." Late at night the widow's sable emissaries arrived one by one, no tidings of the undutiful daughter, when later still, the Negro who had been dispatched to Stephen was heard singing most merrily in praise of Missy and Massa Stephen, so intoxicated that he could not find the gate and tearing down the Virginia fence so as to obtain an entrance into the plantation, which feat he accomplished, detailing particulars relative to the runaway match.

A year passed, the widow would not be reconciled to her daughter, when it came to her ears that she was a grandmamma, and a mutual friend acquainted her that her presence was all that was required at the forthcoming christening to make her children happy. The old lady followed the course suggested to her, and oh what tears of joy were shed when she folded to her heart her "dear, dear, dear beautiful grandson," and christened him "Stephen."

Courtship is carried on in the woods I suppose in about the same manner as any where else. The youth on being accepted, is generally assisted by his parents to erect a log-house; the necessary furniture is obtained and other appurtenances belonging to domestic affairs, with a sufficient stock etc., for a commencement.

We will suppose the marriage ceremony to be celebrated at the domicile of the bride. All the neighbors round are invited—at times to the number of a hundred persons. Early on the bridal morning the guests commence arriving. If there be no minister in the vicinity, the Judge of the district performs this important ceremony. It is an amusing assemblage. The females of the party are closeted with the bride until the appointed time, comforting and consoling her and arranging her bridal dress. The neighbors congregate, when the bride is ushered in with the "Father" and bridesmaids—followed by the "intended" and his particular friends.

The marriage ceremony being performed, the feasting commences, and the one I was invited to was a temperance wedding party. The tables groaned under venison, bears meat, wild turkey, and prairie hens, corn bread and sweet potatoes, coffee the only stimulating beverage.

This repast continued some hours, owing to the great number of visitants and the small quantity of crockery. Things went on moderately gay until about evening, when the "happy pair" made their escape to their own domicile. The great number being temperance folk, with the setting sun were seen jogging to their homes. The fiddle had been playing occasionally during the day, but no stimulating tipple being forthcoming, Paganini had fallen asleep. Some of the "rowdies" of the party had however managed to bring sundry gourds full of whiskey and these were disclosed to view one by one as required. The Fiddler on being awaked and sipped some of the "Old Monongehela," re-tuned his Cremona, rosind his bow, and then they all went to work dancing: "Rosin the Bow," "Jim along Josey," "Tip Coon," etc. etc. This continued until morning, when after breakfast the marriage party separated.

Accoucheurs call themselves *midwives* in some parts of the country, and when they can they send in a pretty bill for *attendance*. A Christening goes off very much in the same way as the marriage party and an excellent apology for a "frolic." This ceremony is performed by a minister, and winds up with a jollification, with long life and success to the embryo Senator or mayhap future President of the country.

I was present at the interment of one of the oldest settlers in Texas. He had come into the country with Austin, and one of the first to plant corn and raise cattle. He had fought in nearly all the battles of the Republic from the storming of the Fort Velasco to the fight of San Jacinto. His wife had gone to the tomb long before him. The spot where many friends met to do the last mournful office for their old friend, was picturesque indeed. The family grave was situated on the estate, fenced in, consecrated by patriotism, valour and honesty, and decorated with rose bushes. Some of the friends opened the grave where the ashes of the wife of the departed lay in peace. The procession was seen winding its way through a grove of giant trees; the corpse borne by the old warrior's relatives, the neighbors following. The body was lowered into the grave, when an old friend of the deceased made us acquainted with his history, his valour and rectitude of life. A prayer followed, when all knelt. The sons were borne away from the grave of the poor old man and the neighbors closed the ground over him. The seasons will change, years will follow, but many will drop the tear upon the emigrant's grave and venerate the flowers that grow upon the tomb in the wilderness.

Wednesday, January 3rd, 1844: Fine. Crockett [Texas] produce is taken to the Trinity 20 miles to Rob[b]in's ferry[17]—25 miles above Cincinnati. From Crockett[18] to Fort Houston[19] pretty and undulating for small farms—reddish soil from Crockett to Fort Houston. Iron ore rich about here in the ridges. From Fort Houston to Kingsboro's [Kaufman] on Bow d'Arc[20] (no inhabitants) low land. Kentucky Colony some 15 miles off.[21] Some 70 to 80 miles to Fannin County Court House[22] [from

[17] Robbin's Ferry was established in 1821 over the Trinity River at the crossing of the old San Antonio and La Bahía roads and named after Nathaniel Robbins. The ferry continued to operate until 1930, when the Clapp's Ferry Bridge was built. *The Handbook of Texas*, II, 483.

[18] Crockett, Texas, was named after David Crockett when the town was established in 1837 on the Old San Antonio Road. Its population grew very slowly over the years, but the 1950 census listed it as having almost 6,000 people. It is the present county seat of Houston County.

[19] Fort Houston, a stockade and blockhouse, was built in 1835, about two miles west of present Palestine, Texas. The fort was an important point of the frontier defense from 1836 to 1839, but was abandoned in 1842. The site eventually became the home of John H. Reagan. William A. McClintock, "Journal of A Trip through Texas and Northern Mexico in 1846–1847," *Southwestern Historical Quarterly*, Vol. XXXIV (1930–31), 231–56.

[20] Bow d'Arc [Bois d'Arc Bayou] rises near Whitewright in eastern Grayson County and flows generally eastward across Fannin County and into Red River at the northwestern corner of the Fannin-Lamar county line.

[21] The Kentucky Colony, previously identified as the W. S. Peters Colony, at this period had approximately 197 families and 184 single men. Peters Colony File (MS., Texas State Archives).

[22] Fannin County Court House (Bonham, Texas) is approximately 100 miles due north of the site of Fort Houston.

Fort Houston]. Indian village [Caddo] on entry to Fannin County. Plenty buffalo all about from Mr. Uzzel of Montgomery.

Thursday, January 4th, 1844: Morning cloudy. Noon, fine. Wind W. Some waggons have arrived today at Huntsville only 3 *months* from Houston. Water navigation forever! Hauling is no go! Had a roam thro' the woods. Pine in abundance (Pinus Terebin Shrub). Oaks, half a dozen varieties,[23] particularly the "overcup oak," the acorn as large as an egg. Hic[k]ory, walnut (white and black), dogwood (of which the Indians made their arrows), but in particular abundance is the Laurus Sassafras, the bark or outside root used as a *tea*.[24] There is a Frenchman in this county who scents white soap with it.

In Louisiana the young leaves, which contain mucilaginous matter and some essential oil used for thickening and giving flavour to a creole soup called "gumbo."[25] At times when the Indians are pressed for food, they eat the young leaves of the sassafras. Wild gooseberry grows 4 feet high, fruit small and good flavour—purple when ripe.

Saturday, January 6th, 1844: Two families with Negros comprising a *suite* of 50 to 60 from Alabama, went thro' this to settle about Grime's Prairie—9 weeks from Alabama, expenses only 150 dollar.

[23] The lower part of the Brazos is the great region for the live oak, and I am informed that on one estate comprising less than a league and belonging to Jones and Company of Galveston contains more of this valuable timber than the only plantation belonging to the United States Government in Florida, said to be some 500,000 acres. The following are the varieties in Texas: 1. live oak (ships). 2. scrub, or mountain live oak (meat for pigs) 3. water oak (for rafts). One of the greatest advantages of the oak, particularly in a new country, is the large quantity of fattening food in the acorn, or as called in this country *mast*. Some shipments of live oak have been made to Britain as *knees* for ships principally, but without regard to form and size. Thus it would only sell as common lumber and did not more than pay expenses, but if contracts were made for specific sizes, the lumber could just as easily be obtained as it is now, when cut at random.—Bollaert.

[24] Seeds of okra are used in Scotland and in Texas as a substitute for coffee when it is scarce.—Bollaert.

[25] Gumbo—okra chopped fine and equal quantity of tomatoes—an onion cut fine, lump of butter, pepper and salt. Stew with water—favourite dish of West Indies and New Orleans.—Bollaert.

Cotton is getting up a little. Cotton principally smuggled into Natchitoches [Louisiana]. If introduced as Texas cotton, [one must] pay 3 cents per pound debenture, and if not shipped in three months the 3 cents is forfeited, but it would be bad management to "traffic" it. Red River takes say 20,000 bales or more into the United States.

Wednesday, January 10th, 1844:[26] Mail arrived last night. Houston's secret message of last November published.[27] The opposition newspapers are going in favour of annexation to the United States now that they see that they will not do anything upon their own hook. It appears that many friends of Old Sam also want that, because they see that Mexico will delay a long time in recognizing this country. Also, it is said that Old Sam "is not very opposed to it." No doubt that the country would progress better with the A—— than with the present state of things. It appears that the patriotic blood which has flowed in the conquest is being forgotten. . . . The massacre of Fannin and his four hundred—the fall of the Alamo, and lastly the decimation of the Mier prisoners. Opposition and the go-a-head principle may shortly make great changes in Texas.

Sunday, January 14th, 1844: Mail rider from the E. lost mail bag in creek between here and Cincinnati. Stream so high and running strong. Rain all day, cold and unpleasant. Wrote to Kennedy. 5 P.M. Mail rider returned. San Jacinto bottom impassable —funny [?] country.

See Kier's poem on Texas. (It is said that Mr. Kier wrote this *poetic* effusion, believing it to be all right. At Houston a copy could be got):

> *Galveston, long and low*
> *And rising in prosperity*

[26] Bollaert's journal contains entries for all of the dates of January, 1844. Those not included merely pertained to the weather, e.g., "cloudy and rainy today."
[27] This must be in reference to "A Speech at the Old Capitol," November 10, 1843, which was published in *The Weekly Citizen*, December 9, 1843. *The Writings of Sam Houston*, III, 455-57.

Where small vessels may safely go
And anchor in security.
And anchor in Anahuac
Where ducks go quack, quack, quack.
Gonzales and Victoria
Are towns upon the Guadalupe
The one is distant from the Bay
The other some thirty miles up

Wednesday, January 19th, 1844: Accompanied Mr. MacD. a few hundred yards from the house towards the little stream which runs from Huntsville Spring (which contains sulphur) to get specimens of the bamboo or China briar,[28] and see the plant. The Indians have a name for it, but call it likewise. It grows from a bulbous looking root like a potatoe by the side of trees and runs up them and festoons them like a vine. The stem is knotted like the cane and has strong thorns irregularly placed upon it. The leaves are thick and form a rich foliage and not very large, with brown tendrils and at this season of the year the berries are green and become blackest as the spring approaches and contain three seeds each. It would form a beautiful garden plant, but the most interesting and important part of this plant exists in its roots; and forms no less a nutritious substance as an article of food than bread for the Indians, and at times used by the pioneer and backwoodsman.

This plant is met with nearly all over this country, and I am informed found likewise in Louisiana and eaten by the Indians. But I think it prefers light sandy soils and then it grows in great beauty and luxuriates by the margins of rivers, creeks, and all small streams; shedding forth its thickly clustered leaves, and dark green, forming a pleasing contrast to the forest trees. It is an evergreen. The flowers I am informed are small and white. (There are other such bulbous roots used as food by the Indians).

Immediately below the stem commences a collection of irregularly formed potatoe-like roots much larger than that vegetable,

[28] So called by the settlers.—Bollaert.

with many long soft fibres, running from them. The bamboo *potatoe* that is most fit for use is of the year's growth. If the plant be left in the ground, the second year's crop exudes from the first year's and is studded irregularly over the first year's. The second year's potatoe becomes hard and when it has 3 or 4 years of age it takes on a woody or fibrous character (like unto the palmetto).

The part of the root used by the Indians for a substitute for bread,[29] and moreover a sort of beer or spirituous liquor has been made from it by some settlers about here. This genus of plant exists in the Southern states, but does not come to the perfection there as it does in this country. [The paste] is made into *bread* in the form of cakes. I am informed that the Indians make several preparations from this valuable root, but I have not been able to obtain particulars. I think this specie is new, if so, I would suggest the specific name of Donaldiana, but if this be a new plant, then I would have it named "Margarita Donaldiana."

The Castor oil plant thrives and looks like a tree; it is cultivated for the oil in many parts of the country. (Castor oil plant 3 years grows 1 foot in circumference, 1 foot from ground, and 15 feet high in Mr. Mac's garden). Much is said relative to the extraordinary healing properties of the "Jimpsum [jimson] Weed" (James Town weed), particularly for sores on horses' backs. It is the *Datura Stramonium*, but I cannot vouch for all I hear about it. the plant grows in this and other parts of the country in great luxuriance.

[29] What I have called the potatoe, and of the year's growth, is carefully cut from the last year's produce and beaten in a mortar to a paste. The mortar is made by putting a small fire on the top of a stump and burning it down to the required size, and the pestle is made of hard wood, hardened still more in the fire.—Bollaert.

XIV

DOWN THE TRINITY TO GALVESTON

[January–April, 1844]

Friday, January 19th, 1844: Left Huntsville for Cincinnati, distant 12 miles. This is a small town on the Trinity surrounded by farms and plantations and is the port, if so it may be called, for this part of the country. A steam boat had just left with some German emigrants for Fort Houston, which locality is highly spoken of for farming and stock raising and in a healthy range of country. There is now in the Trinity River some 40 feet depth of water, and during high freshets 20 feet more.

Saturday, January 20th, 1844: At noon left Cincinnati by steam boat for Alabama.[1] Some ten or twelve miles up the Trinity passed what is laid down as "Oceola,"[2] and marked as containing "coal beds." Much has been said and written upon the existence of coal, particularly on this river. I have examined many of the localities and the substance called coal,[3] which by a stretch of imagi-

---

[1] The town of Alabama is no longer in existence. In 1844, it marked approximately the furthermost point on the Trinity River that steamboats could safely reach. Bollaert's purpose in going upstream with the *Ellen Frankland* steamboat before returning to Galveston was to see as much of this area of Texas as possible. The boat was discharging emigrants and picking up cotton for the return voyage.

[2] Osceola is marked on Arrowsmith's map, unlike Alabama, which was not laid down. However, it, too, soon became a ghost town and apparently never really existed except for one family.

[3] The substance called coal and found on Trinity River, particularly at Oceola the largest deposit of it appears to come under the head of *recent bituminous lignites,* formed by the action of water on wood and other vegetable matters— having none of the chemical characters of the coal-measures, which consist of alternate beds of coal, slate-clay, shale, and sandstone; and rather belonging to the alluvial than what is sometimes termed the Deluvial formation. It may be observed here, that as yet nothing has been discovered in Texas that has any relation to the great coal fields west of the Allegheny Mountains; although it is sometimes asserted that the coal on the Trinity is a continuation of the great American coal deposit and that it extends even to the Rio Grande! I mention these circumstances— to put people on their guard and prevent imposition of this subject in particular.— Bollaert.

nation in the fevered brains of *speculators* has been compared even, if not superior, to the best Walls-End![4]

The geological character of the country, above and below this, is sand; in some places the sand is somewhat indurated and called by some *rock*. I do not know for what reason. What is called *coal* is recently decomposed or bitumanized vegetable matter, having a black appearance, and at times, for short distances, putting on the appearance of being in nearly horizontal layers, but I believe in no cases of any great extent. A company was said to have formed for the working of said mines; a Mr. Price and his family from one of the coal districts of England was induced to come to Texas to superintend, but he and his wife soon died at Oceola. At Cincinnati I found on a painted small board the armorial bearings of this individual.

At dusk came to in the river along side of the bank; the river is broad and deep, being free from rafts or snags.

Sunday, January 21st, 1844: Early in the morning came to Rob[b]in's ferry, 45 miles from Cincinnati. The settlement is placed on the eastern bank of the river, from which is shipped considerable quantities of cotton. Through this place runs the old road from San Antonio to Nacogdoches. The cane[5] grows in great luxuriance upon the banks, shewing that the soil is rich and well adapted for cotton, sugar, tobacco, etc. There is a plentifully wooded bottom with prairies behind. 4 P.M.: Arrived at Alabama, having had to stem a 3 to 4 mile current, 35 miles from Rob[b]in's ferry. Up to this the river has a few narrow turns, but no difficulties present themselves and from its mouth to a great distance above this can be navigated with comparative facility.

Above Alabama on this river is situated the new town of Mag-

---

[4] Wallsend is an important coal mining town situated on the Tyne River four miles east-northeast of Newcastle in Northumberland, England.

[5] The cane of the bottoms in Texas is said by some to be of 7 or more years growth and flowers, goes to seed, and then dies. I have counted up to 30 joints but I am informed that some *old* cane has more and then the stem becomes yellow. Wherever cane grows, the land is considered very rich and well suited for cotton, sugar, tobacco, etc. In winter when pasture is scarce, cattle appear to like the leaves of the cane and thrive on it.—Bollaert.

nolia,[6] being the landing place for Fort Houston, which part of the country is rather a favorite spot with many of the folk on the lower parts of the river, particularly as regards its salubrity. The creeks between Alabama and Magnolia are Hurricane, Elk-hart, and Box.

The town of Alabama is still in its infancy, and to render it prosperous requires a large population of planters; nevertheless, some cotton is grown about here and adjacent country; but, for farming and stock raising purposes, higher up on the river is recommended. It may be stated that as yet two steam boats kept continually running are not sufficient for the trade of the river, so that flat boats are obliged to be resorted to. For about four months of the year the river can be navigated by steamers, but the bars at its mouth has now only 3 feet—thus this steamer when laden with cotton, etc., if she draws more, must unload ere she can get over.

Monday, January 22nd, 1844: 7 A.M.: Left Alabama, arriving at Cincinnati at 1 P.M. Just now the trees are leafless, but hung with thick clusters of mistletoe and that very useful of parasite plants, the Spanish Moss (*Tillandsia Usneoides*), not omitting to mention that the canes are in full leaf, of which cattle are very fond.

Tuesday, January 23rd, 1844: The *Ellen Frankland* getting cotton all day—just now there is much more cotton ready than boats to take it down the river.

Wednesday, January 24th, 1844: Morning cool. The air, on account of the prevalence of light clear northers being colder than the water causes a thick mist to appear on the river which clears off as the sun rises. Left Cincinnati in Steamer *Ellen Frankland* descending the river.

Six miles came to Nelson's Creek on western side, here is a

[6] Magnolia is a ghost town today, some ten miles southwest of Palestine. It was named after the large magnolia tree in the center of the town and at one time had a population of 800 or more. When Palestine acquired a railroad, the town on the Trinity declined rapidly. *The Handbook of Texas*, II, 129.

ferry. Ten miles more to Wrights Bluffs, the site for the intended town of Trinidad.[7] The bluffs are formed of a sandy strata declining some 6° to the S.E. Passing a fine cotton plantation belonging to Mr. Roberts, one mile more brought us to the landing place of Carolina. Here the bluffs are some 150 feet high, the sandy strata indurated sufficiently for building.

Thursday, January 25th, 1844: Sharp frost during the night. The town of Carolina (formerly called Bath)[8] is situated on a prairie surrounded by timbers at the summit, or rather behind, the bluffs. There are some twenty habitations, one of considerable dimensions with a sign board "Carolina Hotel. Dry Goods and Groceries," but entirely deserted.

Rome (not the city of Rome) is the name of a town not far from Carolina, the only inhabitant there being a gin maker (cotton gin).[9] On nearly all the bluffs speculators have marked out town sites, with high and sounding names, such as already mentioned, then Pompei, below Duncan's ferry, Geneva, etc.[10] Generally speaking, if there be a bluff on one side of the river, on the opposite it is low.

Half a mile above Carolina and on the same side is Bidais Creek, at the head of which is Coles' Mill,[11] running through part of Carolina bluffs. Here we found deer, wild turkies, geese, and ducks in abundance; fish is said to be very plentiful in all the creeks about here. 2 P.M.: Started—passed Duncan's ferry and 35

[7] Trinidad is one of the few towns on the Trinity River which Bollaert visited that did not disappear, although its population never exceeded a few hundred people. The small settlement is in western Henderson County.

[8] This settlement today is called Bath, not Carolina. It is located in southern Walker County near the mouth of Carolina Creek. Other than a few dwellings, Bath consists of a church and cemetery community.

[9] Rome likewise became a ghost town and today no remains of its former existence are evident.

[10] None of the communities named after important Italian cities ever materialized, although there is a Geneva, Texas, in Sabine County, but it was not established until 1885.

[11] John P. Coles, from North Carolina, built a mill on Yegua Creek in 1826. He was a member of Austin's "Old Three Hundred," later serving a two-year term in the Texas Senate (1840–41). Bugbee, "The Old Three Hundred," *Quarterly of the Texas State Historical Association*, Vol. I (1897–98), 108.

miles came to Patrick's ferry; here are about a dozen houses. Remained here for the night taking in wood at two dollars the cord. (A cord of wood is 8 feet long, 4 feet in height, and the sticks about 4 feet long).

Friday, January 26th, 1844: 7 A.M.: Left. At noon passed Swartwout.[12] This is rather a considerable village, placed on rather high land, but has no bluffs. In passing the Coshatte Villages, saw Indians of same name some on the banks in their wigwams (constructed of branches of trees and nearly square). The Texan Government some few years since ordered "reserves" to be allotted to these and other friendly Indians,[13] but the intrusion of white settlers has prompted many of the Coshattes to return to the United States, and some have joined other tribes in the interior of Texas. The Coshattes are a mild inoffensive people, attend somewhat to agricultural pursuits and occasionally assist the planters in their vicinity to pick cotton.

Twelve miles from Swartwout is Smithfield;[14] the few habitations thus denominated is a little distance in land. Here are forests of Magnolias. Ran during the day 75 to 80 miles. Cane very fine and in full leaf and good for cattle now; there is little grass.

Saturday, January 27th, 1844: Current of river is now about 2 or 3 miles per hour, it is getting wider, and the banks are beginning to get low, no bluffs & settlements are scarce. Many large alligators, or caymans, basking in the sun on the sand banks along the shores. In many places on the banks of the river, natural levées or embankments are formed, and forming, from the earthy matters brought down by the river.

[12] Swartwout, Texas, previously mentioned, is on the Trinity River in southwestern Polk County at the site of the Alabama-Coushatta Indian village.

[13] The State of Texas did not set up a permanent reserve for the Alabama-Coushatta Indians until 1854, when 1,280 acres were purchased and given to them as the initial unit of the present Alabama-Coushatta Indian Reservation. *The Handbook of Texas*, I, 20–21.

[14] There is a Smithfield (in northeastern Tarrant County) in Texas today, but it is not the same one mentioned here. The Smithfield on the Trinity, like so many of the other settlements Bollaert visited, soon became a ghost town.

4 P.M.: Arrived at the landing place of the town of Liberty,[15] which is situated in a prairie about half a mile from the river. Here is a ferry, and one store. At this place a beef preserving and salting machine, after the plan invented by Mr. Payne of London had been put up.[16] The locality for the works had been badly chosen, so that during a rise in the river not many weeks since, the waters broke in upon the establishment and I now saw it in a ruinious condition, carrying away a bark mill and tar pits. It is very questionable if this spot be adopted to this operation. In the first place, little can be said as to the salubrity of it, and secondly, there is not a sufficient supply of cattle, and hogs so as to make it profitable. With good apparatus, persons who understood the management of it and placed on some part of the western shores of Texas, where cattle could be well raised. I do not see what is to prevent the success of such an undertaking.[17]

Sunday, January 28th, 1844: Leaving Liberty and passing the plantation of Mr. Van Pradelles (on the last bluff on the river), at 4 P.M. arrived at the mouth of Old River,[18] here is a ferry and road to Houston. The land is low and swampy and said to be good for the culture of rice. A mile or so from Old River is the mouth of Trinity River, which empties itself into a large basin; all round this basin there are large collections of drift wood, this with sand and other earthy matters have formed several islands from which the waters of the Trinity issue by seven or more passes, Brown's pass being the principal one and by which the navigation

[15] Liberty, in present Liberty County, was settled as early as 1830 by unauthorized squatters. The town's growth has been very slow but steady since that time, and today it has a population of approximately 5,000. It is an inland port with barge connections with the Houston Ship Channel.

[16] This beef-processing plant was built by James Taylor White in the early 1840's. It furnished beef for Jones and Company, an English beef-packing concern, until destroyed by a flood in 1844. Rosalie Fincher, "History of Liberty County" (unpublished M.A. thesis, University of Texas, 1933).

[17] I am informed that the British Government has entered into very large contracts with parties in Ireland to supply beef and pork at 2d per pound.—Bollaert.

[18] There are several streams in this region of Texas named Old River. The one Bollaert mentions rises in southwestern Liberty County and flows southeast fourteen miles to join the Trinity River in northwestern Chambers County.

of the river is effected. At the present moment there is less than three feet water on the bar of Brown's pass, the channel of which is tortuous and difficult, owing to snags and large logs of drift timber. At highest tides and under the most favorable circumstances, such as freshets and S. E. winds, there is seldom more than four feet of water on the bar, and the general depth two to three feet.

Informed that the *Vista* was on the bar in 10 inches of water. From Van Pradelles to here the land on either side low and swampy—good for rice—trees hung with Spanish moss—few small settlements. At the mouth of Old River is one family. Found a flat boat of Messrs. Jones and Company full of cotton— took her in tow to Brown's pass, and we stay for the night.

Monday, January 29th, 1844: Moved down toward the bar of Brown's pass and found the steamer *Vista* aground across it in two and half feet water. The *Vista* taking out part of her cotton so as to float over the bar, our Steamer at a similar operation.

Anahuac bears E, from Brown's pass 1½ miles.[19] Here are the ruins of Bradburn's fort, occupied by Bradburn, an American in the service of Mexico. The land is moderately high, not subject to overflows, but somewhat swampy in rainy weather owing to a sub-stratum of a clayey nature. There are pretty good grazing lands in this vicinity. About the passes of the Trinity, Anahuac, etc., is what is called the residence of "The great nation of geese." And the number of wild geese, swan, duck, brent, cranes, pelicans, and other birds is enormous. The wild swan is white, has a black patch on the wings (about the shoulder joint) and the tail is black. Turtle and fish are in abundance, and particularly about the passes numbers of large alligators. Dropped down into the pass, but got aground.

Tuesday, January 30th, 1844: Filled a flat with cotton and land-

[19] Anahuac was formerly a military post and where the first land office was opened to give settlers the necessary license for colonizing the lands. [In] 1831, Colonel [John Davis] Bradburn, military commandant of Anahuac, was forced by the settlers to retreat, which he did to Mexico.—Bollaert.

ing bale on bank of the pass. *Vista* steaming last night; she moved a little—airs S. E. cloudy. 450 pounds is reckoned the proper weight for a bale of cotton. Some planters make bales of 600 pounds, thus "shading in" 150 pounds—which ought to be paid in proportion for. The cotton is generally repressed into a smaller space at Galveston. Noon cloudy and occasional rain. Midnight dropped down the pass, but got aground and continued there all night.

Wednesday, January 31st, 1844: 10 A. M. went on board *Vista* but strong S. E. wind prevents us starting. The *E. F.* [*Ellen Frankland*] may be some days ere she leaves, for independent of her being on the bar, she has her cotton to get in.

Like to the mouths of all southern rivers [the Trinity is] almost choked up with drift wood—thus rendering the navigation difficult. I do not think that the navigation of the Trinity can pay, considering the length of voyage and the expences incident to the unloading and re-loading steamers at the mouth, but as plantations increase, some means will be resorted to to facilitate trade. 6 P. M.: Started, but did not run more than 10 miles, came to anchor.

Thursday, February 1st, 1844: Sent a party on shore to cut wood—plenty of game, particularly deer. The fresh water of the Trinity generally extends to a considerable distance out into the bay (Red Fish Bar). At noon came to anchor off the east end of the chain of islands forming Red Fish Bar. This chain of islands is low and sandy, covered with brush wood, with here and there a few trees; they are said to be increasing in size very rapidly and will doubtless ere no very distant period elongate the peninsula forming part of East Bay.

Friday, February 2nd, 1844: Crossed Red Fish Bar at day light. Major [Jack] Hayes on board going to Island [Galveston] to purchase arms etc. out of appropriations made. About noon, owing to strong S. E. winds, arrived in Galveston, having been absent six months.

LIST OF DISTANCES ON TRINITY RIVER

From Dallas (in the Kentucky Settlement near to the Cross Timbers)[20] to:

Magnolia	273 miles
Alabama (about)	80
Rob[b]in's ferry	30
Cincinnati	45
Wright's Bluffs	15
Carolina	15
Patrick's ferry	35
Swartwout	40
1st Coshatte Village	10
2nd Coshatte Village	2
Smithfield	10
At night (stopped)	10
Liberty	72
Van Pradelles	28
Mouth of Trinity River	30
	773

The return to Galveston in early February, 1844, marked the end of Bollaert's travels in Texas prior to his last and most important journey—an examination of the area southwest of San Antonio where the proposed Kennedy Colony was to be located. By now the Englishman had visited most of the populated regions of Texas, except the upper Trinity River. This region held a peculiar interest for him because of the rapid settlement going on there in the Kentucky Colony. Obviously, he was anxious to acquire as

[20] Dr. Denan [?] of the United States Army was sent in 1836 to vaccinate the Indians. [He] informs me that the Cross Timbers might be in about 98° and in width about 30 miles and composed of shrubby growth of timbers and goes on crossing the Arkansas and up to the Missouri about NNE and SSW, undulating with the prairies on each side, but on the Western, these prairies take on a mountainous character. Cross Timbers takes its name from crossing the streams. In such places in [the] Cross Timbers, creeks run thro' them and then the timbers are larger and more plentiful.—Bollaert.

*much knowledge of the latter settlement as possible, but he was
especially interested in finding out about the land, with a pros-
pective view of colonizing in that region.*

*Difficulty of travel to the headwaters of the Trinity, plus the
lack of time, prevented Bollaert from making the journey in person. However, upon his return to Galveston he acquired some
first hand knowledge of the country of present Northeast Texas
from his British friend, Charles Elliot. The latter had traveled
overland from Fort Houston to Dallas the previous spring, returning down the Trinity in a canoe or "dug out." A brief journal
of the trip was kept by Elliot, which in turn was copied by Bollaert
and inserted in his own narrative at this point:*

Pursuing our route from Fort Houston to Dallas we passed
over a sandy broken, and save an occasional spot like an oasis in
the desert, almost uninhabitable country. The route pursuing its
course the dividing highland between the Rivers Trinity and
Neches selects the poorest and most unproductive soil in its passage that could possibly be found. This is not the case a short distance either to the right or left, for we there find a rich and productive soil abounding with excellent timber and spring water.
On our approach to Rock Lookout, the face of the country ex-
hibits an entirely different appearance. From a rolling broken and
rocky district we descend to an almost unbroken soil, a timbered
country, but of a shallow ashy and unproductive soil. A few miles
passed and the prairies of Lacy's fork[21] open upon the view, rich
verdant and mantled with flowers of every hue. From this point
to Red River in a N.W. direction the same general description
will almost invariably apply. That is, the country is prairie, intersected by wooded streams affording timber sufficient for all purposes for many years to come and abounding in limestone springs,
and creeks. The soil is deep black and sandy, having a limestone
foundation at considerable depth. In some places, although rarely,

[21] Lacy's Creek (formerly called Lacy's Fork of Cedar Creek) rises in west-
central Van Zandt County and flows southwest twenty miles to join Cedar Creek
in southern Kaufman County.

we find gravel and stones intermingled with the soil. The prairie east of Bois D'Arc is of the hog-wallow character, on White Rock of a yellow sandy nature, and on the Elm Fork[22] of a deep chocolate colour, all equally rich and productive.

The Cross Timbers running through the colony in a N. E. direction, is a section or belt of timber land of a loose yellow soil covered with an undergrowth of vines, sumach [sumac], red-bud, and indications of productiveness, yet the land is not so lasting as the prairie. Beyond or westward of the Cross Timbers the prairie becomes studded with stony knobs decorated with dwarf live oak shrubbery, but the vallies below and margins of streams are of a high degree of fertility.

The prairie in addition to all the wild grasses known, produces spontaneously wheat, rye, oats, and red clover, not differing materially from the domestic or cultivated varieties. We also find cayenne pepper, flax, and the indigo plant profusely and widely scattered over the country. Among the wild animals that roam almost undisturbed in this region, the bison, or buffalo, and wild horse are conspicuous, the former rolling onwards from our approach like porpoises at sea, and the latter in all their native freedom and wildness careening over the plain in conscious security, now approaching and now bounding away with the speed of the wind. During the vernal season they find abundant sustenance on the prairies and during the winter months they seek shelter from wind and cold in the bottoms where the wild rye and a variety of winter grasses supply them with food.

The timber is plum, hickory, peccan, cedar, bois d'arc, muskeet, ash, hackberry, elm, black walnut, persimmon, every variety of oak, hawthorn, cotton-wood, sycamores, willow, locust, various kinds of grapes and vines of all kinds. Minerals: indications of lead are found on White Rock and other streams, and in a very pure state [it] has been found in the bed of that stream. Iron

[22] Elm Fork of the Trinity River rises in eastern Montague County and flows southeast approximately eighty-five miles through Cooke and Denton counties to a confluence with the West Fork of the Trinity in central Dallas County, just west of the city of Dallas. The stream has been dammed in central Denton County to form Lake Dallas.

321

appears in the Cross Timbers in inexhaustible quantities.[23] Stone coal we are informed is found in large quantities near Bird's Fort,[24] and salt in any quantity may be procured from a lake some 15 or 20 miles above Bird's Fort near the West Fork.

Productions: as yet scarcely any portion of the country has been cultivated to the best advantage. In Fannin County where the climate and soil is similar, they raise wheat, cotton, potatoes, tobacco, corn, oats, rye, etc. etc. In the vicinity of Dallas[25] we found some cornfields in a very flourishing condition, prospects of good crops flattering.

Of the climate we believe to be the finest in the world we will only say that the nights throughout the year are invariably cold. That we preserve fresh meat 4 to 6 days without salt, and that persons who go out to this country in the heat of summer do not become sick, but on the contrary those who start so are invariably restored. Although this country is in or near the latitude of Natchez, Mississippi, the great altitude of the country renders it healthy and the air salubrious.

Memorandum of a Trip down the Trinity River in a canoe or "dug out" in May.

Wednesday, May 10th, 1844: Left Dallas at 4 P.M. Passed

[23] Although a considerable deposit of iron ore exists in the Daingerfield area in East Texas (more than a hundred miles east of the Cross Timbers), Elliot's statement that iron appears in the Cross Timbers in inexhaustible quantities is highly exaggerated.

[24] Bird's Fort was a Ranger outpost erected by Jonathan Bird in the fall of 1841, north of the West Fork of the Trinity River some seven miles above present Arlington, Texas. It was here that Edward H. Tarrant and George W. Terrell met with the representatives of nine Indian tribes in September, 1843, and signed a treaty that was ratified by the Texas Senate on January 31, 1844. Bollaert speaks of the treaty in one or two instances in his journal. Anna Muckleroy, "The Indian Policy of the Republic of Texas," *Southwestern Historical Quarterly*, Vol. XXVI (1922–23), 184–206.

[25] The first settler at present Dallas was John Neely Bryan, who established himself at the present Court House Square in 1841. At the time of Elliot's visit there in the spring of 1843, Dallas consisted of two log houses, two families, and a total population of less than twelve people. John William Rogers, *The Lusty Texans of Dallas*, 25–35.

mouth of White Rock[26] and camped at upper end of Trinity Bluff, say 12 miles.

Thursday, May 11th, 1844: Open run to raft 16 miles ¾ miles long, fall 7 or 8 feet. In the bottoms water swift among the trees and bushes, rendering the navigation extremely dangerous. Three miles below fell into middle slough, which was narrow, deep, and rapid, but gradually increased in depth; passed 8 small rafts, no one exceeding 50 yards in length. Slough supposed to contain a volume equal to that of the river. Made, say 40 miles.

Friday, May 12th, 1844: Passed 4 small rafts. Slough of river on left at 10 miles and another on right at 15 miles, both, or each, of these supposed to contain a greater volume of water than the one we are pursuing. Bluff just below last slough on right bank. Passed Bois D'Arc 4 miles below on left; open but crooked river, low ground and subject to inundation on both sides. Camped on low bluff at 50 miles on right bank.

Saturday, May 13th, 1844: Raft at 10 miles—another at 15 miles, both about 50 yards long. At 20 miles a beautiful long Red Bluff—far above the reach of high water and washed by the river two or three hundred yards—a fine situation for a town. At 35 miles 2 small rafts, and Haines Bluff just below this also is a fine town site, being washed by the river some distance, a high level timbered country broken left bank. At 46 miles a raft 40 yards long and another at 50 miles of 20 yards. Camped on low ground subject to inundation on left bank, say 60 miles. Rained hard during night and next morning.

Sunday, May 14th, 1844: Rained this morning—departed late. 8¼ o'clock and 1½ miles. Bluff right bank, river washes. Saw bluff at 4½ miles and at 6 miles high ground appears on both sides,

[26] White Rock Creek rises in northern Dallas County and flows southeast about twenty miles to the Trinity River. The stream is dammed to form White Rock Lake in the eastern part of the city of Dallas.

probably above high water mark. Creek right bank at 15 miles. Bluff right bank 18 miles high and also very eligible for a town—22 miles, creek, left bank. 31½ miles, bluff, left bank. 34 miles, raft 40 yards. Bluff just below. At 38 miles mouth of Richland[27] larger than the river at the mouth—comes in on right. Drift at its mouth in the river at 40 miles. Bluff at N.W. bend of river on left bank. Camped.

Monday 15th, 1844: Started at 4¾ o'clock. River washes same bluff at intervals for an hour; at 20 miles bluff on left bank touched, same 4 miles beyond. 34 miles, bluff on right bank. 38 miles, raft 30 yards. 41 miles, bluff on right bank. Same bluff 1½ miles below at 50 miles. Camped on bluff, left bank.

Tuesday 16th, 1844: Started at 5 o'clock. 12 miles, bluff on right bank. 9 o'clock reached Magnolia, 21 miles. Total distance 273 miles.

Entries in Bollaert's journal from the time of his arrival in Galveston, February 2, 1844, until he left for the western frontier of Texas, April 26, 1844, are rather irregular. Although he does not explain that he was busily engaged in other matters, he obviously was making preparations for his last and most extensive tour. Meanwhile, he did find some time to note the changes that had occurred during his absence and to record from time to time what he considered important events, as well as trivial ones.

"Although only absent from Galveston six months," Bollaert observed on February 2, "I find that considerable improvements have and are still going on. No longer does the 'picayune' system of bartering continue, but a good cash trade, and owing to the United States not having a commercial treaty with Texas, the harbour is full of European vessels bringing manufactured goods and taking cotton[28] etc., in return. Texas has at present French

[27] This particular Richland Creek rises in southeastern Hill County and flows east fifty miles to join the Trinity River in northern Freestone County.
[28] Produce of cotton this year 100,000 bales, and had the weather been more

*and American ministers, a chargé from England and consuls from
England, France, U. States, Bremen, Holland, Austria,*[29] *and
Belgium. Last October, Colonels Williams and Hockley repaired
to Mexico (at Sabinas some thirty or forty miles west of the Rio
Grande), there to meet with other commissioners on the part of
Mexico to arrange an armistice, a preliminary to a peace with that
country.*

*"In these trans-atlantic countries we are kept alive by what is
called an 'excitement'; the one on the tapis just now is the wish of
the United States cabinet to annex Texas."*

Sunday, February 4th, 1844: Wrote to Sadie.

Saturday, February 10th, 1844: Revenue at Galveston Q^{r}. ending 31 Jany £52–14–7. Report from frontier says that an armistice
for 10 years has been concluded. On 15th December 1843, convention of peace signed at Mexico between it and Yucatan.

Thursday, February 15th, 1844: Excitement of annexation
dying away.

Tuesday, February 20th, 1844: Evening and night "Gulf
storm" with much lightning and thunder and blowing hard from
N.N.E., accompanied with torrents of rain.

March 2nd, 1844: Another anniversary of Texan independence.
It was celebrated in Galveston by the Sunday and other schools,
by the military companies, literary institutions, religious societies
and the citizens generally in a spirit which shows that the
event commemorated was a boon worthy of the most grateful
remembrance.

Although the Declaration of Independence was but a measure
embraced by the people of Texas—then but a handful—as an

favorable, it would have exceeded this quantity. In 1838–39 it was hardly 5,000
bales. In the month of March there were about thirty vessels in port.—Bollaert.

[29] From Trieste the *Amelia Giuseppe*, the first Austrian vessel—the Captain
of which was presented with the freedom of Galveston City.—Bollaert.

only and desperate expedient from the choice presented to them by Mexico, either to fly the country and leave behind them the acquisitions of their privations, toils and sufferings, or submit to a decree of extermination.

With every prospect to discourage them, with every disparity of means, numbers, and military preparation against their enterprize and undertaking, which in case of failure, could only have been pronounced a model of temerity, was crowned with the most complete success, and in the short space of eight years, has transformed into an abode of intelligence, industry, and prosperity, a land which under the dominion of another people claiming to be civilized, had failed to give any evidences of emerging from barbarism, and only began to show signs of improvement on the introduction of the race who now possess it. Texas, which up to within a few years of the revolution, was only known, even to the wisest statesmen of the American continent, from the uncertain and fanciful accounts of wild adventures and ignorant savages, as the lurking places of pirates and outlaws, now engages the attention of the most civilized nations, and claims their warmest sympathies and regards.

Agriculture blesses with abundance the plains that were desolate and unproductive; the axe rings in the forest; the towns resound with the hum of industry, where eight years ago man had no habitation, and the reign of silence and solitude was scarcely ever broken by the voice of a human being. The harbour of Galveston, which then was only known as the rendezvous of pirates, is now white with the sails and gay with the flags of Europe and America, lured hither by the lucrative commerce, awakened by the industry of the hardy possessors of the soil.

Agriculture, arts, trade, learning, and religion are steadily advancing, and show on every hand, as the evidences of their onward march, plantations, farms, and luxuriant fields, rising towns, and busy workshops; ports and bays white with canvass, rivers navigated by swift moving steamers, academies of learning, temples filled with pious people, and pulpits from which learned, gifted, and devout men impart the lessons of religion.

326

These are the fruits of liberty, and all these have been acquired with the independence of a country: "Where the breeze from the South wooes the flowers, as we press those we love in their sweet summer bowers."

March 10th, 1844: Whatever the plottings of the opposition, war party or factions in Texas, may have been relative to the annexation of Texas to the United States; upon the subject all was pretty quiet in Texas until the autumn of last year, when it was whispered about that even President Houston was in favour of that measure. The reason given by the President's friends, was that altho' an armistice was expected from Mexico, peace with that country, preserving the nationality of Texas, was not expected, although Great Britain and France were using their friendly mediation with Mexico for that purpose; and it was generally thought that the United States would assist in settling the question for Texas. But many believed that the view and intentions of the U. States, although intimidating Mexico, was really to have Texas attached to herself.

Now then commenced an *excitement* in the newspapers of the U. States favorable to annexation and a few land-holders and speculators seemed to think that with the change, emigration would flock in, they would sell their lands and make fortunes. But the blow came upon those who had fought, suffered, and had lived in Texas for years, when it was whispered that President Houston was in favour of annexation—reasons were offered, viz: that he saw that there would be new difficulties with Mexico; that she would not, without being coerced by Britain or the U. States acknowledge the independence, that Houston, the Hero of San Jacinto did not wish to risk another campaign or suffer others to command, and that he wished to wind up the affair by annexation. It was known that very influential persons in the U. States were in private and probably public communication with Houston upon the matter. General Murphy, the United States chargé d'affaires is known to be very active; a small American Man of War [was] sent to Galveston to facilitate the carrying of dispatches, etc.

Moreover, out comes the government paper informing the nation that, it will not oppose annexation.

Now, whilst all these things are going on, the British chargé and that of France are in the United States, principally at New Orleans, and it is reported that they are *sick*, thus Brother Jonathon has it all his own way here.

The latter end of February the United States Schooner *Flint* left Galveston harbour for a rendezvous with another United States Man of War, and obtained important dispatches from her. The *Flint* returned to Galveston, the dispatches forwarded to Washington to President Houston. The result of this latter move was that General Henderson[30] was sent to the Government of the United States as a private, but special envoy. A few days afterwards, other dispatches from Houston go to the United States purporting to accede to annexation and that there was only one dissentient voice in the Texas Senate, that Houston would call the Texas Congress together—that there would be no difficulty on the subject and now all that was wanted was the consent of the Senate of the United States to the annexation. Mr. [William] Green, United States Consul, was likewise sent with dispatches to the United States Government—bringing this history up to the beginning of March [1844].

Captain E[lliot] and Count S[aligny] still in New Orleans! The bubble must soon burst. Texas will probably lose her nationality, foreign emigration for many reasons will not flock here, more particularly when the direct trade with Europe is stopped, and worse than all if Jonathan has been playing possum with —————— ——————, Jonathan may chance to get "Jesse."

There has never been so much shipping in the ports of Texas, and principally foreign, as this year, viz: English, Bremen, French, Belgian, Hanover, bringing emigrants and manufactures, and in

---

[30] James Pinckney Henderson was sent to Washington, D.C., in 1844 to work with Isaac Van Zandt in negotiating a treaty of annexation with the United States. The treaty was signed on April 12, 1844, but was rejected by the United States Senate on June 8, 1844, and Henderson, over his protest, was ordered home by President Houston. Elizabeth Yates Morris, "James Pinckney Henderson" (unpublished M.A. thesis, University of Texas, 1931).

return taking cotton, hides, etc. The town of Galveston is rapidly improving and may number 4,000 souls.

This will be a long season, owing to the bad state of the roads not being in a state to allow the rapid transit of cotton, and the navigation of the rivers, but badly attended to.

Saturday, March 23rd, 1844: On the 21st Captain Elliot arrived from New Orleans and still indisposed. Count Saligny still remains in New Orleans causado por un herida recibido a un desafio General Murphy at Houston. The President and Cabinet at Washington [-on-the-Brazos].

The annexation *excitement* appears to be over, but what are the real maneuverings Old Sam only knows and those who surround him. We cannot but suppose that Old Sam and his party know what they are at; nevertheless, there appears considerable uncertainty, and time only will unravel the web—pour moi c'est la même chose.

Tuesday, March 26th, 1844: Blowing hard from S.W. Colonel Williams and Colonel Hockley arrived from Matamoros via Corpus Christi. "The precise terms and conditions for the continuance and termination of the armistice have not transpired." The two countries are to maintain their present pacific position towards each other until commissioners have been appointed and shall have terminated their labours for the establishment of a permanent peace between the two nations.

Wednesday, March 27th, 1844: News from Mexico states that Santa Ana will soon proclaim himself *Dictator,* and then may give us a second act a la Iturbide. Santana reposing all his hopes on his military adherents.

I am informed that Santana is a most parsimonious and miserly [individual], amassing money and lands at a most extraordinary rate. He is not a young man—his riches may assist in sustaining him in tottering power. His wife is described as a most slatternly woman, and generally found *"En Mexican deshabillé."* A pretty pair! On one occasion he invited some friends to dine with him, but requested them to bring their own wine, for he thought strong liquors very bad. What a catch for Father Mathew and his followers—the blood-thirsty, treaty-breaking, ungrately [*sic*] Santana!

His enemies are many, but some how or other he keeps them quiet by armed forces who obey him—creatures who can only rise and keep commands by acceding to his measures. Santana's life has been often attempted, and many ingenious plans have been resorted to. Once a rich musical gold snuff-box with precious stones, in which was secreted a small pistol and so arranged that in winding it up to a certain pitch the pistol would off. Santana, suspecting that all was not right, turned it about, the result being that the conspirator got himself shot dead.

Sunday, March 31, 1844: Neptune arrived—brought reports that the Mexican minister [Juan Nepomuceno Almonte] had demanded his passport from the United States Government and that Mr. Packenham had protested against the manoeuvers of the United States Government for the annexation of Texas. We learn that the Mexican Government is very much disturbed at the prospects of annexation of Texas to the United States, and well informed persons in Mexico believe that every effort will be made by that government to make it a condition on the acknowledgement of the independence of Texas, that she shall remain separate from, and independent of the United States. It is thought that no great difficulty will be found in procuring a recognition on this condition.

Sunday, April 7th, 1844: President Houston arrived in Galveston—General Murphy, Colonels Hockley and Williams—the last two had but lately gone from this to Washington, but had to return with the President. Some are trying to stifle the affair of annexation. I should not be surprized that as far as the United States Cabinet can carry it, the thing is done. (Terrell, when speaking of the Americans on the Texas question says: "Their desire is their right, and their own convenience is their justice").

Mrs. Holl[e]y collecting materials for some juvenile works on Texas, a Mrs. Storm likewise. Mrs. Holl[e]y was about the first, if not the first, to write about Texas, first in a series of letters and then those letters enlarged, making her history of Texas.[31]

Monday, April 8th, 1844: Captain Elliot, the chargé d'affaires, left in *Neptune* for New Orleans and will probably travel in the United States. I encountered General Lamar on March 7th and he told me that "annexation had taken place," and Elliot told us that no such thing had happened. General Hamilton also made speculation on annexation, but it did not work out.

Wednesday, April 10th, 1844: Mail from England arrived on Barque *John Barnes* from Liverpool, left 2nd January. Mr. Grieve[32] tired of the ship, landed at Matagorda and comes by land to Galveston.

Thursday, April 11th, 1844: The President paid us a visit. He told us that he had doubts about annexation, but that everything was still *en embroyo*. We shall see. The President returned to Houston where he left his family. Mr. Grieve arrived.

[31] Mary Austin Holley (New Haven, Connecticut) visited Austin's Colony in 1831, and as a result she wrote *Texas, Observations, Historical, Geographical, and Descriptive, in a Series of Letters Written during a Visit to Austin's Colony, with a View to a Permanent Settlement in that Country in the Autumn of 1831,* published in Baltimore in 1833. Another book, entitled *Texas,* appeared in November, 1836, and proved to be good immigration propaganda. A revised edition of this work, containing much fresh material, was published in 1843. These books and her long series of letters are invaluable accounts of early Texas. Mattie Austin Hatcher, ed., *Letters of an Early American Traveller, Mary Austin Holley; Her Life and Her Works, 1784–1846.*

[32] James H. Grieve, from England, became one of the principal stockholders in the Kennedy Colony, along with William Pringle. After William Kennedy withdrew from the enterprize, a new contract was issued on November 1, 1843 to "William Pringle and James Grieve, and Their Associates" to settle 600 families near the headwaters of the Nueces River. Soon after Grieve's arrival in Galveston, he accompanied Bollaert and others to the site of the proposed colony. The two Englishmen returned to England during the summer of 1844. Neither Grieve nor Bollaert ever came back to Texas. "Colonization Papers," *Executive Record Book No. 48.* (Texas State Archives).

XV

TO THE KENNEDY GRANT, AT LAST

[April–July, 1844]

More than two years had elapsed since William Bollaert arrived
in Texas, yet he was only now starting the venture for which he
had originally come: to examine and report upon the tract of
land granted to William Kennedy in February, 1842, for the purpose of colonizing European emigrants. Kennedy withdrew from
the project a short time later,[1] but the grant continued to be referred to as the Kennedy Colony even though the colonizing company was reorganized on November 1, 1843, without him. The
four-and-one-half-million acres lay along the Nueces and Frio
Rivers and included parts of the present counties of Uvalde,
Maverick, Zavala, Dimmit, Frio, La Salle, and McMullen. This
vast unsettled region in the 1840's was frequented by untamed
Indians, principally Apaches and Comanches. But aside from the
Indian menace and Kennedy's sudden withdrawal from the company, the principal cause of Bollaert's long delay in exploring the
region is obvious from his narrative—Mexico's renewal of the
war with Texas early in 1842. Not until an armistice was finally
reached with that country, and the arrival of James Grieve from
England in early April, 1844, did the exploration finally get
under way.

Bollaert's notes on his last Texas excursion were kept in pencil
in a small three-by-four-inch black leather notebook. The handwriting has faded badly but is still legible. The narrator is fre-

---

[1] Kennedy stated in a letter to Henry Addington, September 24, 1844, relative
to his relinquishing interest in the grant, that "my subsequent appointment as
Her Majesty's Consul at Galveston, led me to doubt the expediency of acting
upon it. Well acquainted with the jealous disposition of the North American
Republicans, and not ignorant that the best intentions afford no sure protection
from interested, or malicious misrepresentation, I decided on relinquishing my
interest in the grant, which I did,—retaining no share of its advantages, direct or
indirect." *British Diplomatic Correspondence Concerning the Republic of Texas,*
367–68.

quently vague relative to the course of travel being pursued; the names he mentions are often impossible to identify, for he abbreviates. Nevertheless, this portion of the narrative proves extremely interesting.

Saturday, April 20th, 1844: Accompanied Mr. Grieve to Houston per Steamer. Left Galveston 5 P. M.—Francois and Dick with carriage[2]—At dusk passed the site of the Battle ground [of San Jacinto].

Sunday, April 21st, 1844: 2 A. M. arrived in Houston. There has been very heavy rains in the interior. Creeks full and roads bad—so it may be a week ere we get off. We may have to take oxen instead of horses for carriage. From the prairie to bottom of river, from 60 to 70 feet from sea level, and from it to level of sea, 12 to 15. Thirty feet of water in Bayou. "Red grass" on the lower part of Brazos—good for fattening cattle.

Coshattes—Ostin, principal chief—a few of them are here trading peltries etc. (They are descended from the Choctaws). Some have just returned to the Trinity to plant corn—had their "corn dance"—got drunk and then sloped. A Coshatte can get $2 at least for a deer.

Monday, April 22nd, 1844: Visited Mr. Greg's plantation on the other side of the Bayou—sandy sub-soil—sugar, corn, and S. potatoes, fine magnolias. Major S—— had a sad spill in a slough. We find that 4 oxen will do better and cheaper for our trip than horses, and [are] about engaging them for $85 the trip of two months. Houston Court [is] sitting—full of lawyers and clients. Trade is not brisk, owing to much cotton finding its way directly to Galveston. Well at the Capitol nearly 70 feet deep. It is a marly strata—pretty good for bricks—only two brick houses in Houston. Surface soil thin and sandy but no appearance of gravel or pebbles.

---

2 François and Dick were hired as hunters for the expedition. Bollaert does not identify them by their last names, although he makes frequent mention of them in the present and subsequent chapter.

Tuesday, April 23rd, 1844: Last night Stephenson mesmerized two simple black youths—plates—water—for want of other amusement in the city—this pleased our friends. Mr. Williams says that the S. shore of Padre Island has in some places three tiers of sand hills, some 50 to 60 feet high and during a norther they suffered much. About 1822, what is now known as Matamoras, was called Rancho de ———— but is now 2 to 3 miles from the river, when then it was on the bank of Rio Grande the river having changed its course this great distance.

The Rio Grande was navigated some 20 years since by an American from Santa Fé. Freshets considerable at times—muskit timber and ebony wood principally. Near to Corpus Christi there is generally a good ford from Padre Island.

I went out to the Coshatte Camp—the men and boys drunk, the women making among other attention to them—cigarettos. Ushan, or Ostin, the chief, very drunk, and he had his face painted black (the war colour) and generally in his tent, but too drunk to get up. Another Indian had one side of his face painted red, the other black—another all red. There were some finely limbed men and boys—the younger squaws pretty good looking and having small feet and hands. The young men had on one of their wrists 5 small rings of iron not quite closed. One of the young men said: "Me little drunk—Ushan much drunk, drunk a heap. Whiskey make Indian bad—want to fight." Men and women [were] dressed in garments made of printed stuff. From their intimacy with the whites they have many of the conveniences of life.

Wednesday, April 24th, 1844: Steamer arrived from Galveston bringing nearly all the San Antonio prisoners, 25 in number (excepting those who have died—about 12) who were released at the instigation of General [Waddy] Thompson, the U. S. Minister, and who brought them away with him in the U. S. Ship of War *Bainbridge.* Mier prisoners still delayed at Perote.[3] Calhoun will

[3] The last of the Mier prisoners were not released from Perote until September 16, 1844. Alexander, "Account of the Mier Expedition" (MS., Archives Collection, University of Texas Library).

be here by the next New York from N. Orleans. Wrote to [William] Pringle and sent letter to Sadie. It appears that E[nglish] and F[rench] ministers in Washington have protested against annexation and General [James] Reily told Newell that Elliot and Saligny had attended Holland—the oldest in the Republic.

Thursday, April 25th, 1844: Sent petition to P. C. Jack[4] for admission to practice at the Texas bar, Committee approved. Dr. Watson[5] informs me that he and [George W.] Bonnell were cut off from their party at Mier, but in effecting their escape, Bonnell *was* killed. Introduced to P——, known among the American trappers as the "Road Finder." He was stolen when very young and lived 9 years amongst the Indians of the Rocky Mountains; has trapped even to the Pacific and taken as many as 17 scalps of Blackfeet Indians. In 1824 a party of Comanches took him to the mines of San Saba—where he saw remains of old mining works.[6] Previously and after this period the Comanches were friendly with White men (not including Mexicans).

[4] Patrick Churchill Jack was appointed district attorney of the First Judicial District of Texas on February 1, 1840, and of the Sixth District on March 15, 1841. He died a few months after approving Bollaert's petition for admission to the Texas bar (August 4, 1844) of yellow fever in Houston. Thrall, *Pictorial History of Texas,* 570.

[5] Dr. Watson's first name is not known. He was not listed on the roster of prisoners in Thomas W. Bell's rare book, *A Narrative of the Capture and Subsequent Suffering of the Mier Prisoners in Mexico* (1845), now in the Texas University Library. However, two or three vague references to him have been found. He did not take part in the battle of Mier, but "remained on the Texas side of the Rio Grande with a small detachment. . . . After the battle he returned to San Antonio with . . . [the] body of troop." Nixon, *A Century of Medicine in San Antonio,* 71.

[6] Two Americans were taken prisoners by the Comanches; they were stripped naked, and in the month of August made to tramp after their victors—one of them was obliged to carry a large brass cooking pot, and this during the burning suns rays blistered his back. The second day he continued the pot carrying, when it became so painful that he made up his mind to throw the pot down and thus disobeying the Indians he would in all probability be scalped and killed. He approached the chief: "Gentleman Indian, Great Captain, Big Chief," to use the beautiful, elegant and chaste language of the poet, "may I be for ever eternally —— —— if I carry your brass pot any longer." And with this he indignantly threw the brass pot at the chief's feet. There was a moment of anxious suspense, when the Indian hugged him, called him "brave" and "brother," gave them back their clothes and put them in the way of the settlements.—Bollaert.

In 1839, 300 persons died of yellow fever in Houston. In 1843, only two persons died of fever (bilious). Majority of diseases brought on by intemperance.

Friday, April 26th, 1844: A Swiss or Polish Jew of a very bad character received 39 lashes with a cow-hide for robbery. There are still other such like indictments against him. Old Sam was petitioned for him, but it did not succeed. He had broken gaol in the United States. Cow-hiding I think is more severe than cat o'nine tails when administered with a strong hand.

The general opinion here is *for annexation* and that Old Sam is now really for it also, it seeming to him to be the only way to settle the question.

Saturday, April 27th, 1844: Had to get new and larger hind wheels and a new tongue to carriage—after dinner left Houston, accompanied a few miles by the Mayor and a dozen other friends. Six miles good road, but the 3 next rather heavy prairie, to Canfields—camped—tent up—cots—table—camp seats etc. This is the first party I believe, that has travelled with such comforts and conveniences. We may require them, but we shall get on but slowly; our four oxen are seemingly sufficient, but if we get into heavy roads our *pic nic* plans may be frustrated. Travelled 9 miles.

Sunday, April 28th, 1844: During night slight rain—wind var: S.W. and light norther, morning cloudy. Turned off at Canfields to Brey's Bayou.[7] Five miles—road only tolerable. No scarcity of flys, mosquitos. Six miles to near the "Fork" of the River[8]—had dinner—took the road to Richmond. Four travellers met today inform us that we cannot cross the Brazos higher up. Saw few

[7] Brey's Bayou is shown on Arrowsmith's map as a creek flowing into Buffalo Bayou from the west. This stream has long since lost its identity, with the expansion of the city of Houston.

[8] What river Bollaert had in mind here is certainly not clear. He undoubtedly meant the fork of the road, instead of the river. The road running west of Houston forks about half-way to the Brazos, one fork running northwest to San Felipe and the other goes straight west to Richmond.

deer—Mr. G[rieve] shot P. hen. Four miles brought us to Kirk's on the edge of the Brazos timber—camped. Met Mr. Settle, who informs us that we shall have a tough job thro' the bottom and looked quite dismayed to see our caravan. Sumach and pepper trees—wild China—black berries—cut-throat grape—make good preserves. Travelled 15 miles.

Monday, April 29th, 1844: Mr. Settle going to Galveston—sent all our mattresses etc. back. Hired 4 oxen ($2) to drag us thro' the sloughs of Oyster Creek.[9] Passed a fine plantation—corn, cotton, and sugar luxuriating—roads pretty bad. If Pringle could only see the omnibus in the many difficulties coming along. Waters of the Brazos rising—8 miles to Richmond ferry. Waters high, 200 yards wide and running a 6 mile current owing to heavy rains in the interior. Plantations looking well and prettily situated. Weather fine—clear, SE—fresh breezes. Fifty feet of water in River and at low water rounded pebbles found. Surface soil clay loam—marly strata, and then the diluvial with pebbles. Fossil bones occasionally found about here. Large cotton wood, associated to the sycamore,—probably of the poplar tribe. Met Messrs. Gilbeau[10] [and party] on their journey to New Orleans via Galveston with specie from San Antonio—pack mules in their plan and a good one, travelling 40 miles per day. They intended going by San Felipe, but the Brazos water so high that it would have been impossible to get thro' the bottom. Crossed to Richmond. It is well situated on a bluffy prairie. This place is but of small account as yet. Met Mr. Sullivan—married a daughter of Mr. Long, who lives near here. Folks along the Brazos preparing for an overflow.

In 1824 about a mile from Richmond there was a great fight between the Choctaws and Carancahuas in which the latter were

---

[9] Oyster Creek rises north of present Richmond in northern Fort Bend County and flows southeast fifty-two miles through Brazoria County to empty into the Gulf of Mexico. This region is still one of the most fertile parts of Texas.

[10] Bollaert identifies [C.H.] Guilbeau, in a miscellaneous note found elsewhere, as the French vice-consul at San Antonio. Guilbeau also served as ad interim mayor of San Antonio during 1841. Lamar, *Papers*, III, 559.

badly whipped. The inhabitants of this place did not speak very favourably of Mr. Maillard[11] and his doings when assisting on the *Richmond Telescope*. Camped 3 miles from Richmond; prairie high and somewhat undulating—pastures good. The Brazos being so high, the gullies in the prairie filled with "back water." Alligator gar of large size in these "back waters" and other fish.

Wilson the Jew who got 39 lashes in Houston passed us today in the bottom and came into our camp, having put up at a farm near us. He was known at Richmond and made to slope. He says he is going to Matamoras—thus the Mexican frontier is a place of refuge for *our* criminals.

Tuesday, April 30th, 1844: Very heavy dews during night—4 miles to first timber. Counted 15 to 20 different flowers in the prairie—and passion flower—some very pretty. Got into a precious *difficulty* in crossing a hollow of first timber—honey suckle in bottoms. I thought it was a gone case—as it is, it is a case of serious dislocation—10 miles across a bend to second timbers. The waters high and covering the path two feet deep the prairie about here covered with a large yellow flower. Fine and clear and strong SE breezes. Noticed a pink and white variety of *Aroma* (of the mimosa species). Prairies without a tree—wood only in the bottoms of rivers and creeks. I do not think these prairies have ever been covered with wood, this substance only growing when there is abundance of water—such as on rivers, creeks etc.—no scarcity of deer, but being in the prairie we do not hunt—prairie hen (a specie of grouse—rather say prairie grouse) wild doves, quail, snipe, plover, etc. The plantations on the edge of the bottoms—plenty cattle—sand hill crane—wild turkey and saw buffalo "chips." Omnibus got bogged—had to take all baggage out. Back water of Brazos 2 feet on road at One Tree camp. Blew hard from SE about sun down and got under lee of some timber. For this we suffered much from mosquitos. *Bars* as used in E[ast] Indies, meshes to[o] large for our mosquitos.

Wednesday, May 1st, 1844: First difficulty with oxen—strayed during the night. The way to travel is with pack mules and they require no corn, like horses. If going on a settling trip, then light jersey waggons with mules—oxen *sont toujours de bête*. We shall have a very long trip of it. The strong wind of last night dissipated all the damp air of yesterday and thus we had no dew. 8 A.M. cloudy, 81°. Prairies begin to rise and near the timbers undulate a little. Bottoms sickly during overflows, but prairies I think are healthy—plenty deer in prairies but rather wild. By great good luck our driver came back with oxen. They had strayed 6 miles and were not easily tracked on account of there being no dew. 7 A.M., started—4 miles passed a creek—had to head it. Two miles to Burdett's plantation, overflowed. They talk of going West, having been so sick last fall. Two miles more to Allen's.[12] He is a tanner and keeps "Public House." His bark mill is merely a hammer to beat the pieces of bark on a block. Purchased corn and dried beef. A few hundred yards further got butter and milk from a very pretty woman—something like *Temira*. Crossed Allen's Creek[13] here, good water; 1½ miles re-crossed the same, having left the San Felipe road 1 mile back. Camped.

Thursday, May 2nd, 1844: Persecuted by mosquitos during the night—Surface soil marly-loam good for bricks and rough pottery. Six miles came to cross road from San Felipe to Columbus[14]—the road travelled appears to go to La Grange, bears N.W. Few deer in prairie. Three miles to first branch of [San] Bernard, fine clear running water. Thick prairie surface soil, reposing on a bed of white marly clay studded with silver pebbles and sand. Noon 89° —fine S.E. breeze. Six miles to the main branch of the [San]

[11] Nicholas Doran P. Maillard has been previously identified as the author of an anti-Texas book, published in London in 1842. He also served as co-editor of the Richmond *Telescope* for a brief period in 1840.

[12] M. N. Allen was granted one-fourth league of land near Wallis, Texas, in 1827. *The Handbook of Texas*, I, 32.

[13] Allen's Creek (also known as Eightmile Creek) rises in southern Austin County and flows southeast for fifteen miles into the Brazos River near Wallis.

[14] The travelers were near present Sealy, Texas.

339

Bernard.[15] The land good bottom, but up and down—deep quick sand—surface soil about here sandy, in bed of river pure sand and few pebbles. We nearly had a spill in the river. Two miles further came to another branch of the Bernard. Two more camped. No mosquitos and slept for the first time since leaving Houston.

Friday, May 3rd, 1844: Three miles brought [us] to edge of Colorado Timbers of Post Oak. Found many new plants and flowers. The Nymphea alba [water lily] in great beauty, with its delicate odour. Here is park-like scenery, but as yet the only Chateaux are those of *Espagne.* Varieties of the mimosa species plentiful. White and red globular flowers.

To "swear like a trooper" is an old simile, but in Texas' case—to swear like a bullock driver when bogged. It is the concentrated essence of blasphemy. Slough in bottom bad; had to go round. Saw a scarlet species of geranium—wild plums and peach.

On our arrival within a mile of the ferry found that there had been a rapid rise in the Colorado and was filling the slough we had to pass. I found it swimming—went to a settlement just by, found some acquaintances. They tell us that there is more than 6 feet of water over the road and it is very bad, that no wheeled vehicle had passed for a long time. Camped. Found two pretty women addicted to "swabbing" but they had the grace to confess it was not a *delicate* accomplishment.

Saturday, May 4th, 1844: River falling slowly—not much game about here. Wells about 30 and 40 feet, 15 of which through a marly gravelly soil, then comes to indurated sand. Water good. Six miles below this some time since was found the *solid* part of a fossil horn; it measured 6 feet. What the entire length was with the hollow part, it is difficult to say. In Montgomery County a similar horn was discovered.

15 The San Bernard River rises in southwestern Austin County and flows southeast 105 miles, forming all or part of the county line between Austin and Colorado, Austin and Wharton, and Wharton and Fort Bend counties. It cuts the road Bollaert and his party were traveling about midway between San Felipe and Columbus.

Sunday, May 5th, 1844: Water belly deep in the sloughs. Surface soil (sandy) beds of gravel, indurated sand. At Columbus crossing. Went to Columbus—dined with Low and Robson.[16] River falling fast. Cavalcade of mules and horses from Corpus Christi for the Houston market.

Monday, May 6th, 1844: Broke up camp—got through Colorado bottom 1 mile—muddy but not bad and with an extra yoke of steers—ferried across bravely and kindly received by Mr. Robson and Low.

Lamar to Refugio, 18 miles; good road, some musquit. A vessel of 200 tons has been within 300 yards of shore in 8 feet water. Mr. Byrne[17] has 2 leagues on S.W. point of St. Joseph's [Island] —residence near the pilot house of Passo Caballo. Mr. Byrne has 2 leagues at La Mar. La Mar appears to have advantages as a port for us. Land at Lamar 25 to 30 feet high—wells can be dug from 4 feet—good grass for cattle. Thirty-two miles from La Mar to Goliad—to Carlos' Rancho[18] on the San Antonio, 28 miles. Settlements about there where cattle for draught can be obtained. We can take advantage of houses for our Emigrants at Lamar.

Tuesday, May 7th, 1844: Twelve miles up the river, sandstone is found hard enough for grindstones and occasionally used for building. Got omnibus repaired. Nos vamos a paso de cangujo. After dinner left Columbus over prairies and undulated post oak ridges—ground covered with good grass and now and then thick beds of marygold—the small geranium continues. Six miles to Skull Creek—dry—1½ more to Townsends—large gravel and stones begin here. Robson and Low bade us adieu and returned to Columbus. We are now out of the muddy part of the country

[16] This is the same Robert Robson whose plantation in Montgomery County had been Bollaert's headquarters during the previous winter. (See footnote 1, Chapter XI.)

[17] James W. Byrne. (See footnote 3, Chapter XII.)

[18] Carlos Rancho is on the San Antonio River where the old trail from Victoria to Refugio crossed the river. It was named for Carlos de la Garza, who had a commissary, barrel house, smithy, and a double log cabin at the site during the period of the Republic. *The Handbook of Texas*, I, 297.

and the *miasma* of the low lands and are regaled with southern or Gulf breezes. Camped 2½ miles more in a small prairie, having good grass. No mosquitos. Fresh S breezes, but myriads of fire flies like so many sparkling gems. Caught some of them. It is a long fly and the interior of hinder part can be illuminated at pleasure and of a brilliant bluish white colour. Travelled 10 miles.

Wednesday, May 8th, 1844: Morning fine and air cool—a freshness not like the coast and bottom lands we have come from. Two miles came to an open log house—full of girls and boys at school. One to Townsends—7 to first Navidad, ½ more at 2nd—1 mile to fork and 4 to Shad Owens[19]—18 to La Vaca, 30 to Gonzales. Cotton wood, or Canadian Poplar—Navidad River, sand bottoms with few pebbles—got a bad strain with the *bus*—cracked and other ways damaged the old wound in fording, or more properly in getting up the bank. One mile to 2nd branch—here we had to McAdamize[20]—6 miles to Rocky Creek—sandstone, clear water—pretty undulating prairies in the Post Oak timbers. Today met with 8 or 10 new sorts of prairie flowers—some very beautiful. Camped 2 miles onwards about head of Nixon's Creek.

Thursday, May 9th, 1844: We are now on the main road,[21] leaving the "settlements" on our left. Water lily in great abundance and beauty in water holes and heads of creeks. (*Kowampopin*, Indian for water lily). Nooned on the La Vaca 8 to 9 miles from camp. There is no scarcity of snakes about but the plant called rattle-snake master is in great abundance—the root is chewed—and has the taste of a strong bitter carrot. Country gone over undulating prairies with groves of post oak-myrtle.

[19] This was Shadrack B. Owen, who had settled in the region a short time before. Owen Branch is named for him. *The Handbook of Texas*, II, 321.

[20] To McAdamize (macadamize) meant to cover a road with a layer of broken road-metal. The process of laying carriage roads according to the system of John Loudon Macadam, a Scottish engineer (1756-1836), was carried out very extensively in the early nineteenth century in England.

[21] This road was familiar to Bollaert by now. It ran in almost a straight line from Columbus to San Antonio (present United States Highway 90) and was the eastern leg of the Old Presidio Road.

To the Kennedy Grant, at Last

Land of the myrtle, acacia vine and
Land of the brave and the free
Joy around thee, for ever entwine.
Hail Goddess of sweet Liberty.

Wild hemp—oats—rye here. Francois and Dick left hunting deer and turkey after what they considered something more interesting—when lo and behold a skunk discharged a large quantity of its fetid matter in Francois' face—Dick got a touch of it. They stopped and washed in a water hole, but we have to keep to windward of them. Crossed the La Vaca where I got lost last year—took a right hand road, but found it leading up the river. Altered course and took up an old trail bearing S.W., travelled along it 6 or 7 miles to Ponton's Creek.[22] When came across a road running E & W. Mr. G. considered it the best to take. Wild turkey, deer, and saw two droves of mustangs. Took on wood and water and camped 2½ miles in the prairie. All the gullies have spring water in them.

Friday, May 10, 1844: When taking the middle watch heard the howl of droves of wolves—good black surface soil, fine grasses, white *aroma* intermixed with flowers upon sandstone undulating prairies with small timbers on the margins of creeks—few islands of timber. Five miles by a cross-road running N.W., came to a summit of the "Big Hill"[23] range and had a view of the beautiful woodlands. Changed course to southward. The gullies as they descend to NW look like white cliffs (the result of the limestone rock of the interior) few peccans on hills—numberless flowers— 4 miles to noon—plenty deer but wild. After dinner thought I saw a road to the left—separated from my party—got upon a creek which I took for Ponton's—got into a wood—night came on and after travelling 8 or 10 miles came upon Mr. Tilley's settle-

[22] This stream, previously identified, was named for William Ponton, a member of Green DeWitt's colony.
[23] Big Hill derives its name from its location on the highest of some rolling hills in present Gonzales County.

343

ment on Mustang Creek (between Smithers and Brushy)[24] tired and fatigued—put up for the night.

Saturday, May 11th, 1844: Mr. T[illey] accompanied me to near the ground we camped yesterday (about 12 miles distant)— no appearance of my party—went with him to Smithers Creek to Mr. Smith's, from whence a party goes on the ———— at Gonzales. My party appears to be on the *LaBahía* trail,[25] by a fire I saw on the prairie.

It appears that we should have taken the right hand road after crossing the LaVaca at Daniel's ford[26]—or the one we crossed 5 or 6 [miles] from the La Vaca. My party will strike a road on the Guadalupe and then go up to Gonzales—by the Cuero Road. Met Mr. Smithers,[27] now an old man, gave me some anecdotes of the state of Texas some 20 years since. Mush and milk for supper.

Sunday, May 12th, 1844: Started with Mr. Smith and two others for Gonzales. Ten miles to Ponton's Creek. Two miles came to our old camp and 4 more near the tip of "Big Hill"— saw our trail even ere we turned off, looking in the direction of the Cuero road saw smoke of two fires—probably signals for me— 4 miles to top of Big Hill ere we got up fell in with road from Daniell's on the La Vaca on the W side with the La Grange Road. Noon'd on hog and corn doings—weak coffee, no sugar—a sort of Indian looking *country*. Camped on Thorn's Creek, 1 mile, sandstone. Clear water, 4 miles to Brockhan's on Peach Creek;[28]

24 Bollaert was considerably off his course. All three of these creeks are several miles southeast of Gonzales, near the main road.

25 The La Bahía Road ran south-southwest from La Grange to Goliad (La Bahía), missing Gonzales by fifteen or twenty miles.

26 This ford across the La Vaca River was named for George Daniels, who settled in the vicinity in 1840. *The Handbook of Texas*, I, 464.

27 Probably Lancelot Smithers, one of the couriers for William Barret Travis before the fall of the Alamo. Williams, "A Critical Study of the Siege of the Alamo and of the Personnel of its Defenders," *Southwestern Historical Quarterly*, Vol. XXXVII (1933–34), 164. Smithers formerly operated a ferry boat at Gonzales.

28 Peach Creek is an intermittent stream rising in southern Bastrop County and flowing south thirty-two miles across western Fayette County to join the Guadalupe River in eastern Gonzales County.

10 to Gonzales thro' Post Oaks—very hot. Some 3 or 4 miles back discovered the trail of our waggon and on arrival at G[onzales] found that they had arrived last night, having got to a settlement and then up the river [San Marcos River]. There are three men to be indicted for murder tomorrow!

Monday, May 13th, 1844: Ferried over Guadalupe—got fresh stock of bacon and corn at Mr. DeWitt's—8 cents bacon, 3 bits corn. Corn is sent to San Antonio to be ground for Gonzales! Nooned 8 miles, having passed a dry prairie—thick surface soil of a pretty good quality in places, resting on standstone—selenite in loose pieces about. Musquit timbers. Six miles more and camped in the post oaks—deer in plenty—no scarcity of skunks and rattle snakes. Noon 82°.

Tuesday, May 14th, 1844: Since we left Galveston there has been a succession of S. E. winds; these are grateful indeed during the heat of the day—as usual much talk of Indians about—the Comanches. Veremos. Two and one-half miles on the road found an imbedded mass of an indurated silicious marl containing large quantities of volute like shell. Land undulates—post oak with musquit undergrowth—fine hickory and good pastures. Many new flowers, but the marygold and wild geranium (something like Sweet William) predominate. Bear grass in flower—white; 16½ to creek, sandy. On west side is marked on a tree 40 miles to San Antonio (some say 75 miles, others 66 to 68); 32–33 miles to Gonzales. Road very sandy at times today and from 2 to 4 very hot. Camped 1 mile from junction. Water bad. 17½ miles.

Wednesday, May 15th, 1844: Near all places w[h]ere there is water, there are mosquitos, then the sand fly, horse fly, ants up to a very large size, but besides this the tick, rather larger than the bed bug, but on animals swells up with their blood to 2 times their size. There is an almost imperceptible bug, that attacks the traveller, covering him with pustules—the itching is very severe, when one rubs and scratches, then the pustules rise and enlarge

345

and a regular inflamation succeeds. Of a morning in particular we all scratch and "Bless the Duke of Argyle." To a casual observer it would appear that there was iron ore about here, but it is only indurated iron sand, sometimes puts on a nodular appearance, but they are only in *situ* and not a regular formation.

Centipede: Had 42 vertebrated legs—20 vertebra, 2 processes at tail, 2 horns, 2 strong forceps and teeth—legs yellow—back dark green, belly dirty yellow. When dismembered the parts walk —body contains a dirty green matter—their bite said to be very venemous and said in some cases to be mortal—poison said to be issued by legs. Rattlesnakes pretty abundant. A medical man in Louisiana it is said put a centipede on a cat, when the cat died of its stings soon afterwards. The Mexicans in particular are much afraid of them, and when camping, lay *acabresto* round their camp or when they are sleeping—*Faith!* Twelve miles to Cibolo[29]— clear water running over a large silicious pebbly bottom, with slabs of sandstone. Having passed the sandy part, came to a clear post oak country full of deer and quail. Banks of the Cibolo very steep, caught cat-fish and perch—turtle—fine bathing and we needed it to wash off the poisonous matter of the bugs. My body was in one mass of inflamed pustules. Flowers in prairies numberless wild lavender—surface soil moderately good and very pretty country, owing to the undulations. I think I see the "Capote"[30] to the right of us—a mill might be placed here. Surface soil sandy—3 large pebbly strata and on banks and bed of river small and large slabs of sandstone. Valley narrow—70 to 80 feet deep. The ascent of the Cibolo steep—long and bad road. 84° noon. Six miles camped.

Thursday, May 16th, 1844: 5 A. M., 78° Three miles from camp on a creek. Surface soil 3 to 4 feet—then layers of sand containing large thick slabs of highly indurated sand. Poorish land—saw

[29] The party was now a short distance south of present Randolph Air Force Base.
[30] This must have been a peak or hill in the vicinity of San Antonio. Whatever it was, it has lost its identity in this region. Capote Peak applies today to a peak in Presidio County, several hundred miles distant from San Antonio.

wolves and vultures. Fourteen miles from camp to Salado, fine clear stream, but I do not think brackish at present.

Many fine settlements might be formed in the Salado valley, good land, water for mills, a good climate and no mosquitos. Noon 85°—sunset crossed the San Antonio and camped in the Plaza.

Friday, May 17th, 1844: Robinson says he told Acklard[31] that I had fixed him as Colonel! and given him a place in history—get sketch of him—Miss Jaques. Emigrants sent out by Castro not finding land located—are working here. A few days since a man was killed not far from this by a party of Mexican cortados. Warm during the day, but a dip in the river delightful.

Saturday, May 18th, 1844: There appears to be some apprehension of inroads of Mexicans and Comanches. Hays and his men have been for some time past actively scouring the country, even to the Rio Grande and one Mexican marauding party driven over the river. The French and German emigrants lately armed, go into the fields, each armed with his gun—queer state of things. Bachelors party at Mr. Spencers, serenaded the ladies. Hays came in from his camp some 10 miles off. Anxiously awaiting news from the seat of government, [he] has 40 men under him—has orders to be near San Antonio and on the look out. There are Mexican troops "Cortadores" who look out after smugglers and with them Hays had a skirmish and sent them off. Hays does not think it would be judicious to commence surveying for us at this moment, but will accompany us thro' the greater part of the Colony and having pointed out, will survey during the summer. For some days past public prayers have been offered up for rain. There has been a long spell of drought, but here they can have recourse to irrigation. Gardening is improving a little, and such is the nature of the soil and climate that every production might be raised. The flour

---

[31] Bollaert has a pencil drawing of Colonel Acklard at this point, but he does not identify him further. Apparently he accompanied the party only from Houston to San Antonio.

consumed here comes from New Orleans but one or two persons have re-commenced raising wheat.

Sunday, May 19th, 1844: Secate blanca—white musquit grass. Secate verda—green musquit. Secate colorado—tall musquit. Had ride with some four lady friends. Beargrass in flower and a fine yellow and red aquatic plant—land cracking with drought. Two fandangos tonight, one on occasion of the marriage of a German butcher. The Major [Hays] is coming to camp, look across the Esequia.

Monday, May 20th, 1844: During night violent thunder storm and heavy rain. Our tent got into a fix—lightning, thunder, rain, mud, and darkness *à choix*. All our traps got wet—had to move into a house. Hays came from his camp, advises us not to leave this for a day or so, for the late rain has swelled the Medina, rendering it impassable.

Tuesday, May 21st, 1844: Morning cool—cloudy—breeze from N.W. A very old woman upwards of 100 and a Karonk boy died yesterday. Well dug at Mr. Jaques 16 feet. The stuff gone thro' resulting from the limestone rocks of the interior—some few miles from this large slabs are quarried and at times nodules of sulphuret of iron some decomposed into oxide.

News today from the coast not favorable to *annexation*. Report that there has been an encounter near Corpus Christi between the "Cortados" and contraband traders. The traders led by Alderete.[32] Killed and wounded some 15 of the "Cortados" or "Comisiones." The father of Alderete was a great enemy to the Comanches and had some great fights with them.

Wednesday, May 22nd, 1844: Reports mention that there are military movements on the Rio Grande and under the direction

---

[32] José Miguel Aldrete probably was the largest landowner in Refugio County at this time. He also possessed large holdings in the *brasadas* of the Nueces. *The Handbook of Texas,* I, 26.

of [General Antonio] Cañales. Woll it is said has been sent to the interior to suppress risings against Santana. At all events, Hays has positive order to keep a sharp look out. It is said the "Wacoes" have been killing our people on Little River.

Thursday, May 23rd, 1844: At times 18 to 20 representatives of as many nations [in San Antonio]—at present: Mexicans, American, French, German, and Irish compose the community of merchants. There are 5 Irish, 3 American, and a French baker —population improving since last year and San Antonio could turn out at least 300 fighting men. Bachelors predominate—thus ladies are at a premium.

Poncho-Jorongo—Mexican blanket. What I have called the limestone of this country, on examination appears to be made up principally of silicious matter—very little calcareous matter—but in some I noticed small muscle shells imbedded.

Friday, May 24th, 1844: Her Most Gracious Majesty's Birthday. Decided that the omnibus [should] go back to Houston. We prosecute our journey with pack mules. I wish we had started without it. It has retarded us, and the expence has been very great. True, we had our comforts, but the delay has been terrible.

Bamboo briar (Toque) found on the Colorado, Brazos, and heavy bottoms—annually new briars or shoots come out of the fresh potatoe-like excrescences. All the Indians use it when they find it. The Carancahuas boil the tender offsets of it—bruise and then cut it up into thin slices—then beaten up into a paste made into cakes—dried in the sun—and heated on a fire when eaten— this with strong ya[u]pon tea, so strong at times as to intoxicate is much relished by the Caranchuas. Evening party to celebrate H.M. birthday. We hoisted our flag, the national anthem was sung, the mint juleps, toasts, and songs followed—Stevenson in the Chair—and the brave Col. Cooke Via.

Saturday, May 25th, 1844: From San Antonio by Flores Rancho, 35 miles to Sequin—then to Gonzales 34—if by the Capote 1 mile further—some give 75 miles from G to Cibolo by lower road, others 72—others again only 66, or 36 to the Cibolo and 30 to Gonzales. But by lower road, altho' sandy, the San Marcos is avoided and is steep banks and 5 or 6 miles gained. The *Cibolo* is some 12 to 15 miles, or where the road crosses, placed in Map [Arrowsmith's] too far west.

Post arrived—its content threw a gloom over the land speculators and political waverers—for it was expected that news would have arrived of the annexation. Some slight military movements on the Arkansas and the dispatch of the U.S. Steamer *Poinsett* to Mexico with proposals to purchase Texas for 5 or 6 million dollars gives hope. The Americans are always talking of *whipping* Britain, but they don't say anything about E[ngland] and F[rance] protesting against their annexing T[exas] to U.S. Strange things may come out of this Texan affair—*Maromeros*, or rope dancers, R. dancing tumbling, theatre.

Sunday, May 26th, 1844: Some of Hay's men came in from scouring the country—no Indian or Mexican sign.

Monday, May 27th, 1844: At last and after asserting ourselves, got the carriage from Goodman el Herrero borracho. A job of say half a day he has been 10 days over—but we may think ourselves lucky for Mr. Elliot has had the face of a clock, for some slight repair, 4 years in his possession. San Antonio, thou art famed for the concentrated essence of indolence and delay. It is one of the most luxurious climates in the world, with excellent bathing and even on the hottest day, a workman has only to rest say from 12 to 2 or 3. But old foreign residents are contaminated—and the only persons who appear to work are the recent importations of Germans and French. The few shopkeepers here appear to dread the establishing of our colony, for they foresee that we can get the Rio Grande trade as well as that of Chihuahua. About midnight a drove of wolves came near the town, setting the San Antonio pack of some 2 to 3,000 dogs of all sorts and sizes upon the bark.

Tuesday, May 28th, 1844: In the hand of any other people,

what a delightful residence and picturesque habitations would have been erected here—say even in the hands of the Moors. The river so clear, running gently, of an equable temperature all the year, and after *fandango* dancing, bathing comes next. Under the shade of overhanging trees in secluded spots may be seen the *Naiads*. The *Dryads* enjoy the silvery stream with more publicity in the evening. After a bathe one feels renovated and feels a beautiful glow. Water as it comes from the springs appears to be slightly heated.

Wednesday, May 29th, 1844: Having purchased a mule and horse and hired 2 pack horses, a muleteer, and Tom Hancock for a woodsman, left San Antonio—7 miles to Leon and 5 to Arroyo del Medio.[33] Myriads of new flowers. The rich musquit grass in abundance and the country alive with deer. Camped on the Medio. Once more I see the rich and flowering prairies, undulating ridges between each rivulet and stream. To the N and N.W. the mountain range. We have escaped from the myriads of flies and I hope it is not out of the frying pan into the fire. No bugs—ants—snakes—centipedes—skunk—scorpions, etc. Mr. James,[34] the Deputy Surveyor joined us. During the evening Major Hays and his Lt. Ben McCulloch[35] and another visited us from their camp 5 miles distant.

Hays intends to be above us and visit us during our peregrinations in the colony. Our party consists of Mr. Grieve, Mr. Stephenson, and self, directly connected with the expedition. Mr. James (Deputy Surveyor), Tom Hancock, our woodsman and hunter, Felipe Jayme, our muleteer, Dr. Cuppler and Mr. Lowe as guests,

[33] The Arroyo del Medio is a creek (Medio Creek) rising in the western part of Bexar County and flowing southeast approximately fifteen miles to empty into the Medina River.

[34] John James was made assistant surveyor of Bexar County in 1839. He surveyed the townsites of Castroville, Boerne, Bandera, and several other settlements west of San Antonio. *The Handbook of Texas*, I, 904.

[35] Ben McCulloch had a long career in Texas, as a representative to Congress, surveyor, Texas Ranger, and officer in the United States Army and later in the Confederate Army. In 1844, he was one of Captain Hays' chief scouts. Webb, *The Texas Rangers*, 84. (See footnote 44, Chapter II.)

and François. We are well formed, armed, and pretty well mounted and now we have got rid of the omnibus I see nothing to prevent us going a head.

Thursday, May 30th, 1844: Heavy dew during night—even cool compared to the temperature of the town of San Antonio. After 16 miles W, somewhat northerly, came to the "Cañon Crossing" of the Medina River, about 3 miles below where the San Geronimo enters the Medina. Crossing the Potranca and Sans—but we are only some 10 miles from the "Presidio Crossing." Thus the Medina on K[ennedy]'s map is made to run too rapidly to N. Fine cool and strong breezes from N. and W. making it fine travelling. Camped. Herds of deer and flocks of wild turkey. Colquon[36] has some land this side of the "Crossing." Saw petrified oyster shells on the banks of river. About Austin there are banks of them, so Mr. James tells me—from which lime is made. Land about here stony and not very good quality—neither is it picturesque. The Lomas—"ridges"—between the streams appear to be higher on the western than on the eastern.

We may be some 80 feet above San Antonio—pastures rough— musquit, live and post oaks, peccan, cypress. San Antonio bears *E* of us. Crossed the Medina River—running down and somewhat rapidly—stony bottom rises sometimes 15 feet. This river has been known hardly to run for 2 years. Eight miles brought us to the Chican Creek, about 7 miles above the "Presidio Road."[37] James espied a "Bee flock" in a live oak; the axe went to work—cut partly thro'—found it a young "form"—the bee in all its stages—and got some fine honey. Since crossing the Medina we have travelled

[36] Bollaert doubtless refers to Ludovic Colquhoun, a former senator from San Antonio who was taken prisoner by General Woll in 1842, and released in March, 1844. Colquhoun's holdings near the "Crossing" on the Medina River would have been near present Castroville. *Biographical Directory of Texan Conventions and Congresses,* 70.

[37] The Presidio Road took its name from Presidio San Juan Bautista opposite present Eagle Pass, Texas. The road extended from the Río Grande to Columbus via San Antonio, and is sometimes confused with the *Camino Real,* which extended from the Río Grande via San Antonio to Nacogdoches (Old San Antonio Road). The latter crosses the Río Grande several miles below Eagle Pass. (See Arrowsmith's map.)

over a wooded hilly country and strikes us that it would be a fine tract for the cultivation of vines. It is said that in the Cañon de Uvalde[38] there are very many species of grape and very plentiful springs at every step, giving rise to rivulets and then creeks, being tributaries to streams to the right and left. Weather very fine and not hot. Hancock took a hunt—brought us in venison—he found 3 bee trees and had a crack at a bear. All these hills strewed with silicious rounded stones and pebbles and in the deep creeks these seen in horizontal layers.

Friday, May 31st, 1844: During night pleasantly cool—about 4 to 500 feet above sea[39]—mustangs about our camp. Eight miles in a S. direction struck the Presidio Road and 8 more brought us to the Honda, or "Deep Dell."[40] As water *is* at the crossing just now, had to go up it some distance and then found a water hole—plenty deer, leopard cats, savage turkies. Land dry and only very good near the water courses. Six miles from El Hondo, then as it presents a series of water holes, some of them large and deep dells; during rainy season it is probable [that it] forms a continuous stream which runs into the Hondo, called El Tahucano—formerly a favourite camping ground of that tribe [Tahuunde]. It is prettily situated, having small timbers of different sorts—musquit and great quantities of prickly pear. From the Hondo to this is one immense *carpet* of flowers—particularly of the Texas Marygold. Saw traces of bear, wolf, and different sorts of cats—few mosquitos just now. What a hunting park could be made out of this locality.

Our camping ground is famed for a "robo" in July 1838. Houston had invited the Mexican families who had resided at San Antonio to return. Our muleteer, Pedro Jayme, was with his four

[38] Cañon de Uvalde is the same as present Sabinal Canyon, in the extreme northeastern portion of Uvalde County on the Sabinal River.

[39] The altitude above sea level of the region that Bollaert and his party were now exploring is approximately 1,000 feet.

[40] Hondo Creek flows into the Frio River in present northwest central Frio County. The travelers were not far from present Batesville, or southeast of Sabinal, Texas.

children and others—some 23 Mexican men and women camped on their way from the Rio Frio—with some 50 horses, corn, and some money. Captain [James H.] Cocke (now Major and collector of customs at Galveston) came into the camp, rested with some 20 followers—matured a plan to rob them—which they did effectively. Cocke killed a poor widow's son, and Cocke pointed his gun at Philip Jayme—he held up his two children when Cocke dropped his piece. Cocke with his spoil went to San Antonio—but was badly received there and soon *cleared* out, but only three of the stolen horses were returned—bonita historia!

Saturday, June 1, 1844: Ever glorious! Six miles came to a fine little stream, the Arroyo Seco[41]—one mile to Tierritas Blancas—a loma of white sand; plenty water about here and mosquitos; here commence the undulating hills, or Puertocitos del Rio Frio —from the summit of are seen the lomas or ridge of Rio Frio—11 miles to Rio Frio—steep banks—caught trout and cat-fish. Had to build a raft of three irregular logs (of cedar) and two cross pieces underneath and bound together with a lazo. Camped at the general camping place—½ mile below is another crossing. Five or six leagues above is the road General Woll[42] entered Texas in 1842 and is generally fordable.

We have now entered upon our grant, but 9 miles above and 7 below the crossing is surveyed by others. On the E. bank of this river [Frio] are portions that are low and during heavy freshets (which rise sometimes 50 and 60 feet) overflow, and this low part becomes sloughs. This is not the case on *our* side of the river, which is generally higher. Pastures pretty good on the river. A variety of wood, including cypress and a wood called "Brazil," used as a dye wood, a plant of which brooms are made—some mosquitos.

[41] Seco Creek (Dry Creek) rises in northwestern Medina County and flows southeast forty-five miles into Hondo Creek in northern Frio County.

[42] The Woll Road was cut north, parallel to the Presidio Road, by General Woll during his approach to San Antonio in September, 1842. Woll's choice of routes was dictated by his desire to reach San Antonio undetected. E. W. Winkler, "The Bexar and Dawson Prisoners," *Southwestern Historical Quarterly*, Vol. XIII, (1909–10), 290.

Sunday, June 2nd, 1844: Our muleteer is full of admiration of this part of the country . . . 65 miles from Bejar by the Presidio Road. Travelled 3 miles on the Presidio Road and then 7 miles N.N.W. Struck the Olinos [Olmos],[43] or Elm Creek from that timber growing upon it. Several smaller creeks running into it. Just now not even the Olmos Creek is running. The land upon the creek good for locations, as it declines on both sides and easterly fine musquit prairies. This spot, in honor of our Bos[s], I call "Camp Grieve." Antelopes seen for first time. Deer, wild turkies, quail, hares (mule rabbits) rabbits, rats, snakes. Crossed many mustang trails going down to Elm Creek. "No lo digas" Tell it not, Creek is called half way between San Antonio and Rio Grande—6 miles from this it runs into the Leona. Sighted rifles in case of a difficulty. We have been a temperance party since leaving Bejar, but Mr. G. had stored away some sherry—when we drank "success to the colony." Eight miles N.E. thro' heavy brush upon the very steep banks struck the Frio—very picturesque—no pasture or we should have camped for the night. Filled our gourds—ascended but found that we were in a slough and the mosquitos too thick. Found on the bank of river a solitary Indian wigwam. Got out into a musquit prairie—2 miles W. camped (Camp Mosquito), good pastures.

Monday, June 3rd, 1844: Two miles N.E. to River. Easy descent, pastures at the water's edge and thro' fine country, out of sloughs and not subject to overflow—banks in places steep—now sand—bed of river rounded pebbles—clear stream. We are below the Arroyo de Uvalde [Sabinal River] and some 14 or 15 miles from Presidio Road, and this ford Felipe Jayme wishes to call Paso del Toro, from tracks of a wild bull he discerned about here. Above is a steep barranca—caught large quantities of trout—cat—perch, myriads of minnows. Hancock discovered 5 Mexicans, most probably "Cortados." One advanced to examine our trail of this

[43] There are five creeks in Texas named Olmos Creek. This particular one is an intermittent stream rising in southwestern Uvalde County and flowing south ten miles into Cato Creek in northern Zavala County.

morning and then they probably concluded that it was part of Hay's company, when they *put* off S.W. Left Paso del Toro—3 miles W.S.W. in a slough, some mosquitos. Six miles thro' a chaparal, turning round to the Rio Frio again—very pretty, but now the stream is more placid and less of it. By map in straight line, 17 m[iles] from Presidio Road. Hancock makes it 15, thus we are below, but from the quiet state of the stream, it may be possible we are above the Arroyo de Uvalde, large trout in river— Grieve and Jayme went down the river and found the Arroyo de Uvalde called by the muleteer "El Sabinal" owing to the quantity of cypress in it 400 yards below us. Trout Camp—from the numbers in the pool of river somewhat different from English trout. It is said that there are great quantities of cypress and cedar on the Arroyo de Uvalde. During the freshets, [logs] could be floated down easily into the Frio, into the Nueces, and to the Coast. When freshets run, then there are no falls in the rivers. Land silicious and under its beds of indurated sand and rounded pebbles as yet we have seen no rock in *situ*—all ———— or alluvial. *Peccans.*

Tuesday, June 4th, 1844: Left Rio Frio and kept along our boundary line as near as we could—15 miles, somewhat south of west [we] struck the Leona River; came upon two small water holes in upper part of a valley that runs into Rio Frio, below the Presidio Road, and Mr. G. thinks would be fine for grazing. Antelopes,—and a few deer—rats. The Valley of the Leona has a fine vegetation—fine ferns—average depth of river about here 10 feet—deep pools—rocky bottom—falls occasionally—rises perhaps 6 to 8 feet more. Constant stream—very few fords—waters cool—passed one range of hills—undulating country; we think we are below Woll's Road and some 8 or 10 miles below the source or springs of the Leona.[44] This river does not increase in width much during its course—average width 30 to 40 feet and at its mouth is more like a canal than a river, with banks only 3 or

[44] If Bollaert is correct, he and his party were now a few miles below present Uvalde, Texas.

4 feet. This river is entirely located [on the map]; this speaks well of the land in the valley and the constant supply of water—musquit, live oak, peccan, good grass, and muskit mulberry. Some parts of river famed for its trout. To get to it we had a terrible scramble thro' very "God d——n mean brush"—banks pretty steep, but not difficult to water horses. I do not think much of the land upon this our upper boundary, added to the grant, *but we might get some 20 more miles up the Frio and then over to the Leona or Nueces; this would comprise some valuable land.*

Fat Cat-fish Camp: It is a common saying that the fish of this river can be fried in their own camp. Fish so large ran away with some of our hooks. Leona excellent for mill races, etc. Large masses of silicious rock in river, and on banks layers of pebbly matter. Prickly pear more or less all over the country; saw a few of another species (long one). Shingles could be made on the Uvalde [Sabinal] of cypress—tanks for water. Up camp—got through brush on river bank—"very *mean*"—reconnoitered and found it too late to go to the head of the Leona. Camped 2 miles N.W. at a water hole in a canada, or small valley, leading into the Leona just above today's camp. Water in hole—hot—but good; musquit grass, water, and open country. Suspicious looking trail hard by running up the country. Our hunter, Tom Hancock (made prisoner at Santa Fé and Mier), found a bee tree at the water hole.

Bee Tree Camp: Today it has been very hot and no breeze. Two and one-half leagues to the loma and 2 more to the head of the Leona about W.N.W. The Leona appears much more extended N.W. than laid down, thus giving more land to the Grant.[45] The Nueces is said to be only 8 miles W of it.[46] Saw large quantities of Spanish flys—no scarcity of mosquitos.

[45] Bollaert's observations are correct. The Leona is shown on Arrowsmith's map as a stream approximately thirty miles long, whereas it actually extends through central Uvalde and northeastern Zavala counties for some seventy miles before joining the Frio River in southern Frio County.

[46] The Leona and Nueces are approximately eight miles apart near the headwaters of the former stream. The distance widens to about twenty-five miles in southeastern Zavala County.

Wednesday, June 5th, 1844: Five or six miles N.W. over heavy loma came to banks of Leona. Met a Mexican Anti Galan near Woll's Road. Good ford. Mexican says that springs are 4 or 5 miles above and that to the Frio it is only 9 miles—thus maps are wrong. Woll's Road good. To the Nueces 4 leagues—here, canadas but no water. From Springs to the Nueces about W.N.W. —good land on this part of river. Camped on E side of River on Woll's Road—well beaten road. The Mexican Tom found was retiring to the Rio Grande. We cross-questioned him. It appears that the party we took for "Cortados" had robbed our *prisoner* who lives now in San Fernando [Chihauhua]—had been robbed of 3 horses. He started in pursuit with his father and 2 other friends; they left him at the Nueces, and he went on to San Antonio—stopped there 2 days and is retiring to San Fernando with a letter (dated 31 May) with some coffee, etc. as a present. We have not held a council of war upon him yet. He gives a pretty good account of himself.

Comanches:

About a month since 300 Comanches and their families came into Presidio[47] to trade 3 or 400 horses and mules, and have gone down between the Rio Grande and Nueces mustang hunting. The principal chief is named Ysamonica and the chief interpreter Santana. Woll has issued orders not to make war upon them— they rob poor Mexicans on the upper side and sell on lower part of river—game has been scarce in their country and they eat mustangs.

Presidio 2 leagues from River—from here to Rio Grande 66 miles. This river (La Leona) appears from all account to be one of the Gardens of Eden of Texas, the river neither increasing or decreasing much and irrigation could be easily carried on.[48] Three

[47] This should not be confused with present Presidio, Texas, southern Presidio County. Bollaert is referring to the Presidio of San Juan Bautista, near present Eagle Pass, Texas. See footnote 37 above.

[48] Bollaert is not only a good prophet here, but he demonstrates the attributes of a keen observer. This region today is in the heart of the "Winter Garden of Texas," one of the largest producers of vegetables in the United States.

miles on Woll's Road—El Huerfano (The Orphan), W.S.W. 5
miles, but the whole of the Huerfano seen 1 mile further. Journeyed 5 miles along the road then 3 to 4 east and struck the Frio
River. River moderately broad and placid, plenty fish—pebbly
bottom—very large masses of silicious rock with fine crystals of
quartz. We are about 2 miles below the Woll Road. Had a council of what to do with Mexican. Some were for ———— him—
others to keep him with us, fearing he might be a spy. At last
agreed to let him go. On our road found that he had had a mule
along with him and left at some distance from the river to explore,
and probably he had a cargo of tobacco smuggling into Mexico.
From Woll's Road to our left undulating and prairie country and
in the back ground ranges of mountains. Land good, but saw no
water in canadas. Camp Castle Hill—in a gully 200 yards from
river. No dew. Saw ranges of mountains to our left 15 or 20
miles off.

*So far the exploring party had been wandering around in the vi-
cinity of the common corner of present Uvalde, Zavala, and Frio
counties. Even today, this region (between present Pearsall and
Uvalde) is thinly populated and contains much mesquite, although irrigation has transformed it considerably since Bollaert
was there more than a century ago. From their present Castle Hill
Camp, the travelers gradually proceeded down the Frio and
Nueces Rivers until they reached present Corpus Christi on
June 24, 1844.*

XVI

HOMEWARD BOUND

[June–July, 1844]

Thursday, June 6th, 1844: Morning cloudy. The 2nd and 3rd cloudy morning we have had since we have been out. Rock of river like hone-stone—light soil. It would be easy to purchase—say from Woll's Road on Leona up to Springs [Uvalde]—for trading town, etc. Just behind our camp there is an isolated hill—rocky—on the summit is a rude fort dug down in the rock. Came in a zig-zag about S. S. E. 8 or 10 miles came to the head of a canada-creek leading to the Frio (Olmos). We had not seen any deer during the morning; large quantities of ferruginous matter in rock.

Saw deer and then came on the water hole—found no water, but when on a hill saw a barranco, being E, made for it and found it the Rio Frio; some 8 miles below Trout Camp on same river picked up a lame horse. Passed an old waggon trail not far from river—owing to bends in the Frio we think our line cuts it twice, if not oftener, and thus throws in more land save 15 miles by 12.[1] Found old Indian camp—river just running, but very deep pools and full of fish. Much of land came over today good, but no running water just now. This is probably a Comanche camp—when they return from hunting mustang in the lower country and pillaging. Last year they marauded at Corpus Christi and Laredo. They are now SW of us. We may meet them! All round this (Comanche Camp) is strewed with bones of mustangs and only one *beef* they had eaten. Removed for the night one mile higher up for pasture—all about here found Comanche camps, probably of last year when they returned from the Coast. The banks of the Frio are generally steep and deep. Irrigation could not be profitably resorted to, but there are vallies, canadas, sloughs, and gullies

---

[1] An examination of the map of the Kennedy Grant reveals that the Frio River cut the northeast boundary of the tract only once.

in abundance and one crop might be easily got—the rest of the year for pasture.

Friday, June 7th, 1844: In Mr. G. watch—alarm—and all got under arms. Nothing occurred. Scarcity of game. Indians have thinned them off. Two miles until we got to the lomas of the Frio, then 5 miles, fine pasture prairies to the head of the Pringles creek and hills. Formerly the creek was called "El Topo" (now called Pringle Creek), for it was on this part of the Leona about Presidio Road that the mail met and exchanged bags for the Rio Grande and Natchitoches; likewise called "No lo digas"—from "What news?" Three miles down valley to a water hole. Passed some good pastures. The Comanches it is supposed have eaten 20,000 mustangs during the last 5 years. They *barbecue* mustangs sometimes whole by digging a large hole in the ground, putting stones in, making them hot, then in goes the mustang, other stones laid on, and then a big fire. Sometimes as a tid-bit, the head. Crossed the creek (Pringle Creek), zig-zagged down, but in a straight line 5 or 6 miles S.E.; pastures good. Water only in holes in creek. Passed all sorts of trails.

Snakes are not so common as I had been led to believe. We see one or two a day, and hear about as many more, but just as one of our party was making up his *pallet* (not bed) a large rattle snake welcomed him to the terra incognita. Death to the vermin was decreed, and off went his head. Rattle Snake Camp on Pringle's Creek.

Saturday, June 8th, 1844: E by E.S.E., some perhaps little more southerly; some 7 miles cut the Presidio Road. Two bold tracks, but grass growing over it. Fine country, pretty open. No water. Three miles, musquit and good pastures, open country to Esperanza Creek ("No lo digas"—Pringle's Creek). Six more of same country to Los Olmos (Camp Cupples). Water at present in holes but pastures good. For the first time since we have been traveling few showers of rain.

On the W side of Olmos Creek runs a range of hills (Grieves

Hills); about here they form many ridges, commencing at the head of creek and terminating on the forks of it and the Frio. Wherever there is a river or creek, there is a dividing ridge (loma) generally higher as one goes westward. The head of La Leona may be 100 to 150 feet above San Antonio[2], this spot (Pringle's Camp, perhaps 50). But there appears to be a declination S.E. about here (see rivers and their tributaries taking that direction).

Sunday, June 9th, 1844: Went down W side of Elm Creek 8 or 10 miles where it enters the Rio Frio.[3] At the juncture are rich groves of elms in particular, live oak. It may be seen in going towards the Frio and Elm that when considerable freshets exist they cover large tracts of land, forming generally large sloughs (which sloughs make a bed and then enter the river again). By descending, one gets to the prairie.

The land travelled over today is good but Mr. G[rieve] says wants a stiff subsoil to retain the water. This accounts for so much at present almost useless land, without dams were made. Saw deer, wolves, leopards, rattle and other snakes, wild turkey with their brood about *two weeks* old. *No mosquitos.* Some very large elms 20 feet girth. Camped on Rio Frio about 1 or 2 miles from the junction with Elm Creek. *Camp Kennedy.* Found fine shady bowers, pretty good pastures—no tracks or trails, river running smoothly, deep and 20 to 30 feet wide with large pools. River runs S until the Leona comes into it—rough brush on the banks— plenty cat-fish and very fine. Banks from water 60 to 80 feet— sand mixed with clay. In some parts of Mexico it may be seen, and in parts dryer than this part of the country, that they prefer a barren country without running water, being esteemed healthier. They dig gullies, leading to large tanks or dams, and thus irrigate land. Moreover, the cattle raised in such situations after feeding on the prairies are obliged to come up to the farm for water, and

[2] The headwaters of the Leona River are somewhat above 900 feet, compared to 700 feet above sea level for San Antonio.

[3] The party had now moved down southeasterly across the Frio County line. Elm Creek unites with the Frio River in western Frio County.

thus they are made tamer than those that are allowed to run wild on the prairies and drink at rivers and creeks.

Some such sort of system must be resorted to for parts of our colony—*dams* only want making and one crop annually can be easily obtained *without* irrigation. Left Rio Frio over fine prairies and undulating and hilly lomas, not much brush, fine pastures—musquits—no water now—many canadas leading into the Frio and Leona. Camped 10 miles S W. *Campo sin agua*—15–16 miles below Presidio Road.

Monday, June 10th, 1844: Four miles S by W brought us to the Leona, 5 or 6 to the junction with Frio; banks steep but not high. Cloudy and small rain—great droves of deer and mustang trails, hares, rabbits, moccasin. G—— shot a large R. snake full of eggs half as large as a hen's egg—sultry. (Camp Wasp) With only a few small streams, what agricultural operations could be carried on—soil rich and light, but colored somewhat with oxide of iron.

Several species of the centipede seen—one today appeared to have more than 200 [tentacles] and smaller than the one examined on 14th May. Plenty cat-fish here—few trout. Showers and thunder storm in the distance. Left camp, went down 2 miles—all along old Indian camps, forded Leona; here our mule made a rush, got into river, only 2 feet deep, but running swift, upset cargo, powder, and Mr. G's portmanteau got into the river. Felipe made a dexterous grab at it and saved it going down river—lost axe. Weather sultry and brewing a storm—our wood craft called into play—rigged up tents—lost one fourth of our powder—tobacco wet and some meal. During first watch a leopard, wolf or coon jumped over Hancock. Alarm.

Tuesday, June 11th, 1844: Day light, blew strong from S.W. and then came on a storm with heavy rains. Ticks and red bugs in abundance. Some 10 years since the Leona did not run, and then came on all at once and has continued running a beautiful stream. Here, I call Camp and Paso Peccan (Nogul) of which there are many and very fine. The river here 20 feet wide, 2 to 3 feet deep—

363

banks 10 feet and sloping—fine lands— as all is on this river. If San Antonio is called "El Diamante de Oeste," this may be called "La Perla." Wild turkeys in abundance.

Robinson has a silver mine 100 miles above San Antonio and it is supposed that all about it is a mineral region. Our camp is a perfect *Monmouth* St.—our fixings drying in a blistering sun. Dr. Cupples had violent fever last night from sun exposure and Mr. Lowe has been some days on the sick list with "chills." We rest here today to recruit, for when leaving here for the Nueces, we go into a tierra incognita and will find water scarce. The Comanches, when they are out hunting or war, carry with them some preparation which it is reported heals wounds rapidly.

If wanting to deceive by sign, if only say 10—make 5 or 6 fires and then the enemy will calculate 25 or 30.

Wednesday, June 12th, 1844: One mile from the Leona crossed "Todos Los Santos" Creek—water holes—fine land—goes up to near Presidio Road and enters Leona 2 or 3 miles down; deer in "cords"—killed a fine fat doe within a day or two of fawning. After being in the timbers and brush of the Leona, came to musquit and pretty open country. Nine miles over undulating musquit prairie to a dry creek—having water holes directly below us— antelope—wolves, locusts, hares, rabbits—fine and cool weather —Elm and live oak. Many mustang and wild cattle tracks, but there being no water on the prairies have driven them off to the margins of different rivers. Land soft and reddish from oxide iron. No stone or pebbles. As yet had no opportunity to see sub-strata. Six miles more over musquit lomas—camped. No water. Course today about S. Eight miles S. came to a creek; water too salt[y] to drink! pretty fix! Five more and slough to the Nueces. Camped. Travelled 30 miles by map. Twenty-three, say 30 from Laredo Road 35 by map and 40 by road. Dr. C. thinks that this spot is 200 feet above[4] the Frio at Camp ——— on Leona. I do not think it is so high. When it rains then water is to be found across from the Leona—during summer months the traveller is recommended

[4] Bollaert must mean "200 feet below" rather than "above."

to take a large gourd full from the Leona—by the Laredo Road.[5] Those learned in water finding may meet with some. On approaching the banks, found the pastures either eaten up by the mustangs or burnt up with drought. The land is pulverulent and contains large quantities of oxide iron—musquit wood and its grass— towards the river the Cactus Opuntia. On river about here, elms, lances [lacewood], oak, etc.

During our ride today saw no eligible spots for settlers. Mr. G——'s birthday.

Thursday, June 13th, 1844: During night sultry. We were all pretty feverish and occasionally plagued with mosquitos. During the latter part of autumn and winter the rains overflow many parts of banks of river and during heavy freshets from thunder storms sometimes in summer. Hancock tells me that the country about the head waters of the Nueces is very pretty and settlements for those who love the "Far West." This river, like some other streams in Texas has the property like that of Avernus in Sicily—of losing itself and then some 25 miles below rising again. Some 80 or 90 [miles] by road up Nueces from Presidio Crossing is an old Spanish Mission[6]—(it is supposed mines were worked about here). There is no lake at the head of Nueces, but there is one spring. Mountain regions on the Nueces and other waters in vicinity rocky and bad. The vallies only good. Thirty miles from head of Nueces to the Las Moras—[7] over the high range of Las Moras Mountains. Left *Camp* Plimpton, went down the slough and soon got out of the land that overflows. Mustangs have been

[5] The Laredo–San Antonio Road originally ran considerably east of present United States Highway 81, the route most frequently followed today. The former road constituted the southeastern boundary of the Kennedy Grant. (See Appendix I.)

[6] According to Arrowsmith's map, the deserted Spanish mission was located near present Uvalde, Texas. It should have been placed farther north on the Nueces River. This mission was the one of San Lorenzo de la Santa Cruz, also known as El Cañon Mission. It was founded near present Barksdale, Edwards County, in 1762, and abandoned in 1768. Herbert Eugene Bolton, *Texas in the Middle Eighteenth Century*, 94–95.

[7] Las Moras Mountain is in central Kinney County, immediately north of the town of Brackettville. Its Spanish name means "the mulberries."

down to the slough to drink this morning. Thanks to their numberless tracks got out of the brushwood, which is pretty hard upon our trousers. Good cattle ranges all about here (horned).

I think there are bluffs on which habitations might be built or a little way back in the high land. One crop at least could be obtained, and most extensive stock ranges and a river to take produce to the coast.

Travelled about 8 miles reconnoitering, but almost 6 miles down river camped on a gully—fresh water—apparently a spring —good pasture. Generally all over the country ground much burnt up by sun and saline materials in the soil. Rough thickets of musquit—thorns of all sorts and Cactus Opuntia "d——n rough work." Travelled 8 miles straight down river—rough brush—saw one specimen of mescal.[8] Came to a long and large Bayou—inlet from the river during overflows and acts as a water course during rains (Bayou, bayonco, etc. terms employed here). Land bluffy and near river; too hot for red bugs or ticks. White heron, hawks, smaller birds, some new flowers, wolves, deer, turkies, quails. Camped on road on E side of Bayou—*Camp Bollaert.*

Friday, June 14th, 1844: Much lightning and thunder and black rolling clouds—during middle watch threatening of rain. All up. Camp manufacturing—only few drops—blew over with wind from N. E. Morning cloudy.

All over the country the many varieties of *chaparral* (acacia or mimosa) thrive to the great horror of the woodsmen and it requires considerable knowledge of *woodcraft* to pursue one's course. We are perhaps the first to traverse this section of country. Even the Indian would not venture to travel thro' it.[9] Eight miles —having taken some 4 or 5 miles over pretty open country—came to a small creek with water holes. Saw some hares (buck rabbits) —6 miles further open country, but large quantities of cactus (3

[8] The party was now moving down the Frio through south central Frio County and northeastern La Salle County.

[9] The travelers were now approaching the great "Brush County" of South Texas. Except for large areas that have been cleared of mesquite and cacti, much of the county appears the same today as it must have a century ago.

species)—some *maguey* and a little musquit—noticed a geranium. *Buck Rabbit Camp*—river being 3 miles S.E. and from our last camp E. 6 miles. *No water*, few deer; shot two young wolves out of 3. Musquit grass burnt up. We are now on a succession of elevated prairies. The timbers of the Nueces seen as a dark green hill—cloudy; travelled 10 miles SE by S. making 8 *miles good* to the Nueces—over open country by a slough or bayonco. We seem to think there is some eligible land about here and near the river.

Saturday, June 15th, 1844: Last night after sunset the gnats and small flies nearly blinded us. The effluvia from the slough nearly choked us. Frogs (bull), crickets, and such like small fry commenced their inharmonious notes. No breeze and very sultry. No sooner had we had supper and bethought to seek repose upon our pallets, with the idea that a few snakes, scorpions, centipedes, and lizards—independent of wolves, panthers, and such like— when myriads upon myriads of "galley-nipper" mosquitos commenced their discordant buzzing and stinging—which was kept up until morning. No one slept altho' much fatigued. We moved about sullenly from one place to another, growling imprecations upon our "hellish" visitors. It is said that if one seats himself quietly and no speaking and away from others, that for even an hour the mosquito rushes heedlessly by, but should they hear a noise or see a movement, then commences their gyrations and stinging. In honor of the above I call this *Camp Pandemonium*.

The grant only embraces the E. bank of the Nueces, but if the Government would not allow some parts of the opposite bank to be included, land scrip or head rights could be purchased and located where required. Bottom land rich light colour—away from it on the undulating prairies and lomas, land sterile and covered with pebbles and broken pebbles of silicious material. Sometimes pure quartz—occasionally on the hills—large masses of a silicious rock and soil often coloured red from the degradation of a silicious rock, containing much ox-iron.

We have not seen any mustangs, but we have heard them and

seen their numberless trails and here and there the bones of the wild horse strewed about. Should these lands be covered with any earthy materials, voila! fossil bones. Mr. G. and Hancock went reconnoitering, report favourably of land—met with some heavy thickets—and that we were opposite a long creek that runs into the Nueces. So we are in a straight line some 13 miles from the Laredo Road. Struck the Laredo Road 7 miles from camp and 1½ from River.[10] Pretty open road over a wilderness country and crossing several lomas that go down to the river. Light soil, covered with a silicious pebble. Camped ½ a mile from river on the edge of a large slough—having water from river; good for rice plantation. Saw some few of the maguey plant in flower, about 20 to 25 feet to top of stem. *Camp Maguey.* I am informed that it is nearly open prairie to Laredo (60 miles) and the creeks generally brackish if the country has not had rain.

Sunday, June 16th, 1844: Got no sleep for mosquitos—had breakfast at 3 A.M. and before sunrise off. Country open, much maguey. Five miles came to Sause[11] Creek. Water in holes and brackish—when it rains then the water is pretty good—fine broad valley and good stock range.

Perhaps artesian wells might be sunk at the head of valley which would ensure a continuous stream. Thirteen miles over 6 or 8 ranges of hills. Each valley having water holes owing to late rains and drinkable. Nooned in the Cañada del Guadalupe. Timber here makes its appearance and water holes large and long. To this, good sheep ranges, if one could be assured of protection, particularly against Indians—grass, musquit, and although large quantities of cactus and some thorny brush, sufficient clear land for grazing. After rising the loma E of the Sause, there appears to be a declination to S.E. 17 miles to Rio Frio. Crossing several canadas with water holes, pastures improving and fine for sheep farms, on either side of the road. Found on road chalcedony, silicious

---

10 They were now about twenty-five miles southeast of present Cotulla, Texas.
11 This should be Sauz Creek, an intermittent stream which rises in southeastern La Salle County and flows south fourteen miles into the Nueces River.

pebbles, quartz, and silicified wood, and when within 5 miles of the Rio Frio saw outbursts of the San Antonio limestone. Camped on a pretty bluff a few yards from river. Owing to rains above, the river is swelled.

Monday, June 17th, 1844: We had anticipated mosquitos, but there were none, altho' there are sloughs about us. Fine farms could be made on either side of the River, with fine pastures behind. Thus, a farm only having 500 acres on the river could have thousands of acres back for pasture.

The Nueces about the Laredo road ought to be put farther westward [on Arrowsmith's map].

From the Frio eastward, over 4, 5 and 6 miles there are rivulets and fine pastures. Such a disposition of things is waiting in the colony. Good night's rest—no mosquitos—built raft and crossed river at the ford. It is not general to have to make raft—only during or after heavy rains—plenty cat-fish, but our bacon grease out today and thus we had no fat to fry them in. *Short commons* is commencing its appearance.

When starting, 4 Mexican Peons, who had escaped from prison in Laredo preparatory to their being sent to the army, and going to Bejar, told us that General [Pedro] Ampudia[12] had been killed in Matamoras and the Sub-prefect of Mier and Norias in Zacatecas. One mile on road to San Antonio Mr. James, Dr. C. and Felipe left us for Bejar, we on our way to Corpus Christi— 3 or 4 miles crossed the Leona Creek where our pack mule bogged —had to unlade him—heavy brush to creek, found we could not get to the San Miguel.[13] Camped 1 mile down the Leona Creek; plenty deer, turkey, hares, rabbits.

Tuesday, June 18th, 1844: Headed E through brush, but came

[12] Pedro Ampudia was commander of the Mexican forces stationed at Matamoros at the time of the Mier Expedition. He defeated the Texans at Mier, and in January, 1843, marched them as prisoners to Matamoros. The rumor of his assassination was "highly exaggerated," for he died of natural causes in 1868. *The Handbook of Texas*, I, 42.

[13] San Miguel Creek rises in eastern Frio County and flows southeast until it joins the Frio River in northeastern McMullen County.

down on the Frio, bore up 12 miles straight, cut the San Miguel Creek 3 or 4 miles above junction with Frio—just now running stream, but ceases in dry weather—cotton wood found on its banks. Seven or 8 miles to La Parita [Creek]—horrible road—few bad water holes (Parita de la Piedra[14] is lower down). Nooned; we think we are 2 or 3 miles above the junction of Frio with Nueces[15]—rocky hilly ridges coming down to river. The vallies of San Miguel and La Parita and on banks of Frio good lands. The Frio appears deep and pretty broad and looks as if backed up by the Nueces. This is a wild country indeed, and the only consolation is that we are steering homeward. Nine miles E, or down the river, came to a waterfall in a slough not far from the Nueces. Indian signs seen today at starting. Turkey buzzards hovering and prairies on fire on other side of Nueces. Fell twice upon Indian trail—thought it prudent to slope off from it. Comanche Camp just above us. Apaches called Seraticks by Americans.

Wednesday, June 19th, 1844: Heavy dew at sunrise. 35 miles down Sⁿ Antonio to Calvearo Rancho St. Patricio to Calves ranch 3 days or 70 miles—San Patricio to Goliad 55. From Goliad to Victoria 35 miles. For the last two days unsuccessful with game—dined and supped off a turkey but Mr. G. popped two charges into a young buck at a water hole 8 miles from this morning's camp. Country pretty open—we don't exactly know where we are.[16] Two miles farther after going thro' a tremendous brush and tropical valley, came to a clear running stream—five miles from its junction with Nueces. Fresh meat and cool running water! Allah Kereem!! Chiltipin, or green red pepper, first seen here. Washing day, rather of the *dab* order. Bottoms of Nueces not broad and in them exist "the great nation of thorn thickets—

[14] Piedra Creek is an intermittent stream rising in eastern La Salle County and flowing south sixteen miles into the Nueces River. The Spanish name means "stone."

[15] The party was now near Three Rivers, Texas (Live Oak County), where the Nueces, Frio, and Atascosa rivers come together.

[16] Bollaert and his companions could not have been very far from present George West, Texas, in central Live Oak County.

cactus, palmetto, and some species of plants, *all* thorn—rattle snakes not very numerous but very large. Saw a large black spider said to be worse than rattle snake. (Dr. Wiederman of San Antonio would let a rattle snake bite him, but not this spider— spider *horrenda*—large as a small crab, long black hairy legs.) Ten miles S.E. pretty open country—plenty deer and tame. Came to the Nueces by a slough of great extent and thickly wooded with live oak, elm, cotton wood, musquit and fine pastures. Camped on a picturesque knoll thickly wooded and just here all the trees hung with Spanish moss. River flowing and say 20 to 30 feet deep, if not more. How interesting had we descended the river in a "dugout." As far as I have seen the Nueces and I am informed that it is navigable, say for steamboats, fully 7 or 8 months in the year. The Leona could [be navigable] to its source. Fine lands about here.

We may be 15 or 20 miles from San Patricio.[17] During heavy freshets these woods appear to be under water some feet, but there are "lomas," or ridges of hills, running at right angles to the river that are not, and on which towns might be placed.

Thursday, June 20th, 1844: When watering horse in river this morning an alligator took my mare Fanny Baker's nose for a bait, made for it. Fanny snorted, when the alligator turned a sumerset and made off down stream. Heavy dews—1½ [miles] struck the road from Laredo to Goliad; ½ mile struck a creek with waterholes; brush "pretty mean." Six miles farther struck an old Mexican encampment—for we saw maize growing—probably Ampudia's party when Woll came in. The gullies now are dry. By mustang and Indian trails 7 miles more, nooned. No water—clear country with musquits—timber after timber is seen—gully after

[17] San Patricio is on the north bank of the Nueces River. It was founded in 1830, in southwestern San Patricio County, and served as the headquarters for a small force under James Grant and Francis Johnson during the Goliad campaign. Later, a battle was fought here, in which the Texans were defeated by a Mexican army under José Urrea. Although San Patricio became an important town in the era of the Republic, it began to decline about the time of the Mexican War. Today its population is less than fifty, with only one business house. *The Handbook of Texas*, II, 559.

gully, and no water. This under a blistering sun is no particular joke. Just before we camped saw a fine horse in the prairie—some stray mustang.

This part of the country was famed some 3 or 4 years since for mustangs and wild cattle. They appear to have changed their range, probably on account of being hunted, and dry season having no water. Course up to noon E.S.E. with a moderately open country, traversing lomas, we did not strike the river until 2 hours after sunset, having travelled 18 to 20 miles S.E. Got to river, and what with brush, steepness, and bogginess could not water horses. We assuaged a parching thirst, and then took to our pallets—thankful in having found water. All the country travelled over today had no water—fine pastures and woodlands. Saw a smoke rise up suddenly about S.S.E. of us. Tom Hancock our hunter stopped short, looked graver than usual—"D——n them, they have discovered us—this is a signal for other parties to prepare and meet and send women and children back—Comanches, I 'spose." We bore off a little more S. I do not think it was a Comanche, but a Lipan fire.

Friday, June 21st, 1844: Heavy dew; commenced about 2 A.M., continued until long after sunrise. Tom H[ancock] says that when he was soldiering on this part of river during the war he had chills and fever. Tom Hancock at 8 years of age when going to see his brother who had a stock farm in Illinois was made prisoner by the Winnebagos; these had killed his brother just before and some other white people. Tom remained in captivity 18 months with 2 white girls. He was treated pretty well, and did not get so much whipping as the other Indian boys. Hunting, fishing, and shooting frogs was his great delight. The Indians have prophets and stated times of prayer—they count time by moons. Women do all the work, often get smartly whipped. [The Winnebago] trade at Chicago—[they are] more friendly to British than Americans.

United States dragoon had a fight with them and killed 300 warriors, this brought them to a treaty and they gave up their prisoners.[18] Tom says he "knocked about" with General Leavenworth's men—was *quite wild,* went home and only found his mother—she died in two months. He went to school and had much difficulty to relearn English. He then was apprenticed to a cabinet maker—too hard for him—knocked about in Illinois and Mississippi—came to Texas just after the battle of San Jacinto— was on the expedition under [Antonio] Cañales, fought 3 battles —Mier and Saltillo. Taken by the Comanches whilst out hunting —they brought him to San Antonio—went on Santa Fé expedition, made prisoner, taken to Mexico and worked in that city, until released in June 1842—was taken by General Woll and worked in chains—made two ineffectual escapes—got a bad Mexican consumptive fever—was liberated last spring—but says now that he is "used up" and is only 23. He has [is] small, delicately made, dried up, but has the eye of a hawk. Poor Tom! I'm afraid thy days are numbered—quiet, modest, intelligent, and when he can be brought out, his conversation truthful and interesting.

One mile down river, after making some ineffectual breaks to get to river—found a spot, but very boggy—black alluvial bottom soil. We guess we are about 8 or 10 [miles] from San Patricio. Tom says 40! Large sloughs all about river, so that when it rises these are full and the country even to 6 or 8 miles is boggy. Had to give my mare water in my hat at one place, being too boggy. Alligators and alligator gar of great size. They have been known to bite persons severely when bathing. Few cat-fish—stream thick and running. Four miles. Went fishing, lost 3 hooks owing to branches often under water. Banks pretty precipitous and dense vegetation. Five miles E. Five miles SSE. A thunder storm with rain caught us on the river, but could not break thro' the thicket. Camped under some musquits and no water. The storm has cooled the air and made it agreeable.

Saturday, June 22nd, 1844: Morning fine and cool. For the last

18 The Winnebago chief, Red Bird, led his warriors against the settlement of Prairie du Chien, Wisconsin, in 1827. His forces were soon trapped by two American armies near present Fort Winnebago and surrendered. By 1832, the Winnebago had ceded most of the Wisconsin lands in return for hunting grounds in the Far West. Ray Allen Billington, *Westward Expansion, A History of the American Frontier,* 298–301.

2 or 3 days country more open and fine pastures but away from river want of water, altho' there are sloughs which run inland 8 to 10 miles; still when it rains forms streams, and when the river is high are filled with back water. In the rainy season the whole of the country near the river has the reputation of being boggy.

The best travelling is on the other side of the river and Tom says it is 80 miles from the junction of the Frio and Nueces to San Patricio. Six miles SE came to some back water—2 miles more S. E. struck river at the first open spot we have seen on the river. Range of hills on each side of river with ridges coming down to water. Lomas—between them sloughs or creeks—about here a silicious rock is seen under the thick stratum of soils and bottom land but no retentive sub-soil, thus as soon as rains fall they filter deeply thro' and reach the main rivers—plenty deer—turkies. Great burns on either side of river. Undulating prairie country. Whirlwinds—made 12 miles S. E. along river, camped early owing to Mr. Lowe's and Tom Hancock's horses "giving out." Tom's horse was lent by Hays—old—one eye, etc. Mr. L. a d——d old mustang he bought in Galveston, saddle, and bridle included, for $18. He was told that it would give out and the wonder is that it has lasted so long.

Found here the large mustang grape—not yet ripe—has an orange flavour.

Sunday, June 23rd, 1844: Heavy dews—night cloudy—and cool. Morning hot and no breeze. We are all looking worn out and pretty dirty and long beards. Five miles struck the San Patricio Road to Goliad. One-half a mile from San Patricio one house and it in ruins—the rest down and enclosures falling to pieces—covered with weeds 15 feet high—½ mile to river, which may be 15 to 20 feet deep and 80 to 100 wide. It has been known to almost cease running in parts and General Wavell,[19] late of the Mexican

---

[19] General Arthur Goodall Wavell was born in Scotland in 1785, and became a soldier of fortune. He served at various times in the armies of Spain, Chile, and Mexico. He terminated his services with the Mexican Army in 1833, and made repeated attempts to get a grant of land in Texas, but never succeeded in getting his claim validated by the Texas government. E. C. Barker, "General Arthur

Army, when he crossed there was only 5 inches depth at ford. Alligators and alligator gars jumping about. Found two large planks of cottonwood at the crossing—rigged up a raft and got our traps over. Camped. We have been out of meal for some days —venison, wild turkey, and water. Today as a treat we have a few spoonfulls of rice—hog and hominy. Venison only and water are far from inducing poetry, but as Seneca says: "It may be all for the best." Just after our meal, having eaten all our food, two turkies came within a few yards of us—crack went the rifle—down went the turkies. Thus we have our supper *nil desperandum*. Slight thunder storm with rain. Comanches,[20] when they make

Goodall Wavell and Wavell's Colony in Texas," *Southwestern Historical Quarterly*, Vol. XLVII (1943–44), 253–55.

[20] [The Comanches] attribute an inferior modicum of divinity to the sun, and suppose all febrile diseases to emanate from it. They have no distinction of days or seasons. They believe in witchcraft, attribute diseases to the "blasting breath" of some secret enemy. They hate the Ketchies of the Trinity. When remaining for any time in a place they live in buffalo skin tents; when travelling, or a temporary stay, of boughs of trees. Polygamy to an unlimited extent, no fixed ceremonials of marriage. The principal warriors have from 6 to 8. Carno Santua (the son of Amsua) left 10 widows to lament his death. The squaw is ostler, catching and saddling the horses, butcher, cook, etc., etc. The Comanche hunts, robs, and fights. Some of the squaws use the arrow. Squaws more ferocious than the men. They love to torture male prisoners. "Come to the dance" well known shout or yell when torturing prisoners. In 1818 supposed to capture annually 10,000 horses and mules from the Spaniards—arms are short light guns, lances and Bows and arrows; shields of buffalo hide that will resist a ball sometimes. The Comanches at war always with the Osages and Pawnees. The Comanche has strong attachment to kindred and lament for a long period over their dead. The widowed squaws—themselves with knives or sharp flints. The warrior's property is generally burnt at his death thus to transfer to the heavenly hunting grounds for their use. In 1816 the smallpox raged among them when about 5,000 horses and mules were immolated. Comanche vain of his person when painted and "dandyfied" which he likes much. Squaws do not dress up. They do not cultivate the land and subsist principally on buffalo and deer. Their only real article of domestic furniture is the copper pot they boil their meat in. They eat roast meat. They dry and jerk their meat for winter or for travelling. They have plenty salt from springs and salt resulting from the evaporation from the Upper Brazos. Kind of bread from the pods of the locust tree. Eat Peccan, black, red haws, prickly pear and a few roots from spontaneous fruits.

They sometimes visit the Wacoes (on the Brazos) trafficing in horses, for beans, melons and maize. Few diseases among them. Men of a 100 years still go out hunting buffalo—fine climate—and spiritous liquors have not been introduced among them. Their language consists of some 400 words, many of which are of Spanish and English origin. Destitute of verbo; they are supplied by gestures and grimaces. And to write it correctly would have to undergo many improvements.— Bollaert.

their annual trade and depredation on the Rio Grande, collect salt from the great lakes. There are other smaller salt lakes towards the coast. There are saline springs in the Comanche country as well. Travelled 8 or 9 miles over prairie and camped in musquit timbers—no water and prevented sleeping by mosquitos.

Monday, June 24th, 1844: Off at day break; 8 miles thro' brush and prairie, heading Pintas Creek, which is only a slough. Came upon a lagune (hot water), and then struck the road from lower crossing of Nueces. Caught a young kid asleep—makes us a breakfast. Owing to late rains water here and there on the prairie, bluffs above the bay and good pastures. Deer of Texas peculiar to it—the young kid or fawn spotted like a fallow deer.

The general road from San Patricio to Corpus Christi is to stand out well from river so as to avoid slough and cut the Matamoras Road. Evening, 4 or 5 miles from Corpus Christi. Four miles on road came to an old corral—pretty country—groves of musquit and live and post oak! One more mile to Corpus Christi. Found many old friends—Clay, Davis, Stevenson, Kinney, etc.;[21] kindly received. We have been travelling between "Scylla and Charybdis." On 27th May this place was visited by 25 Lipans[22] to steal horses etc. wounding Colonel Cooke thro' the eye. There were only 8 men at the "Rancho." On 30th ulto the Lipans reappeared and drove off cattle and horses. Thirty went in pursuit, 10 came up and re-captured horses, killed and wounded 5 Indians. Indians pursued, then came a desperate fight, 3 of our party killed, 5 wounded; 20 of Indians killed and wounded.

The Lipans have gone towards San Antonio. Hays has had a brush with the Comanches. Mexico has refused to enter into any treaty about Texas.

Tuesday, June 25th, 1844: This place Corpus Christi—3 leagues of it was purchased from a Mexican in 1839 by Colonel Kinney

---

[21] This was Henry Lawrence Kinney, who built a fort and trading post near the site of present Corpus Christi in 1840. (See footnote 20, Chapter III.)

[22] Some say they were Comanches.—Bollaert.

who commenced trading with the Mexican frontier, or rather supplying traders (smugglers) from there. Continual have been the vicissitudes of this place from both Mexicans and Indians, even up to the present moment. At present there are some 30 or 40 fighting men, a few cannon, and Colonel Kinney's house fortified. It is supplied with water from a spring, the course of which is dammed up, a presa, or reservoir, and Colonel K.'s plantation makes a good shew in Indian corn, pumpkins, melons, sweet potatoes, beans, tomatoes, chiltipins and sea-island cotton. Tobacco and sugar will grow well. Generally speaking there is a want of streams, but in the vallies or gullies of the lomas are springs, which can be dammed up and in the vicinity of these gullies good crops can be obtained.

A town in embryo called "Grayson"[23] 1 mile N.W. was laid off on paper only, Corpus Christi being the only settlement. There are some half dozen American stores, including a German, and a grog shop or two. All appear to be on good terms and friendly with each other.

The revenue cutter "Santana," Captain Simpton, arrived at pass and brought down in the Picayune Mr. Klaener, Bremen Consul, Merriman, Rosgood, Saner, Jones, Menter, etc. Some on business, some on pleasure, not forgetting some of the 200 joyful ————.

Wednesday, June 26th, 1844: Even now when the Nueces has a deep stream, the pass has only 2 feet water, and at times quite dry, particularly after northers. Colonel K[inney] thinks it would not be difficult to widen the channel, but even then the mouth is very extended. Good Fandango and supper at "Uncle Bob's." News arrived late at night of 2 more fights about 10 days since, 40 miles from San Antonio on the Pinta[24] between a party Co-

[23] The town of Grayson never developed beyond the "paper stage."
[24] Pinto Creek is in Kinney County. It is also known as Piedra Pinto Creek, and is an intermittent stream rising northwest of the Pinto Mountain and flowing southwest to the Río Grande. Bollaert's information is not correct; he doubtless is referring to the fight which Hays had with a band of Comanches under Yellow Wolf on June 8, 1844, on the Pinto Trace between San Antonio and Gonzales. The chief was killed by Ranger Richard A. Gillespie, and not Hays, as reported. James Kimmins Greer, *Colonel Jack Hays,* 105–107.

manche of 70 to 80 warriors and Hays and his men. He had one killed, 3 w[ounded], the enemy 20 or 30 killed and many wounded. The Chief, seeing Hays, asked him to come and have a talk. H. went out; when the Indian tried to spear him, H——shot him.

Thursday, June 27th, 1844: From parties who are coming in, they report much Indian signs all about. At Kinney's fort and other spots looking well to their arms. Hays came accidentally upon his Comanches and they finding one of his men alone, Peter Foyer, a Frenchman, killed him.

Friday, June 28th, 1844: Afternoon left Corpus Christi—weather threatening and wind ahead. Made little of it, had to come to anchor, blow and gale and rain all night. We got all wet.

Saturday, 29th, 1844: At day break found we were only a few miles from Corpus Christi; bore up for it to dry our clothes, etc. Noon, left and at sun down came along side the *Alert*, late *Santana*, inside Aransas Pass and opposite the houses. Lost my blanket over board—high tides—island and reefs made up of shells.

Sunday, June 30th, 1844: Twelve miles to McGloin's[25]—13 miles to inside of pass 25 miles and 5 miles to the bar. Took on beef and vegetables.

Monday, July 1st, 1844: Day light got under weigh and about 8 A. M. got over bar in 8 and 8½ feet (high tide) bar at low water, 6 feet. This is not an easy entrance; it is changeable. Cheyne, a pilot, lives inside the pass, SW side of St. Joseph's Island. Shoals of red fish and other larger—pursuing ship jack, mullet, and others small, these in their flight take to shallow water and are pursued

---

[25] This was James McGloin, one of the founders of the town of San Patricio (1830), and a prominent landholder and empresario. With James McMullen, McGloin contracted to colonize an area along the Nueces River near its mouth, and helped many new Irish immigrants get a start in the area. "Translations of Empresario Grants," (MS., General Land Office, Austin, Texas).

by myriads of pelicans and man-of-war birds, who, perceiving their flight, easily catch them. Large shoals of shells and when covered with sand, form islands. Bars change annually—particularly after heavy rains and storms. 5 P.M., off P. Caballo.

Tuesday, July 2nd, 1844: Daylight off the Brazos and then to Galveston—regularly worn out and nearly dead—

So ended William Bollaert's tour of frontier Texas. In a box of loose-leaf paper, deposited with his journal and notes, scattered entries of a diary kept by Bollaert until 1849 are found. The diary is incomplete; some of it is written in Spanish. Bollaert left Galveston on the Texas barge, John Barnes, *early Wednesday morning, July 10, 1844. He arrived at London docks in the afternoon of September 15, 1844, a sea voyage of sixty-two days.*

APPENDIX I

Colonization Contract Between the Republic of
Texas and William Pringle, James Grieve, and Associates

[*November 1, 1843*][1]

WHEREAS, by the fourth section of an act of Congress passed the fourth day of February, A.D., eighteen hundred and forty-one, entitled "An act granting land to Emigrants." The President of the Republic of Texas is authorized to contract with certain persons therein named for the purpose of colonizing and settling a portion of the vacant and unappropriated lands of the Republic.

And whereas, by another act of Congress passed the fifth day of February, A.D., eighteen hundred and forty two, entitled "An act amendatory of an act granting land to Emigrants," approved February fourth, one thousand eight hundred and forty one, the provisions of the act first above recited, so far as relate to the authority thereby given to the President to enter into a Contract with W. S. Peters and others named in said act, to introduce Colonists upon certain terms therein expressed and set forth, are extended to such other company or companies as may be formed and organized, for like purposes, as the President may in his judgment approve.

Now, therefore, this contract and agreement, made this first day of November, A.D., one thousand eight hundred and forty three, at the town of Washington, between Sam Houston, President of the Republic of Texas, on the part of said Republic, of the first part, and William Pringle, James Grieve, and their associates, of the second part— Witness:

That for and in consideration of the grants and privileges, rights and immunities hereinafter mentioned, the said parties of the second part, contract and agree to introduce, or cause to be introduced, a Colony of six hundred families, or single men over seventeen years of age, within three years from the date of this contract, and to have

[1] Except for the omission of the name William Kennedy, this contract is almost identical with the original one made between the Republic of Texas and Kennedy in February, 1842. "Colonization Papers," *Executive Record Book No. 48* (Texas State Archives).

the same settled within the limits of the tracts of land, hereinafter specified and set apart for said parties, of the second part, all of which said families, or single men, are to be free white inhabitants of a foreign country, and to reside within said limits.

In consideration whereof the said party, of the first part, hereby designates, assigns and sets apart, for the said parties, of the second part, and for the settlement of the said Colony, the three following described tracts of land, that is to say—tract No. 1. Commencing at a point where the upper Presidio Rio Grande road crosses the river Nueces, and extending thence in a direct line to the head spring of the river Leona, including the said spring, thence in a direct line to the point of confluence of the Aroyo de Uvalde with the Rio Frio, thence down the main branch of the Rio Frio to the crossing of the road from San Antonio to Laredo, thence along the line of said road to the river Nueces, thence along the east bank of the said River to the point of beginning.

Tract No. 2. Consisting of one fourth part of a tract twenty miles in breadth on the east bank of the Rio Grande, commencing on the Rio Grande five miles below the crossing of the road from the salt lakes of San Patricio County to Comargo, and stretching upward along the left bank of the Rio Grande to a point ten miles above the Dolores Ferry, which tract is to be divided into four equal parts, each fronting on the Rio Grande, which are to be numbered 1, 2, 3, and 4, the numbers commencing at the lowest point on the Rio Grande; the portions now set apart and designated as tract No. 2 to William Pringle, James Grieve, and their associates is the part No. 2 of the above division.

Tract No. 3. Now set apart to William Pringle, James Grieve, and their associates, is part No. 4 of said division.

And the said party of the first part, further contracts and agrees, in behalf of the Government of Texas, to give and to grant to each family so introduced by the said parties of the second part, who shall reside within the said described limits, six hundred and forty acres of land, to be located in a square as nearly as possible, within said limits, and to each single man over the age of seventeen years so introduced, three hundred and twenty acres of land, each of which said grantees shall be entitled to receive from the Government of Texas a full and absolute title to the same, whenever they shall have built a good and comfortable cabin upon it, and shall keep in cultivation and under good fence, at least fifteen acres on the tract for which they are to receive title.

And the said party of the first part, further contracts and agrees to allow the said parties, of the second part, as a compensation for their services, and in recompense of their labor and expense, attendant on the introduction and settlement of the families introduced by them, a premium of ten (10) sections of land for every hundred families, and in the same ratio of half sections for every hundred single men, so introduced and settled, but no fractional number less than one hundred will be allowed any premium, which said premium lands must be selected from the vacant lands within the limits of the tracts of lands above deisgnated and set apart for the settlement of the said Colonists.

And the said party of the first part, further contracts and agrees, in behalf of the Government of Texas, to give and grant to each settlement of one hundred families made under the provisions of the before recited acts, in conformity with the conditions of this contract, one section of six hundred and forty acres of land, each of which said sections shall be located as near the centre of the settlement, receiving the same, as may be practicable and shall be used by the said settlements to aid and assist them in the erection of buildings for religious public worship.

And it is hereby mutually agreed by the parties to this contract that all legal locations that may have already been made within the boundaries, so designated, or that may hereafter be made and surveyed, previous to the first day of February next, shall be respected and any locations or surveys made by the said parties of the second part, or their emigrants, on such locations, shall be null and void.

And it is further agreed between the said parties to this contract that all lands lying within the limits of the tracts which have been designated and set aside for the said parties, of the second part, which shall not be appropriated, according to the terms of this contract, to the emigrants or for premium or church lands, shall, after the expiration of three years, revert to and remain the sole property of the Government of Texas as a part of the public domain.

And it is further agreed between the parties of this Contract that unless the parties, of the second part, shall have introduced two hundred families, that is to say, one third of the whole number of families, which they have contracted to introduce within the limits of the Republic, before the expiration of one year from the date of this contract, then the said parties, of the second part, shall forfeit all the lands and immunities, rights, and privileges, of whatsoever kind, name and nature, that they may have previously acquired, by virtue of this contract, but no forfeiture, on the part of the parties, of the second part, shall in any manner prejudice the rights of such families and single persons as they may introduce who shall be entitled to their respective quotas of land in the same manner as if the said parties of the second part, had completed their contract.

And it is further agreed between the parties to this Contract that the following shall be the definition of the word "family," as it is used in this instrument, namely, first, a man and his wife; second, a widower and two or more children, if males, under the age of seventeen years, if females unmarried, third, a widow the same as a widower, either of which three classes shall be considered as constituting a family in the construction of this contract.

And it is further agreed between the parties to this contract that the said parties, of the second part, shall not be permitted to introduce any emigrant who has been guilty of any atrocious crime, or is of bad moral character, nor shall they, nor any of the families or persons, introduced by them, be permitted to sell or give any spirituous or intoxicating liquors to any Indian or Indians, nor shall they furnish them in any manner with powder, lead, fire arms, or with any kind of warlike weapons, upon pain of forfeiting, upon conviction thereof, all the lands they may have acquired, by virtue of this contract.

And it is further mutually agreed between the said parties that the parties, of the second part, shall be found to have designated and surveyed all the lands required for the settlement of the families they are authorized to introduce, by virtue of this contract, also for premium and church lands within two years from the date of this contract, after which it shall be permitted to any citizen of the country to locate and settle upon any lands which may remain unappropriated within the limits of the tracts designated and set aside for said parties, of the second part.

And it is also understood and agreed upon between the parties of this contract that each alternate section of land in the tracts Nos. two (2) and three (3) on the Rio Grande except for the premium and church lands shall be reserved and forever set apart for the use and benefit of the Republic of Texas.

And it is also understood and agreed upon that the said parties, of

383

the second part, will have the privilege to introduce and settle upon the lands, herein designated, an additional number of four hundred families, or single men over seventeen years of age, provided the said parties of the second part, shall within one year from the date of this Contract, give to the party of the first part a written notice of an intention so to do, which additional numbers shall be introduced and settled agreeably to the terms of this Contract, as provided for the six hundred families, or single men over seventeen years of age, herein above specified.

And whereas, by the thirteenth section of an act entitled "an act granting land to emigrants" passed on the fourth day of February A.D.: one thousand eight hundred and forty one, power is given to the President to extend the time for the introduction of the first one third of the whole number of families, or single persons, over the age of seventeen years and whereas, the emigrants to be introduced and settled, under this contract, are to be brought from Europe.

Therefore, the party of the first part, agrees to extend the term for the time of six months over and above the time of one year, above specified, to the parties, of the second part, for the introduction of the said families or single persons.

And it is further agreed between the said parties of this contract that if it shall be found to conflict with any of the acts aforesaid, it shall so far be considered null and void; and the said acts shall govern the construction to be placed upon it, but this shall not be considered as extending to, or affecting, any other part of this contract that may be consistent with said acts, which shall be and remain in full force.

> In testimony whereof
> we have hereunto set our
> hands and affixed our seals
> at the Town of Washington,
> this first day of November,
> in the year of our Lord one
> thousand eight hundred and
> forty three

(signed) SAM HOUSTON
(signed) *For* WILLIAM PRINGLE
JAMES GRIEVE
WILLIAM KENT [?]

APPENDIX II

Decr. 1846

Notes for a Life of Wm Kennedy

BY W. BOLLAERT

Wm Kennedy has three brothers, Hugh, partner with Mr. Oliver, chemist & druggist in Chartres St., New Orleans, (1846—now on his own acc^t.), James, a surgeon residing in London, Samuel, brought up under James, who went to New Orleans as a Medical man, but owing to a "difficulty" (of rather a serious nature was indicted for wilful murder & declared guilty—he appealed and was then acquitted (he was allowed to escape from Prison), left the United States, returning to England—and this day, Sunday 27 Decr 1846 preparing to sail in the "Leonidar" to India there to establish himself)—(went to India & China, returned home, & in 1849 took charge of an Emigrant ship to Australia—died in Sydney)—Susan, who married a year or two ago a chemist & Druggist in Paris (a Frenchman).

The father of these was a manufacturer of considerable standing having concerns at Paisley, Glasgow, Belfast &c. William was educated at Belfast & in his early days showed considerable symptoms of mental power—learning with great rapidity & positively understanding *all* that he attempted to learn. Sheridan Knowles was one of his teachers. We next find him studying at Glasgow & entered for the Kirk, but having preached his obligatory sermon decided much to the grief of an aunt that "divinity" was not his vocation. His knowledge of the dead languages, Classics & Mathematics was great the latter prompting him subsequently to study the Art of War in actual service in Germany.

Not long after leaving College an Uncle who resided in Tyrone died leaving to William the greater part of his fortune—a patrimony of some extent—a small town in the bargain.

Young & inexperienced & of a too jovial disposition for a time the "patrimony" administered bountifully to his hospitable habits & all those in that part of the country looked upon him as their Chief—and had it have been his wish, none they would have liked better to have led them in case of a "difficulty," such things being not uncommon in Ireland & continues so.

385

His Treasury was decreasing, but ere it was too low he made provision for the education of his Brothers & Sister & he has to be proud of the commercial position of Hugh & medical fame in particular of his brother James.

His classic reading led his mind to ponder upon the past & coming events in the Eastern world & his Ambition was now turned to perfecting himself in the military art in Europe so that he might arrive on eastern ground a practical as well as a theoretical soldier. For this object he collected together such part of his fortune he then could & taking with him a humble servitor & companion, proceeded to Paris in 1823, requesting permission to enter the French army under the Duke of Angouleme, then on the eve of going to Spain to assist Ferdinand the 7th to put down Liberalism. He did not succeed in this for some reason or other was not permitted to join the French Army. After passing some time in Paris & becoming acquainted with its wonders—& his funds getting low—his servitor left him, when he left France for Germany, making himself acquainted with the inmates of the various universities.

Returning to England to look after his remaining property & being at Glasgow he accidentally met with his old teacher and friend Sheridan Knowles, who was then delivering a Course of Lectures on Elocution in that City. Knowles discovering that his favourite pupil wanted occupation, suggested to him the idea of succeeding him in a Course of Lectures on Elocution, for which Knowles knew he was well fitted; but Kennedy had misgivings of his own abilities, but Knowles got the better of "his modest worth" and induced him to do so, which he did in the Glasgow Theatre—his lectures were crowded, many of his auditors were his old college mates who hailed "Will Kennedy's" re-advent amongst them with joyous acclamation. An advertisement now appeared for an Editor for the Paisley Advertiser, *a Tory paper*—there were more than 200 applicants, he was amongst them & was the fortunate one (he remained several years connected with the Paisley Advertiser and out of about £250 or £300 per an: shared largely in the maintenance of his Brothers & Sister). It was now independently of his editorial occupations which gave great strength to his party, he devoted his talent to literature, coquetting with the Muses, & prepared material for the publication "The Arrow of Rose," "Fitful fancies," "My Early days" and another small work and numberless Songs, Sonnets, and other literary contributions—studying in particular the scientific development of the drama—much did he write & unfortunately destroyed—one play & a beautiful one it is—the "Siege of Antwerp" which was performed at Hull in 1841?—

Wishing for change of scene & in the hope of bettering his fortune he came to London engaging with Mr. Alexander on his Morning Journal in the publication of the St. James Chronicle, writing for other papers at the same time contributing gems of prose & poetry to the Albums then so much in fashion—particularly the Continental Album. For a period he was one of the parliamentary reporters for the "Times" and was sent by that journal to Bristol during the riots there when Sir C. Wetherell was Recorder—the ability he displayed in his advices from there may be seen in that paper of that period, & even to this day he retains the consideration of persons connected with that monster of mutter. He had again a wish to go to the East—which was not gratified & we soon find him as Editor at Hull of the Hull Advertiser—he became Sheriff—conducting it with Reform principles—his abilities made this a journal of some consequence to the government & his efforts were noticed by the late Lord Durham, who on being appointed to the Governorship of Canada, took him out with him to that country, appointing him with Chas. Buller as Municipal Commissioners—Vide their report to the Government—Lord Durham having been played false with by the people at home very soon after his arrival in Canada—threw up his command in disgust—returned to England but soon after died, which death was undoubtedly accelerated by a policy to which his heart was a stranger to—he was a victim—On Durham leaving Canada, Kennedy did so too, but ere he left the New World, journied thro the United States, saw his brother Hugh at New Orleans and then went to Texas the history of which country had been for years interesting to him, more particularly the last campaign of G¹ Houston which terminated in 1836 by his overthrow of Mexican power in Texas. (Vide Introduction to his His: of Texas.)

He promised La Mar the President and the Texans to write for the information of Europe—a history of Texas and he nobly performed his promise—the writer of these notes has travelled far and wide over that country and never opened Kennedy's Texas with[out] learning something new and remaining his debtor for the perusal of such beautifully written pages, one seldom sees.

On the appearance of this work Capt Houston late of the Guards, solicited him to go to Texas & purchase land for him there, this he accepted, but on his arrival & examining minutely into affairs deemed it not judicious at the period to do so. He went to Austin, during the presidency of Sam Houston, who conferred on him the honor of Consul General from the Republic to Great Britain, at the same time putting at his disposal more than 5 millions of acres of land West of San Antonio, under a colonising agreement, hoping that he would be able to induce emigration from Europe.

He returned to England, and particularly at the request of President Houston was nominated to the post of British Consul at Galveston[1]—Capt. Elliot to that of Consul General. (On his return from Canada he married Marianne Bettison a daughter of one of the proprietors of the "Hull Advertiser.")

Kennedy soon saw that the question of annexation was getting ripe and even outstepped, if that term can be used, his province of Consul —in his anxiety to inform his Gov[t] of the true state of affairs & the coquetting of Sam Houston—Texas became annexed—Elliot now chargé d'affaires left & was promoted to Govr of Bermuda. Kennedy had several attacks of severe illness, in part brought on by his anxiety at the state of affairs and an indifferent climate in the Autumn of the year at Galveston—(I have no doubt that he was a little dissipated in his life—Drink! Drink! Drink!!) when he took advantage of leave of absence & is now in England (Dec[r] 1846) searching for health—

Refer to Sam Kennedy (& Hugh & James)

Mr. Pringle—who has—the best collection principally of M.S.
Mr. McManus—formerly in the
Polus [?] of Hull
Sheridan Knowles
De Haber
Mrs. Kennedy

---

[1] Bollaert related in later life that, at Kennedy's request, he had acquired information for the British Admiralty on the coasts of Texas. In 1844 the Hydrographic Office of the Admiralty published a map, *The Coast of Texas, from documents furnished by* W. H. Kennedy, Esq., HM Consul at Galveston. In the copy in The Newberry Library the handwritten words, "W[m]. Bollaert, F.R.G.S. to" have been inserted after "furnished by," and after "Galveston" has been added, also in handwriting, "who forwarded them to the Admiralty. Presented by Admiral Beaufort to W[m]. Bollaert, 1850." Admiral Sir Francis Beaufort was hydrographer to the navy.

Appendix II

Mr. Bettison
Mr. Collins—Editor of Hull Advertiser
"Hull Advertiser"

1849—June—Since Kennedy's return he has principally resided at Glasgow, and I am sorry to know what Mr. Pringle tells me, that for some time the poor man has been *under care* in Glasgow, and that his mind is very disturbed. His wife has returned to Hull and it appears that the Foreign Office does not continue his salary. This is serious, and although he will improve I doubt whether he can ever recover.

It cannot be denied that Kennedy is a man of genius and that of a high order, if his life had been of a regulated character, his facility of composition would not have needed the drudging perseverance that a literary life entails on an author. His discriminating powers were of a high order, & he easily separated the grains from the chaff. Through life he appears to have been very proud & ambitious—but genius must bend somewhat to the ordinary rules of action, otherwise in most cases the results are of a melancholy nature. Wm Bollaert. 1851 (July 1) W.K. I hear is still under restraint in Paris where he has a sister married.

BIBLIOGRAPHY

Manuscripts and Documents

Alexander, John R., Account of the Mier Expedition. Archives Collection, University of Texas Library.

Bollaert, William. Cherokee Memos: to publish for an article on the Cherokees, 1843 (20 pp. Various sizes. Manuscripts and clippings). This manuscript and the following ten are in the Edward E. Ayer Collection of The Newberry Library.

——. Diary, April 20–July 2, 1844. (150 pp. 14.3 cm.)

——. Miscellaneous Notes Concerning Texas. (16 pp. Various sizes.)

——. Notes and View of Galveston Island. (33 pp. Various sizes.)

——. Notes and Memoranda, January 24, 1837–March 31, 1838. (199 pp. 20.1 cm.)

——. Notes for a life of William Kennedy. (9 pp. 31.5 cm.)

——. [Notes on Texas, 1843–1844.] From Galveston to Columbus–Austin and Journey to San Antonio. (224 pp. Various sizes.)

——. Personal Narrative of a Residence & Travels in the Republic of Texas by W. B. During the years 1840–2 & 3–4. (237 pp. Various sizes, some clippings and sketches.)

——. Private Journals, 1831–49. (349 pp. Various sizes.)

——. "Texas in 1842—by a Traveller." (37 pp. 24.7 cm.)

——. Texas Sketches. (38 pencil drawings and charts. Various sizes.)

Bejar Archives. Archives Collection, University of Texas Library.

Brown, Frank. Annals of Travis County and the City of Austin. Archives Collection, University of Texas Library.

Colonization Papers. Executive Record Book No. 48. Texas State Archives.

Davenport, Herbert. Notes from an Unfinished Study and Fannin and His Men. Archives Collection, University of Texas Library.

Diplomatic Correspondence of the Republic of Texas. Texas State Archives.

Department of State Records of the Republic of Texas. Texas State Archives.

Executive Letter Book No. 40. Texas State Archives.

General Land Office Records. Austin, Texas.

390

Bibliography

Index to Navy Muster Roll. Texas State Archives.
James Morgan Papers. Rosenberg Library, Galveston, Texas.
Kemp, J. L., San Jacinto Roll. Texas State Archives.
Montgomery County Scrapbook. University of Texas Archives.
Peters Colony File. Texas State Archives.
Scrapbook of Colorado County. University of Texas Archives.
S. M. Williams Papers. Rosenberg Library, Galveston, Texas.
Texas Colonization Papers. Texas State Library.
Translations of Empresario Grants. General Land Office, Austin Texas.

Unpublished Theses
(University of Texas Library)

Fincher, Rosalie. "History of Liberty County" (M. A. thesis, University of Texas, 1933).
Frantz, Joe B. "The Newspapers of the Republic of Texas" (M. A. thesis, University of Texas, 1940).
Leach, James H. "The Life of Reuben Marmaduke Potter" (M. A. thesis, University of Texas, 1939).
Morris, Elizabeth Yates, "James Pinckney Henderson" (M. A. thesis, University of Texas, 1931).
Rosson, Opal. "The Life of Andrew Janeway Yates" (M.A. thesis, University of Texas, 1939).

Newspapers
(All newspapers listed were published in Texas and are on file in the University of Texas Library)

Austin *City Gazette*, 1839–42.
Austin *Texas State Gazette*, 1849.
Austin *Western Advocate*, 1843.
Civilian and Galveston Gazette, 1842–45. (Variant title: *Civilian and Galveston City Gazette*.)
Galveston *Texas Times*, 1842–43.
Houston *Morning Star*, 1839–46.
Houston *Telegraph and Texas Register*, 1837–46.
Washington *National Vindicator*, 1843–44.
Washington *Texian and Brazos Farmer*, 1842–43.

Books

Adams, Ephraim Douglass, ed. *British Diplomatic Correspondence Concerning the Republic of Texas, 1838–1846*. Austin, 1917.

Bancroft, Hubert Howe. *History of Mexico*. 6 vols. San Francisco, 1883–88.

———. *History of the North Mexican States and Texas*. 2 vols. San Francisco, 1884–89.

Bell, Thomas W. *A Narrative of the Capture and Subsequent Suffering of the Mier Prisoners in Mexico*. N.p., 1845.

Bemis, Samuel Flagg, *A Diplomatic History of the United States*. New York, 1950.

Biesele, Rudolph L. *The History of the German Settlements in Texas, 1831–1861*. Austin, 1930.

Billington, Ray A. *Westward Expansion, A History of the American Frontier*. New York, 1949.

Biographical Directory of the American Congress, 1774–1927. Washington, 1928.

Biographical Directory of Texas Conventions and Congresses, 1832–1845. Huntsville, Texas, 1942.

Bolton, Herbert Eugene. *Texas in the Middle Eighteenth Century*. Berkeley, 1915.

Christian, Asa Kyrus. *Mirabeau Buonaparte Lamar*. Austin, 1922.

Clark, Joseph L. *A History of Texas, Land of Promise*. New York, 1939.

Dixon, Samuel H., and Kemp, Louis W. *The Heroes of San Jacinto*. Houston, 1932.

Dobie, J. Frank. *The Mustangs*. Boston, 1952.

Falconer, Thomas. *Letters and Notes on the Texan Santa Fé Expedition, 1841–1842*. F. W. Hodge, ed. New York, 1930.

First Biennial Report of the Texas Library and Historical Commission, March 29, 1909, to August 31, 1910. Austin, 1911.

Frantz, Joe B. *Gail Borden: Dairyman to a Nation*. Norman, 1951.

French, James S. *Elkswatawa; or, the Prophet of the West*. 2 vols. New York, 1836.

Friend, Llerena B. *Sam Houston, The Great Designer*. Austin, 1954.

Gambrell, Herbert. *Anson Jones, the Last President of Texas*. Garden City, 1948.

Garrison, George P., ed. *Diplomatic Correspondence of the Republic of Texas*. 3 vols. Washington, 1908–11.

Green, Thomas Jefferson. *Journal of the Texian Expedition against Mier*. Austin, 1935.

Greer, James Kimmins. *Colonel Jack Hays; Texas Frontier Leader and California Builder*. New York, 1952.

Gregg, Josiah. *Commerce of the Prairies*. Max L. Moorhead, ed. Norman, 1954.

Hill, Jim Dan. *The Texas Navy in Forgotten Battles and Shirtsleeve Diplomacy*. Chicago, 1937.

Hodge, Frederick Webb, ed. *Handbook of American Indians North of Mexico*. 2 vols. Washington, 1907, 1912.

Hogan, William Ransom. *The Texas Republic: A Social and Economic History*. Norman, 1946.

Holley, Mary Austin. *Letters of an Early American Traveller, Mary Austin Holley: Her Life and Her Works, 1786–1846*. Mattie Austin Hatcher, ed. Dallas, 1933.

———. *Texas, Observations, Historical, Geographical, and Descriptive, in a Series of Letters Written during a Visit to Austin's Colony, with a View of a Permanent Settlement in That Country in the Autumn of 1831*. Baltimore, 1833.

Houston, Sam. *Autobiography*. Donald Day and Harry H. Ullom, eds. Norman, 1954.

———. *The Writings of Sam Houston*. Amelia W. Williams and Eugene C. Barker, eds. 8 vols. Austin, 1938–43.

Johnson, Francis White. *A History of Texas and Texans*. Eugene C. Barker and Ernest W. Winkler, eds. 5 vols. New York, 1914.

Jones, Anson. *Memoranda and Official Correspondence Relating to the Republic of Texas, its History and Annexation, Including a Brief Autobiography of the Author*. New York, 1859.

Kemp, Louis Wiltz. *The Signers of the Texas Declaration of Independence*. Houston, 1944.

Kendall, George Wilkins. *Narrative of the Texan Santa Fé Expedition*. 2 vols. New York, 1844.

Kennedy, William. *Texas: The Rise, Progress, and Prospects of the Republic of Texas*. 2 vols. London, 1841.

Lamar, Mirabeau Buonaparte. *Papers. . . .* Charles Adams Gulick, Jr., and Harriet Smither, eds. 6 vols. Austin, 1920–28.

Maillard, Nicholas Doran P. *The History of the Republic of Texas*. London, 1842.

Nixon, Patrick Ireland. *A Century of Medicine in San Antonio.* San Antonio, 1936.

——. *The Medical History of Early Texas, 1528–1853.* Lancaster, Pennsylvania, 1946.

Pike, Zebulon M. *The expeditions of . . . to the headwaters of the Mississippi River.* Elliott Coues, ed. 3 vols. New York, 1895.

Power, Tyrone. *Impressions of America, 1833–1835.* 2 vols. Philadelphia, 1836.

Richardson, Rupert Norval. *The Comanche Barrier to South Plains Settlement.* Glendale, 1933.

Rogers, John William. *The Lusty Texans of Dallas.* New York, 1951.

Schmitz, Joseph William. *Texan Statecraft, 1836–1845.* San Antonio, 1941.

Sheridan, Francis C. *Galveston Island; or a few Months off the Coast of Texas: The Journal of Francis C. Sheridan, 1839–1840.* Willis W. Pratt, ed. Austin, 1954.

Smith, Justin H. *The Annexation of Texas.* New York, 1941.

Thrall, Homer S. *A Pictorial History of Texas.* St. Louis, 1879.

Wade, Houston. *The Dawson Men of Fayette County.* Houston, 1932.

Warren, Harris Gaylord. *The Sword Was Their Passport: A History of American Filibustering in the Mexican Revolution.* Baton Rouge, 1943.

Webb, Walter Prescott. *The Texas Rangers.* Boston, 1935.

——, and others, eds. *The Handbook of Texas.* 2 vols. Austin, 1952.

Wooten, Dudley G., ed. *A Comprehensive History of Texas, 1685–1897.* 2 vols. Dallas, 1898.

Wortham, Louis J. *A History of Texas, from Wilderness to Commonwealth.* 5 vols. Fort Worth, 1924.

Yoakum, Henderson K. *History of Texas, from Its First Settlement in 1685 to Its Annexation to the United States in 1846.* 2 vols. New York, 1855.

Articles

Adams, Ephraim Douglass, ed. "British Correspondence Concerning Texas," *Quarterly of Texas State Historical Association,* Vol. XV (1912), and *Southwestern Historical Quarterly,* Vols. XVI–XXI (1912–17).

Barker, E. C. "General Arthur Goodall Wavell and Wavell's Colony in Texas," *Southwestern Historical Quarterly*, Vol. XLVII (1943–44), 253–55.

Binkley, W. C. "The Last Stage of Texas Military Operations Against Mexico, 1843," *Southwestern Historical Quarterly*, Vol. XXII (1918–19), 260–71.

Bollaert, William. "Arrival in Texas in 1842, and Cruise of the Lafitte," *Colburn's United Service Magazine* (November, 1846), 341–55.

———. "Blackbeard's Island or, the Fatal Retreat," *Colburn's United Service Magazine* (November, 1847), 449–52.

———. "History of Texas. By a Traveller. Part I," *Colburn's United Service Magazine* (January, 1847), 70–80.

———. "History of Texas. By a Traveller. Part II," *Colburn's United Service Magazine* (April, 1847), 516–27.

———. "Life of Jean Lafitte, the Pirate of the Mexican Gulf," *Littell's Living Age*, Vol. XXXII (1852), 433–46. (Also in *Colburn's United Service Magazine*, October and November, 1851.)

———. "Notes on the Coast Region of Texas Territory," *Journal of the Royal Geographical Society of London*, Vol. XIII (1840) 226–44.

———. "Observations on the Geography of Texas," *Journal of the Royal Geographical Society of London*, Vol. XX (1851), 113–35.

———. "A Visitor in Texas," *Chamber's Edinburgh Journal*, n.s. (May, 1853), 331–32.

Brown, Alma H. "Consular Service of the Republic of Texas," *Southwestern Historical Quarterly*, Vol. XXXIII (1929–30), 299–314.

Buckley, E. C. "The Aguayo Expedition into Texas and Louisiana, 1719–1722," *Quarterly of the Texas State Historical Association*, Vol. XV (1911–12), 1–65.

Bugbee, Lester G. "The Old Three Hundred," *Quarterly of the Texas State Historical Association*, Vol. I (1897–98), 108–17.

Bulletin of the Antivenom Institute of America, Vol. IV (1930), 72.

Dabbs, J. A. "Additional Notes on the Champ d'Asile," *Southwestern Historical Quarterly*, Vol. LIV (1950–51), 347–58.

Dunn, W. E. "The Founding of Nuestra Señora del Refugio, the Last Spanish Mission in Texas," *Southwestern Historical Quarterly*, Vol. XXV (1921–22), 174–84.

Erath, George Bernard. "Memoirs of Major George Bernard Erath," Lucy A. Erath, ed., *Southwestern Historical Quarterly*, Vol. XXVII (1923–24), 27–51.

Eve, Joseph. "A Letter Book of Joseph Eve, United States Chargé d'Affaires to Texas," Joseph Milton Nance, ed., *Southwestern Historical Quarterly*, Vol. XLIII (1939–40), 365–77.

Fisher, Rebecca J. Gilleland. "Capture and Rescue of Mrs. Rebecca J. Fisher, née Gilleland," *Quarterly of the Texas State Historical Association*, Vol. III (1899–1900), 209–13.

Hackett, C. W. "The Marquis of San Miguel de Aguayo and His Recovery of Texas from the French, 1719–1723," *Southwestern Historical Quarterly*, Vol. XLIX (1945–46), 193–214.

Hendricks, S. B. "The Somervell Expedition down the Río Grande, 1842," *Southwestern Historical Quarterly*, Vol. XXIII (1919–20), 112–40.

McClintock, William A. "Journal of a Trip through Texas and Northern Mexico in 1846–1847," *Southwestern Historical Quarterly*, Vol. XXXIV (1930–31), 231–56.

Muckleroy, Anna. "Indian Policy of the Republic of Texas," *Southwestern Historical Quarterly*, Vol. XXVI (1922–23), 184–206.

Sinks, Julia Lee. "Rutersville College," *Quarterly of the Texas State Historical Association*, Vol. II (1898–99), 124–33.

Smither, Harriet. "The Alabama Indians of Texas," *Southwestern Historical Quarterly*, Vol. XXXVI (1932–33), 83–108.

Spell, Lota M. "Samuel Bangs: The First Printer in Texas," *Southwestern Historical Quarterly*, Vol. XXXV (1931–32), 267–78.

Spellman, L. U. "Letters of the 'Dawson Men' from Perote Prison, Mexico, 1842–1843," *Southwestern Historical Quarterly*, Vol. XXXVIII (1934–35), 246–69.

Sterne, Adolphus. "Diary of Adolphus Sterne," Harriet Smither, ed., *Southwestern Historical Quarterly*, Vol. XXXI (1927–28), 63–83.

Warren Harry. "Colonel G. Cooke," *Quarterly of the Texas State Historical Association*, Vol. IX (1905–1906), 210–19.

Williams, Amelia W. "A Critical Study of the Siege of the Alamo and of the Personnel of its Defenders," *Southwestern Historical Quarterly*, Vol. XXXVII (1933–34), 157–84.

Winkler, E. W. "The Bexar and Dawson Prisoners," *Quarterly of the Texas State Historical Association*, Vol. XIII (1909–10), 292–324.

Woll, Adrian. "Brigadier General Adrian Woll's Report of his Expedition into Texas in 1842," Joseph Milton Nance, ed., *Southwestern Historical Quarterly*, Vol. LVIII (1954–55), 523–52.

INDEX

Aberdeen, Lord: *see* Gordon,
George Hamilton
Abolitionists, unpopularity of, in
Texas: 163
Adaes Indians: *see* Adaices
Indians
Adaices Indians: 234 & n.
Adams, John: 276
Adams, John Quincy: 276
Addington, Henry: 332 n.
Africa: xiii, 136
Agriculture, observations on:
286–89
Agricultural products: 322
*Agricultural Tour in the United
States and Canada, 1841*
(Barclay): 285
Agua Dulce Creek: 213 n.
Alabama: 270, 307
Alabama, Texas: 311 & n., 312 f.
Alamán, Lucas: 136 & n.
Alamo, the: 63 n., 216, 234 f.,
236 n., 237, 258, 297, 308,
344 n.; battle for, 221–22;
description of, 222–24
Alamo del Parras, Coahuila,
Mexico: 236 n.
Alazan Creek: 237
Alba, Duke of: *see* Toledo,
Fernando Alvarez de
Albert, Prince Consort of Queen
Victoria: xviii
Aldrete, José Miguel: 348 & n.

Alert (sailing vessel): 378
Allegheny Mountains: 311 n.
Allen, Capt. John K. (Texian
Navy): 57 n.
Allen, M. N.: 339 & n.
Allen's Creek: 339 & n.
Almonte, Juan Nepomuceno: 330
Alva, Duke of: *see* Toledo,
Fernando Alvarez de
Alvarez, Juan: 172
Amanda (French warship): 101,
122
Amelia Giuseppe (sailing ves-
sel): 325 n.
Amended War Bill: 124
American colonies: 77
Ampudia, Gen. Pedro: 159, 171,
369 & n.
Amusements: 81
Anahuac, Texas: 317 & n.
Anderson, John D.: 259 & n.
Anderson, K. L.: 301 n., 302 n.
Andes Mountains: xvii
Andrews, Stephen Pearl: 163 & n.
Angouleme, Duke of: *see* Bour-
bon, Louis Antoine de
Annexation to U.S., rumors of:
330–31
Anthropology Society (Great
Britain): xviii
Antigua: 5 & n.
Antilles, the: 5
Antiquarian, Ethnological and

397

*other Researches in New Gra-
nada, Ecuador, Peru and Chile,
with Observations on the Pre-
Incarial, Incarial and other
Monuments of Peruvian
Nations* (Bollaert): xix
Anton Chico, New Mexico: 24
Apache Indians: xi, 172, 234, 256,
    332, 370
Apothecaries' Company (Lon-
    don, England): xii
Aquayo, Marquis of, failure of to
    settle San Antonio: 235–36
Aransas, Texas: 299
Aransas Bay: 42n.
Aransas County, Texas: 42n.
Aransas Pass: 44n., 378
Aransas River: 42n.
Archer (Texian warship): 57n.
Arequipa, Peru: xii
Argentina: xvii
"Argia—or Creon the Tyrant of
    Thebes; A Tragedy" (unpub-
    lished work by Bollaert): xix
Arista, Gen. Marciano: 28 & n.,
    43, 106, 120, 123
Arkansas: 194
Arkansas River: 319n.
"Arkansas tooth pick" (Bowie
    knife): 246n.
Arlington, T.: 322n.
Armijo, Gov. Manuel: 25 & n.,
    142
Armistice with Mexico, pro-
    claimed by Sam Houston:
    173–74
Armstrong, George: 261n.
Arroyo del Medio Creek: 351 & n.
Arroyo de Uvalde: 356, 381

Arroyo Seco: *see* Seco Creek
Atacama: *see* Chile
Atascosa River: 370n.
Atlantic (sailing vessel): 144
Atmospheric railway, description
    of: 275 & n.
Attacapan Indians: 236n.
Aury, Louis-Michel: 15 & n., 16
Austin, John: 85, 87 & n.
Austin, Moses: 17, 63, 160
Austin, Stephen Fuller: 17, 39n.,
    73n., 181 & n.
Austin, Texas: xi, 23, 25, 28f.,
    52, 55n., 62, 83 & n., 86 & n.,
    110f., 138, 140, 142, 148, 154,
    156f., 165, 183, 185, 190ff.,
    195ff., 208, 248, 276, 388
Austin, William Tennant: 111
    & n.
Austin City *Gazette*: 156, 199n.
Austin County, Texas: 275,
    339n., 340n.
Austin family: 280
Austin (Texian warship): 91,
    142, 157, 166, 169f., 176, 177
Australia: 3, 385
Austria: 325
Avernus, Sicily: 365
Avoco Valley, Ireland: 237 & n.

Bache, Richard: 135 & n.
Bahamas Islands: 5
Balize: 90, 102
Bamboo trees, description of: 309
Bambridge (U.S. warship): 334
Bandera, Texas: 351n.
Barclay, Robert: 285 & n.
Barkely, Richard A.: 209n.
Barksdale, Texas: 365n.

Barrataria (headquarters for pirates): 14f., 96
Barton, William: 197 & n.
Barton's Springs: 106, 197
Bastrop, Texas: 188, 189 & n., 190, 196, 199, 276
Bastrop County, Texas: 344n.
Bates, Thomas: 33, 34 & n.
Batesville, Texas: 353n.
Bath, T.: 112, 314 & n.
Bay of St. Bernard: 91
Bayonne, France: xiv, 72
Beagle (sailing vessel): xiii
Bears: 253
Beavers: 255
Bejar, Texas: 298, 355, 369; assault of, 241
Belfast, Northern Ireland: 385
Belgrade, Texas: 110 & n.
Belgium: 103 & n., 129, 137f., 163, 325
Bell, Thomas W.: 335n.
Bermuda: 388
Bernard River: 87
Bettison, Marianne: 388
Bexar, Texas: 28, 32, 49n.
Bexar County, Texas: 28n., 214n., 226n., 228n., 229n., 251n., 351
Bidais Creek: 314
Bidais Indians: 115, 116n.
Big Creek: 114
Bilious fever: 201
Billingsley, Capt. Jesse: 215
Bingham, Major Francis: 111 & n.
Bird, Jonathan: 322n.
Bird's Fort: 322 & n.
Bison: 248n.

Black, John S.: 292 & n.
Blackfeet Indians: 335
Bocanegra, José María: 136 & n.
Boerne, Texas: 351n.
Bois d'Arc Bayou: 306 & n., 321, 323
Bollaert, Alice Henderson: xvii
Bollaert, Andrew Jacob: xii
Bollaert, Caroline Bingley Melanie Kate: xvi
Bollaert, Charles William Alexander: xvi & n.
Bollaert, Emily Martinez: xvii
Bollaert, Francisca Maria Augusta: xvi
Bollaert, Henry Jacob: xii
Bollaert, Jane Sarah: *see* Marsden
Bollaert, Nathan: xii
Bollaert, William: aptitude of, for chemistry, xii; South American experiences of, xii–xiii; experiences of, in Portugal, xiv; Texas experiences of, xv; marriage of, xvi; voyage of, to Texas, 4; arrival of, in Galveston, 11; enlists as "waister" in the *La Fitte*, 38; journey of, to Matagorda, 62ff.; catches malaria, 199ff.; acts as interpreter in case of Calange *v.* Clauzel, 219–21; departure of, from Texas, 379
Bollaert family: xi
Bollard: *see* Bollaert
Bonavista, Texas: 72
Bonnell, George W.: 197 & n., 265n., 335
Bonnian, Jean: 227

Boone, Daniel: 197
Borden, Gail: 52, 135 & n., 163
Borden (Texian warship): 36n.
Bourbon, Louis Antoine de,
    Duke of Angouleme: 386
Bourgeois d'Orvanne, Alexander:
    100 & n.
Bowie, Jim: 222f., 231, 246n.
Bowie, Pleasant: 246n.
Bowie, Razin: 246n.
Bowie knife: 246n., 253
Box Creek: 313
Boxer (U.S. warship): 128
Boylan, Capt. James D. (Texian
    Navy): 38 & n., 56n., 59 & n.
Brackenridge Park, San Antonio,
    Texas: 229n.
Bradburn, Col. John Davis:
    317n.
Brande, Prof. William Thomas:
    xii
Brashear, William C.: 178
Brazil: xvii, 275
Brazoria, Texas: 30, 83, 87 & n.,
    140, 201f.
Brazoria County, Texas: 337n.
Brazoria County Militia: 30n.
Brazos County, Texas: 50n.
Brazos Farmer: 170n.
Brazos River: 31n., 39n., 85, 87,
    134, 139, 148, 153, 157, 163,
    179, 180f., 191, 196, 200n.,
    261n., 262, 264ff., 279, 307n.,
    333, 336 & n., 337, 338 & n., 379
Brazos Road: 111
Bremen, Germany: 325
Brenham, Dr. R. F.: 128 & n.
Brey's Bayou: 336 & n.

Brighton, England: 101
Britishers: 276, 372
British Museum, London, Eng-
    land: 183
British West Indies: 5n.
Brown, George William: 30 & n.
Brown, Capt. William S. (Tex-
    ian Navy): 56n.
Brushy Creek: 344
Brutus (Texian warship): 56n.
Bryan, John Neely: 322n.
Bryan, William: 132 & n., 170 &
    n., 178
Bryant (sailing vessel): 152
Buffalo: 248n., 255
Buffalo Bayou: 20 & n., 109,
    267n., 336n.
Buller, Charles: 387
Bulloch, Richard: 102
Burleson, Gen. Edward: 49 & n.,
    50ff., 154, 156f., 189f., 204,
    231n.
Burnet County, Texas: 197n.
Burnett, David G.: 21 & n., 276
Burr, Aaron: 105
Byrne, James W.: 261n., 262,
    341 & n.
Byrne, William Odin: 261 & n.,
    262, 266n.

Caddo, Texas: 307
Calder, Robert James: 178
Caldwell, Mathew: 154, 156, 183,
    215f.
Calhoun County, Texas: 40n.
California: 142, 225n., 237
Calvearo Rancho St. Patricio:
    370
Cameron, Ewen: 48, 172 & n.

Camp Castle Hill: 359
Camp Kennedy: 362
Camp meetings: 294–95
Campos (Tonkeway chief): 189
Camp Plimpton, Texas: 365
Camp Wasp, Texas: 363
Canada: 3, 91, 285 & n., 387f.
Cañales, Gen. Antonio: 121ff.,
   349, 373
Canary Islands: 236
Candy pulling, description of:
   295
Caney Creek: 72, 87
Canfields, Texas: 336
Cape Horn: xiii
Capote Mountain: 214
Capote Peak: 346n.
Carancahua Indians: *see* Karan-
   kawa Indians
Carlos I (pretender to the Span-
   ish Throne): xiv, xv, xix
Carlos Rancho: 341 & n.
Carolina, Texas: *see* Bath, Texas
Caroline (sailing vessel): *see*
   Sarah Barnes
Carter, Jane: xii
Castañeda, Gen. Francisco: 212
Castle Hill Camp, Texas: 359
Castro, Henri: 90 & n., 102, 213,
   221, 230, 347
Castroville, Texas: 351n., 352n.
Cate Creek: 355
Cedar Creek: 74, 320n.
Centralist party (of Mexico): 25
Ceuta, Morocco: xvii
Chambers, Trafford: 136
Chambers County, Texas: 316n.
Cheltenham, England: 112
Cherokee Indians: 90, 141, 240

Cherokee Lands: 110, 121, 138
Chicago, Illinois: 372
Chican Creek: 352
Chihuahua, Mexico: 122, 240n.,
   350, 358
Chile: xiii, xvii, xviii, 374n.
Chilipin Creek: 213n.
Chiltipin Creek: 213n.
China: 385
Choctaw Indians: 90, 333, 337
Christenings: 305
Cibolo River: 214 & n., 244f.,
   248n., 250, 258, 346, 350
Cincinnati, Texas: 292 & n., 306,
   308, 311ff.
Civilian and Galveston Gazette:
   13n., 28 & n., 29n., 34n., 35,
   128 & n., 276n.
Claiborne, Gov. W. C. C.: 15
Clapp's Ferry Bridge: 306n.
Clyde (British vessel): 8
Coahuiltecan Indians: 234n.
*Coast of Texas, from documents
   furnished by W. H. Kennedy,
   Esq., H M Consul at Galves-
   ton, The* (map published by
   the British Admiralty): 388n.
Cobb, Henry Adolph: 125, 167
   & n.
Cocke, Capt. James H.: 354
Coles, John P.: 314n.
Coles' Mill: 314 & n.
Colita (Coushatta chief): 84 &
   n.
Collin County, Texas: 276n.
Colombian Archipelago: 5
*Colonization Contract Between
   the Republic of Texas and Sam
   Houston and others:* 380ff.

Colorado County, Texas: 210, 242 n., 243 n., 340 n., 275

Colorado Hills: 190

Colorado River: 20, 70, 110, 137, 148, 154, 180, 182 ff., 187, 189, 190 n., 193 ff., 200 n., 202, 209 & n., 230, 238, 239, 243 n., 260 ff., 266 ff., 272, 287, 340 f.

Colquhoun, Ludovic: 352 & n.

Columbia, Texas: 16, 38 n.

Columbus, Texas: 110, 137, 180, 182 & n., 199, 200, 202, 208 n., 258, 260 f., 266 f., 339, 340 n., 341, 342 n., 352 n.

Comal County, Texas: 214 n.

Comanche Chiefs, slaughter of, at La Espada Mission: 235

Comanche Indians: xi, 50 n., 84, 165, 174, 189, 191 f., 198, 224, 227 & n., 229, 232, 234 n., 235, 237–38, 246, 250 f., 256, 269, 279, 335 & n., 345, 347 f., 358, 360 f., 364, 370, 372 f., 375 & n., 376 & n., 377 n., 378; characteristics of, 375 n.

Comanche Peak: 133

Comargo, Texas: 381

Comino Real (Road): 352 n.

Concepcion, Mission of: 225, 231 & n., 233

Congestive fever: 201

Conroe, Texas: 265 n.

Cooke, Col. William G.: 128 & n., 240 & n., 376

Cooke County, Texas: 320 n.

Cooper, James Fenimore: 210 n.

Copano Bay: 29, 36, 42, 44 n., 213 n., 233

Cordillera Road: xiii

Cordilleras Mountains: 193 ff.

Corpus Christi, Texas: 29, 43 f., 48 & n., 50, 55, 86, 104 n., 111, 121 f., 174, 329, 334, 341, 348, 359 f., 369, 376 & n., 378

Cotulla, Texas: 368 n.

Cós, Gen. Martin Perfecto de: 231 n.

Coshatte Indians: 115 & n., 289, 333

Cotton: 271, 286 ff., 308

Cotton gins: 278

Council House fight, at San Antonio: 166 & n., 229 n.

Court House Square, Dallas, Texas: 322 n.

Coushatta Indians: 84 & n., 315 & n.

Cowan's Ferry: 87

Cowen, James William: 87 n.

Cramayel, Viscount Jules Edouard de: 164 & n., 174 & n.

Creole Indians: 97, 236 f.

Crisp, Capt. Downing H. (Texian Navy): 56 n., 62 & n., 63, 143, 160

Crockett, David: 64, 168 & n., 222 & n., 223, 306 n.

Crockett, John Wesley: 168 & n.

Crockett, Texas: 306 & n.

Cross Timbers: 83, 319 & n., 321, 322 & n.

Cruger, Maj. Nicholas: 102

Cuba: 10, 144, 175

Cuero Road: 344

Culebra Creek: 226 & n.

Cutter (sailing vessel), Bollaert journeys to Matagorda in: 62 ff.

Cypress Bayou: 119

Daily Advertiser: 30n.
Daingerfield, William H.: 157
Dallas, Texas: xi, 319, 320 & n., 322 & n., 323n.
Dallas County, Texas: 276n., 320n., 323n.
Dalston, England: xvi
Dancing: 295–96
Daniels, George: 344n.
Davis, Gen. James: 119, 121, 244f., 250, 376
Davy, Sir Humphrey: xii
Dawson, Capt. Nicholas: 149, 214
Dawson's Company: 298; slaughter of, 239
Deal, England: 4
Declaration of Independence (Texian): 325
Decrow, Daniel: 39n.
Decrows Point: 39 & n., 69, 173
Deer: 252–53
Denmark: 5, 8
Denton County, Texas: 276n., 320n.
Devereux, Col. Julian Sidney: 266 & n.
De Witt, Green C.: 210n., 211 & n., 259n., 343n., 345
De Witt Colony, Texas: 210n., 211 & n.
Dickinson, Lieut. S. A.: 222n.
Dimmit County, Texas: 322
Doctors: 300
Dollar, value of, in sterling currency: 269
Dolores Ferry: 381

Dolphin (U.S. warship): 125f., 159f., 164
Dona Maria II, Queen of Portugal: xiv
Dor, Judge John M.: 107 & n.
Doyle, Sir John Milley: xiv
Doyle, Percy W.: 264 & n.
Dragonfly, description of: 175
Drinks, list of: 55n., 56n.
Ducros, Texas: 100 & n.
Duncan's Ferry: 314
Dutch Ball, description of: 26–27
Duval County, Texas: 213

Eagle Pass, Texas: 352n., 358n.
East Bay: 318
Ecuador: xviii
Edmund, P.: 133 & n.
Edwards County, Texas: 365n.
Edwards Plateau: 243n.
Egg nogs: 293
El Cañon Mission: *see* San Lorenzo de la Santa Cruz
Electra (British warship): 160
El Hondo, Texas: 353
Elk-hart Creek: 313
Elkswatawa, the Prophet of the West (French): 210 & n.
Ellen Frankland (steam vessel): 311n., 313, 318
Elliot, Capt. Charles: 120 & n., 130, 132f., 136, 155, 160, 163f., 167, 169, 320, 322n., 328f., 331, 335, 350, 388
Ellis, Richard: 26 & n.
Elm Creek: 355, 362n.
Elm Fork: 320n.
Emigrants, early, in Texas: 20–21, 269f.

England: xi, xii, xiv, xvi, xvii, 3, 5f., 109, 121, 130, 133 & n., 135f., 138, 140, 163f., 173f., 204, 241, 248n., 275f., 297, 312 & n., 325, 331 & n., 332, 350, 386f.; *see also* Great Britain

Epsom, England: 281

Equadorian Land Company: xvii

Esperanza Creek: 361

Espiritu Santo Bay: 87

Ethnological Society (Gt. Britain): xviii; *Transactions* of, xviii–xix

Ethnological Society (U.S.A.): xviii

Europe: xi, xiii, 3 & n., 20f., 80, 164, 221, 301, 326, 328, 386

Eves, Joseph: 130, 153

Exchange, the, Galveston, Texas: 84

Exchange Hotel, New Orleans, Louisiana: 91 & n.

Expedition of Pedro de Ursua & Lope de Aguirre in Search of Eldorado and Amagua in 1560–61 (Simon): xix

Eye, Judge Joseph: 108 & n.

Fannin County, Texas: 231, 306n., 307, 322

Fannin County Court House, Bonham, Texas: 306 & n.

Faraday, Michael: xii

Farm prices: 268–69

Fayette County, Texas: 344n.

Federal Party (Mexico): 158, 161

Ferdinand VII, King of Spain: 16n., 386

Ferguson, Alan: 29 & n.

Fevers, antidotes for: 200–202

Filisola, Gen. Vicente: 223

Fire hunting: 112n., 277

Fisher, Henry Francis: 126 & n.

Fisher, Capt. William S.: 149

Flint (U.S. warship): 328

Florida: 307n.

Fort Bend County, Texas: 337n., 340n.

Fort Houston, Texas: 306 & n., 307, 311, 313, 320

Fort Winnebago, Texas: 373n.

Foyer, Peter: 378

France: xi, 5, 39, 92, 100, 129f., 138, 157, 163, 174f., 175 & n., 178, 221, 234f., 297, 325, 327, 380, 386

Frankland and Company: 292

Franklin, Benjamin: 134, 135 & n.

Freestone County, Texas: 324n.

French, James S.: 210

Frio County, Texas: 332, 353n., 354n., 356, 357n., 359, 362n., 364, 366n., 368, 369n.

Frio River: 332, 353n., 354, 356, 357 & n., 359ff., 362 & n., 364, 366n., 368, 369 & n., 370 & n., 374, 381

Frolic Privateer (sailing vessel): 102

Funchal (sailing vessel): 101, 144

Galicia (Spanish province): 236

Galveston, Texas: xi, xv, xvi, 3, 11, 14ff., 21, 24f., 27, 29n., 30n., 37, 42, 49n., 50, 51 & n.,

52, 56n., 57f., 62, 73, 84, 88f., 96, 99, 110, 119, 123, 132, 134, 138, 140, 142, 143-44, 145-47, 148, 150, 152f., 155ff., 165, 168, 170, 173, 175, 178f., 181, 202, 257, 262, 264, 267, 274, 276, 280, 283, 286 & n., 292, 297, 301, 311, 318ff, 324, 325 & n., 326ff., 331 & n., 332n., 333f., 337, 345, 354, 374, 379, 388 & n.; Bollaert's impressions of life in, 18-20; minutes of emergency meeting held in, March 9, 1842, 31-32; citizens of, prepare for Mexican invasion, 34-35

Galveston Bay: 15, 20

Galveston Island: *see* Galveston, Texas

Gálvez, Don José Conde de: 14 & n.

Game, in Texas: 252-57

Garcia, Luciano: 107 & n.

Garza, Carlos de la: 341n.

Geneva, Texas: 314n.

George West, Texas: 370n.

Georgia: 266

German settlements, in Texas: 275

Germany: 385f.

Gibbs, Sanford: 285n.

Gibbs, Thomas: 285n.

Gibraltar: xvii

Gilleland, Johnson: 50 & n.

Gillespie, Col. Barry: 83n.

Gillespie, Richard A.: 377n.

Gladstone, William: 5n.

Glasgow, Scotland: 385f., 389

Glasgow Theatre, Glasgow, Scotland: 386

Goliad, Texas: 23, 28, 50 & n., 233 & n., 237f., 241, 341, 344n.; Battle of, 222n., 371n.

Goliad Mission: 233

Gonzales, Texas: 21, 87, 140, 149, 208n., 210, 211n., 213, 258f., 342, 344 & n., 345, 349f., 377n.; Battle of, 212n.

Gonzales County, Texas: 33n., 259n., 260n., 343n., 344n.

Gordon, George Hamilton (4th Lord Aberdeen): 120 & n.

Grande Condé (sailing vessel): 151

Grant, James: 371n.

Grapes: 245

Grass Fight, near San Antonio: 231 & n., 232

Gray, F. S.: 33

Grayson, Texas: 377 & n.

Grayson County, Texas: 276n.

Great Britain: 25, 129, 158, 230, 287, 307n., 327, 350, 388; Admiralty of, 388n.; Foreign Office of, 389; *see also* England

Green, Gen. Duff: 121 & n.

Green, Thomas Jefferson: 299

Green, William: 328

Grey Fox, description of: 253

Grieve, James H.: 331 & n., 332f., 337, 351, 356, 362, 380f.

Grieves Hills: 362

Grimes, Sen. Jesse: 265 & n.

Grimes County, Texas: 265n., 292n.

Grimes Prairie: 265n., 307

Grosvenor Square, London, England: 241
Ground hogs: 254
Guadalupe (sailing vessel): 142, 177
Guadalupe County, Texas: 214n.
Guadalupe Mountains: 210
Guadalupe River: 20f., 87, 200n., 211n., 213f., 244n., 246, 248, 258f., 344 & n.
Guadalupe Valley: 242ff., 252
Gualateca (Texian warship): 57n.
Guantajaya silver mines, Tarapaca, Mexico: xii
Guilbeau, C. H.: 337 & n.
Guizot, François Pierre: 122 & n.
Gulf of Mexico: 17, 27n., 95, 99, 136, 213, 237, 268 & n., 337n.
Gutiérrez, Bernard: 237n., 238
Gutiérrez, José Bernardo: 216n.

Haber, Baron Maurice de: xiv
Hackney, England: xvii
Haight, John C., letter of: 33
Haines Bluff: 323
Hakluyt Society publications: xix
Hall, Robert: 261n.
Hall, Warren D.: 106 & n.
Hamilton, Gen. William B.: 101 & n., 103, 178, 331
Hamilton Creek: 197n.
Hancock, Thomas: 351, 357, 363, 368, 372, 374
Hanseatic States: 138, 163
Harbord, Sadie: 138
Hardin, William: 178
Hardman's Ferry: 187

Harrisburg, Texas: 108, 151
Harris County, Texas: 267n.
Hatch, George C.: 209 & n.
Havana, Cuba: 164
Haviland, Capt. J.: 38
Hays, John Coffee: 33 & n., 52, 156, 225 & n., 227 & n., 241, 244, 318, 356, 376, 377n., 378
Hayti: 5
Headrights: 269 & n.
Heard, Capt. William J. E.: 31 & n.
Henderson, Gen. James Pinckney: 328 & n.
Henderson County, Texas: 314n.
Herrara, José Manuel: 216n.
Hill, Jim Dan: 34n.
Hill County, Texas: 324n.
History of the Navy of the United States (Cooper): 105
Hitchcock, Capt. Lent Munson: 38 & n.
Hockley, George Washington: 59 & n., 151 & n., 152f., 239n., 257, 325, 329f.
Hodge, F. W.: 234n.
Holland: xi, xvff., 138f., 163, 174, 325, 335
Holliday, John J.: 131 & n., 180 & n., 331 & n.
Hondo Creek: 353 & n., 354n.
Honey Creek: 197 & n.
Horse race, description of: 280–82
House of Representatives (Texas): 77, 110, 288
Houston, Sam: xv, 3, 21, 23, 25 & n., 26, 27n., 31n., 33n., 35f., 49 & n., 51f., 55n., 58, 62, 63 &

n., 83n., 88f., 101 & n, 104 & n.,
105f., 107 & n., 108, 114, 119,
121, 122 & n., 124, 148, 150,
164n., 167, 169, 170 & n., 172,
183, 189, 196, 212, 239n., 264
& n., 269 & n., 300f., 308, 327f.,
330, 336, 353, 380, 387f.; fore-
bearance of, 52–54; armistice
with Mexico proclaimed by,
173–74; efforts of, to restrain
"War Party", 297–99
Houston, Texas: xv, 17, 20, 38n.,
52, 55n., 62, 83 & n., 101,
104ff., 110f., 118f., 127, 137,
139, 140f., 142 & n., 153, 163,
165, 179, 264, 267, 274, 280,
288, 301, 307, 316, 329, 333,
336 & n., 340f., 349
Houston County, Texas: 306n.
Houstonian, The: 28
Houston Ship Canal: 20n.
Howard, Maj. George Thomas:
229 & n.
Hoyt, Capt. N. (Texian Navy):
57n.
Huckins, Rev. James: 103 & n.
Hull, England: 387, 389
Hull Advertiser (Hull, Eng-
land): 387ff.
Hunter, Dr. Johnson Calhoun:
70 & n.
Hunters, advice to: 246–47
Huntsville, Alabama: 284n.
Huntsville, Texas: 284ff., 311
Huntsville Hotel, Huntsville,
Texas: 285
Huntsville Spring: 289, 309
Hurricane Creek: 313
Huston, Felix: 298 & n.

Illinois: 20f., 372, 373
Immigrants, types of, suited for
Texas: 109; agricultural pros-
pects for, in Texas, 116–18
Impressions of America
(Power): 71
Independence (Texian war-
ship): 56n.
India: 385
Indians: 131, 140, 225n., 232,
234ff., 244, 247, 255f., 309f.,
319n., 383
Indigo: 264
Industry, Texas: 262 & n.
Invincible (Texian warship):
56n.
Ireland: 140, 261n., 275, 385
Ironside (sailing vessel): 70
Iturbide, Augustin de: 241 & n.

Jack, P. C.: 335 & n.
Jack, William Houston: 30 & n.,
35
Jackson, Col. Alden: 32, 33
Jackson, Terrell, 233n.
Jacksonville, Texas: 262, 263n.
Jagua: 254
Jamaica: 9n., 10
James, John: 351 & n.
Jayme, Pedro: 351, 353f., 356
Jefferson, Thomas: 105
Johannes, Samuel: xii
John Barnes (sailing vessel): 178,
331, 379
Johnson, Francis: 371n.
Johnson, Thomas: 275
Johnston, Gen. Albert Sidney:
30, 34, 298 & n.

Jones, Anson: 49 n., 101 & n., 264, 301
Jones and Company: 307n., 317
Jordan, Samuel W.: 123n.
Journal of the Royal Institution (London, England): xii

Karankawa Indians: 14, 41, 73 & n., 276n., 337, 349
Karlsruhe, Germany: xv
Kaufman, Texas: 306
Kaufman County, Texas: 320n.
Kemper, Samuel: 216 & n.
Kendall, George William: 24n.
Kendall County, Texas: 244n.
Kennedy, Hugh: 385ff.
Kennedy, James: 385f.
Kennedy, Samuel: 119 & n., 138, 150, 156, 332 & n., 385, 388
Kennedy, William: xv, 3 & n., 13 & n., 17, 25 & n., 100 & n., 106, 108, 119 & n., 121, 124, 130, 133, 161f., 167, 171, 278, 308, 331n., 352, 380n., 385ff., 389
Kennedy Colony, Texas: 243n., 269n., 319, 331n., 332, 365n.
Kenney, Col. H. S.: 86 & n.
Kentucky: 241, 262n., 276n.
"Kentucky Colony": *see* Peters, W. S., colony of
Kentucky Settlement: 319
Kerrville, Texas: 248n.
Ketchie Indians: 375n.
Kickapoo Indians: 115, 116n.
King's College, London, England: xiii
Kinney, Henry Lawrence: 48 & n., 376 & n., 377 & n.
Klaenner, D.: 167 & n.

Knapp, Samuel Lorenzo: 105
Knowles, Sheridan: 385f.
Koronk Indians: *see* Carancahua Indians

La Bahía, Texas: 233n., 344n.
La Bahía Road: 306n., 344 & n.
Lacy's Creek: 320n.
Lacy's Fork: 320 & n.
La Espada de San Francisco, Mission of: 225, 232f.; slaughter of Comanche chiefs at, 235
Lafayette County band: 151 & n.
Lafayette County Volunteers: 154, 156
Laffite, Jean: 14–16, 38ff., 84n., 90, 160
La Fitte, Jean: *see* Laffite
La Fitte (steam vessel): 29, 34 & n., 35ff.
La Grange, Texas: 154, 183, 184 & n., 199, 261, 339, 344n.
La Grange Road: 262, 344
Lake Creek: 266
Lake Dallas: 320n.
Lake Nyasa (East Africa): xiii
Lallemand, Charles François Antoine: 17 & n.
Lamar, Gen. Mirabeau Buonaparte: 21 & n., 23, 31n., 34 & n., 36, 50 & n., 122, 160, 167, 185f., 187 & n., 189, 240, 262, 276, 297f., 331, 387
Lamar, Texas: 341
Lamar County, Texas: 306n.
Land grants, in Texas, Houston's conflict with legislature over: 269n.
Land values, in Texas: 269–70

La Parita Creek: 370
La Parita Valley: 370
Laredo, Texas: 52, 149, 257, 298, 360, 371, 381
Laredo Road: 364, 365 & n., 368f.
La Salle County, Texas: 332, 366n., 368n., 370n.
Las Moras Mountains: 365 & n.
"Last of the Incas, The: A Play in Three Acts" (unpublished work by Bollaert): xix
La Vaca, Texas: 342
La Vaca River: 209 & n., 211n., 260, 342f., 344 & n.
Lawrence, William: 135 & n.
Lea, Nancy Moffette: 150
Leger, Dr. Theodore: 201, 202 & n.
Leininger, Count Victor von: 135, 137n, 164
Leon, Guadalupe, story of, told to Wm. Bollaert: 64ff.
Leon, Texas: 351
Leona Creek: 369
Leona River: 33, 355f., 357 & n., 358, 360, 362 & n., 363ff., 381
Leona Valley: 356
Leon Creek: 226 & n., 227
Leonidar (sailing vessel): 385
Leon Springs, Texas: 243n.
Leopard cats: 254
Lewis, Col. J. R.: 266 & n., 267
Lewis, William P.: 24 & n.
Liberty, Texas: 316 & n.
Liberty (Texian warship): 56n.
Liberty County, Texas: 316n.
Life of Aaron Burr, The (Knapp): 105

Life of George Washington, The (Marshall): 105
Lima, Peru: xvii
Linnean Society (London, England), *Transactions* of: xix
Lipan Indians: 213, 256, 376
Lipantitlan, Texas: 118 & n., 119 & n., 121, 123, 129
Lipscomb, Judge Abner Smith: 119 & n.
Lirima Range: xiii
Lisbon, Portugal: xiv
Little River: 191, 349
Live Oak County, Texas: 370n.
Live Oak Point: 44 & n., 48, 50
Liverpool, England: 4, 11, 136, 178, 286, 331
Livingston, David: xiii
Llano Mines: 198
Llano River: 198
Lobache and Company: 89
Lockmar, Antonio: 221, 241
London, England: xii, xiii, xv, xvi, 3f., 25n., 106, 379, 385, 387
Long, Gen. James: 16 & n., 159 & n., 237
Lookout Peninsula: 261n.
Louis XV, King of France: 92
Louisiana: 15, 19, 126f., 144, 236, 293, 307, 309; brief history of, 92
Louisville, Kentucky: 276
Louthrop, J. T. K.: 56n., 176 & n.
Love, James: 31 & n., 32
Low, Richard: 210 & n.
Low Countries: 221
Lymington, Hampshire, England: xii
Lynch, Nathaniel: 267n.

Lynchburg, Texas: 267 & n., 274
Lynch's Ferry: 267n.
Lytton, Edward George Earl
   Lytton Bulwer: 18n., 19

Macadam, Loudon: 342n.
McCulloch, Lieut. Ben: 33 & n.,
   351 & n.
McGloin, James: 378 & n.
McIntosh, George S.: 133 & n.
McKinney, Thomas F.: 50 & n.,
   104n.
McLeod, Carl Hugh: 130, 156 &
   n.
McMorran, Susannah: xvi
McMullen, James: 378n.
McMullen, John: 219 & n., 232
McMullen County, Texas: 332,
   369n.
McMullen-McGloin Colony,
   Texas: 219n.
McNeel, John Greenville: 87 &
   n.
Macready, William Charles: 190
   & n.
Madison, James: 15
Madison County, Texas: 265n.
Magnolia, Texas: 312–13, 324
Magnolia Creek: 313
Maillard, Nicholas Doran: 338 &
   n.; criticisms of Texas by, 139–
   42
Malaria: 200n.
Margaritta Island: 17
Marie Elizabeth (sailing vessel):
   89, 102, 144
Marin, Don Tomas: 177
Marriages: 302–305
Marsden, Jane Sarah: xii

Marsden, William: xii
Matagorda, Texas: 16, 62, 70, 85,
   87, 101, 122, 127, 140, 174, 185,
   261n., 266n., 331
Matagorda Bay: 27n., 39n., 40n.
Matagorda County, Texas: 39n.
Matagorda Island: 27n., 40n.
Matagorda Peninsula: 27n.
Matamoros, New Mexico: 53,
   106f., 156, 178, 193, 239, 257,
   329, 334, 338, 369 & n.
Matamoros Road: 376
Mathew, Rev. Theobold: 182 &
   n.
Maverick County, Texas: 332
Mayfield, James S.: 154, 156
Medico-Botanical Society (Gt.
   Britain): xviii
Medina County, Texas: 354n.
Medina River: 33, 149, 226 & n.,
   227, 348, 352 & n.
Medio Creek: 226 & n., 227, 351
   & n.
Merchant (steam vessel): 132
Meridia, Mexico: 169 & n.
Merriman, F. H.: 161 & n.
Methodists: 294–95
Mexican Army: 373n., 375
Mexican Civil Wars: 237
Mexican hogs: 253
Mexican Indians: 217
Mexican Navy: 158
Mexican Revolution: 140, 280
Mexicans: xi, 3, 27, 36, 43, 55, 73,
   84ff., 88, 123, 129, 131, 145,
   150, 154, 156, 161, 180, 183,
   185, 198, 212, 214ff., 222, 225
   & n., 227, 231 & n., 237, 241,
   245, 335, 347, 377

Mexican War: 225 n., 371 n.
Mexico: xi, 3, 16 & n., 23, 25, 36, 48, 51, 66, 73 & n., 81, 88, 95, 97, 104 f., 120 f., 128 ff., 132 & n., 134, 138, 143, 152, 154, 156, 158 n., 164, 170, 172 f., 175, 177 f., 181, 185, 193, 198, 204, 227 n., 228 n., 236 & n., 239, 251, 257, 264 & n., 276, 288 n., 297, 299, 308, 317 & n., 320, 325, 327, 329 f., 332, 350, 362, 373, 374 n., 376
Mexico City, Mexico: 23 f., 64, 158, 172
Middleburgh, Holland: xi
Mier, New Mexico: 106, 127, 149, 159, 162, 296, 299, 335, 357, 369 & n., 373
Mier Expedition: 197 n., 369 n.
Mier prisoners: 169 & n., 172, 276 n., 308, 334 & n.
Milam, Ben: 241
Mill Creek: 261 & n., 262
Miller, Burchard: 126 & n.
Miller, Washington D.: 33 & n., 49 n.
Mills, Robert: 160
Mina, Gen. Francisco Xavier: 16 & n.
Missions, on San Antonio River, description of: 225-26, 231-34
Mississippi: 272, 287, 293
Mississippi River: 88 f., 91, 96, 99, 102
Missouri: 194
Missouri River: 319 n.
Missouri Trail: 143
Mobile, Alabama: 34 n., 40
Mobile Bay: 91

Montague, David: 178
Monterey, Mexico: 28 n.
Montgomery, James: 265 n.
Montgomery, Gen. Richard: 265 n.
Montgomery, Texas: 114, 137, 153, 265 & n., 266, 268, 271, 275, 279, 307
Montgomery County, Texas: 4 n., 20, 109, 110 & n., 242 n., 265 n., 266 n., 270, 284 & n., 292 n., 320 n., 340 & n.
Montserrat Island: 5
Moore, Commodore Edwin Ward: 56 & n., 57 n., 62, 106, 160 & n., 166, 169, 170, 176, 177 & n., 178
Moore, Capt. John H.: 212 & n.
Moore, Sir Thomas: 237 n.
Moors: 351
Morehouse, Brig. Gen. E.: 178; letter of, to Col. Jackson: 32 & n.
Morgan, Col. James: 132 & n., 135, 166 & n., 170 & n., 177 f.
Morris, John D.: 28 & n.
Morris, Judge Richard: 34 & n., 102, 145 f.
Mosquito Hawk: *see* Dragonfly
Mount Bonnell: 197
Mount Vernon County, Texas: 265
Murphy, Gen. William Sumter: 174 & n., 264 & n., 327, 330
Muskhogean Indians: 115
Mustang (steam vessel): 264, 276
Mustang Creek: 344
Mustangs: 255-57

Nacogdoches, Texas: xi, 141, 182, 352n.
Nangle, William B.: 222n.
Napoleon I, Emperor of France: 17, 73, 92, 237
Narrative of the Capture and Subsequent Suffering of the Mier Prisoners in New Mexico, A (Bell): 335n.
Nashville, Texas: 264, 265n.
Natchez Indians: 84
Natchitoches, Louisiana: 308
Natchitoches River: 361
National Register: 33n.
National Vindicator, extracts from Nov. 27, 1843 ed.: 275n., 276
Navasota River: 265
Navidad, Texas: 342
Navidad River: 208, 342
Negro ball, description of: 299–300
Negroes: 20, 95n., 155, 171, 269f., 273, 286, 288, 293–94; condition of, in Texas, 271–72
Negro nurseries: 272
Nelson's Creek: 313
Neptune (steam vessel): 62, 157, 161f., 169, 330f.
Netherlands, Dutch revolt against Spanish in: 221n.
Newberry Library, Chicago, Illinois: 388n.
Newcastle, England: 312n.
Newmarket, England: 281
New Mexico: 23, 25n.
New Orleans, Louisiana: 4, 15, 17f., 21, 24n., 31, 35, 55, 56n., 88ff., 100, 106, 108, 123, 128ff.,

133, 135f., 155ff., 163, 166, 170, 173, 209, 227n., 231n., 271, 288, 293, 301, 307n., 328f., 331, 335, 348, 385
New Philipines: 236
New Year Creek: 263 & n.
New York, N. Y.: 135, 152
New York (steam vessel): 31, 62, 99, 102, 106, 108, 158, 161, 172f., 335
Nieuw Nederlandsch Biografisch Woordenboek: xi–xii
Nixon, John T.: 260n.
Nixon's Creek: 208, 260 & n., 342
Nolan River: 133
North Carolina: 314n.
Nueces River: 121f., 127, 134, 138, 142, 156, 241, 331n., 332, 348n., 356, 357 & n., 358f., 364, 365 & n., 367, 368 & n., 369, 370 & n., 371 & n., 374, 376f., 378n., 381
Nuestra Señora del Espirito Santo de Zuñiga, Mission of: 233n.; *see also* La Bahía
Nuestra Señora de Loreto, Mission of: 233n.
Nuestra Señora de Los Dolores de Los Ais, Mission of: 233n.
Nuestra Señora del Refugio, Mission of: 42 & n., 43, 233n.

Oahquash (Waco chief): 165
Oak trees: 307 & n.
O'Brien, Owen: 55 & n.
"Oceola": *see* Osceola
Ogden, Frederick W.: 300 & n.
Old Presidio Road: 208n., 342n.

Old River (Liberty County, Texas): 316 & n., 317
"Old Sam": *see* Houston, Sam
Old San Antonio Road: 352n.; *see also* San Antonio Road
Olmos Creek: 251n., 355 & n.
Olmos Springs: 251 & n.
"On the Different Sorts of Hunting and Species of Game in Texas" (anonymous essay): 252–57
Oporto, Portugal: xiv
Opposums: 254
Oregon Territory: 142
Orinoco River: 17
Osage Indians: 375n.
Osceola, Texas: 311 & n., 312
Otters: 255
Our Lady of Guadalupe of Zacatecas, Mission of: 224, 234
Owen, Clark L.: 52
Owen, Shadrack B.: 342 & n.
Owen Branch: 342n.
Oyster Creek: 111, 337 & n.

Pacific Ocean: 43, 143, 237, 335
Packenham, R.: 134
Padre Island: 334
Paisley, Ireland: 385
Paisley Advertiser: 386
Palestine, Texas: 306n.
Panama: xvii
Panthers: 254
Parades, Gen. Mariano: 172
Paraguay: xvii
Paris, France: 103, 109, 275, 385f,. 389
Pass Cavallo: 27 & n.
Patrick's Ferry: 315

Pawnee Indians: 375n.
Peach Creek: 344 & n.
Pearsall, Texas: 359
Peccary: *see* Mexican Hog
Pecos River: 24 & n., 133
Pedro I, Emperor of Brazil: xiv
Pellegrini, Snider de: 120 & n., 122, 151
Perez, Antonio: 225
Pérez, Manuel: 225n.
Perote, Mexico: 209n., 334n.; prison at, 161 & n.
Perote Castle, Mexico: 209, 264
Persimmon trees: 289
Peru: xii, xiii, xix
Peters, W. S.: 276n., 380; colony of, 276 & n., 306 & n.
Philabeaucourt, Baron Ernest: 39n., 120 & n.
Philip II, King of Spain: 221
Pickwick Papers (Dickens): 210
Piedra Creek: 370 & n.
Piedra Pinto Creek: 377n.
Pike, Zebulon Montgomery: 228n.
Pinckard, Ferdinand: 168
Pintas Creek: 376
Pintas Spring: 251
Pinto Creek: 377 & n.
Pinto Trace: 377n.
Planter's Exchange, Huntsville, Texas: 285
Plaza, San Antonio, Texas: 209n., 228n., 229, 230
Plimpton, Charles: xvi
Poinsett (steam vessel): 350
Pole cats: *see* Skunks
Polk County, Texas: 315n.

Pompei, Texas (proposed town site): 314
Ponton, William: 210 & n., 343n.
Ponton's Creek: 343f.
Port Isabel: 102
Post Oaks, Texas: 345
Potomac (Texian warship): 56n.
Potomac River: 96
Potter, Ruben M.: 31, 34, 135 & n.
Power, James: 41 & n., 101, 108, 127 & n., 152
Power, Tyrone: 71 & n.
Power and Hewetson Colony: 41
Prairie du Chien, Wisconsin: 373n.
Prairie fire, description of: 74–75
Presidio, Texas: 358n.
Presidio County, Texas: 346n., 358n.
Presidio Crossing: 365
Presidio Road: 38, 258, 352 & n., 353, 354n., 355f., 361, 363f.
Prevost, Theodosia: 105
Pringle, William: xv, xvi, 137 & n., 331n., 335, 380f., 389
Pringle's Camp: 362
Pringle's Creek: 361
Privateering: 88
Puerto Rico: 6, 9

Quintana: 85, 87
Quito: xvii

Rabbits: 255
Race courses: 280
Rancheros, description of: 217
Randolph Air Force Base, Texas: 346

Reagan, John H.: 306n.
Recorder's Office, New Orleans, Louisiana: 93
Red Bird (Winnebago chief): 373n.
Red River: xi, 83, 110, 133, 157, 271, 306n., 308, 320
Refugio, Mission of: 233
Refugio, Texas: 23, 233n., 237, 341 & n.
Refugio County, Texas: 26
Reilly, James: 124 & n., 178, 335
Reinosa, Texas: 102
Republicano (sailing vessel): 169
Reyes, Gen. Isador: 107
Richard Creek: 324n.
Richmond, Texas: 179, 336 & n., 337 & n., 338 & n.
Richmond *Telescope*: 338 & n.
Rickards, Little and Company: xvi
Rio Grande River: xi, xiii, 23, 29, 36, 52, 66, 102, 107, 126f., 148f., 154f., 160, 193, 221, 227n., 231, 235, 239n., 240n., 256f., 297f., 311n., 325, 334, 335n., 347f., 350, 352n., 355, 358, 361, 376, 377n., 383
Rise, Progress and Prospect of the Republic of Texas, The (Kennedy): xv, 3 & n.
Robbins, Nathaniel: 306n.
Robbins Ferry: 306 & n., 312
Robinson, Judge James W.: 164 & n.
Robson, Robert: 242n., 243n., 244 & n., 245, 248, 250, 258f., 266f.

"Robson's Castle," Colorado County, Texas: 243n; *see also* "Scotch Hermitage"

Rocky Creek: 342

Rocky Mountains: 61, 335

Roman Catholic Church, missions ceded to, in 1841: 233

Rome, Italy: xv, 129, 138, 194

Rome, Texas: 314

Rosillo, Texas: 216n., 238; Battle of, 237

Round Rock: 197n.

Royal College of Physicians (London, England): xvi

Royal Geographical Society (London, England): xiii, xvii, 5n., 102; *Journal* of, xiii; *Transactions* of, xviii

Royal Institution (London, England): xii

Royal Society of Arts (London, England): xviii

Ruta, Rev. Martin: 184 & n.

Rutaville, Texas: 184 & n., 199

Sabinal, Texas: 353n.

Sabinal Canyon: 353 & n.

Sabinal River: 353n., 355

Sabinas, Mexico: 239n., 325

Sabinas (Cypress) Creek: 244 & n., 245, 250

Sabine River: xi, 88, 96, 107, 110 & n., 137, 230

Sacaroppa, Texas: 16

St. Charles Hotel, New Orleans, Louisiana: 91f.

St. Croix: 8

St. Eustache: 5

St. George's Church, Stanford, England: xvi

St. Hubert (hunter's patron saint): 211 & n.

St. James Chronicle (London, England: 387

St. Joseph's Island: 262, 341, 378

St. Kitts: 5

Saint-Louis (Delaware chief): 165

St. Louis, Missouri: 23, 193

St. Louis Hotel, New Orleans, Louisiana: 91

St. Luis Island: 43, 84

St. Mary Mounthaw, Parish of, England: xii

St. Miguel: 133

St. Saba: 5

St. Thomas, Bollaert's impressions of: 4 & n., 5–6

Salado, Battle of: 154n., 215 & n., 216

Salado River: 169, 214, 226, 239f., 298, 347

Saligny, Count Alphonse de: 100 & n., 102, 106, 108, 328f., 335

Saltillo, Battle of: 169, 373

San Andres River: 191, 264

San Antonio, Texas: xi, xv, 3, 20, 23, 25, 27 & n., 28 & n., 29, 34, 36, 39, 51f., 58, 66f., 73, 86n., 106, 110, 120, 133, 138, 140, 142, 145, 149f., 154ff., 185, 189, 200, 208n., 209, 212 & n., 213, 242n., 243, 248, 250, 251 & n., 257f., 262, 268, 270, 274f., 297f., 306n., 312, 319, 335n., 337 & n., 342n., 345, 346n., 349f., 351 & n., 352 & n., 354 &

n., 355, 358, 362 & n., 364, 369 ff., 373, 376, 377 & n., 388; captured by Gen. Woll, 148; description of, 216 ff.; history of, 235 ff.

San Antonio (Texian warship): 56n., 142, 172 & n., 177 & n.

San Antonio Bay: 40n.

San Antonio de Bejar: 216n.; *see also* San Antonio

San Antonio de Padua: *see* Alamo, the

San Antonio de Valero: *see* Alamo, the

San Antonio Mission: 224, 233

San Antonio River: 215 & n., 217, 225 f., 228 & n., 229, 233, 236, 241 f., 341 & n., 347

San Antonio Road: 306n.

San Augustine: 300

San Bernard (Texian warship): 56n., 61, 128, 142 ff.

San Bernardo Bay: 40n.

San Bernard River: 57, 74, 85, 181, 339, 340 & n., 341

San Felipe, Texas: 336n., 337, 339, 340n.

San Felipe de Austin, Texas: 181, 261n., 262 & n.

San Fernando, Texas: 236

San Fernando Mission: 224

San Gabriel River: 191 & n., 264

San Jacinto, Battle of: 3, 31n., 38n., 39n., 63n., 84n., 108 & n., 129, 138, 167, 222n., 223, 280, 305, 333, 373

San Jacinto (Texian warship): 56n.

San Jacinto River: 114, 267 & n., 308

San José Mission: 216, 225, 232 & n., 233 f.

San Juan (sailing vessel): 160

San Juan Bautista, Presidio of: 352n., 358 & n.

San Leon, Texas: 179 & n.

San Lorenzo de la Santa Cruz: 365n.

San Luis: 36, 88

San Marcos River: 211n., 213, 345, 350

San Miguel, Texas: 24

San Miguel Creek: 369 & n., 370

San Miguel River: 225

San Miguel Valley: 370

San Patricio, Texas: 14, 48, 119, 219n., 370, 371 & n., 373 f., 376, 378n.

San Patricio County, Texas: 29n., 213

San Patricio Road: 374

San Pedro Creek: 228 & n., 236

San Saba, Texas: 224, 237, 335

San Saba mines: 196

San Saba Mission, rumors of hidden treasure in: 191–92

San Saba Valley: 192, 194

Santa Anna, Gen. Lopez de: 23, 25, 36n., 63n., 73, 123 ff., 128, 131, 132 & n., 136, 154, 157 f., 161, 169, 171, 172 & n., 173, 177, 212, 221, 239, 241n., 264, 275 f., 296 ff., 329 f., 349, 358

Santa Anna (Texian warship): 36, 38, 41, 49, 51, 156, 377

Santa Gertrudis Creek: 111

Santa Marta: xvii

Santana: *see* Santa Anna
Santa Fé, New Mexico: 23f., 84, 88, 142f., 149, 193, 334, 357
Santa Fé expedition: 21–23, 24n., 28n., 131 & n., 133, 181, 197n., 240, 373
Santa Fé prisoners: 125f., 128, 130 & n., 132 & n., 134, 181
Santo Domingo: 9
Sarah Barnes (sailing vessel): 175
Saratoga, Texas: 112
Sauz Creek: 368 & n.
Schmidt and Company: 89
"Scotch Hermitage": 244, 266; *see also* "Robson's Castle"
Scotland: 307n., 374n.
Scott, Sir Walter: 194
Scylla (sailing vessel): 174f., 177
Sealy, Texas: 339n.
Seco Creek: 354 & n.
Seeger, Capt. William (Texian Navy): 56n., 172 & n.
Seguin, Texas: 212, 214, 258, 349
Seis Canciones Españolas del Peru y Chile (Bollaert): xix
Seminole Indians: 90, 98
Senators: 77
Seneca, Marcus Annaeus (Roman philosopher): 375
Shakespeare, William: 9n.
Shannon, Col. Jacob: 265 & n.
Shaw's Hotel, Galveston, Texas: 55
Sheperd's Bush, London, England: xvii
Sherman, Sidney: 178
Sierra Madre Mountains: 66, 104, 256, 297

Simon, Pedro: xix
Skull Creek: 208 & n.
Skunks: 254
Slave auction, description of: 94–95
Smith, Ashbel: 132 & n., 133, 183 & n., 301
Smith, Thomas I.: 292n.
Smithers, Lancelot: 344 & n.
Smithers Creek: 344
Smithfield, Texas: 315 & n.
Snake Island: *see* Galveston
Snively, Col. Jacob: 191 & n.
Society of Antiquaries (London, England): xviii
Somervell, Gen. Alexander: 51, 149, 159, 178, 296ff.
Spain: xiv, xvii, 5, 65, 92, 235, 374n., 386
Spaniards: 234n., 236, 238
Spanish Americans: description of, 217–18; food of, 218–19
Spanish Moss, description of: 72
Spanish Royalists: 216
Sporting Magazine (London, England): xix
Sporting Review (London, England): xix
Squirrels: 254
Stewart, Charles Bellinger: 161 & n.
Stuart, Hamilton: 29 & n.
Swartwout, Texas: 110 & n., 114, 137, 140f., 315 & n.
Sweden: 5
Sydney, Australia: 385
Sydnor, John S.: 29 & n., 31

Tahuunde Indians: 210f., 353

Talleyrand, Perigord (French statesman): 73

Tamaulipas, Mexico: 122f.

Tampico, Mexico: 264

Tarrant, Edward H.: 322n.

Tarrant County, Mexico: 276n., 315n.

Tawakonie Indians: *see* Wichita Indians

Tay (sailing vessel): 8

Taylor, Capt. John W.: 56n., 90

Tecumseh (Shawnee chief): 210

Tehas Indians: 234 & n.

Tejas Indians: *see* Tehas Indians

Telegraph and Texas Register: 38n., 106, 276

Terrell, George Whitfield: 165 & n., 292n.

Terrible (Texian warship): 57n.

Tertillia Peaks: 226

Teulon, George K.: 137 & n., 156, 199

Texan and Brazos Farmer: 165 & n.

Texans: 28n., 84, 121, 152, 173, 189, 212, 227n., 231 & n., 297, 369n., 387

Texan Wars: 237

Texas: xvff., 3ff., 25n., 34n., 43, 63n., 71, 73, 78, 81, 88, 91, 95f., 105ff., 111, 120, 123, 129, 135, 137f., 149, 154f., 157, 160, 161 & n., 163, 166, 168, 171, 173f., 178f., 184, 190f., 197f., 200 & n., 204, 209, 211, 214n., 230, 234, 237, 239n., 240f., 243n., 248n., 251, 256 & n., 258, 261n., 262n., 264n., 268, 269n., 270ff., 275f., 278, 280, 286f., 292n., 293, 295, 297f., 300f., 307n., 308, 311f., 315 & n., 316, 319, 324ff., 328, 330, 332, 335n., 337n., 344, 350, 354, 355n., 358, 365, 366n., 373, 374n., 376, 381f., 388 & n.; importance of early, to England, xi; political scene in, 21–22; invasion of, by marauding Mexican party, 27n.; uses of titles in, 76ff.; agricultural prospects in, for immigrants, 116–18; criticism of, by N. Maillard, 139–42; derivation of name, 234n.; game in, 252–57; annexation to U.S., rumors of, 327–28

Texas, Observations, Historical, Geographical, and Descriptive, in a Series of Letters Written during a Visit to Austin's Colony, with a View of a Permanent Settlement in that Country in the Autumn of 1831 (Holley): 331n.

Texas Commissioners: 239 & n.

Texas Indians: *see* Tehas Indians

Texas Mounted Volunteers: 225n.

Texas Navy: deployment of, during Mexican crisis, 35–36; composition of, 56n.

Texas Navy in Forgotten Battles and Shirtsleeve Diplomacy, The (Hill): 34n.

Texas Rangers: 33n., 225n.

Texas Revolution: 262n., 280

Texas Sentinel: 197n.

Texas Times: 80 & n., 168 & n.

Texas University Library: 335n.
Texas Volunteers: 189
Thespian Company of Matagorda: 86
Thompson, Capt. Henry L.:
(Texas Navy): 56n.
Thompson, Gen. Waddy: 130 &
n., 134, 334
Thorn's Creek: 344
Three Rivers, Texas: 370n.
Times, The (London, England):
8, 387
Titles, use of and attitude toward, in Texas: 76ff.
Tlascalan Indians: 236n.
Tobasco: 88f.
Toledo, Fernando Alvarez de,
Duke of Alba: 221 & n.
Toluca (Mexican) Regiment:
223
Tom, Toby: (Texian warship):
57n.
Tomkins, Judge Augustus M.:
147 & n.
Tonkaway Indians: 190, 203,
208, 211, 241, 256
Tortola Island: 7
Town Creek: 265n.
Townsend, Henry: 89
Townsend, Texas: 341f.
Travis, Texas: 262
Travis, William Barret: 344n.
Travis County, Texas: 197n.
Tremont Hotel, Galveston,
Texas: 19, 23, 131, 171; Bollaert's description of contest
in, 58–60
Tres Palacios Bay: 70 & n.

Trials, held in Galveston: 145–
47
Trieste: 325
Trinidad: 314 & n.
Trinity Bluff: 323
Trinity River: xi, 84, 110 & n.,
112, 179, 200n., 265, 289, 292
& n., 306, 311 & n., 314n.,
315n., 316 & n., 317ff., 320 &
n., 322n., 323, 324n., 333,
375n.
Tug (steam vessel): 62
Tyler, President John: 264

Ugalde, Col. John de: 238
Union Springs: 112
United Services Magazine (London, England): xviii
United States Army: 319n.
U.S. Highway 81: 365n.
U.S. Highway 90: 342n.
United States of America: xi, 20,
23, 25 & n., 34, 52, 61, 73, 77,
83f., 97, 105, 118, 124, 128ff.,
136, 138, 141, 145, 158 & n.,
162, 168, 170, 172ff., 211,
228n., 231n., 239n., 264, 269f.,
272, 274ff., 278, 280, 285, 289,
297, 300, 308, 324f., 327f.,
330f., 336, 350, 358n., 385, 387
United States Senate: 328 & n.
United States Volunteers: 297
University of Chile: xviii
Urrea, José: 371n.
Ushan (Coshatte chief): 334
Uvalde, Texas: 356, 359, 365n.
Uvalde County, Texas: 332,
353n., 355, 357n., 359
Uvalde Springs: 360

Valparaiso, Chile: xiii, xvii
Van Ness, George: 28 & n.
Van Zandt, Isaac: 164 & n., 166, 328
Van Zandt County, Texas: 320n.
Vasquez, Juan: 237n., 238
Vásquez, Rafael: 23, 30n.
Velasco, Texas: 84 & n., 135, 157, 181
Vera Cruz, Mexico: 62, 126, 128, 131 & n., 135, 142, 158, 161, 169, 174f., 209
Verandah Hotel, New Orleans, Louisiana: 91
Verde Creek: 244n.
Vesta (steam vessel): 292
Victor (British warship): 99, 101
Victoria, Queen of England: 171, 275
Victoria, Texas: 28f., 31, 52, 341n., 370
Victoria Mission: 233
Vindicator: 300
Virginia: 30n., 293
Virginia Point, Texas: 179 & n.
Virgin Islands: 4n.
Vista (steam vessel): 317f.

Waccos Indians: 50, 349
Wache, Louis: 135
Wade, Capt. John M.: 38 & n.
Waister, definition of: 37n.
Waldeck, Count Boos: 135, 136 & n., 137 & n., 160 & n.
Wales: 140
Wallace, J. W. E.: 212
Waller County, Texas: 263n., 265n., 292, 314n.
Wallis, Texas: 339n.

Wallsend, England: 312 & n.
Walnut Creek: 188
War Bill, 1842: 120n., 122
Warfield, Charles A.: 142 & n.
"War Party": 57–58, 83, 104, 110, 124, 138, 164f., 168, 170, 174, 274; Houston's efforts to restrain, 297–99
Wars of Succession in Portugal and Spain, from 1826–1840, The (Bollaert): xix
Washington, D.C.: 153, 328, 385
Washington, George: 77f.
Washington, Texas: 20, 33n., 48, 89, 153, 164f., 174, 264, 265 & n., 275f., 288, 293, 300, 328ff., 380
Washington County, Texas: 263n., 265 & n.
Washington-on-the-Brazos: *see* Washington, Texas
Washington (Texian warship): 36, 38, 41, 57n.
Waterloo, Texas: 193 & n.
Wavell, Gen. Arthur Goodall: 374 & n.
Webber, John: 190n.
Webber's Prairie: *see* Webberville
Webberville, Texas: 192, 199
Webster, Daniel: 130n.
Webster-Ashburton Treaty: 129n.
Wedding, description of: 289–92
Weekly Citizen, The: 308n.
Western Advocate: 199 & n.
Western Rangers: 225
West India Steam Packet Company: 6

West Indies: 7, 17, 140, 276, 307n.
Wetherell, Sir C.: 387
Wharton (Texian vessel): 30f., 51, 56n., 57n., 142, 157, 166, 169f., 176f.
Wharton County, Texas: 31n., 340n.
Wheelright, Capt. George Washington (Texian Navy): 56n., 81 & n.
White House, Washington, D.C.: 96
White Rock Creek: 323 & n.
White Rock Lake: 323n.
Whitewright, Texas: 306n.
Whiting, Maj. Samuel: 164 & n.
Wichita Indians: 246, 256
Wicklow County, Ireland: 237n.
Wilbarger, Joseph Pugh: 192 & n.
Wild cattle: 255
Wild hogs: 254
Williams, Samuel May: 89n., 104 & n., 170, 239n., 257, 325, 329f.
Wilson, John: 89
Wilson County, Tennessee: 225
Wilson County, Texas: 214n., 260n.
Winnebago Indians: 373 & n.
Woll, Gen. Adrian: 56, 148f., 151, 154, 155 & n., 156, 159, 185, 209 & n., 215, 217, 239 & n., 241, 352n., 354 & n., 358, 371, 373

Woll's Road: 354n., 356, 358ff.
Wolves: 255
Woods, H. G.: 209n.
Wright, Jeff: 119
Wrights Bluffs: 314
Wynn, Martha: 168

Xaramene Indians: 234 & n.
Xerxes I, King of Persia: 81

Yates, Andrew J.: 29, 30 & n., 31
Yegua Creek: 314n.
"Yellow Jack" fever: 92 & n.
Yellow Wolf (Comanche chief): 377n.
York, John: 262 & n.
Yorkshire County, England: 140
Ysamonica (Comanche chief): 358
Yucatán, Mexico: 17 & n., 35, 56n., 62, 107, 124, 126, 142, 154, 157f., 161, 166, 169ff., 176f., 276, 325

Zacatecas, Mexico: 369
Zanoni (Lytton): 19, 99 & n.
Zanzibar: xiii
Závala, Lorenzo de: 14 & n.
Zavala (Texian warship): 36, 51, 56n.
Zavala County, Mexico: 332, 355, 357n., 359
Zuñiga y Guzman Sotomayer y Sarmiento, Balthasar Manuel de (Viceroy of New Spain): 216n.

of which *William Bollaert's Texas* is Number 21, was started in 1939 by the University of Oklahoma Press. It follows rather logically the Press's program of regional exploration. Behind the story of the gradual and inevitable recession of the American frontier lie the accounts of explorers, traders, and travelers, which individually and in the aggregate present one of the most romantic and fascinating chapters in the development of the American domain. The following list is complete as of the date of publication of this volume:

1. Captain Randolph B. Marcy and Captain George B. McClellan. *Adventure on Red River:* Report on the Exploration of the Headwaters of the Red River. Edited by Grant Foreman.
2. Grant Foreman. *Marcy and the Gold Seekers:* The Journal of Captain R. B. Marcy, with an account of the Gold Rush over the Southern Route.
3. Pierre-Antoine Tabeau. *Tabeau's Narrative of Loisel's Expedition to the Upper Missouri.* Edited by Annie Heloise Abel. Translated from the French by Rose Abel Wright.
4. Victor Tixier. *Tixier's Travels on the Osage Prairies.* Edited by John Francis McDermott. Translated from the French by Albert J. Salvan.
5. Teodoro de Croix. *Teodoro de Croix and the Northern Frontier of New Spain, 1776–1783.* Translated from the Spanish and edited by Alfred Barnaby Thomas.
6. A. W. Whipple. *A Pathfinder in the Southwest:* The Itinerary of Lieutenant A. W. Whipple During His Explorations for a Railway Route from Fort Smith to Los Angeles in the Years 1853 & 1854. Edited and annotated by Grant Foreman.
7. Josiah Gregg. *Diary & Letters.* Two volumes. Edited by Maurice Garland Fulton. Introductions by Paul Horgan. Out of print.
8. Washington Irving. *The Western Journals of Washington Irving.* Edited and annotated by John Francis McDermott. Out of print.
9. Edward Dumbauld. *Thomas Jefferson, American Tourist:* Being an Account of His Journeys in the United States of America, England, France, Italy, the Low Countries, and Germany.
10. Victor Wolfgang von Hagen. *Maya Explorer:* John Lloyd Stephens and the Lost Cities of Central America and Yucatán.

11. E. Merton Coulter. *Travels in the Confederate States:* A Bibliography.
12. W. Eugene Hollon. *The Lost Pathfinder:* Zebulon Montgomery Pike.
13. George Frederick Ruxton. *Ruxton of the Rockies.* Collected by Clyde and Mae Reed Porter. Edited by LeRoy R. Hafen.
14. George Frederick Ruxton. *Life in the Far West.* Edited by LeRoy R. Hafen. Foreword by Mae Reed Porter.
15. Edward Harris. *Up the Missouri with Audubon: The Journal of Edward Harris.* Edited by John Francis McDermott.
16. Robert Stuart. *On the Oregon Trail:* Robert Stuart's Journey of Discovery (1812–1831). Edited by Kenneth A. Spaulding.
17. Josiah Gregg. *Commerce of the Prairies.* Edited by Max L. Moorhead.
18. John Treat Irving, Jr. *Indian Sketches,* Taken During an Expedition to the Pawnee Tribes (1833). Edited and annotated by John Francis McDermott.
19. Thomas D. Clark (ed.). *Travels in the Old South,* 1527–1825: A Bibliography. Two volumes.
20. Alexander Ross. *The Fur Hunters of the Far West.* Edited by Kenneth A. Spaulding.
21. William Bollaert. *William Bollaert's Texas.* Edited by W. Eugene Hollon and Ruth Lapham Butler.

William Bollaert's Texas

is set in Linotype *Electra*, a product of William Addison Dwiggins' lettering skill, and one of the few native American type faces used in machine composition for book texts. It is used here in the 11-point size, with two points of leading, or space, between the lines.

On the title page *Electra* combines with Warren Chappell's *Lydian*, set by hand. *Lydian* is a calligraphic kind of display type; that is, a letter based on forms written with the broad-edged pen. The broad-edged pen is the most versatile letter-making tool. Before the invention of printing all books were written with this kind of pen, cut from a feather, usually that of a goose.